THE SHRINKING POLITICAL ARENA

THE SHRINKING POLITICAL ARENA

Participation and Ethnicity in
African Politics, with a
Case Study of Uganda

Nelson Kasfir

UNIVERSITY OF CALIFORNIA PRESS
Berkeley • Los Angeles • London

University of California Press
Berkeley and Los Angeles, California
University of California Press, Ltd.
London, England
Copyright © 1976 by The Regents of the University of California
ISBN: 0-520-02576-8
Library of Congress Catalog Card Number: 73-85790
Printed in the United States of America

For Harry and Charlotte
with love

CONTENTS

PART II

ETHNIC POLITICAL PARTICIPATION
IN UGANDA: GROWTH AND CONTRACTION

PREFACE

Getting people out of politics must strike most rulers as an attractive idea at some point in their careers. Getting them out of ethnic politics will seem even more attractive because it offers rulers the chance to become statesmen. Whether personal advantage or public policy acts as catalyst, leaders sometimes try to reduce the volume of national and local participation.

Their prospects seem but wishful thinking because any attempt to contract participation in politics, and especially in ethnic politics, offends two notions proclaimed by common sense and sanctified by social science. The first notion is that once people begin to participate in politics, they cannot be dislodged. The second is that ethnicity everywhere is such an intractable social force that it cannot be removed from politics until people forget their ancestry. Furthermore, few social scientists and virtually no politicians would publicly discuss the behavioral implications of policies intended to reverse the growth of participation because these policies are regarded as inherently undesirable.

Victories in the worldwide spread of the right to engage in political activity are usually considered signposts on the path of world history. Those who pass through national struggles are not expected to relinquish newly acquired opportunities lightly. Once it has been won, who would give up the right to decide his own fate?

Ethnicity is thought to be equally unyielding to political direction. Not so many years ago both politicians and academics rested comfortably in the belief that ethnic loyalties and regional nationalisms had occurred in a stage long since transcended in the industrialized states. But today, with ethnicity resurgent everywhere, and not just in the Third World, coping with ethnic political participation has become a universal task.

If the political demands growing out of nationalism or ethnicity or "tribalism" are as inexorable as the resilience of the
cultures they are taken to symbolize would suggest, the states-
man must either compromise or crush. State authority must be
surrendered or nationalism defeated; to many politicians and
academics there seems no other possibility. And if this is true in
America and Europe, how much more must it be the case in
Africa? For there observers think they see primordial cultures
deeply rooted in the participants' identities, and thus conclude
that the path toward unity under any sort of effective central
coordination will be exceptionally difficult.

Armed only with this framework of conventional wisdom,
any observer would find postindependence politics in Uganda
exceptionally puzzling. For in the latter half of the 1960s, there
was not only a growing transformation of the regime that
steadily reduced the volume of participation but also a sustained attempt by Ugandan leaders to take ethnicity out of
politics. These two courses of action overlapped, though the
latter was not simply a special case of the former.

Transforming the Ugandan regime meant that a variety of
government structures identified with independence were dismantled. Most of these had provided opportunities for people
to enter politics and, to varying degrees, to influence policy.
The government seemed to succeed in getting them out of
politics. In this respect Uganda followed a pattern that appeared
to be endemic throughout subsaharan Africa. But how could
governments poor in both resources and skilled manpower implement such an unlikely policy throughout their countries?
Was it possible that people who had acquired some degree of
political consciousness in the agitation and elections that led to
independence would acquiesce in these changes?

Although Ugandan officials would have denied that they
were placing obstacles in the path of participation in general —
at least until the military took power — they were forthright
about the purposes of the measures they introduced to dampen
ethnic expression from the crises of 1966 until the coup of
1971. Whatever its importance in the precolonial period (a
matter of some debate), ethnic political participation had become central to Ugandan politics during colonial rule and the
first years of independence. But later, public assertion of ethnic

demands seemed to fall off sharply. Was it possible that for a while Ugandans found bases for political activity other than their ethnic identity?

To resolve these seeming contradictions between Ugandan facts and social science wisdom, we must rework our notions of participation and ethnicity. Participation turns out to be a complex concept that can be broken down into several components on which governments can sometimes have significant impact, either stimulating or reversing the growth of political involvement. It is possible to get people out of politics, though it is another issue entirely to determine whether and when it would be desirable to do so.

Ethnicity is also more complicated than is generally assumed. It leads an intermittent though often intense existence, dominant in certain situations and absent in others. A variety of conditions will determine whether people living in Moscow, New York, Calcutta, or Lagos will seek political reward on the basis of ethnic identity. Governments, either intentionally or unintentionally, influence many of these conditions — sometimes dissuading, sometimes persuading people of the relevance of their ethnic orgins. This book, then, concerns the political consequences of the conceptions that people accept as social reality and the possiblities of changing these conceptions through political engineering.

Everyone who writes about Africa, and particularly about ethnicity, has to decide whether to follow popular usage or anthropological convention in referring to ethnic units. People speaking African languages, particularly in Bantu linguistic areas, use different prefixes to refer to a single person, to more than one person, to the place in which they live, and to descriptive adjectives.[1] Anthropologists do away with these

1. In Bantu languages generally *Mu-* is the prefix added to refer to an individual, *Ba-* or *Mi-* to denote the plural, *Bu-* to identify a territory, and *Ki-* to indicate that the word is used as a descriptive adjective — thus, *Muganda, Baganda, Buganda,* and *Kiganda.* To simplify usage somewhat, I have dropped the *Ki-* prefix and used the collective word for the people as the form for adjectives (for example, Baganda customs rather than Kiganda customs). I have not substituted an *r* for *l,* as is sometimes done in western Ugandan Bantu languages (for example, *Runyankore* instead of *Lunyankole*) with the exception of references to languages used on Radio Uganda, where the change seems to have been officially adopted.

PREFACE

prefixes and use the core of the name of the ethnic unit (a nonword) in each of these cases.

I have decided to follow popular usage current in East Africa rather than anthropological practice. Dropping prefixes can lead to confusion of people with place names. Perhaps a more important reason is that in a book which articulates a notion of ethnicity depending in part on the identities that people perceive for themselves and others, it would be a mockery to use a term that carries no meaning to any of them.

Reference to the *Bakonzo* instead of the *Bakonjo* (except as a government–designated census category) is an extension of this point, since the people in question regard themselves as Bakonzo. The *Bakonjo* spelling — now accepted by the government and most other Ugandans — derives from the language of the people whom the Bakonzo often identify as their oppressors.[2] My usage is not entirely consistent, and I refer, for example, to the Chagga and the Luo without a prefix. However, anthropologists are not always consistent either and often use a prefix when referring to the territory regarded as the "home" of members of an ethnic unit.

I have received generous assistance from many quarters and particularly from Ugandans — government officials, scholars, Makerere students, and farmers in many parts of the country — who have taken time from their own pursuits to fully answer questions and gently correct mistaken impressions. Today it would be imprudent to acknowledge by name any of those now in Uganda — a small indication of the personal dangers created by the present regime.

A number of colleagues took the trouble to review carefully earlier versions of several of the chapters presented here. I am especially grateful for the close scrutiny and important criticisms offered by Michael Davies, Richard Hook, Samuel Huntington, and particularly Crawford Young. I have also been guided by the helpful suggestions of David Baldwin, Dennis

2. The distinction provides an example of the researcher's problem of deciding whether the identity of an ethnic unit depends upon the perceptions of those who are members or those who are outsiders. The problem is taken up in chapter two.

Cohen, Henry Ehrmann, James Fernandez, Garth Glentworth, Frank Holmquist, Sidney Kasfir, Martin Kilson, Gene Lyons, Roger Masters, William Mayer, W. H. Morris—Jones, Christian Potholm, Paul Puritt, Ken Sharpe, Frank Smallwood, Denis Sullivan, Yash Tandon, Michael Twaddle, Neil Warren, and Joshua Zake.

Rupert Emerson has been more helpful than he knows. Not only did he comment on many chapters, but he also convinced me that an earlier manuscript could be expanded into a book — though I suspect that he had a somewhat different one in mind. If my writing style has improved with revision, at least some of the credit ought to go to the inspiration provided by that fine American scribe, Word Smith. Members of the Political Science Seminar at the University of Zambia provided an instructive attack on an earlier version of my notion of ethnicity. A seminar at Temple University organized by Harriet B. Schiffer provided the opportunity to present the first version of chapter six, and one at the University of Manchester offered the chance to test the concepts in chapter one.

Makerere University provided me with facilities, and members of its staff gave me the continuous encouragement which is indispensable for scholarly enterprise during the four years I taught there. I deeply appreciate the ambitious and often courageous lengths to which James Coleman and Ali Mazrui went to maintain a strong intellectual commitment at the university. I am indebted to the Rockefeller Foundation and the Carnegie Corporation for supporting my appointment as a visiting lecturer. The Department of Political Science and Public Administration made financial assistance available in support of much of the research that is presented here.

I am also grateful for the support and encouragement that I have received while teaching at Dartmouth College. Both sufficient time to complete this book and financial assistance to cover preparation of the final manuscript were provided by the college. The Institute of Commonwealth Studies in the University of London provided a quiet haven and stimulating seminars — both incalculable contributions. Donna Musgrove began the typing and Anne Barnes guided it to a conclusion. Alain Hénon of the University of California Press and Susan Crow smoothed innumerable rough edges. I am grateful to all four.

In lieu of the conventional final acknowledgment, I wish to solemnly record here that I have promised not to thank my wife for carrying out her usual duties in return for an agreement that she will not thank me for being a husband when she writes a book of her own. With so much assistance from so many different sources I can take little credit beyond the responsibility for errors in what follows.

N. K.

London, June 1974

PART I
PARTICIPATION AND ETHNICITY

PARTICIPATION, DEPARTICIPATION, AND POLITICAL DEVELOPMENT

The aspiration to widespread political involvement shared by national leaders, former colonial rulers, and outside observers in the springtime of African independence has withered in the winter of unrepresentative army and one-party rule. Few are the Tanzanias where the participatory ideal continues to be the basis of political planning. There is greater fear of political participation now, and less of it. Adequate explanation of African political change must rest heavily upon the steadily diminishing role played by political participation.

The advent of independence brought hasty efforts by the colonial powers — particularly Britain and France — to introduce new structures which would channel popular demands into responsive policies. These structures included government and opposition parties, national parliaments, local councils, trade unions, cooperatives, and elections. Their efforts were reinforced by the demands of nationalist leaders who created their followings by attacking the limitations of the existing franchise. Decolonization meant national control, which in turn meant widespread popular participation. But the vigor and importance of all these institutions have declined considerably over the past ten years. In consequence, departicipation, the elimination of people from political life, has become increasingly common in independent African countries.

Since political participation has been an article of faith for many theorists of political development, the significance of departicipation has been overlooked. In their eyes systems become more developed as more individuals take part in political activities. Finding a "participation explosion" which they believed would lead to a "world . . . political culture of participation," Gabriel Almond and Sidney Verba developed a theory,

3

4 PARTICIPATION AND ETHNICITY

based on the cumulation of traits, that passes from parochial to subject to participant political culture.[1] Another writer argues that the increased distribution or spread of power within the political system must be considered an essential feature of the very definition of political development.[2] Popular participation in the form of a "democratic association" has been described as an "evolutionary universal" for large-scale societies.[3] Even the American foreign aid effort has recently come to include "participation" as a basic criterion for judging projects in developing countries.[4]

If we accept the conventional wisdom that more participation means more political development or modernization, does less participation mean political decay or "traditionalization?" If we opt for a different definition of political development, does departicipation create greater capacity for rulers to meet their crises? Are African leaders attempting to manage their polities by reducing the pressures to which they must respond? Can they successfully impose a departicipation strategy in the face of what seems to be the most entrenched of political forces — ethnic identity?

Over forty years ago Harold Lasswell argued that there might be merit in a departicipation strategy, or, as he put it, in practicing "preventive politics":

> The time has come to abandon the assumption that the problem of politics is the problem of promoting discussion among all the interests concerned in a given problem. Discussion frequently complicates social difficulties, for the discussion by far-flung interests arouses a psychology of conflict which produces obstructive, fictitious, and irrelevant values. The

1. *The Civic Culture* (Boston: Little, Brown, 1965), pp. 2, 16-18, 30. See also Lucian W. Pye, *Aspects of Political Development* (Boston: Little, Brown, 1966), p. 45.

2. Frederick W. Frey, "Political Development, Power and Communications in Turkey," in *Communications and Political Development,* ed. Lucian W. Pye (Princeton: Princeton University Press, 1963), p. 301; but see also p. 303.

3. Talcott Parsons, "Evolutionary Universals in Society," *American Sociological Review* 29 (June 1964): 353-356.

4. "Emphasis shall be placed on assuring maximum participation in the task of economic development on the part of the people of the developing countries, through the encouragement of democratic private and local governmental institutions." Section 281, *The Foreign Assistance Act of 1961,* as amended in 1966.

problem of politics is less to serve as a safety valve for
social protest than to apply social energy to the
abolition of recurrent sources of strain in society.

This redefinition of the problem of politics may be
called the idea of preventive politics. The politics of
prevention draws attention squarely to the central
problem of reducing the level of strain and maladap-
tation in society.[5]

Departicipation is not unambiguously desirable, as Lasswell
goes on to suggest. That issue will be taken up in the last
chapter. The issue to be considered now is the nature of
participation and departicipation and its relationship to political
development. Since current definitions and usage leave no room
for departicipation, new approaches more applicable to the
present argument are necessary. The first step, then, is to create
the tools.

1. POLITICAL PARTICIPATION

To participate is to be involved in politics. This definition is
wide-ranging, since no political act is excluded.[6] However, when
the analytic distinctions implicit in participation are carefully
specified, the concept becomes a more precise and useful tool.
In addition, this definition has the virtue of focusing on the
issue investigated here. To participate is to enter the political
arena, and to departicipate is to leave it. Looking broadly at

5. *Psychopathology and Politics* (Chicago: University of Chicago Press, 1930),
pp. 196-197.

6. Geraint Parry relies upon the same definition. His analysis of participation is
extremely helpful. Unfortunately, it came to my attention too late to be used here.
"The Idea of Political Participation," in *Participation in Politics*, ed. Parry (Manchester: Manchester University Press, 1972), pp. 3, 17. Sidney Verba and Norman H.
Nie also follow this usage, though they stop short of calling the making of official
decisions and the overthrowing of governments part of participation. *Participation in
America: Political Democracy and Social Equality* (New York: Harper & Row,
1972), p. 2.

To define what *political* means introduces a range of problems that has engaged
philosophers for over two thousand years. The term can be applied so broadly that
no activities involving the relationships of two or more persons can be excluded. In
most inquiries, however, *politics* is implicitly restricted to the particular context that
forms the basis of a given study. Here, the context is basically governmental action at
national or local levels. Participation in the international and village arenas also falls
within my definition but is not considered here. Nor is the political participation of
foreign companies and foreign governments in domestic national and local affairs,
though they exercise considerable influence on many occasions.

political involvement enables us to include political activities ignored by other studies of participation. The subject ranges as widely as the distance between talking about politics and holding a monopoly of power to make enforceable decisions. Approaching administrative officials, directly influencing government decisions, and taking to the streets are aspects of participation.

What is known about participation in industrialized countries has limited relevance for understanding politics in developing states. One of the most significant differences between the Western European and the new states is that the former gradually adopted measures extending the franchise to all groups, while the latter generally entered independence on the basis of the principle "one person, one vote." Thus, studies of Western Europe and the United States focus on the extension of the franchise and consequent voting patterns,[7] which form one of the least relevant dimensions of participation in most African countries. Of greater importance are questions of education, government jobs, and development. Political participation in Africa turns on the ability to influence directly decisions concerning the allocation of secondary and university places, top positions, and new development projects. Patronage and recruitment are sharper issues than the franchise.

The wide range of behavior that must be taken into account in discussions of participation can be illustrated by arranging participatory activities into a continuum based on degrees of probable involvement.[8] The following list is somewhat arbitrary in its ordering and in its division of activities. Weaker types of

7. For example, Reinhard Bendix, *Nation-Building and Citizenship: Studies of Our Changing Social Order* (New York: John Wiley, 1964); T. H. Marshall, *Class, Citizenship, and Social Development* (Garden City, N.Y.: Doubleday, 1964); and Stein Rokkan, "The Comparative Study of Political Participation: Notes toward a Perspective on Current Research," in *Essays on the Behavioral Study of Politics,* ed. Austin Ranney (Urbana: University of Illinois Press, 1962), pp. 47-90.

8. The items in this continuum were selected primarily from the following discussions and scales of political participation: Robert A. Dahl, *Who Governs? Democracy and Power in an American City* (New Haven: Yale University Press, 1961), pp. 270-301; Lester Milbrath, *Political Participation: How and Why Do People Get Involved in Politics?* (Chicago: Rand McNally, 1965), pp. 16-29; Stein Rokkan, et al., *Citizens, Elections, Parties: Approaches to the Comparative Study of the Processes of Development* (New York: D. McKay, 1970), p. 67; Norman Nie, G. Bingham Powell, Jr., and Kenneth Prewitt, "Social Structure and Political Participation: Developmental Relationships," Part I, *The American Political Science Review* 63, no. 2 (June 1969): 364. See also Verba and Nie, *Participation in America,* p. 31.

involvement may turn out to be more influential on occasion. The problem is to work out measures that will permit comparison. This is not a simple undertaking, since the various types of participation constitute different kinds of behavior and thus are not easily ranked in terms of one another. In the first instance, though, it is sufficient simply to suggest the diversity of activities that must be considered:

1. Talking about politics and persuading others
2. Attending political rallies and meetings
3. Acting in accordance with government rules (paying taxes, observing health regulations)
4. Seeing a party or government official about a problem
5. Joining an organization that plays a secondary role in politics (trade union, cooperative)
6. Voting
7. Joining a political organization
8. Contributing time or money to a political campaign
9. Taking a government or party job
10. Influencing the allocation of resources or the grant of fundamental rights by government (peaceful demonstrations, violent protests)
11. Making critical political decisions
12. Taking over the government through coup d'etat
13. Taking over the polity through revolution

Participation can begin only after an initial lack of awareness, typical of parochial societies, has been overcome. The threshold for participation might be called spectatorship.[9] Just as spectators at a football game do not provide any direct input and cannot affect the result, the majority of the population of most countries most of the time has little involvement. Others may gain sufficient enjoyment simply by following the strategic moves of players directly involved. Those who are satisfied with current outcomes rarely feel the need to participate more actively. An artful government may contrive measures that answer needs before people become aware of them and thus reduce

9. See David S. Gibbons, "The Spectator Political Culture: A Refinement of the Almond and Verba Model," *Journal of Commonwealth Political Studies* 9, no. 1 (March 1971). Gibbons makes the useful point that spectators can easily become participants and then become spectators again depending on the political situation facing them. Ibid., p. 33.

demands made upon itself. On the other hand, certain kinds of apparent nonparticipation can have direct impact on political decisions. Boycotts of elections and walkouts from national assemblies are intended to be participatory acts.

Above the lowest level of involvement, political structures of some sort are essential to make participation effective. [10] Remove the structure and participation becomes much more difficult. Involvement in "administrative" activities is a type of participation. When members of the public conform to government administrative procedures in carrying out their daily business and leisure concerns, they are participating, though at a low (but not insignificant) level of impact on policymaking. Solution of an individual's grievance by the administrative official he importunes may indicate more political involvement than voting or joining a party.

Making critical political decisions is often seen as a distinctly different sort of activity from participation, but the difference is actually a matter of degree, not kind. Increasing influence means increasing participation in decision making. A monopoly over the process of allocating resources is the logical endpoint in the measurement of participation. Coups d'etat and revolutions demonstrate greater involvement than does possessing the monopoly of decision making only in the sense that they alter procedures as well as policy.

As a variation of political participation, revolution underlines the point that participation may or may not be organized through the procedures of the polity. Those attempting to overthrow the existing polity are similar to "praetorians" who merely want to take it over in that both ignore existing institutions while pursuing state power. Protests and violent actions may also occur at levels of lesser political impact in order to draw attention to particular demands. These may follow established procedures for handling disputes (petitions, court actions) or may confront the government by deliberately operating illegally. For the study of political development it is of fundamental importance to learn whether participation occurs

10. For a useful argument demonstrating that variations in political structure affect the volume of participation, see Judith V. May's discussion of data from local communities in the United States. "Citizen Participation: A Review of the Literature," stenciled (Davis: Institute of Governmental Affairs, University of California, 1971), pp. 19-30.

within or without political structures — whether it is institutionalized.

How, then, can we determine the amount of political participation in a particular situation when it will undoubtedly include
several of these different kinds of involvement? We need to
analyze the notion of participation into its components in order
to specify dimensions which, when taken together, will indicate
its "volume."[11] In theory exact comparisons of the volumes of
participation in two different cases might be possible. In practice we must be cautious, since isolating components of participation is not likely to produce a common standard by which
they can all be measured. But identifying the components is a
necessary first step.

The categories employed in the study of influence and power
provide a useful source for distinctions among the factors com-
prising participation.[12] With some modification these categories
are particularly appropriate, since participation is usually an
attempt to exercise influence. Furthermore, unlike many other
notions in political science, the categories of power and influence have remained in use for several years. The components
that produce a specified volume of participation, then, are
these:

1. *Personae* — who is involved?
2. *Scope* — over what issues?
3. *Bases* — with what resources?
4. *Weight* — with what impact?
5. *Propensity* — with what personal goals and at what anticipated costs?

Personae refers to the set of persons involved.[13] A crude
measure is, of course, the number of those participating in a
particular instance. But the indicator can be made more inter-

11. I am grateful to Denis Sullivan, who suggested this term.

12. Harold D. Lasswell and Abraham Kaplan, *Power and Society: A Framework for Political Inquiry* (New Haven: Yale University Press, 1950), pp. 71-102, esp. pp. 73-76; and Robert A. Dahl, *Modern Political Analysis,* 2d ed. (Englewood Cliffs, N.J.: Prentice-Hall, 1970), pp. 14-34, esp. pp. 18-19.

13. The term *personae* has been substituted for Lasswell and Kaplan's term *domain.* The latter is usually restricted to the persons affected by an exercise of power or influence. In discussions of participation those who are attempting to affect others, rather than those who are affected, are usually the focus of inquiry. A full discussion necessarily concerns both, since weight can only be analyzed by considering the government's (or other affected party's) response.

esting by considering the social composition of those who are involved as opposed to those who eschew involvement.

The scope of participation raises the question of the range of issues that draw particular individuals or groups into political activity. Consideration of scope may indicate that participation is restricted to certain problems or that it covers the full range of issues confronting the polity. Scope is likely to be total for a revolutionary movement, highly specific for an interest group, and intermediate for a political party.

The bases of participation are as various as the resources available to participants and as useful as their skill in employing them permits. Wealth, status, communication facilities, and literacy are important aids to effective participation. They suggest one reason why there is an important relationship between participation and economic development or modernization. Other resources are not so obvious. The coherence of those affected and available to participate may be significant. Proximity of the affected people to the seat of government may be equally important. Control over the presentation of an issue — its "agenda" — may be crucial.

The weight of participation concerns the impact of involvement on policies or decisions made or, in other cases, deferred.[14] This dimension is the most complex aspect of participation and entails consideration of several distinctions. Participation can be divided into symbolic and material involvement, depending on whether it is merely ceremonial or is intended to affect the decision-making process directly. Elections in which the outcome is determined in advance or powerless but prestigeful commissions on which members of minority groups are included are examples of symbolic participation.[15] Governments sometimes use symbolic participation to mask a reduction in the opportunities for material participation. Coerced attendance at mass rallies in Black Star Square and a supine

14. Lasswell and Kaplan define *weight* (of influence) as "the degree of participation in the making of decisions. . . ." *Power and Society*, p. 77. In their view influence becomes power when coercion (severe sanctions) is present. Ibid., pp. 74 and 97. In that sense "coercive participation" is equivalent to "power."

15. "Formal coöptation" is an important aspect of symbolic participation. See Philip Selznick, "Coöptation: A Mechanism for Organization Stability," in *Reader in Bureaucracy*, ed. Robert K. Merton, Ailsa P. Gray, Barbara Hockey, and Hanan C. Selvin (Glencoe, Ill.: Free Press, 1952), pp. 135-139.

national assembly that restricted its efforts to ratification were signs of a shift from material to symbolic participation shortly after independence in Ghana. The weight of material involvement can be further broken down into many levels, as the thirteen types of participation listed above suggest.

Participation can be manipulated, voluntary, or habitual. The distinction overlaps to some extent the difference between symbolic and material participation. To suggest the category of manipulative participation raises the question of whether political mobilization or more extreme forms of coerced involvement should be labeled "participation." In the conventional view voluntarism is the essential element, and mobilization or manipulation by leaders must be kept separate from participation.[16] However, the people who become involved in any political issue always have different levels of knowledge, energy, and motives. These differences are likely to lead to efforts by some to bend their fellow participants toward their conception of the goals to be achieved. There has probably never been a case of totally voluntary participation on a significant issue involving large numbers of people.

Even if this were not so, it would be a mistake to ignore manipulated participation. Political institutions that are not prepared to handle additional actors may be weakened by the influx of those commanded to enter politics. This consequence occurs whether the new actors enter the political arena of their own free will or at the insistence of their landlord, union official, or party organizer. Large numbers of people participate in various political activities in the USSR, and the same was true for Nazi Germany. Governments in various new states insist upon mass labor contributions in development projects and mass demonstrations in support of new government initiatives. In election campaigns traditional notables and other brokers often bring uncomprehending but loyal peasants into politics. [17] Some political systems can cope with mass involvement in

16. For example, Myron Weiner, "Participation and Political Development," in *Modernization: The Dynamics of Growth,* ed. Weiner (New York: Basic Books, 1966), pp. 206 and 215.

17. For a discussion of different types of mobilization into politics in India see Lloyd I. and Susanne Hoeber Rudolph, *The Modernity of Tradition: Political Development in India* (Chicago: University of Chicago Press, 1967), pp. 24-27.

institutionalized channels, while others cannot. Thus, it seems more useful to widen the notion of participation to include coerced and manipulated varieties.

Material participation is sometimes direct and sometimes indirect, depending on whether the participation is the act of the individual or of his formal or informal representative. The individual may regard his representative as an adequate substitute for his own activity in politics.[18] Thus, the linkage between the government and the individual may develop through elected or appointed officials or through self-appointed bosses, brokers, or messengers who often appear in confrontations over intensely felt grievances. Another important form of representation concerns government positions held by persons whom a participant perceives to accept his own values or traits. For example, the more positions filled by those identified as Baganda, the more some Baganda may feel represented in the Ugandan government.

Finally, propensity to participate refers to the willingness of individuals to initiate or continue acts of involvement. Their participation may be habitual or the result of uncomprehending obedience to a superior. In other cases actors make an estimate of the value they place on the pursuit of a goal and the costs they believe they are likely to incur. Their sense of political efficacy is a primary consideration.

Calculations of value are likely to include estimates of the desirability of the goal, the pleasure received in engaging in political activity, and the probability that participation can help to achieve the intended objective. In order to assess the probability of success, actors must determine the expected response of those they are attempting to influence through their participation. How likely is it that government officials or members of parliament will respond in the way that the participant intends?

Calculations of costs are likely to include estimates of alternative opportunities in which actors might invest their time and money. Actors must also calculate the penalties they may suffer should their friends, political rivals, or government disapprove

18. Representation as a type of political participation can be further subdivided. See Hanna F. Pitkin, "The Concept of Representation," in *Representation,* ed. Pitkin (New York: Atherton Press, 1969).

of their participation. Moving to higher levels of involvement with greater impact on policymaking is likely to increase the costs to participants. The overall assessment of these values and costs made by each actor will determine not only his willingness to participate, but also the intensity of his participation.

Ethnic political grievances, which are discussed at some length below, provide an illustration of the distinctions that have just been drawn. The personae will come mainly from those who perceive themselves as members of the ethnic unit but may include others who have an interest in their success. Those who also see themselves as members of that ethnic unit but do not become involved may have different social characteristics from those who do.

The scope of this participation will presumably be focused on relatively specific issues, though it may be considerably broader if it is based on the claim of systematic exclusion from all sectors of the society. The bases, or resources, of those participating may enable them to make a sustained and sophisticated campaign for their goals or may be inadequate for more than a futile gesture. Of great importance is the question of whether the ethnic claim itself will be accepted by others as legitimate and thus whether it will be a resource or an impediment.

The weight or impact of the involvement is more likely to amount to material rather than symbolic participation, assuming that the injustice is deeply felt. It may be direct or indirect, depending on whether the participants approach officials through ethnic middlemen or mass confrontations. It is likely to involve a combination of those who voluntarily participate and those who have been manipulated by local leaders or, perhaps, by the government itself when the impetus for change comes from official quarters.

The type of involvement which the participants will employ to force consideration of their case will be a basic determinant of their weight in affecting the decision. They may be able to make successful use of violent protests or even of armed secession; their leaders may quietly approach an appropriate administrative official; they may limit their efforts to organizing a political campaign to educate the government or to voting against the incumbent members of parliament.

Lastly, the propensity of each actor to commit himself to participation in the hopes of rectifying this grievance may be a virtually automatic response based on his traditional values (if those values currently determine his ethnic identity). Alternatively, his participation may be the outcome of his calculation of likely benefits and expected costs. Much will depend on the attitude of government officials toward ethnic participation. If the government's resistance is judged to be great, the perceived costs of participation will be that much higher. Thus, the participants may or may not have intense feelings about the grievance.

Analyzing involvement in terms of each of these dimensions permits us to determine the particular volume of participation under study and gives useful explanations for its characteristics. It also permits us to compare instances of participation in different circumstances in the same political unit or in different political units. The dimensions do not amount to a theory of participation, but they are building blocks for constructing one.

2. DEPARTICIPATION

As the reversal of participation, departicipation refers to the reduction or elimination of political involvement as a consequence of choice, apathy, or coercion. It is a process and thus a continuous variable.[19] If departicipation were taken to its logical endpoint, the consequence would be the elimination of all participation — by definition the end of that political system. Although individuals or groups may be sufficiently satisfied with their government to lessen or relinquish their involvement voluntarily, it is more likely that departicipation will occur as a result of government policies. Forcing people out of politics is a strategy available to the leadership in many countries for enhancing its capacity to rule and making its tenure more secure.

19. Because it is a continuous variable not necessarily related to a specified institutional complex, participation/departicipation is a more discriminating concept than the democracy/authoritarianism dichotomy. Since the preservation of democracy may require limits on participation to avoid polarization and since authoritarianism may be combined with high levels of symbolic participation (and in any event must be combined with some material participation), it would be a mistake to regard participation/departicipation as parallel to (though more subtle than) democracy/authoritarianism. The two sets of concepts overlap but are not equivalent.

Departicipation may result from reductions on any of the dimensions of participation – personae, scope, bases, weight, or calculations of costs and probability of success. In most cases the government is likely to have a more direct effect on weight and, to some extent, on propensity than on the other factors. It can do so because it is in a position to alter the incentives, penalties, and procedures that govern the volume and rate of participation. Abolishing the means of participation at higher levels of impact on policymaking produces departicipation so long as other factors remain the same. For example, increasing the length of time between elections results, *ceteris paribus,* in departicipation. In many African countries the leaders of government have dismantled participatory structures such as elections, legislatures, parties, and local governments and have greatly reduced the autonomy of trade unions and cooperatives. At the very least these actions enormously increase the obstacles to participation and therefore are prima facie evidence of departicipation.

Since departicipation is, however, a negative process, in an analytic rather than a value-oriented sense, it is difficult to establish or measure. Departicipation on one dimension may be accompanied by additional participation on another, or even on the same dimension. Suppose, for example, a government cancels an election and the public responds with violent demonstrations that alarm political leaders. The form of participation has shifted, but it is not clear that any departicipation has taken place. Coercive measures may drive people out of politics or may merely drive them underground. A number of theoretical difficulties with departicipation suggested by this example are worth brief consideration. In each instance the dimensions of participation analyzed in the previous section permit the inquiry into departicipation to be posed more precisely.

First, the removal of one person from politics may result in the addition of another. For example, a new socialist government might reduce the political involvement of businessmen and substitute that of heretofore disenfranchised workers. Or, a military coup might eliminate the structures through which the populace participated while it brings soldiers into the political arena – either collectively or individually. Uganda under President Idi Amin is a particularly striking example.[20] A more complex variation on this question occurs when a change in policy results in the elimination of a small number who participate with an intense sense of commitment and the introduction of a larger number of participants with less political motivation. Several African leaders have justified detention or harassment of intensely committed political actors on the ground that such actions permitted these leaders to strengthen the commitment of the masses to national unity.

At first glance these examples concern the dimension of personae, but they are complex because they concern more than that. It is clearly insufficient, of course, to examine those removed without also considering those added. Departicipation would appear to have taken place when the total number of participants has become smaller. But this is not necessarily so. The smaller number may participate more effectively if they possess more resources than those they displaced. An equally daunting dilemma grows out of the question of intensity. Consider the case put immediately above in which a smaller number of highly motivated actors are forcibly removed from the political arena to make way for the more numerous but less intensely committed. This problem is analogous to the issue raised by "Madisonian democracy" — how to balance the interests of the few who feel intensely against the opposite opinion of an apathetic majority.[21] Both dilemmas can be seen only by analyzing participation into its several dimensions.

A second set of difficulties is raised by intended departicipation through reduction in scope. Common sense suggests that the removal or disappearance of a political issue results in departicipation. But we must ask how the levels of activity of participants on other issues have changed as well as consider the consequences of the removal of the original issue. For example, white American youth who first participated in politics through the civil rights movement of the early 1960s later moved into antiwar protest partly as a result of their expulsion from the movement by blacks. When the Ugandan government insisted that local district councils cease debating questions concerning

20. See chapter nine.
21. See Robert A. Dahl, *A Preface to Democratic Theory* (Chicago: University of Chicago Press, 1956), pp. 4-33.

their constitutional positions and relative prestige, there was, for a time, an upsurge in discussion of the allocation of primary schools and boreholes (wells).

If we could show that the only change in the political situation was the removal of one issue from the arena, departici-pation would have taken place. But other considerations rarely remain exactly the same, particularly if the issue removed is highly controversial. Where the removal introduces new issues (perhaps concerning the right of the government to tamper with participation on the original issue), involvement may increase. Or the smaller number of issues on which participants can focus may heighten their sense of efficacy and thus cause them to redouble their efforts. Thus, where one issue has replaced another, it is often not so easy to determine whether the present or the prior situation affords greater scope for participa-tion.

Third, there are similar difficulties with the dimension of weight. The removal of the means of participating at a particu-lar level of impact (for example, a ban on political parties) suggests departicipation. However, the abolition of one parti-cipatory structure may lead to such adroit use of another that it is difficult to tell whether there has been any reduction in involvement. For example, members of a group whose leaders arc rcmoved from positions of great power may intensify their efforts to win the next election in order to regain their previous influence over policy. If they succeed in arousing many of their quiescent followers, their impact on policy may be even greater than it was before.

None of these difficulties is easy to resolve. Each of them is complex because more than one dimension of participation is involved. Some of them pose a dilemma in determining whether political change led to participation or departicipation because changes took place in two (or more) dimensions *in opposite directions*. In other cases the problem is to follow out all the consequences of intended departicipation in order to determine whether it occurred or whether participation actually expanded. In most cases an informed judgment should be possible even if a precise quantification of the volume of participation remains unlikely for lack of a measure common to all five dimensions.

The postindependence African cases are easier to evaluate

because the elimination of participatory structures has been so thorough that few of these theoretical difficulties arise. Although exceptions like Tanzania merit closer scrutiny, the systematic removal of political structures through which people formerly participated amounts to departicipation in the absence of new forms of political involvement. Since the legacy of colonial rule offers little legitimacy for new forms of participation that might take place of the structures removed, the presumption that participatory techniques insure departicipation is formidable. In Rupert Emerson's words:

> For practical purposes what is sought is not the positive collaboration of the people in choosing those who are to govern them or in deciding policy issues but rather a 'populist' regime in which the people, guided and indoctrinated from above, support the existing order by acclaim and play their assigned part in whatever programs the leaders and governments may lay out for them.[22]

The degree of departicipation is not uniform from one subsaharan African state to another and fluctuates over time. These differences are important to an understanding of the extent of departicipation and the shape it assumes in unique national settings. There are many overall similarities (discussed in chapters nine and ten), but the process of departicipation in one state cannot be understood simply by examining another. Still, it is difficult to consider politics in the black African states without noticing that almost everywhere a radical reduction has occurred in the involvement in decision making of individuals outside the administrative branch of the central government.

3. POLITICAL DEVELOPMENT AND DEPARTICIPATION

How is departicipation related to political development? The answer is elusive — the more so because writers on political development have assumed that departicipation will not occur. Many of them regard participation as an integral feature of

22. "The Prospects for Democracy in Africa," in *The State of the Nations: Constraints on Development in Independent Africa,* ed. Michael F. Lofchie (Berkeley and Los Angeles: University of California Press, 1971), pp. 255-256.

modernization. Since modernization, in their view, is irreversible, there is no reason to consider departicipation. To remedy this oversight, we must consider their resistance to the notion of the reversibility of participation and provide a precise meaning for the concept of political development.

Participation has always been considered an important aspect of political development and often essential to its definition. When the inquiry into political development emerged from the study of economic development, it took over the same paradigm — the shift from tradition to modernity.[23] Under the influence of technological, social, and economic factors mostly from outside the society, the pressure to become modern was seen as inexorable and part of a "world culture." Increasing participation was regarded as an indicator and perhaps a cause of development, while broad access to the institutions of authority was believed to be a characteristic of the modern polity.[24] For example, the growth of democracy was linked to economic development, and social mobilization was analyzed in a variety of contexts. "Although it may appear paradoxical," assert two recent writers, "the principal 'remedy' for instability [during the development process] is increased popular participation."[25]

However, major difficulties soon became apparent in the tradition-to-modernity continuum.[26] The persistence of various

23. See W. W. Rostow, *The Stages of Economic Growth* (Cambridge: Cambridge University Press, 1960); and Robert A. Packenham, "Approaches to the Study of Political Development," *World Politics* 17, no. 1 (October, 1964).

24. S. N. Eisenstadt, "Bureaucracy and Political Development," in *Bureaucracy and Political Development*, ed. Joseph La Palombara (Princeton: Princeton University Press, 1963), p. 99; Martin Kilson, *Political Change in a West African State: A Study of the Modernization Process in Sierra Leone* (Cambridge: Harvard University Press, 1966), pp. 282 and 287; James S. Coleman, "The Political Systems of the Developing Areas," in *The Politics of the Developing Areas*, ed. Gabriel Almond and Coleman (Princeton: Princeton University Press, 1960), pp. 538-544; and Karl Deutsch, "Social Mobilization and Political Development," *The American Political Science Review* 55, no. 3 (September 1961). Although Deutsch did not equate social mobilization and modernization, many researchers who applied his measures of social mobilization have not been so careful.

25. Norman T. Uphoff and Warren F. Ilchman, "Development in the Perspective of Political Economy," in *The Political Economy of Development*, ed. Uphoff and Ilchman (Berkeley and Los Angeles: University of California Press, 1973), p. 116. See also pp. 104-107 and 115-118.

26. See Samuel P. Huntington, "The Change to Change: Modernization, Development, and Politics," *Comparative Politics* 3, no. 3 (April 1971); Rudolph and

combinations of so-called traditional and modern factors suggested that "modern" characteristics did not simply replace
"traditional" features. Overlapping traditional and new norms
often led to unexpected results not likely to create "modern"
patterns. What had earlier been considered a world culture
turned out to be a Eurocentric version of modernity. Many
paths of social change became apparent, but that recognition
meant that a single continuum could not contain them.

With the discovery of these problems, an attempt was made
to broaden the tradition-to-modernity paradigm by capturing
the complexity of the modernization process in a series of
"crises" that together might be regarded as comprehensive. [27]
One of these crises was the question of participation. The issue
was how the society extends power – in the form of the
franchise – to unrepresented groups. The ensuing struggle with
those who resist widened access helps to shape the polity. Thus,
participation was seen as a major crisis, but one that could be
resolved only through successful inclusion. Otherwise the nation
has not become developed.

The new solution, however, created its own problems. Viewing participation as a crisis to be overcome suggests that the
only stable solution for the polity is mass participation, a
formulation that again equates participation with development.
In addition, no one could agree on how many crises there were
in the development process, since no logical procedure was
specified for deriving crises. Nor did anyone suggest a way to
measure progress in solving one crisis in terms of the degree of
success in solving another. Without such a tool it is not possible
to decide whether one country is more developed than another.

The first step in escaping from this cul-de-sac is to recognize
that the factors generally labeled *modernization* can create
serious problems for the political system. Modernization means
increasing man's capacity to control his environment. But while

Rudolph, *The Modernity of Tradition;* C. S. Whitaker, Jr., *The Politics of Tradition:
Continuity and Change in Northern Nigeria, 1946-1966* (Princeton: Princeton Univer-
sity Press, 1970); and Fred Riggs, *Administration in Developing Countries* (Boston:
Houghton Mifflin, 1964).

27. See Leonard Binder, James S. Coleman, Joseph LaPalombara, Lucian W. Pye,
Myron Weiner, and Sidney Verba, *Crises and Sequences in Political Development*
(Princeton: Princeton University Press, 1971); and Rokkan et al., *Citizens, Elections,
Parties,* chap. 2.

education, mass communications, cash crops, and new job opportunities may widen some forms of control, they often produce social frustration expressed in rising rates of participation as well. However, both traditional and recently adopted political structures may be rejected by new participants whose aspirations cannot be easily satisfied. As a result the polity may deteriorate and become progressively less capable of carrying out its appropriate tasks. Paradoxically, the quest for greater social and economic control may lead to a breakdown of political control. In this sense social and economic modernization can lead to political decay, not − as the tradition-to-modernity paradigm requires − to development.

Introducing the notion of political decay greatly increases the explanatory power of the concept of political development.[28] The critical question is whether the polity is able to settle disputes and allocate resources within its established procedures or whether participation takes place outside these procedures. The effectiveness of established channels depends on the value placed upon them by participants. The more political procedures are valued intrinsically, the more they are institutionalized and the better they will be able to process popular demands.

Political development, for the purposes of this book, has been achieved when existing political institutions can encompass political participation. In decadent polities participation outstrips the capacity of institutions, while in developed polities the two are in balance. In addition, there can be political decay in the case of "overinstitutionalization," where participation is reduced far below the capacity of political institutions. Achieve-

28. Samuel P. Huntington, *Political Order in Changing Societies* (New Haven: Yale University Press, 1968), chap. 1. Critics who argue that Huntington is concerned solely with stability overlook his emphasis on the necessity of building political institutions that can handle growing participation. Huntington recently disavowed the use of "political development" to refer to either participation or institutionalization. "Change to Change," p. 304, n. 42. This may be too hasty. The notion of development focuses inquiry on the question of whether there are structured patterns through which the relationship between participation and institutionalization changes or remains constant.

Huntington's argument is directly challenged on the basis of rather limited evidence from India in Paul R. Brass, "Political Participation, Institutionalization and Stability in India," *Government and Opposition* 4, no. 1 (Winter 1969). I am grateful to Howard Erdman for calling this article to my attention.

ment of this balance may be long-lasting or momentary, and it may appear in the poorest or most traditional of states or disappear in the wealthiest or most industrialized of states. Since the question of balance depends entirely on the relationship of participation and institutions in a particular state, it is also free from the ethnocentric bias that identified development with Western institutions in many earlier studies.

There is an important difficulty that arises out of the intimate link posed here between modernization and participation. If the process of modernization necessarily increases political participation and if modernization is both inevitable and irreversible, it follows that the growth of political participation is inevitable and irreversible. If this conclusion holds, there is little sense in discussing departicipation. Many writers, including Huntington, have accepted the first premise.[29] The second has been an almost universal article of faith, derived from the eighteenth-century rationalist conception of progress. Consider, for example, the definition of modernization "as a continuous series of changes accompanying the growth of knowledge and its effects on man's ways of getting things done".[30]

To reverse this process would imply that man can forget what has gone before and lose capabilities previously possessed. In the twentieth century we find this hard to imagine. But in Europe between A.D. 400 and 1000 there was a cumulative loss in many forms of knowledge that had existed during Roman hegemony. At one time or another flourishing civilizations all over the world have intellectually declined. Social and economic

29. *Political Order,* p. 55; and Myron Weiner, "Participation and Political Development," in *Modernization: The Dynamics of Growth,* ed. Weiner (New York: Basic Books, 1966), p. 211.

30. C. E. Black, *The Dynamics of Modernization: A Study in Comparative History* (New York: Harper & Row, 1966), p. 55. Or consider this approach: "Above all, modernization involves belief in the capacity of man by reasoned action to change his physical and social environments." Huntington, *Political Order,* p. 99. Several writers have specifically asserted that modernization is irreversible. See, for example, Arthur Jay Klinghoffer, "Modernisation and Political Development in Africa," *The Journal of Modern African Studies* 11, no. 1 (March 1973): 3 and 10.

In a later article Huntington briefly suggests the possibility of "primitivization," the reverse of modernization. "Change to Change," p. 298. If the idea of decay adds to our understanding of development, we might profit from closer study of examples of the reversal of modernization. The definition of modernization discussed in chapter three, section 2, below allows for the possibility of reversal.

development projects in the new states may also result on balance in setbacks in the modernization process. For example, investments in education may increase total unemployment; those in showplace projects may greatly reduce scarce productive resources; and those in irrigation projects may seriously depress energy levels through the spread of diseases like bilharzia. The society may find itself with less capacity to control its environment than it previously had and thus be less modernized. On this basis it is possible to argue that modernization is reversible and consequently that political participation is as well.

Political participation has, however, often been regarded as irreversible for less fundamental reasons than the nature of modernization. Those who participate in politics acquire a measure of power which, it is presumed, cannot be taken from them. Almond and Verba premise their entire argument on this assumption. [31] Huntington is explicit: "Power which has been dramatically expanded cannot then be dramatically reduced. Once led out of the cave, the masses cannot again be permanently denied the sunlight." [32] There remains controversy between those who believe that political development is promoted by increased participation and those who argue that it is usually retarded. All seem to agree, however, that the expansion of participation is a one-way street. Nevertheless, the evidence from postindependence African states, discussed in chapters eight and nine, overwhelmingly contradicts this proposition. Departicipation has occurred; many Africans have left the political arena.

There are probably complex relationships between departicipation and social and economic modernization. Departicipation may vary primarily with economic and social factors, or it may be largely a function of leadership strategies. It is likely that all are involved. Departicipation may be more probable at low levels of modernization than at higher ones. It may occur more frequently in a stagnant economy than in a rapidly growing one. Departicipation may appear predominantly in countries in which the factors commonly associated with modernization are

31. *The Civic Culture*, pp. 2, 29, and 373.
32. *Political Order*, p. 308.

themselves declining. For the most part this study will not consider these questions, but they are certainly worthy of further inquiry.

Because of the absence of analytic grounding for departicipation, there have been few references and no discussions of the concept in the literature on political development.[33] One writer suggests that efficient administration may contribute to political "sedation" by depressing political involvement. Government officials may introduce policies that slow social mobilization. Some evidence of "political demobilization" and decay in Africa has been presented. The notion of a "premobilized modern system," which was introduced to explain polities where "the trappings of political modernity − parties, interest groups, and mass media − have been imposed upon highly traditional societies," is a useful formulation.[34] Ironically, perhaps the best available source on sophisticated techniques of departicipation is the United States Commission on Civil Rights, which examined the ways in which southern states limited the right of blacks to use their newly acquired franchise during the 1960s.[35]

To return to the question that opened this section, how is departicipation related to political development? For those working within the tradition-to-modernity paradigm, the possibility of departicipation is unlikely to arise; but if it should, it would be viewed as a temporary setback. On the other hand, if political development is understood to be the balance between

33. Ralph Braibanti, "Administrative Modernization," in *Modernization,* ed. Weiner, p. 167; Samuel P. Huntington, "Political Development and Political Decay," *World Politics* 17, no. 3 (April 1965): 419-421; Christian P. Potholm, *Four African Political Systems* (Englewood Cliffs, N.J.: Prentice-Hall, 1970), pp. 278-286; and Dennis Austin and William Tordoff, "The Newly Independent States," in *Participation in Politics,* ed. Parry, pp. 268-270.

Myron Weiner recently reviewed the concept of participation in the development process but did not consider the possibility of departicipation. The closest he came was to observe that "most governing elites in the developing areas have chosen to restrict rather than enlarge political participation." "Political Participation: Crisis of the Political Process," in *Crises and Sequences,* ed. Binder et al., p. 197.

34. Gabriel Almond and G. Bingham Powell, Jr., *Comparative Politics: A Developmental Approach* (Boston: Little, Brown, 1966), pp. 284-287.

35. These included consolidating counties with black majorities to those with larger white ones; extending the term of office of incumbent white officials; abolishing offices for which blacks decide to run; increasing filing fees; adding requirements

participation and institutionalization, then departicipation may promote political development. When participation has increased to the point where political structures can no longer handle the demands pressed upon them, either better structures or less participation is required to avoid political decay. Which of the two is likely to be the better approach depends on the situation. However, acquiring better political structures necessarily means deinstitutionalization, since it will require time to build popular loyalty to new procedures. Where organizational capacities are low, departicipation may be the more effective strategy.

To put the second alternative more precisely, departicipation is likely to result in fewer political structures as well as less participation. Consequently, deinstitutionalization may also accompany departicipation. If a government decides to departicipate by abolishing elections, it will have reduced one form of political involvement and also removed a participatory structure that may have been institutionalized. It remains an empirical question to discover whether the political change has led to a better balance between participation and institutions. The point is that departicipation is being tried in Africa and may have positive consequences for political development.

4. CONCLUSION

Participation, departicipation, and political development are necessary tools for understanding the strategies employed by African governments to force people out of political life. Since ethnicity is often regarded as the bedrock of African politics, the application of these concepts to ethnic politics provides a test of their utility. Can a government hope to succeed in a policy of ethnic departicipation? Is ethnic departicipation

---

for getting on the ballot; withholding pertinent information about elective office; delaying certification of nominating petitions; posting bond requirements that bonding companies would be unlikely to undertake; reapportionment; at-large elections; and full-slate voting (i.e., a procedure which invalidates the entire ballot if a vote is not cast for every office on the ballot). "Political Participation: A Study of Participation by Negroes in the Electoral and Political Process in Southern States since the Passing of the Voting Rights Act of 1965," Report (Washington, D.C.: U.S. Government Printing Office, 1968). Some of these techniques showed up in African countries; others are irrelevant because of the use of more basic techniques of departicipation, such as not holding elections.

merely one aspect of a general effort to reshape the polity inherited from colonial rulers? These questions are considered in later chapters.

Participation, taken broadly, refers to activity in the political arena. The critical distinction is between involvement and its absence. Participation may be analyzed in terms of personae, scope, bases, weight, and propensity. It may be symbolic or material, direct or indirect, voluntary or manipulated, and it may be expressed through structures that afford varying possibilities of impact on policymaking. To compare the volume of participation in two or more situations requires careful attention to these dimensions.

Departicipation is the reversal of participation, the reduction of political involvement. It can be measured in terms of the same dimensions. However, since departicipation means the absence of at least part of a preexisting activity, it is harder to evaluate than participation. The difficulty lies in determining whether the volume of participation is smaller or has merely taken on a different shape. This problem is particularly complex where different dimensions of participation change in opposite directions or where a departicipatory action sparks off additional participation.

Departicipation has not been discussed in the literature on political development, nor can it be until writers drop the assumption that the expansion of participation is necessarily irreversible. The fundamental question of political development is whether participation and political institutions are in balance. Where participation outruns institutionalization, there is political decay. Where participation is restricted to levels far below those which existing political procedures are capable of handling, there is overinstitutionalization.

In subsaharan black Africa most leaders act as if they perceive participation – particularly ethnic participation – as a distinct threat to the nation. They respond by introducing policies that cause many Africans to depart from the political arena. With a few significant exceptions it seems unlikely that more effective participatory structures will be devised that will soon be highly valued by the people in these countries. The choice, then, is between a long spell of political decay in Africa and departicipation. The latter, of course, may lead to even worse problems for citizens who can no longer hold their leaders to account. However, reducing participation to the level where it can be encompassed by existing institutions may make a measure of political development possible, as well as lay the groundwork for more appropriate institutions than African countries have possessed up to now.

◇

TWO

ETHNICITY

The insignia of ethnicity are inescapable, but ethnic identity is not. Everyone is born into a culture, a language, a territory, and a political organization. Only some, however, are known by these facts of life. The political relevance of ethnicity, then, is problematic. Only where ethnicity seizes the political imagination does it become the basis for political participation.

By the same token ethnicity can also cease to fuel political participation. Some African leaders have tried to achieve departicipation through policies that reduce involvement organized in terms of ethnic loyalties. These policies contradict the notion that participation always leads to political development — one of the basic propositions of writers in the tradition-to-modernity paradigm.

To capture the elusive nature of ethnicity requires examination of the various meanings that have been imposed upon this concept. Given the multitude of identities that have been constructed upon the notion of common ancestry a precise definition of ethnicity may be an evanescent goal. It is well to remember Nietzsche's warning: "Only that which has no history is definable."[1] Still, without applicable concepts, explanation cannot proceed.

1. THE PROBLEM

At a minimum the use of *ethnicity* avoids misleading issues that inflame all discussions of tribalism in modern African politics. First, *tribe* and *tribalism* are emotionally freighted with a connotation of the primitive, the absence of civilization. "All of

1. *On the Genealogy of Morals,* trans. and ed. Walter Kaufman (New York: Random House, 1969), p. 80.

28

them [definitions of tribe] no doubt would reflect an implicit subjective judgment by the user of the word that people he is talking of are 'primitive.' . . ."[2] Analysis is inhibited by the suggestion of inferiority, even though the words are in constant use in African countries. Second, the societies that anthropologists originally classified as tribes were remote, self-sufficient, and culturally distinctive.[3] Few Africans now lead lives so untouched by outside influences that they could possibly qualify as tribesmen in this sense. Third, there are often conflicts *within* what are popularly regarded as tribes. The groups engaged in these struggles may also unite on the basis of ethnic criteria, though on a smaller scale.

As a conceptual tool ethnicity is not burdened by the all too available assumption of monolithic social groups necessarily beholden to atavistic customs. The fundamental question, then, is this: if few Africans are currently members of traditional tribes, in what sense can they be classified as belonging to an ethnic unit? For some writers this is an easy question to answer. P. C. Lloyd begins a recent essay by noting that "Africa's new states have many characteristics in common and one of these is that all are composed of a number of clearly distinguishable ethnic groups."[4] Another writer confidently asserts that "the effective and traditional African community is the tribe, of which a very large number can be definitely distinguished on the basis of language and other cultural traits."[5] And in an

2. Herbert Chitepo, "The Passing of Tribal Man: A Rhodesian View," *Journal of Asian and African Studies* 5, nos. 1-2 (January-April 1970): 10. The view is overstated, but consider, for example, Julian Steward's discussion: "The concept of primitive or 'tribal' culture is based on three fundamental aspects of the behavior of members of tribal societies." He adds that " 'tribal society' herein really has negative connotations. 'Tribes' lack state organization, class structure, literacy, and other features commonly ascribed to 'civilized' societies." *Theory of Culture Change: The Methodology of Multilinear Evolution* (Urbana: University of Illinois Press, 1955), p. 44, and n. 3, p. 44.

3. See Aidan Southall, "The Illusion of Tribe," *Journal of Asian and African Studies* 5, nos. 1-2 (January-April 1970): 28. This is probably the best discussion to date of the difficulties in understanding the meaning of the concepts of tribe and tribalism.

4. "The Ethnic Background to the Nigerian Crisis," in *Nigerian Politics and Military Rule: Prelude to the Civil War*, ed. S. K. Panter-Brick (London: Athlone Press, 1970), p. 1.

5. Carl J. Friedrich, *Man and His Government: An Empirical Theory of Politics* (New York: McGraw-Hill, 1963), p. 544.

extremely influential essay, Clifford Geertz argues that primordial bonds, "the product, in most cases, of centuries of gradual crystallization," possess "a deeply abiding strength in most of the new states. . . ."[6]

But how are we to reconcile these views with the fact that many major ethnic aggregates, such as the Bangala in Zaire and the Baluhyia in Kenya, were *created* in the past century and others, like the Kikuyu in Kenya, the Bagisu in Uganda, and the Yoruba and Ibo in Nigeria, did not find unity (that is, did not become a single "tribe" for political purposes) until well after the beginning of the colonial period? Furthermore, what does a Ugandan mean when he says that "it is very discouraging to learn that some of us [Banyarwanda] due to unfavourable conditions *have changed to being either Bakiga or Bahororo* . . ."?[7] And how can we explain President Idi Amin's claim that "everybody in Africa is free to become a member of the Nubian tribe" and his assertion that members of several ethnic units scattered all over Uganda have already done so?

If ethnic groupings are the product of deeply felt loyalties built out of objective characteristics developed over long periods of time, how is it possible for individuals to change their group? One answer might be that social conventions have somewhat permeable boundaries and a few persons will pass from their own group into some other. Another approach, though, would be to suggest that the question may be wrongly formulated. In postindependence African politics we are often not dealing with ethnic groups in the sense of stable, coherent, and long-persisting entities, and — contrary to Geertz's argument — these entities are often not primordial.

If false concreteness is attributed to the concept of tribe, the process of ethnic participation is likely to be misunderstood. Most actors and many observers commonly assume that ethnicity creates the basis for continuous political loyalty to tightly knit groups. Given this premise, the issue is not the nature of ethnicity, but whether it is the natural element on

6. "The Integrative Revolution: Primordial Sentiments and Civil Politics in the New States," *Old Societies and New States: The Quest for Modernity in Asia and Africa,* ed. Geertz (New York: Free Press, 1963), pp. 119 and 114.

7. Esau S. Mfitumukisa, *Uganda Argus,* 8 November 1971, p. 2 (italics added); and Amin, *Voice of Uganda,* 23 April 1974, p. 1. The Nubians are discussed briefly in chapter eight.

which to build new national loyalties or the source of factions that destroy them. For example, Kofi Busia, while prime minister of Ghana, wanted to extend "the brotherhood of family or tribe to the wider brotherhood of the nation." A supporter of the Kabaka argued that the former kingdom of Buganda should be preserved through adoption of a federal system in Uganda, since "loyalty to the nation is only forming, whereas tribal loyalty is an accomplished and ingrained fact."[8] In emphatic agreement W. Arthur Lewis argues that

> any idea that one can make different peoples into a nation by suppressing the religious or tribal or regional or other affiliations to which they themselves attach the highest political significance is simply a nonstarter. National loyalty cannot immediately supplant tribal loyalty; it has to be built on top of tribal loyalty by creating a system in which all the tribes feel that there is room for self-expression.[9]

Other observers, however, note the dangers of ethnicity for the polity. Edward Feit thinks that "the British government acted as Hobbes's Leviathan. . . . Once [the] compact was dissolved and no new Leviathan appeared, the tribes began to revert to a 'state of nature' with each against the other." [10] Similar fears bring Rupert Emerson to the observation that the response of a tribe led by successful entrepreneurs may be "to tighten its ranks in order to safeguard its gains while those less favored seek to press their own cause by organizing their community for concerted self-defense."[11]

8. "Speech at the Inauguration of the Second Republic at Black Star Square, Accra," reprinted in *Weekly News Bulletin* (Kampala: Ghana High Commission, 15 November 1969), p. 4; "The Background to the Events Leading to the 'Suspension' of the Uganda Constitution by Dr. A. Milton Obote, Prime Minister of Uganda in February, 1966," stenciled (Mengo, 11 March 1966), p. 3.

For reasons of this sort political scientists have often called upon leaders of African states to adopt "some species of novel ethnic federalism." Friedrich, *Man and His Government,* p. 544.

9. *Politics in West Africa* (New York: Oxford University Press, 1965), p. 68.

10. "Military Coups and Political Developments: Some Lessons from Ghana and Nigeria," in *Governing in Black Africa: Perspectives on New States,* ed. Marion E. Doro and Newell M. Stultz (Englewood Cliffs, N.J.: Prentice-Hall, 1970), p. 228.

11. "The Problem of Identity, Selfhood, and Image in the New Nations: The Situation in Africa," *Comparative Politics* 1, no. 1 (April 1969): 307.

The point is that whether actors and observers are in favor of, or opposed to, ethnic participation, they rarely think that ethnic units, *as groups*, can be ignored. "Tribalism," says Colin Legum, "is Africa's natural condition, and is likely to remain so for a long time to come — certainly for the rest of this century. . . ."[12] Ethnicity penetrates, it would seem, to the very core of identity. But whether these units actually form groups that play a sustained role in African politics and whether ethnicity is based on fundamental values are issues too complex to be taken as unquestioned assumptions.

2. INADEQUATE CRITERIA OF ETHNICITY

The nature of ethnicity has aroused much controversy among anthropologists. Their debate, interestingly enough, has a familiar ring for political scientists. Many of the difficulties of identifying ethnic bonds turn on the same issues as the determination of class bonds in highly industrialized states.

Class membership can be inferred through either subjective or objective measures. The problem presented by the former — class consciousness — turns on the question of whether each presumed member (as well as the researcher) has the same perception of class in mind. This obstacle can be overcome by relying on objective measures — occupation, education, or income. But these criteria raise the opposite question: do they have the intended meaning to the persons studied? Objective measures also raise other issues. Which set of occupations or ranges of income or education make up each class? How can distinct class boundaries be determined when the objective variables that constitute them are continuous? Also, if more than one variable is used, does the class enclose those who are included by one standard but excluded by another? Presumably, a joint approach involving both subjective and objective measures could overcome these obstacles, though discrepancies between both sets of measures would remain.

Exactly the same issue of subjective versus objective determinants dominates the controversy over the meaning of ethnicity in Africa (and elsewhere, under the label of "nationalism"). Two other underlying themes also fuel the controversy. First, discussions of ethnicity may use definitions based on elite

12. "Tribal Survival in the Modern African Political System," *Journal of Asian and African Studies* 5, nos. 1-2 (January-April 1970): 102.

behavior, on mass behavior, or on the interaction of the two. Frequently, only one of these three is intended. As suggested in the next chapter, the dispute on this issue is often ideological, with liberal scholars focusing on masses and radicals on elites. Second, the definition of ethnicity depends heavily on one's conception of man as motivated either by rational calculations of his self-interest, or by fundamental values rooted in his subconscious, or by some combination of the two. Some of the more recent contributions to the anthropological literature have shifted from a value-oriented approach to one which considers the rationality of choices made from the range of options open to an individual in a given situation.

The various assumptions made in terms of these three dimensions (subjective-objective, mass-elite, and values-rationality) affect the definitions of ethnicity that have been employed in Africa, as well as their applications to politics. These definitions can be most easily organized for discussion according to their emphasis on objective criteria, generated either internally or externally to the ethnic unit, or on subjective characteristics.

A variety of objective criteria, including language, territory, political organization, culture, common name, and descent legend, have been proposed.[13] Each trait suggests an explanation for the claim of common ancestry of individuals who cannot demonstrate actual relations of kinship. For the most part these criteria are created internally by the people whose identity is being examined. But there are also cases of external criteria, notably colonial administrative classifications, that have been imposed upon — and have thus redefined — people. Although useful in particular cases, none of these seems to be generally applicable, either singly or in combination. Consequently they are insufficient bases for a definition.

Culture, long the anthropological premise for classifying people, is often still regarded as "the essence of tribe."[14] Behind

13. Although race can also be the basis of ethnicity (so long as the inheritance of physical characteristics is accepted as part of the definition), it will not be considered. Outside of southern Africa the monopoly of political power is held by the majority race. The argument presented here is concerned with the issues raised by ethnicity in the context of political participation by black Africans only.

14. P. H. Gulliver, "Introduction," in *Tradition and Transition in East Africa: Studies of the Tribal Element in the Modern Era,* ed. Gulliver (London: Routledge & Kegan Paul, 1969), p. 20. He adds that regionalism is an additional factor that must be taken into account in understanding "tribes" in East Africa. Ibid., pp. 19-24.

the mask of national behavior, argues Victor Uchendu, "lie deep-seated tribal value-systems which continue in many subtle ways to influence the attitudes and behaviours of our elites. These in turn strengthen the tribal society and culture." [15]

However, there are serious conceptual difficulties in making ethnicity equivalent to culture. First, there may be two ethnic aggregates accepted as distinct political groups, such as the Batoro and Banyoro in Uganda, which have identical cultural practices (and, for that matter, languages). Second, cultural practices often grade gradually into those of another group, so that boundaries are hard to establish. [16] Third, certain cultural practices necessarily involve members of a different ethnic aggregate. For example, in Uganda Bakonzo use Baamba circumcisers. Are the Baamba to be regarded as "Bakonzo" for certain purposes? Fourth, culture changes over time and over ecological variance; yet the ethnic aggregate may persist and include these differing cultural patterns. [17] Finally, there is often a selection process in which certain cultural practices are peculiar to the identity of a particular ethnic aggregate. But it is rarely clear why certain traits are essential and others merely shared in common with those possessing different ethnic identities. Similar problems afflict the use of descent legends to specify ethnic aggregates, as the details may vary, subtly or blatantly, from one teller to another.

Language is another basis for defining ethnicity. It is subject to many of the same difficulties faced by definitions based on culture. Complicated problems emerge in attempts to establish boundaries between languages and determine whether related dialects are part of language A or language B or are themselves third and fourth languages. [18] Sometimes an accepted ethnic aggregate is made up of people speaking two or more mutually unintelligible languages. The Baamba live in interspersed villages in which either Bwezi or Bulibuli is spoken. Because of pre-

15. "The Passing of Tribal Man: A West African Experience," *Journal of Asian and African Studies* 5, nos. 1-2 (January-April 1970): 56.

16. Gertrude E. Dole, "Tribe as the Autonomous Unit," in *Essays on the Problem of Tribe,* ed. June Helm (Seattle: University of Washington Press, 1968), p. 86.

17. Fredrik Barth, "Introduction," in *Ethnic Groups and Boundaries: The Social Organization of Culture Difference,* ed. Barth (London: George Allen & Unwin, 1969), pp. 12, 14.

18. Dole, "Tribe as the Autonomous Unit," p. 84.

colonial conquest and assimilation, several languages are spoken among the Azande, the Lozi, and the Alur. Often the ethnic aggregate is identified before or during the process of establishing a standard language for the group. In these cases a single language is usually perceived as a requirement of the prevailing definition of ethnicity, and thus members of the aggregate — determined in some other way — attempt to reconcile divergent dialects in order to create a "pure" language.[19]

Another criterion put forward to define ethnic units is traditional political organization. E. E. Evans-Pritchard defines the tribe as the largest community that accepts arbitration as the means of settling disputes and that would combine against similar communities and against strangers in times of war. [20] The price of such a precise definition is that it produces hundreds of "tribes" in place of the one that was previously acknowledged. [21] Such a definition may sometimes help in examining traditional systems but not in explaining present political units, where there are usually different bases for establishing arbitration. [22] Furthermore, this definition takes no account of the changes wrought by recent influences, since it requires that an individual's ancestry be traced back to the earlier group in order to determine his ethnic identity. In most instances the exercise would teach us nothing about his ethnic participation in postindependence politics.

Finally, within the category of internal objective criteria, territoriality has been offered to define ethnicity. I. M. Lewis suggests that tribe "has become a technical term denoting a territorially defined political unit. . . ."[23] Although it is tempting to permit geography to settle the problems of social science, such a solution leaves us with the complex question of migra-

19. J. S. La Fontaine, "Tribalism among the Gisu: An Anthropological Approach," in *Tradition and Transition in East Africa,* ed. Gulliver, p. 184.
20. "The Nuer," in M. Fortes and E. E. Evans-Pritchard, *African Political Systems* (London: Oxford University Press, 1940), p. 278.
21. Southall, "The Illusion of Tribe," p. 43.
22. Nor is it always applicable in precolonial systems. "Units of government and primordial groups did not necessarily coincide in traditional Africa." Aristide Zolberg, "Patterns of National Integration," in *Governing in Black Africa,* ed. Doro and Stultz, p. 177.
23. This, of course, introduces a second (political) criterion as well. It is not clear how much relevance Lewis thinks the term has in contemporary African conditions. "Tribal Society," *International Encyclopedia of the Social Sciences,* vol. 16 (New York: Free Press, 1968), p. 146.

tion, particularly to urban areas. Is a man still a member of his ethnic unit when he leaves its "territory?" The evidence discussed in chapter three suggests that for many migrants ethnic affiliation is so changed by the requirements of city life that traditional ethnic units no longer have the same, if any, meaning. New ethnic units may form in the towns.

In most African cities there is a complex mixture of people from different traditional ethnic units. Territoriality can no longer serve as the definition of ethnicity when different units occupy the same area. Nor can the argument be saved by noting the close relationships many city dwellers maintain with their country relatives unless those links can be shown to be continuously more influential than the newer urban ethnic solidarities. Even precolonial ethnic aggregates may not have escaped this problem, since there was much migration and intermixture at that time as well.

Setting district and county boundaries on the basis of administrators' conceptions of tribe is an *external*, though objective, criterion (in the sense that it did not emanate from the minds of the people making up the unit). The official boundaries, plus other colonial policies of imposing indirect rule and gathering census data on the basis of these "tribes," tended to reify some units that were never in existence before.

Southall describes the emergence of the Baluhyia in western Kenya, which occurred between 1935 and 1945: "Before that time no such group existed either in its own or anyone else's estimation. . . . This new supertribe was closely linked to the colonial administrative framework. . . ."[24] Colonial administrators and scholars played the central role in developing the "Bangala" and Mongo as ethnic units in what was then the Belgian Congo.[25] Thus, Raymond Apthorpe asserts that "certainly in Anglophone Africa, what happened was that the colonial regimes administratively *created* tribes as we think of them today. . . ."[26]

If the colonial administrators were solely responsible for the creation of current ethnic units, we could easily solve our

24. "The Illusion of Tribe," p. 34. Further examples of formation of larger ethnic units due to outside influences will be discussed in the next chapter.
25. Charles W. Anderson, Fred von der Mehden, and Crawford Young, *Issues of Political Development* (Englewood Cliffs, N.J.: Prentice-Hall, 1967), pp. 31-34.
26. "Does Tribalism Really Matter?" *Transition* 7, no. 6 (October 1968): 18.

definitional problems. But again there are difficulties. Not all administrative demarcations identify ethnic units. For example, several districts (and counties) in Uganda possess more than one ethnic aggregate. Some districts are perceived as ethnic units (Acholi and Lango, for example), while others are not and have never achieved ethnic recognition, though not for lack of trying (West Nile and Bukedi among others). Without further criteria, how can one tell which administrative units define ethnic aggregates and which do not?

Reliance on several factors makes the definition of ethnicity more complex but suggests the possibility of avoiding the weakness of any single criterion. The most explicit recent effort to develop a multiple set of objective criteria for the definition of ethnicity is probably the "cultunit" proposed by Raoul Naroll. It includes those who speak a common, distinct language and belong to the same state or, where there is no state but rather a common sociopolitical organization, the same contact group. [27]

If the multiple-criteria approach avoids some problems, it creates others. It suggests, on the assumption of exact correspondence of language, political organization, territory, or whatever criteria are relied upon, that the common system is a closed one, an inference which is almost always false. Or the assumption itself is false, which suggests that each criterion implies a *different* unit with different, though overlapping, members.[28] Furthermore, no combination of the objective criteria will be sufficient to explain urban ethnicity (aside from the cases of pure traditional transplants from the countryside).

The alternative to objective determinants of ethnicity is to consider the group consciousness of participants — that is, when people perceive themselves to be an ethnic group, they become one. And when outsiders perceive people as belonging to an ethnic group, the group exists. Several writers insist on some variant of subjective identification as the basis of ethnicity. [29]

27. "Who the Lue Are," in *Essays on the Problem of Tribe,* ed. Helm, p. 72. Naroll originally proposed a longer list of criteria to determine ethnicity. "On Ethnic Unit Classification," *Current Anthropology* 5, no. 4 (October 1964).

28. Dole, "Tribe as Autonomous Unit," p. 88.

29. James S. Coleman, *Nigeria: Background to Nationalism* (Berkeley and Los Angeles: University of California Press, 1958), p. 426; Crawford Young, *Politics in the Congo: Decolonization and Independence* (Princeton: Princeton University Press, 1965), p. 234; Barth, "Introduction," p. 13; and Walker Connor, "Self-Determination: The New Phase," *World Politics* 20, no. 1 (October 1967): 30.

From this perspective "an ethnic group is identical with the *theory* which its members have of it."[30] The strength of this approach is that it focuses on the major factor we would expect to find in ethnic political participation — individuals who perceive their role in politics on the basis of ethnic loyalty.

Here, though, the problem is matching perceptions of different presumed members — as well as those of outsiders. Does each believe he belongs to the same entity as the others? Do nonmembers agree? The question is testable but not resolvable without additional criteria. It is possible to devise instruments which determine the ethnic identity an individual accepts. [31] But this definition cannot account for discrepancies growing out of different opinions about the inclusion of others held by those accepting a particular ethnic identity. If outsiders see themselves as part of the same unit as insiders while the latter reject them, who are the members of the group? Consider, for example, the case of those Banyarwanda who desire to assimilate but who are rejected by the Baganda.

There exist more complex cases which also demonstrate the inadequacy of this definition. Suppose there are several subgroups of which members of A see themselves in alliance with B and E, while members of B perceive themselves in alliance with C and D.[32] Baamba village alliances demonstrate just this sort of pattern. Finally, there is a mass and elite problem. Generally, an ethnic elite will assert that there is one strongly united group. But members of the masses included by this elite may not perceive themselves as part of the same group or indeed of any group larger than their own villages.

30. Paul Mercier, "On the Meaning of 'Tribalism' in Black Africa," in *Africa: Problems of Conflict and Change,* ed. Pierre van den Berghe (San Francisco: Chandler, 1965), p. 487.

31. For example, see the psychological tests used in Marshall Segall, Martin Doornbos, and Clive Davis, *The Dynamics of Self-Identification among the Banyankole in Uganda* (forthcoming), and in Otto Klineberg and Marisa Zavalloni, *Nationalism and Tribalism among African Students: A Study of Social Identity* (Paris and The Hague: Mouton, 1969).

32. Dole, "Tribe as the Autonomous Unit," p. 85; and Edward Winter, "The Aboriginal Political Structure of Bwamba," in *Tribes without Rulers: Studies in African Segmentary Systems,* ed. John Middleton and David Tait (London: Routledge & Kegan Paul, 1958), pp. 153-158.

3. PUTTING THE PIECES TOGETHER

If neither a pure subjective criterion nor any combination of objective criteria is sufficient to make ethnicity a useful analytic tool, we must find a method to combine the two or reject the concept as unprofitable. A technique that can bridge the two sets of criteria has been developed to study the ethnic categories people use in dealing with one another in particular encounters. This approach finds ethnicity existing only when those under scrutiny define their situation in terms of ethnic indicators and act on that determination. In essence this view grows out of Evans-Pritchard's explanation of the contingent and shifting formation of Nuer political alliances in terms of the "genealogical" *situation* in which two hostile Nuer find themselves.[33]

The notion of ethnic categories came from an experiment carried out by J. Clyde Mitchell to determine the social distances among twenty-one Central African "tribes" (identified on the basis of lineage descent) perceived by respondents chosen from each of them.[34] The respondents grouped the "tribes" into different categories depending on the level of prestige accorded to each, the geographical distance separating their territories, and the degree of similarity in traditional cultural practices.

The important point is not the variation in bases of the categories, but the fact that the respondents found it necessary to resort to them. As Mitchell explains, they use these categories because they regard " 'tribe' as the primary category of social interaction, that is, the first significant characteristic to which any African reacts in another," but cannot handle the complexity implied by persons who see themselves as coming

33. "The Nuer." I am grateful to Conrad Reining for making this connection clear to me.

34. *The Kalela Dance,* The Rhodes-Livingstone Institute, paper no. 27 (Manchester: Manchester University Press, 1956). Mitchell became interested in the Kalela dance because it was popularly regarded as a tribal dance, yet the dancers wore European clothing and acted out certain European roles. "The paradox . . . raised the whole question of what tribalism meant *in that situation."* Mitchell, "Some Aspects of Tribal Social Distance," in *The Multitribal Society,* ed. A. A. Dubb (Proceedings of the Sixteenth Conference of the Rhodes-Livingstone Institute: Lusaka, February 1962), p. 5.

from a multitude of groups.[35] Social situations become more manageable through the creation of large ethnic units that contain a variety of smaller units that an anthropologist might distinguish on the basis of objective ethnic characteristics.

For Mitchell the categories are established by outsiders. Insiders — that is, members of a particular "tribe" — need not categorize, since they share norms and values. According to recent studies, ethnic categories have been employed in similar fashion in a rural trading center and a district capital in Uganda.[36] Because the indicators used to establish the categories were incorrect or inadequate in several cases, it was clear that many people were being perceived as members of groups different from those in which they would classify themselves. These categories do not indicate any necessary relationships between the categorizer and the categorized. Thus, they are not intended to suggest the notion of "supertribes."[37] However, the statistical results of Mitchell's experiment suggest that the categories may have become infused with social responses and therefore may have created the basis for ethnic political participation.

Taken by itself, a theory based on the categories that emerge from interaction is totally inadequate to the task of defining ethnicity. It is intended as an explanation of ethnicity only in those areas in which people using a variety of languages and customs mix — that is, in urban areas. It explicitly excludes some behavior that it concedes to be ethnic. Thus, it regards certain personal relationships based on shared norms as some "other" form of ethnicity to be defined in an unspecified manner. It takes the view of the outsider and never the insider. Like other phenomenological approaches to ethnicity, it cannot handle the situation in which different actors (here limited to outsiders) conflict over the boundaries of the categories they apply.

35. *Kalela Dance,* p. 32; and "Tribe and Social Change in South Central Africa: A Situational Approach," *Journal of Asian and African Studies* 5, nos. 1-2 (January-April 1970): 89.

36. Joan Vincent, *African Elite: The Big Men of a Small Town* (New York: Columbia University Press, 1971), p. 167; and D. R. Pain, "Ethnicity in a Small Town" (paper delivered to the East African Universities Social Science Council Conference, Nairobi, December 1972).

37. See J. Rouch, "Migrations au Ghana," *Journal de la Société Aricanistes* 26, nos. 1-2 (1956): 163-164, cited in I. Wallerstein, "Ethnicity and National Integration in West Africa," in *Africa: Problems of Change and Conflict,* ed. van den Berghe, p. 474.

Finally, and ironically, Mitchell used lineage descent, an objective indicator of ethnicity, to determine which "tribes" would be included in his survey. His categories merely group together other ethnic units determined in a far more casual manner. One has to understand the results of Mitchell's work to demonstrate nothing more than the proposition that given an objective determination of tribe, people will regroup those "tribes" of which they are not members into ethnic categories. These categories may or may not have social significance in certain situations in urban areas.

However, there are three important points to be drawn from his work which lead to a more precise, yet comprehensive, conception of ethnicity in its political manifestations. First, the emphasis on understanding the actors' behavior in terms of the *situation* with which they are coping is fundamental. Second, the categories with which they (that is, *all* actors – both insiders and outsiders) define their response to that situation are clues to their behavior. Third (and going beyond Mitchell's research results), their definitions are not necessarily individual responses only but may be cemented into social solidarity which may then provide the ground for political action.

To examine ethnicity in terms of the situation enormously complicates analysis because it means that the actors' self-definitions in the given situation may or may not involve ethnic considerations. Consequently, ethnicity becomes a variable, intermittently politically salient. Vincent puts this well: "Ethnicity in operation is, like all else social, a tool in the hands of men; it is not a mystic force in itself; there is nothing sacrosanct about the African tribe."[38] To accept this argument leaves open the possibility that ethnic political participation may issue from deeply held values or from a rational calculation of the advantages to be gained in particular situations.

Men in traditional precolonial systems may also have possessed several identities which varied according to the situation. Thus, an individual's definition of his behavior, or role, may have varied depending on whether he was interacting with his family, with a near or distant neighbor with whom he was feuding, with a chief from whom he received orders, or with a stranger with whom he was bartering. Ethnicity was an appropriate role in certain cases and not others (and perhaps *useful* to

38. *African Elite,* p. 10.

achieve desired goals in a third set of cases). Thus, Michael
Moerman argues: "To the serious student of society, the prefer-
ring of any identification should be a problematic phenomenon,
not a comforting answer. The question is not, 'Who are the
Lue?' . . . but rather when and how and why the identification
of 'Lue' is preferred."[39]

To pose the issue in this way removes obstacles that pre-
vented us from accepting the definitions of ethnicity suggested
earlier. We do not need a criterion that will presume the
existence of ethnicity at every moment. We can examine situations to determine whether ethnicity is the response of particular actors and why this should be so. Naturally, we still need to
know what ethnic identity is assumed in those cases, and
therefore we still need to specify the concept.

The categories through which people define the roles of
others may determine their own responses. If the other actors in
a situation are perceived as acting in ethnic roles, one way to
reduce complexity in understanding and acting in that situation
is to adopt a self-definition using the same criteria. In political
disputes it may also secure the one base to which certain of
one's opponents have no legitimate claim. Also, the stereotypes
people assume about others often suggest courses of action
which they are likely to take themselves.

We need not, however, argue solely from categories imposed
on others to the political behavior of the individual. People also
impose categories on themselves, and these categories may or
may not be consistent with those they impose on others. In
accepting this view of categories as either a mode of perceiving
others, or as an identity to be adopted by the actor, we can
ignore Mitchell's distinction between the ethnicity of categories
and the "tribalism" of shared personal relationships. When
shared, norms dictate categories that persons assume for themselves.

When the ethnic role will become important to an individual
cannot be predicted a priori. Objective ethnic indicators such as
language, sense of territory, or common descent may be far
more salient to someone after he has left his traditional home
than before. There are other cases in which the sense of tradi-

39. "Being Lue: Uses and Abuses of Ethnic Identification," in *Essays on the
Problem of Tribe,* ed. Helm, p. 160.

tion is sufficiently relevant to those in the home area that they remain strongly cognizant of the community to which they feel they belong. The Baganda provide a good example of the continuity of a traditional feeling of unity, though many of their customs have been modified by more recent social and economic influences. There is a third type of case, in which ethnicity based on the home area does not develop and a completely new ethnic unit is formed to take its place. Most new ethnic units have grown out of urban situations. In all three types of cases, there are changes in the ideology of ethnicity growing out of colonial and postindependence influences, but it remains possible for traditional factors to play an important role — or to be replaced by new pseudotraditions. There are examples of each of these types in the ethnic aggregates existing in Uganda, and these will be discussed in later chapters.

But no categories imposed by the individual will be reliable predictors of *social* action until they become the basis of a felt social bond. Immanuel Wallerstein suggests that "membership in an ethnic group is a matter of social definition, an interplay of the self-definition of members and the definition of other groups."[40] But beyond this interplay there has to be some mobilization of loyalty which — at least for that situation — draws together a large number of people on the basis of specific (existing or fictitious) characteristics.

La Fontaine provides an example in her interpretation of the coalescence of ethnicity among the Bagisu:

> "Tribal culture" provides an ideology of unity rather than any real identity of interests, by symbolizing the moral community. The Gisu are not united by a common language and rituals rather they are united when opposed to non-Gisu and represent this by reference to language and culture. The cultural symbols of tribalism are thus abstractions from cultural reality, not its basic elements.[41]

Ethnicity is situational since it appears only when Bagisu confront outsiders. At this time objective traits — language and culture — become symbols around which people rally. For the

40. "Ethnicity and National Integration in West Africa," in *Africa: Problems of Change and Conflict,* ed. van den Berghe, p. 474.
41. "Tribalism among the Gisu," pp. 189-190.

duration those who have been mobilized are not just an aggregate of individuals who can be identified as possessing the same trait. They have formed an ethnic *group*.

In later chapters I will cover some of the reasons that lead to the formation of this "ideology of unity." For the moment it is sufficient to assert that it is an essential element in the conception of ethnicity. Looking at ethnicity from this perspective, we could say that it does not exist until people feel it exists for themselves and then only if they are willing to act upon it for some social or political purpose. It is likely that ethnic categories used by outsiders will be shaped by, and may for a time reinforce, this social solidarity.

At this point a more useful concept of ethnicity can be specified. It consists of four elements:

1. certain objective characteristics associated with common ancestry, such as language, territory, cultural practices, and the like (in some cases newly created or recently standardized),
2. which are perceived by both insiders and outsiders as important indicators of identity,
3. so that they can become the bases for mobilizing social solidarity, and
4. which, in certain situations, result in political activity.

The concept seems to be applicable in situations outside Africa, since Andrew Janos uses a similar approach in his discussion of ethnicity in Eastern Europe:

> Most frequently used in reference to language, its meaning is sometimes extended to cover common social, cultural, and physical characteristics transmitted as a matter of inheritance and capable of producing social solidarities based on affect. So defined, ethnicity has both subjective and objective dimensions, for it refers both to perceptible traits and to perception whereby the former assume social relevance.[42]

42. "Ethnicity, Communism, and Political Change in Eastern Europe," *World Politics* 23, no. 3 (April 1971): 493. Janos warns of the difficulties in relating objective to subjective characteristics. However, the virtue of this approach is that it permits such difficulties to be handled as empirical problems.

Thus, ethnicity exists only where it is the basis of community, though the motives for belonging to that community could be based on rational self-interest or fundamental values. Where social solidarity cannot be produced, there can be no ethnic group, though there might be ethnic political action by individuals acting alone. When the situation creating the basis for ethnic involvement disappears, the ethnic group may also disappear, though other factors could stabilize its existence. This leaves us with an extraordinarily complex research task, for in Morton Fried's words: "We can readily recognize that ethnic groups are transitory phenomena with variable memberships oscillating about shifting mythic charters. Simultaneously we can recognize that such associations do possess at least contemporary reality and may raise demands that have to be dealt with on the political level."[43] The research problem is not impossible, of course. The more that objective ethnic characteristics converge in a given population and the more that they vary from those held by outsiders, the more likely it is that a distinctive ethnic unit will emerge — assuming the situation lends itself to the formation or activation of an ethnic unit.

To return to a previously mentioned problem with most approaches to ethnicity, how can disputes *within* ethnic units also be ethnic conflicts? With this approach intraethnic conflict may also be based on ethnic mobilization. The situation will determine which objective characteristics are perceived as important and thus which units become relevant. These might be subunits that compete among themselves for valued goods but unite on the basis of overarching characteristics to repel outsiders. The unit is ethnic so long as objective characteristics such as language or customs are used to define it. If other characteristics such as wealth or social status are used to mobilize people, ethnicity is not an applicable concept.

Finally, let us return to the earlier suggestion that it is misleading to understand ethnicity in terms of "primordial groups." Both words create difficulties. Primordial qualities are objective characteristics that may or may not be possessed by an ethnic unit. Intense loyalty may be pledged to a newly formed unit with fictitious credentials. The influence of

43. "On the Concepts of 'Tribe' and 'Tribal Society,' " in *Essays on the Problem of Tribe,* ed. Helm, pp. 10-11.

modernization resulting from the colonial situation has transformed those qualities that might be regarded as primordial. In all cases the question is empirical, not definitional.

Of greater significance is the danger of conceiving of ethnicity as inevitably leading to politicized "groups." To do so suggests that something like interest-group politics in America describes the behavior of ethnic aggregates in Africa. This is not a useful analogy if American interest groups are pictured as coherent units that are constantly involved in politics in order to protect and promote the interests of their members. African ethnic groups exist intermittently.[44] They sometimes disappear, leaving their members available for political participation through new ethnic (or other types of) units. The danger lies in endowing ethnic groups with a false concreteness that obscures their fluidity. To make these points, however, is not to deny in any way the extraordinary power with which ethnic units can put forward demands and directly challenge the legitimacy of the state when their members are mobilized. Ethnic political participation is intense participation.

4. CONCLUSION

The nature of ethnicity is often oversimplified in discussions of African politics. Creating a picture of easily distinguishable and continuously functioning rival ethnic groups fails to account for both the existence of many smaller ethnic units and the ability of individuals to shift in or out of an ethnic identity. Examination of the definitions offered for ethnicity demonstrates that neither internal nor external objective criteria nor consciousness of group membership is sufficient. Instead, ethnicity must be viewed as the social solidarity resulting from an ideology of unity based on actual or fictitious cultural, geographical, or political characteristics.

Ethnicity may become salient in some political situations but not in others. Individuals urgently assembled to press ethnic appeals may coalesce into groups existing for longer or shorter periods of time. Some of these groups may be based on the revival of traditional unity, while others will be brand-new. Recognizing the fluidity of ethnic action is the first step toward understanding its political impact, as well as the strategies adopted by political leaders to reduce that impact.

44. See the brief discussion of "nonassociational interest groups," in Almond and Powell, *Comparative Politics*, pp. 76-77.

THREE

◇

ETHNICITY AND AFRICAN POLITICS

How important is ethnicity in African political behavior? Before considering its role in Uganda, we need to decide whether it is merely a superficial rationalization for other political variables or a fundamental cause. The decision requires a look at the implications of the view of ethnicity developed in the preceding chapter and at two alternative explanations that are sometimes regarded as more basic than ethnicity. These are modernization and class.

If full reliance is placed on either of these latter explanations, ethnicity must be relegated to a minor role primarily as a facade hiding more salient factors. If African politics is understood as the consequence of socioeconomic modernization, ethnicity may be perceived as part of the more or less rapidly eroding traditional past. If African politics is viewed in terms of class formation or class conflict, ethnicity is likely to be explained as the "superstructural" expression of vested economic interests. In both cases ethnicity is seen as an irrelevant variable, at best a consequence, not a cause, of fundamental political change.

Alternatively, if we assume that ethnicity at times may be an independent variable, it may be more useful to consider the interrelationship between ethnicity and modernization and between ethnicity and class in the political process. There are cases in which modernization creates situations in which ethnic appeals are made to serve new, nontraditional goals. Similarly, despite the conventional notion that class and ethnicity are mutually exclusive variables, they may both be present in some political situations and either reinforce or blunt the impact of each other.

As we shall see, not only have arguments based on concepts of modernization and class unduly restricted the scope of eth-

47

nicity in the explanation of African politics, they have also distorted its meaning. In regard to the three themes in which ethnicity generally has been discussed (objectivity versus subjectivity; mass versus elite; and fundamental values versus self-interest), the modernization and the class perspectives rest on assumptions that are irreconcilable. The definition of ethnicity used here has the advantage of leaving the exact combination of variables involved in each of these themes to empirical investigation. Thus, the argument of this chapter is that ethnicity is a salient and often independent factor in African politics, interrelating with modernization and class in complex fashion.

1. ANALYSIS OF ETHNICITY IN AFRICAN POLITICS

As I suggested in the previous chapter, ethnicity becomes politically important when people are mobilized on the basis of objective characteristics such as culture, language, territory, and the like. Mobilization means the conscious acceptance of membership in the same social unit by holders of (or, more precisely, claimants to) a particular trait. This consciousness may continue for a brief or a long time and be felt intensely or superficially, depending on the circumstances or situation.

This approach helps to clarify several puzzling features of ethnic involvement in African politics. First, it suggests a useful framework to explain the extraordinarily fluid character of political ethnicity − its sudden buildup to intensity and its equally sudden (though often temporary) disappearance. Second, this approach provides a way to specify the group actually participating in politics and thus goes part of the way toward answering the question that Lloyd Fallers posed just before independence came to tropical Africa: "What, indeed, is the 'real' unit, the unit which *matters*?"[1]

The fluidity of ethnic political action makes it highly unpredictable and thus frightening to African governments. Ethnicity is felt to be more the tidal wave of African politics than the tidal ebb and flow. Thus, leaders often try to legislate it out of existence. Politics in Ghana and Uganda exhibit this characteristic with particular clarity.

Following the formation of the National Liberation Movement (NLM) among the Ashanti in the mid-1950s, for example,

1. "Africa: Scholarship and Policy," *World Politics* 9, no. 2 (January 1957): 290.

ethnic loyalty was so intense that five thousand Convention People's Party (CPP) supporters and non-Ashanti residents in Ashanti areas were forced to flee to the coast.[2] Several other ethnic parties appeared in Ghana at this time. Kwame Nkrumah, whose party, the CPP, was perceived to draw its core support among the Fanti in the south, pushed through legislation to attack this problem by making ethnic parties illegal.[3] In spite of indications of the extraordinary intensity of ethnic loyalties at this time, a decade later the question, according to one observer, was whether the military government that took power from Nkrumah had "inadvertently . . . allowed the *almost* buried 'tribal' feeling to resurface."[4]

Uganda presents a similar pattern (described in chapter five): ethnic movements became intense forces in politics and then melted away. To some degree their subsidence was the consequence of a determined political effort by central government officials. Here also legislation made ethnic parties illegal.[5] The surprising point was the degree of the government's success in reducing the public assertion of ethnicity. Although ethnic considerations returned to Ugandan politics with the Amin coup in 1971 — demonstrating that they remained the basis of potential political participation — for a few years they mattered far less.

Viewing ethnic political mobilization as responsive to certain kinds of situations and not to others is a useful approach because of its flexibility. Thus, one might conceptualize the

2. Martin Kilson, "Authoritarian and Single-Party Tendencies in African Politics," *World Politics* 15, no. 2 (January 1963): 274. Many of the causes of the formation of the NLM were economic (particularly the low price paid to cocoa farmers), but the basis on which it was organized and much of the fear felt by its supporters can be explained in ethnic terms only. For this point and for the formation of other ethnic parties see Dennis Austin, *Politics in Ghana, 1946-1960* (London: Oxford University Press, 1964).

3. *The Avoidance of Discrimination Act* (December 1957). See David E. Apter, "Ghana," in *Political Parties and National Integration in Tropical Africa,* ed. James S. Coleman and Carl G. Rosberg, Jr. (Berkeley and Los Angeles: University of California Press, 1964), p. 280.

4. Robert E. Dowse, "The Military and Political Development," in *Politics and Change in Developing Countries: Studies in the Theory and Practice of Development,* ed. Colin Leys (Cambridge: Cambridge University Press, 1969), p. 244. Italics in original. W. E. F. Ward argues that "among the mass of the people, there are no tribal feelings stronger than the feeling between Scots and English today. . . ." "Tribalism in Ghana," *Venture* 18, no. 5 (June 1966): 22.

5. *The Penal (Amendment) Act,* sec. 41 and 42 (February 1966).

activation of various types of political participation in terms of the type of identity or role assumed by the individual in particular circumstances. By the same token identities can cease to be relevant for a period of time. In this way we can avoid the inadequate formulation that the only political alternatives to "a civil politics of primordial compromise would seem to be either Balkanization, *Herrenvolk* fanaticism, or the forcible suppression of ethnic assertion by a leviathan state. . . ."[6] In some situations, which may be shaped by creative leaders, there is an additional alternative — ethnicity may cease to matter.

In employing situational analysis, we can see that ethnicity varies in another way that also contributes to its fluid character. Those who insist on traditional values as the cement binding one member of an ethnic unit to another necessarily stress the invariant continuity of moral obligations and thus of ethnic loyalty. Instead, however, there may be a relatively weak and diffuse loyalty that imposes no particular requirements to help another from one's area. "Allegiance to common values," J. S. La Fontaine points out, "imposes no specific obligations between tribesmen; rather it implies a generalized loyalty which can be mobilized in particular situations as a moral sanction or to legitimize a claim for support."[7]

A brief look at the variation in the importance of ethnicity for urban workers in Kampala demonstrates this fluidity. R. D. Grillo found that mere membership in the same ethnic group is not sufficient to prevail upon one worker to recommend another for a job. In other situations, however, ethnic identity becomes a weapon in political struggles — for example, in battles over trade union office.[8] During the colonial period, competition over employment opportunities in Kampala was based on ethnic identity, primarily between Baganda and Luo from Kenya. However, after independence this rivalry was translated

6. Clifford Geertz, "The Integrative Revolution: Primordial Sentiments and Civil Politics in the New States," in *Old Societies and New States: The Quest for Modernity in Asia and Africa,* ed. Geertz (New York: Free Press, 1963), p. 157.

7. "Tribalism Among the Gisu," in *Tradition and Transition in East Africa: Studies of the Tribal Element in the Modern Era,* ed. P. H. Gulliver (London: Routledge & Kegan Paul, 1969), p. 187.

8. "The Tribal Factor in a Trade Union," in ibid., pp. 318-320.

from categories of ethnicity to those of nationalism (Ugandans versus Kenyans).[9]

Once ethnicity becomes a salient factor in politics, people increase its intensity by adopting ethnic explanations of succeeding events. Ethnicity then becomes a self-fulfilling prophecy, inspiring competing organizations and scapegoating. [10] Poor employment prospects, inequity and uncertainty concerning government treatment in economic and security matters (particularly use of the police and army), perceived changes in social stratification, and government willingness to deal with people on an ethnic basis help to produce situations in which ethnic political participation emerges. The removal of these factors may lead to the disappearance of the ethnic group for political purposes. As Paul Mercier observes, "most often, tribalism is a series of defensive reactions which can quickly disappear when fears of inequality disappear." [11] The government can play a similar role, as Ugandan political leaders attempted to do between 1966 and 1971, by discouraging any political organizations making ethnic appeals and thus reducing ethnic participation.

If the situation forms the context for ethnic political mobilization (or for its absence), then factors in the situation also determine when and what sort of ethnic groups will form and whether they will be entirely new entities or intimately related to older loyalties. Their boundaries may vary, and it is possible for a man to belong to more than one ethnic unit – for example, in a town and in his rural home – though it is unlikely

9. David J. Parkin, "Tribe as Fact and Fiction in an East African City," in ibid., pp. 275-276. The issue became an international imbroglio between Uganda and Kenya for a short time in mid-1970. See *Uganda Argus,* 11, 14, 17 July 1970 and 19 August 1970.

10. Robert Melson and Howard Wolpe, "Modernization and the Politics of Communalism: A Theoretical Perspective," *The American Political Science Review* 64, no. 4 (December 1970): 1115. Robert Dahl makes much the same point for New Haven politics of a generation ago. "The politicians acted out a self-fulfilling prophecy; by treating ethnic distinctions as fundamental in politics, they *made* them fundamental." *Who Governs? Democracy and Power in an American City* (New Haven: Yale University Press, 1961), p. 54. Italics in original.

11. "On the Meaning of 'Tribalism' in Black Africa," in *Africa: Problems of Change and Conflict,* ed. Pierre van den Berghe (San Francisco: Chandler, 1965), p. 495.

that he will declare active loyalty to more than one at any given time. These units may be formed for a variety of purposes — traditional or new — and by a variety of organizers. Thus, an analysis of the groups involved in ethnic political participation must begin with a careful investigation of whom each unit contains and to what extent people can act together on its moral premises.

For this reason theories built on the notion of cultural pluralism are misleading. The original statement of this position was put forward by J. S. Furnivall and depended on the complete separation of peoples — "they mix but do not combine."[12] They have separate social institutions for all phases of life except the market. In Furnivall's view there is also political inequality, since "the union [of the different cultural groups] is not voluntary but is imposed by the colonial power." The withdrawal of colonialism, he felt, would mean "the whole society relapsing into anarchy."

In order to make use of this approach after independence, other writers substituted local political inequality — South African white settlers or an indigenous cultural group — for Furnivall's colonial stratification. Thus, M. G. Smith argues that a society characterized by pluralism has two components: (1) fundamental and clustered differences in the institutional practices of members and (2) deep and rigid inequalities in social and political life along the lines of these institutional cleavages.[13] Other writers drop the condition of inequality and insist only that there be "a relative absence of value consensus, a relative clarity and rigidity of group definition or segmentation, and the relative existence of institutional duplication between the various segments of society."[14]

Even in their weaker form, all versions of this theory begin

12. *Colonial Policy and Practice: A Comparative Study of Burma and Netherlands India* (New York: New York University Press, 1956), pp. 304 and 307.

13. "Institutional and Political Conditions of Pluralism," in *Pluralism in Africa*, ed. Leo Kuper and M. G. Smith (Berkeley and Los Angeles: University of California Press, 1969), p. 27.

14. D. G. Morrison and H. M. Stevenson, "Cultural Pluralism, Modernization, and Conflict: An Empirical Analysis of Sources of Political Instability in African Nations," *The Canadian Journal of Political Science* 5, no. 1 (March 1972): 87. The authors are drawing upon the argument of Pierre van den Berghe, "Towards a Sociology for Africa," *Social Forces* 43 (October 1964).

with the assumption that each ethnic unit forms a separate and self-contained community. That premise is often a risky venture in black African states. There are, of course, instances where ethnic units function as separate communities for a period of time in response to a particular situation, though, with the notable exception of racial units, they rarely become institutionalized. There is no profit, however, in adopting a theory that turns a range of possibilities into a rigid assumption. The cultural pluralists cannot handle the many cases of ethnic units that never were (or cease to be) separate communities. Also, the condition of thoroughgoing political inequality founded upon social stratification does not exist in most black African states today — though it may develop.[15]

The danger in the approach based on cultural pluralism is reification. In one recent study, for example, present-day ethnic units are distinguished on the basis of traditional cultural variance in order to discuss *current* political instability.[16] No one could deny the importance and variety of cultural practices in Africa today. These practices produce culturally plural states. But heterogeneity of culture does not necessarily produce highly separable and continuous ethnic groups. We must keep in mind that ethnicity is a fluid, not a fixed, condition of African politics — both as a definition of group boundaries and as a cause of intense political demands.

2. MODERNIZATION AND ETHNICITY

Modernization creates new possibilities for activating or intensifying ethnic consciousness. To demonstrate this proposition, the concept of modernization must be freed from the notion that tradition and modernity are polar opposites. In addition, ethnicity must be considered as a variable separate from tradition, not as a synonym for it.

When first applied to Africa, the notion of modernization was thought to be the process of replacing traditional values with those of industrialized nations. This view follows logically

15. The notion of cultural pluralism can be applied more successfully to the white-dominated societies of southern Africa.

16. Morrison and Stevenson, "Cultural Pluralism, Modernization, and Conflict," esp. pp. 90-94.

from the idea of colonial rule as modernization. Its mirror image is a view of tribal life in which tradition defines ethnic identity. Africans who gain a Western education or migrate to towns are regarded as "detribalized," shorn of their ancient ties and receptive to various Western influences. Claiming that schools, churches, trade unions, and political parties are "collectivities which have begun to knit the disparate tribal elements into common units," one writer draws the conclusion that "the more that Africans identify themselves with these groups, the less important tribal affiliation becomes."[17] Of a piece with this view is the notion that those who remain in rural areas are obdurate in their resistance to rapid innovation: "Under the terrifying pressure of Western techniques and ideas Africans in many territories instinctively close the ranks for self-preservation; and the only ranks they know are those of the tribe. Hence the aggressive reassertion of tribal identity and prestige."[18]

The animating conception of ethnicity uniting these views can be specified in terms of the three themes suggested above. In the conventional wisdom of writers on modernization, ethnicity and tradition are closely identified. This close connection leads them to assert that ethnicity is the function of objective, preexisting characteristics, not subjective ideology. They also argue that ethnicity tends to be preserved by the rural masses and is dropped by the urban educated elite. And writers on modernization hold that ethnicity issues from deeply held values, "rooted in the non-rational foundations of personality," [19] not from pragmatic calculations of self-interest.

However, the relationship of modernization and ethnicity turns out to be considerably more subtle and complex than this formulation suggests. One reason for this is that the relationship between tradition and ethnicity is also subtle and complex. Both theorists and researchers have shown that traditional and

17. Daniel F. McCall, "Dynamics of Urbanization in Africa," *The Annals of the American Academy of Political and Social Science,* no. 298 (March 1955), pp. 158-159.

18. Vincent Harlow, "Tribalism in Africa," *Journal of African Administration* 7, no. 1 (January 1955): 20.

19. Geertz, "The Integrative Revolution," p. 128.

modernizing influences may be interrelated in various patterns. If that premise is correct, we may look for the interrelationships between ethnicity and modernization, since traditions (both ancient and newly created) are influential in determining ethnic identifications.

The first step (as suggested in chapter one) is to adopt a different definition of modernization. By defining it as the increasing capacity to control the problems facing particular societies (or individuals), we can avoid the ethnocentrism implicit in equating modernity with the values and technology achieved by Western industrialized nations. Effective control in an African country may require techniques quite different from the latest engineering advance developed in the West. However, it would be foolish to assume that Africans cannot effectively borrow Western ideas, even though these may result in new social patterns — often unanticipated, sometimes unpalatable. Perhaps the most significant Western imports into Africa have been the psychological, social, and economic values and practices associated with the "cash nexus" and increasing wealth. [20] In most cases these values and practices have been significantly transformed in their new applications. The empirical question of modernization is to discover whether and in what ways their application has actually increased control of the problems facing the society and, equally important, *whose* control over *whose* problems.

Given this definition, it becomes fallacious to assume that tradition is necessarily in conflict with Western influences or is displaced or weakened by them. Rather it is often the case that traditional and Western factors form "a more indeterminate reality in which one blends into the other and varies with the play of contextual forces and events in time." [21] In his study of Sierra Leone, Martin Kilson demonstrates how chiefs take advantage — often over the protests of their traditional clients — of the opportunity to convert their customary rights into liquid

20. See Martin Kilson, "African Political Change and the Modernisation Process," *The Journal of Modern African Studies* 1, no. 4 (1963): 427.
21. Lloyd I. and Susanne Hoeber Rudolph, *The Modernity of Tradition: Development in India* (Chicago: University of Chicago Press, 1967), p. 66. See also C. S. Whitaker, Jr., "A Dysrhythmic Process of Political Change," *World Politics* 19, no. 2 (January 1967).

capital and thus to invest heavily in producing cash crops. [22] Lloyd Fallers poses the case of the Baganda — extraordinarily receptive to Western practices, yet strongly loyal to many of their traditional customs. [23] These customs, including those of recent origin, are an essential resource for ethnic political participation. Consequently, understanding the role of ethnicity in politics will often depend upon unraveling the causal links between all three variables — ethnicity, tradition, and the factors of modernization.

In the first place ethnicity can reinforce the determination to modernize. And the process of modernization often reinforces — or creates new possibilities of — ethnicity. If people associate the social and economic advancement of others with a common ethnic identity, they may be anxious that their own ethnic compatriots catch up. The Ibo are the best-known case of "responsive modernization" based to some extent on a feeling of ethnic deprivation. [24] But similar cases exist all over Africa as a result of the differential pattern of colonial modernization. Several Ugandan examples are discussed in the next chapter. The uncertainty produced by "being behind" creates a situation in which an ethnic definition of the relevant unit is likely to be adopted, and on that basis investment into education and economic ventures is often stimulated.

The reverse, the reinforcement or creation of ethnicity as a consequence of modernization, is even more important. Social mobilization resulting from education, new wealth, mass media, or urbanization transforms group memberships by widening the individual's horizons. Upon coming to the city or joining a rural cooperative, an individual will take on new loyalties. This does not mean he necessarily drops his older bonds. The old and the

22. *Political Change in a West African State: A Study of the Modernization Process in Sierra Leone* (Cambridge: Harvard University Press, 1966), pp. 57-59; see also pp. 66-67.

23. "Ideology and Culture in Uganda Nationalism," in *Political Modernization: A Reader in Comparative Political Change,* ed. Claude E. Welch, Jr. (Belmont, Ca.: Wadsworth, 1971).

24. James S. Coleman, *Nigeria: Background to Nationalism* (Berkeley and Los Angeles: University of California Press, 1958), p. 143. See also Paul Anber, "Modernisation and Political Disintegration: Nigeria and the Ibo," *The Journal of Modern African Studies* 5, no. 2 (September 1967): 168.

new may coexist. "Communal transformation entails the multi-plication rather than the substitution of social identities."[25] In one sort of a situation the new identity may be triggered, while in another the old one may hold sway.

The increasing pace of social change is likely to make people more concerned about their identity and more prepared to form groups on the basis of ties which they have acknowledged but in which they have taken little interest in the past. The political consequences can be enormous. Melson and Wolpe argue per-suasively that in Nigeria "modernization, far from destroying communalism, . . . reinforces communal conflict and creates the conditions for the formation of entirely new communal groups. . . . Nigeria's political crisis is traceable directly to the widening of social horizons and to the process of modernization at work within national boundaries."[26]

The positive influence that the factors of modernization have on ethnic consciousness can best be discussed by looking first at the towns and then at the countryside, even though I shall later stress their linkages. Urbanization is one aspect of social mobi-lization which significantly alters the nature of ethnicity and the boundaries of units based on ethnic definitions. In Max Gluck-man's succinct statement, "An African townsman is a towns-man, an African miner is a miner: he is only secondarily a tribesman."[27] That is, as soon as an individual ventures outside the range of direct influence of his rural compatriots, he re-sponds to a set of stimuli in which his previous ethnic identity plays a minor role. Instead, he sometimes reacts as a worker on the basis of economic interests and at other times as a member

25. Melson and Wolpe, "Modernization and Communalism," p. 1126. In this context Karl Deutsch's notion that social mobilization is a *two*-stage process involv-ing the shedding of traditional values before the forming of new attachments is misleading. "Social Mobilization and Political Development," *The American Political Science Review* 55, no. 3 (September 1961).

26. Melson and Wolpe, "Modernization and Communalism," p. 1113.

27. "Tribalism in Modern British Central Africa," in *Africa: Problems of Change and Conflict,* ed. van den Berghe, p. 348. Gluckman's point is that urban ethnicity must be understood as the consequence of the social context of the town. However, he argues that "class relationships are becoming increasingly important" at the expense of ethnic ties. Ibid., p. 355. Later anthropologists have been less certain of this point.

of a new ethnic unit.[28]   Peter Gutkind insists that "what Africans do in towns, their behavior and the structures they create,
are invariably designed to meet urban conditions. At best they
are only superficially traditional."[29]

The argument is overstated, however, since tradition may
play a more or a less significant role in the life of urban
migrants, and members of urban ethnic units may have a variety
of important linkages with those in the countryside. The differing importance of rural traditional customs to urban migrants is
illustrated by three ethnic residential clusters in Kampala. [30]
The first consists of Banyankole "target workers" who are not
committed to an urban life-style. They spend relatively brief
periods working in the city, have limited contact with people
from other ethnic units, and transplant as much of their rural
life as they can (including the style in which they build their
huts). The second cluster is made up of Bahaya prostitutes who
necessarily have contact with all other units but keep up their
Bahaya ties as well. Their intention is to return ultimately to
their rural area. The third consists of Luo migrants whose goal is
to earn enough money to move to a better suburb in Kampala.
With one group focusing their attention on city life, another
looking back to their country home, and the third remaining
ambivalent, we might expect three different responses in situations to which an ethnic identity might be relevant.

Enjoying the pleasures of urban life and coping with urban
problems are both likely to cause migrants to modify cultural
practices learned in their villages. However, as Fredrik Barth
warns us, "the important thing to recognize is that a drastic
reduction of cultural differences between ethnic groups does
not correlate in any simple way with a reduction in the organizational relevance of ethnic identities, or a breakdown in
boundary-maintaining processes."[31]   The convergence of cul-

28. J. C. Mitchell, *Tribalism and the Plural Society: An Inaugural Lecture* (London: Oxford University Press, 1960), p. 24. See also A. L. Epstein, *Politics in an
Urban African Community* (Manchester: Manchester University Press, 1958).

29. "Preface: The Passing of Tribal Man in Africa," *Journal of Asian and African
Studies* 5, nos. 1-2 (January-April 1970): 6.

30. Parkin, "Tribe as Fact and Fiction," pp. 286-292.

31. Fredrik Barth, "Introduction," in *Ethnic Groups and Boundaries: The Social
Organization of Culture Difference,* ed. Barth (London: Allen & Unwin, 1969), pp.
32-33.

tural patterns in the town does not necessarily result in the loss of ethnic distinctiveness. Indeed, the notion of "supertribalization" was coined to call attention to the fact that urban migrants to African cities — far from being "detribalized" — have often increased their ethnic consciousness. [32]

For example, migrants to African cities often cannot depend on municipal authorities to provide social services for them. Instead, they have formed voluntary associations to provide social insurance for funerals and for men out of work and information about jobs and accommodations. Often these associations are tribal unions, formed by migrants from a particular region. In these cases there is the additional purpose of keeping alive their songs, history, language, and beliefs. [33] In West Africa urban unskilled workers have preferred these ethnic associations to trade unions — a preference which helps explain the weakness of the latter. [34]

In many cases, however, ethnic voluntary associations cannot be so easily traced to a specific traditional society that could provide an ethnic identity for migrants before they left their rural homes. If there are only a few individuals from one area, they will have to join with others to make the voluntary association work. The new unit will most likely correspond to a geographical area or linguistic unit, but it may never previously have been the basis for solidarity. [35] This "regrouping" is one consequence of migration to the city. It may take place because the demands of urban living require new forms of response, because people reduce the bewildering mosaic of ethnic identi-

32. J. Rouch, "Migrations au Ghana," *Journal de la Société des Africanistes* 26, nos. 1-2 (1956): 163-164, cited in I. Wallerstein, "Ethnicity and National Integration in West Africa," in *Africa: Problems of Change and Conflict,* ed. van den Berghe, p. 474.

33. On voluntary associations in African cities generally, see Immanuel Wallerstein, "Voluntary Associations," in *Political Parties and National Integration,* ed. Coleman and Rosberg, Jr.; and Kenneth Little, *West African Urbanization: A Study of Voluntary Associations in Social Change* (Cambridge: Cambridge University Press, 1965), esp. pp. 24-46.

34. P. C. Lloyd, *Africa in Social Change: Changing Traditional Societies in the Modern World* (Harmondsworth: Penguin, 1967), p. 213.

35. Wallerstein, "Ethnicity and National Integration," p. 474. Problems of administrative control among mixed populations in urban areas may further reify (and perhaps actually create) new and larger units. In Mulago and Kisenyi, two small communities in "Greater" Kampala, unofficial ward headmen were often appointed

ties to manageable proportions, or because colonial officials establish new ethnic units for the purpose of administration. As voluntary associations cater to the demands of these new "geo-ethnic" units, many urban residents are likely to develop vested interests in their new identities. [36]

The countryside still contains most of the population in all African nations, but it is not immune to the new conceptions of ethnicity growing out of the urban experience. "Urban feed-back," resulting from the return of migrants, often creates or intensifies political consciousness of rural ethnic units larger than those previously felt to be relevant. [37] Although target workers, who return to live in their rural areas after accumulating sufficient cash, are likely to carry new ethnic conceptions with them, there are other ways in which urban residents influence country dwellers. The very consequences of modernization — postal, telephone, train, and road networks — reinforce the connections between urban and rural ethnicity.

P. H. Gulliver notes that "virtually all urban dwellers in East Africa continue to maintain close links with the rural, tribal areas." [38] Of the urban, male, wage-employed population in

by the parish chief on a "tribal" basis in addition to the chief's official headmen, appointed on a territorial basis. These men helped the chief in cases involving members of their "tribes" and sometimes were promoted to official status. A. W. Southall and P. C. W. Gutkind, *Townsmen in the Making: Kampala and Its Suburbs* (Kampala: East African Institute for Social Research, 1957), p. 186. Mitchell's point that in towns the complex mixture of people must be reduced to a few manageable categories (see discussion in chapter two above) has obvious application here.

36. Melson and Wolpe, "Modernization and Communalism," p. 1120. They suggest the use of "geo-ethnic" to describe new urban groups based on nontraditional or neo-traditional communities of origin. Ibid., p. 1124.

37. Ronald Cohen and John Middleton, "Introduction," in *From Tribe to Nation in Africa: Studies in Incorporation Processes,* ed. Cohen and Middleton (Scranton, Pa.: Chandler, 1970), p. 26.

38. "Introduction," in *Tradition and Transition in East Africa,* ed. Gulliver, p. 25. C. C. Wrigley makes the same point for Baganda in the mid-1950s: "There is no sharp dividing line between town and country, or between agriculture on the one hand and commerce and the professions on the other." "The Changing Economic Structure of Buganda," in *The King's Men: Leadership and Status in Buganda on the eve of Independence,* ed. Lloyd A. Fallers (London: Oxford University Press, 1964), p. 51.

Many other urban workers in Kampala send their wives to their rural homes for at least half the year to cultivate their land. For many, strong links with the countryside are their "ultimate social security." David Parkin, *Neighbours and Nationals in an African City Ward* (London: Routledge & Kegan Paul, 1969), pp. 29 and 189.

Nairobi, two-thirds spend at least one week, and one-third over a month, annually in their rural home area.[39] The same connections have been pointed out for West African countries as well. The urban elite invariably have kin living in rural areas and often participate in the affairs of their former communities on visits.[40] Commoners (in terms of their traditional society) who have succeeded in the city often return to their home areas to seek titles and badges of traditional prestige.[41]

"Rather than breaking down . . . the traditional forms, the modern communications systems have been instruments for maintaining them."[42] Money to maintain traditional obligations is mailed home. Sorcerers, women from the area who are likely to become prostitutes, and those "requiring" traditional cures are sent home by tribal unions. Traditional products, such as yams and palm wine, are sent to the city. The post, the telephone, and the telegraph may be used to transmit instructions concerning traditional religious problems in the rural area.

The impact that the formation of new ethnic units in the city has on rural perceptions of ethnic boundaries has not received very much attention from researchers. Nevertheless, there is no question that ethnic units in the countryside today are far different from their precolonial predecessors. The factors involved extend beyond modernizing influences, however. Polit-

39. Marc H. Ross, "Politics and Urbanization: Two Communities in Nairobi" (Ph.D. diss., Northwestern University, 1968), p. 70, cited in Colin Leys, "Politics in Kenya: The Development of Peasant Society," *British Journal of Political Science* 1, no. 3 (July 1971): 315. In another study cited by Leys, Thomas S. Weisner examined a matched pair of samples of urban and rural Kenyan residents and found that they tended to be single families with two households, one rural and the other urban. "One Family, Two Households: A Rural-Urban Network Model of Urbanism" (paper delivered to the University Social Science Council Conference in Nairobi, December 1969).

40. P. C. Lloyd, "Introduction: The Study of the Elite," in *The New Elites of Tropical Africa,* ed. Lloyd (London: Oxford University Press, 1966), p. 31. In Sierra Leone urban-based professionals are often the sons of chiefs. Kilson, *Political Change in a West African State,* p. 71. The same fact has been noticed in Ghana and Uganda.

41. Kilson, *Political Change in a West African State,* pp. 69-70. Lloyd makes the same point for the Yoruba in *Africa in Social Change,* pp. 212-213.

42. Leonard Plotnicov, "Rural-Urban Communications in Contemporary Nigeria: The Persistence of Traditional Social Institutions," *Journal of Asian and African Studies* 5, nos. 1-2 (January-April 1970): 68. The remainder of this paragraph summarizes Plotnicov's argument. Many of the same communications functions have been noted for the Luo Union in Kampala. Parkin, *Neighbours and Nationals in an African City Ward,* pp. 153-154.

ical competition, particularly the effort to expand central government expenditure and increase the number of jobs, may have been even more important in the creation of new and larger rural ethnic units. The establishment of district boundaries and census units by colonial officials has been a significant cause as well. Together modernization, political competition, and colonial administration have produced new and wider loyalties for rural inhabitants.

While modernization has helped to create new ethnic units and to heighten the sense of identity in older ones, tradition has not been forgotten. The use of traditions to justify contemporary political demands has been characteristic of both colonial and postindependence politics. There is an unnecessary difficulty here created by anthropologists who insist that *all* contemporary ethnic units are the product of the colonial situation.[43] The implication that there is no direct connection between precolonial ethnic units and those that exist today is clearly false for many peoples, especially those living in relatively centralized kingdoms like Ashanti, Alur, Buganda, and Bunyoro. In the latter cases the definition of the traditional unit is essential, though certainly not sufficient, to an understanding of the current unit. Where the process of growing ethnic consciousness leads to expanded boundaries or even to a new unit — as in the case of the Batoro or the Baluhyia, respectively — tradition remains an important justification, though precolonial traditional history must either be ignored or warped to fit contemporary political necessities.

Traditions — whether ancient or newly minted — become tools in the arsenal of politicians intent on acquiring ethnic constituencies. The purification of language, the return to traditional names and customs, and the strengthening of the traditional legitimacy of generally innovation-minded ethnic political leaders promote mobilization of political participants. It makes little difference for political purposes whether the tradition

43. See, for example, Elizabeth Colson, "Contemporary Tribes and the Development of Nationalism," in *Essays on the Problem of Tribe,* ed. June Helm (Seattle: University of Washington Press, 1968), pp. 201-202.

exists in the historical culture or is a present-day particularism.[44]

The important question is how tradition becomes a political resource to reinforce newly arising claims.[45] The answer depends on the specific circumstances facing the potential ethnic unit. The most extreme case of the creation of an ethnic unit after colonial rule began is that of the Bangala of Zaire. An ethnic unit with no traditional referent grew out of the widespread use of Lingala, the Zaire river language, and the mistaken belief of early colonial administrators that a coherent social group lived along a wide stretch of the river's banks. The Bangala became conscious of this identity during the colonial period. They played an important role in increasing political participation in Kinshasa during the early 1960s.[46]

Many other aggregates have had a linguistic relationship, a traditional authority system, or some other potentially unifying rationale, but no precolonial political unity. The Ibo, Yoruba, Kru, Mongo, Kikuyu, Baluhyia, Wasukuma, Wanyamwezi, Bagisu, Iteso, Lugbara, Bakiga, and Banyarwanda gained a sense of consciousness as ethnic entities in the colonial period.[47] The

44. However, fundamental traditional values may shape political attitudes in significant ways, including the propensity to participate and to act effectively in postindependence political life. Very little is known about this. Robert LeVine's work on status mobility in Nigeria suggests that tests of this sort of hypothesis could be devised. *Dreams and Deeds: Achievement Motivation in Nigeria* (Chicago: University of Chicago Press, 1966).

45. The reverse case — the use of new techniques to protect traditional life — is suggested by the strategy of the American Iroquois, who "remain socially outside the dominant culture but use the legal techniques of the modern state in an attempt to preserve the integrity of this 'outside' position." Reinhard Bendix, *Nation-Building and Citizenship: Studies of Our Changing Social Order* (New York: Wiley, 1964), n. 18, p. 45.

46. Charles W. Anderson, Fred von der Mehden, and Crawford Young, *Issues of Political Development* (Englewood Cliffs, N.J.: Prentice-Hall, 1967), pp. 31-33.

47. See ibid., pp. 33-38 (Mongo, Kru, Ibo); Anber, "Modernisation and Political Disintegration," p. 178 (Ibo); Thomas Hodgkin, "Letter to Dr. Biobaku," in *Odù*, no. 4 (1957), p. 42, cited in Wallerstein, "Ethnicity and National Integration," p. 477 (Yoruba); Gulliver, "Introduction," p. 22 (Kikuyu); Aidan Southall, "The Illusion of Tribe," *Journal of Asian and African Studies* 5, nos. 1-2 (January-April 1970): pp. 33-38 (Baluhyia, Wasukuma, Wanyamwezi, Yoruba); La Fontaine, "Tribalism Among the Gisu," p. 186 (Bagisu); Joan Vincent, *African Elite: The Big Men of a Small Town* (New York: Columbia University Press, 1971), p. 262 (Iteso); John Middleton,

Chagga elected a paramount chief for the first time in the 1950s.[48] The Bakonzo developed an areawide sense of political consciousness and organization just before Uganda gained independence (see chapter five below).

The expansion in scale of ethnic units makes ethnic leaders more credible in the national arena. Thus, tradition can be used to organize and mobilize an ethnic constituency. The reason why language and cultural practices are useful political resources is that they permit mobilization around unambiguous symbols. Of course, it helps if the "tradition" in question is unambiguous. Thus, ambitious individuals may deliberately undertake the task of standardizing the language spoken by all members of the ethnic unit or establishing particular customs as symbolic of the tribe.

The Bagisu paid particular attention to developing a single language for political purposes. "It was felt to be, and clearly was, a tribalistic movement designed to give the Gisu language equal standing with better-known African languages, such as Luganda."[49] Competition with Buganda for colonial, and later independent governmental, favors stood behind efforts in this direction in many parts of Uganda, as chapter four illustrates. The favors in question are anything but traditional. They concern control over development and the production of wealth. "Generally, only their language is conservative; their views are modern."[50] Strategic use of the past marked the response of Baganda to the first deportation of their Kabaka, Mutesa II, in 1953. Barkcloth, a traditional form of dress of the Baganda, was worn again (though – symbolically – it was often worn *over* European dress). Other traditional customs were also revived. [51] Tradition was being used to heighten the consciousness of

"Political Incorporation among the Lugbara of Uganda," in *From Tribe to Nation in Africa,* ed. Cohen and Middleton, p. 67 (Lugbara); and Donald Denoon, "The Perception of Ethnicity and Change" (paper delivered to the Universities Social Science Council Conference in Kampala, December 1971), pp. 11-12 (Bakiga, Banyarwanda).

48. Harlow, "Tribalism in Africa," p. 19.

49. La Fontaine, "Tribalism among the Gisu," p. 184.

50. Mercier, "On the Meaning of 'Tribalism' in Black Africa," p. 495.

51. Audrey I. Richards, *The Multicultural States of East Africa* (Montreal: McGill-Queen's University Press, 1969), p. 48. See also Richards, "Traditional Values and Current Political Behaviour," in *The King's Men,* ed. Fallers, pp. 322-324.

Baganda in order to mobilize their political opposition to the colonial government.

A final point needs to be made about the role of tradition and pseudotradition in the formation of ethnic units. If tradition can be successfully converted into a political resource by one ethnic unit, the process is likely to be imitated by another hoping to gain similar benefits. Indeed, even while claiming to follow ancestral traditions, leaders may seek to model their behavior and political demands on the successful performance of other ethnic units. This may have the paradoxical consequence of reducing differences among ethnic units while increasing the sense of distinctive ethnic identity that the members of each possess. "Ethnic learning" has occurred in most African countries and has a multiplying effect on political participation. Precisely this process took place in Uganda as people formed ethnic units and then attempted to adopt symbols that resembled those of the Baganda because the latter formed the most successful *political* unit. The Baganda regarded their Kabaka as the focal point of their autonomy, so each additional ethnic unit attempted to develop pseudotraditions that would justify a supreme ceremonial figure for itself.[52]

Ethnic learning in Uganda is not so different from the politics of status emulation among castes in India. Formation of caste associations encourages lower castes to achieve the same status as traditionally higher castes — usually by "finding" a traditional justification for upward mobility. The Rudolphs suggest a subtle additional consequence as well. Through the pragmatic politics pursued by caste associations, Indians have become "capable at various levels and in the context of various systems of calculating political advantage in the pursuit of moral and material ends. . . ."[53] Ethnic associations may function to shift the basis on which their members rest their ethnic identity from that of deep psychic identity to that of rational calculation of self-interest. Ugandan examples suggest similar shifts in attitudes, as well as some surprising later reversals.

52. Three other ethnic units in Uganda had a strong traditional claim to monarchy in Ankole, Bunyoro, and Toro. However, several others — even traditionally acephalous political systems and those composed of two or more traditional cultural patterns — also demanded kings. This point is discussed further in chapter four.
53. Rudolph and Rudolph, *The Modernity of Tradition,* pp. 36 and 62.

Ethnic learning need not be limited to tradition. Once an ethnic unit has mobilized a group consciousness and formed some sort of organization, it is likely to adopt the tactics of its opponents, even when these are inimical to its traditional principles. In Ghana the NLM, representing the Ashanti fears of suppression, quickly copied the political tactics of the older CPP. A hard-hitting, abusive newspaper, flags, songs, salutes, and paramilitary troops were organized.[54] The Northern Peoples Congress (NPC) in Nigeria, originally a patron party, began using the mass-party techniques of its opponents, the Action Group (AG) and the National Convention of Nigerian Citizens (NCNC).[55] When the Bakonzo decided to secede from Uganda on the principle of ethnic autonomy, they adopted the features of contemporary government, using a combination of the newly independent Ugandan regime and what was then the Toro kingdom administration as their model.

3. CLASS AND ETHNICITY

Discussing the relationships between class and ethnicity in Africa is more complicated than the previous discussion of modernization because there is controversy over the very existence of classes. Radical analyses often begin on the assumption that classes affect political behavior and expend little effort in delineating the social phenomena that justify the concept.[56] In general, class analysts accept and emphasize even more strongly the centrality of the changes in social and economic structure discussed by the writers on modernization.[57] They differ fun-

54. Austin, *Politics in Ghana,* pp. 269 and 291 n.

55. Henry Bienen, "One-Party Systems in Africa," in *Authoritarian Politics in Modern Society,* ed. Samuel P. Huntington and Clement Moore (New York: Basic Books, 1970), pp. 108-109.

56. See, for example, Giovanni Arrighi and John Saul, "Socialism and Economic Development in Tropical Africa," *The Journal of Modern African Studies* 6, no. 2 (August 1968); and Richard L. Sklar, "Political Science and National Integration – A Radical Approach," *The Journal of Modern African Studies* 5, no. 1 (May 1967). The failure to specify the concept of class before applying it in Africa and an attempt to rectify this omission are presented from a Marxist perspective in V. L. Allen, "The Meaning of the Working Class in Africa," *The Journal of Modern African Studies* 10, no. 2 (July 1972).

57. They would, for example, agree that "the marks of class are independent of the marks of tribal membership." McCall, "Dynamics of Urbanization in Africa," p. 158. The pun, at any rate, is excellent.

damentally, however, over the implications of these changes, and they also put less emphasis on tradition. For example, although traditional class structure (for example, in Northern Nigeria, Ankole, or Rwanda) may contribute to the class advantages of an individual or group, radical writers rarely regard that as salient for contemporary Africa.

Often those arguing from a radical point of view insist that a choice between analytic tools must be made. To accept class is to reject ethnicity. African political participation, it seems, must be explained in terms of one or the other, but not both simultaneously. Reflecting upon the Nigerian conflict – conventionally considered the most extreme case of the political impact of ethnicity – Stanley Diamond concludes:

> In any event, the basic dynamics of the Nigerian situation have never been predominantly tribal. The Hausa-Fulani-Yoruba-Ibo process of political conflict and accommodation before, during, and following formal independence is a function of the class, national, and neo-colonial nature of the struggle in Nigeria, of the African struggle at large. Recourse to the explanatory principle of "tribalism" is a Western reification which blocks our view of African reality, and deflects our attention from our own responsibility.[58]

The argument presented in this section suggests, on the contrary, that both class (mobilization on the basis of objective economic interests) and ethnicity are often operative in the same political situation and that they may either reinforce or work against each other. To argue so depends upon an examination of the classes into which present-day Africans could be divided and – equally important, but often overlooked – the degree to which class position creates political consciousness.

In class analysis ethnicity is regarded as an ideological tool rationally manipulated by the emerging bourgeoisie to mystify peasants. Without insisting that it is the only form ethnicity takes, Sklar emphasizes that "tribal movements may be created

---

58. "Reflections on the African Revolution: The Point of the Biafran Case," *Journal of African and Asian Studies* 5, nos. 1-2 (January-April 1970): 27.

and instigated to action by the new men of power in fur-
therance of their own special interests which are, time and
again, the constitutive interests of emerging social classes. Tribalism then becomes a mask for class privilege."[59] Going further, Archie Mafeje uses a more orthodox Marxist approach
both to call attention to the central role the elite plays in the
manipulation of ethnicity and to rule out any substantive meaning for African political analysis that ethnicity may be thought
to possess: "If anything, it is a mark of *false consciousness* on
the part of the supposed tribesmen, who subscribe to an ideology that is inconsistent with their material base and therefore
unwittingly respond to the call for their own exploitation. On
the part of the new African elite, it is a ploy or distortion they
use to conceal their exploitative role."[60]

These views suggest a consistent radical position for the three
themes in which ethnicity may be understood. Radical analysts
tend to see ethnicity as a subjective, rather than an objective,
phenomenon. Since classes are based on objective economic
relations, acting on the basis of ethnic loyalties can only be
subjective.[61] Second, ethnicity must be understood in terms of
the elite (or bourgeoisie), not the masses. Finally, since
ethnicity from this point of view is a tool used by the elite to
consolidate its class position, it is clearly a question of rational
self-interest and has little to do with fundamental values or
psychic identity. Modernization analysts (as the reader will
recall) argue that ethnicity has to be understood as an objective
phenomenon, characterizing the masses at the level of fundamental values — the polar opposite of the position held by class
analysts within each of the three themes.

59. "Political Science and National Integration," p. 6.
60. "The Ideology of 'Tribalism,' " *The Journal of Modern African Studies* 9, no.
2 (August 1971): 259. Italics in original. Mafeje regards "tribalism" as divorced from
"tribe" (the self-sufficient isolated rural community) and thus uses it in approximately the same way as I use "ethnicity." Ken Post also dismisses "tribalism" as
"false consciousness." " 'Peasantization' and Rural Political Movements in Western
Africa," *Archives Européenes de Sociologie* 13, no. 2 (1972): 248.
61. An orthodox Marxist might qualify this statement to allow for an earlier
stage in which the *narodnost* (or the "people") with a common territory, language,
and culture (but not economy) would be based on *objective* ethnic relations.
I. Potekhin, "The Formation of Nations in Africa," in *Social Change: The Colonial
Situation,* ed. Immanuel Wallerstein (New York: Wiley, 1966).

In order to assess the radical position, we must next consider what the notion of class can mean. Just as in our discussion of ethnicity and modernization, it is useful to draw a distinction between city and countryside in looking at class. In both cases Marxist analysis needs to be "slightly stretched" — to borrow a phrase from Frantz Fanon.[62] There are three likely candidates for classes in the cities. One consists of the wealthy, of those who took over the positions of departing colonialists. A second is made up of wage laborers, and the third consists of those involved in intermittent or illegal activities and those not employed at all.

In discussing the middle classes in Africa, we are necessarily discussing the existence of an urban class. While chiefs in various countries (notably Sierra Leone, Northern Nigeria, and Buganda in Uganda) have amassed relatively large amounts of' capital in the countryside, most of the members of the upper or middle ranks are government employees. As such, their orientations are directed toward the capital city. They certainly possess the objective indicia of high social class — a virtual monopoly over higher education, professional and top bureaucratic occupations, economic wealth, and political control. By these criteria the "upper level of the new African elite is distinct from the lower strata of the elite as well as from the bulk of the African population."[63]

However, they have relatively little control over the means of production. Foreign enterprises dominate the commercial sectors in many African countries.[64] To the extent that Euro-

62. *The Wretched of the Earth,* trans. Constance Farrington (New York: Grove Press, 1968), p. 40. Fanon was referring to the coincidence of wealth and race in the colonial situation when he made the remark.

63. Kilson, *Political Change in a West African State,* p. 69. Coleman argues that Western education was the central factor in the emergence of a new class. *Nigeria,* pp. 115-116.

64. Reginald H. Green and Ann Seidman, *Unity or Poverty? The Economics of Pan-Africanism* (Harmondsworth: Penguin Books, 1968), pp. 109 and 105-124. See also Andrew M. Kamarck, *The Economics of African Development* (New York: Frederick A. Praeger, 1967), p. 36. The major exceptions are countries like Uganda and Tanzania in which state corporations own the largest industrial complexes. However, state capitalism is not likely to produce a vigorous bourgeois class either. Also, if one rejects the present African elites as hopelessly capitalistic, as radical analysts do, then the current efforts to nationalize foreign enterprise under the guise of socialism amount to the consolidation of bourgeois control of the means of production.

peans, Lebanese, or Indians dominate important economic functions, the African bourgeoisie cannot play the historic role of its European counterpart. Indeed, if one takes seriously the premise of neocolonial control of African economies, it is unlikely that they ever will. A "comprador" middle class may be all they can aspire to be.

An additional problem in considering large traders and the holders of high government positions as a class is the brief time during which they have had access to great social advantage. Compared with people in industrialized countries, they simply have not had much opportunity to become socialized to their class. Political decolonization has been accompanied more by class formation than by the expected behavior of securely established classes. With the exception of elites in Liberia and Sierra Leone (and the special case of South Africa), perhaps, those occupying high status appear to lack shared consciousness of their class membership. They are new to each other as well as to their status. They continue to respect traditional obligations to assist poor kin, "usually in ways that mitigate a great widening of the social distance between the upper and middle categories and the poorer sections."[65] In addition, the underprivileged have not fully grasped the increasing difficulty that will accompany their efforts to achieve upward social mobility in the future. They do not vigorously oppose the elite and thus do not heighten its (or their own) class consciousness.[66]

Subjective perception, then, may be lagging behind objective economic position. The point is vital, because radical writers often claim that class-based political participation follows logically and inevitably upon economic differentiation.[67] However, discrepancies in wealth and life opportunities are not sufficient evidence to prove that class consciousness exists, much less to prove that political action occurs on the basis of such consciousness. There are two separate questions here: what are the objective differences in wealth and opportunities and how do people respond to these differences?

65. Kilson, *Political Change in A West African State,* p. 88.
66. Lloyd, *Africa in Social Change,* p. 315. See also Richard Sandbrook, "Patrons, Clients, and Factions: New Dimensions of Conflict Analysis in Africa," *The Canadian Journal of Political Science* 5, no. 1 (March 1972): 119.
67. For example, Allen, "The Meaning of the Working Class in Africa," pp. 177 and 178.

These arguments are less likely to hold as time goes on. As people of high status become more accustomed to privilege, they may seek its defense through common political action. Reduction in the channels of mobility is likely to stimulate consciousness of class interests. Evidence of the closure of this aggregate is already beginning to appear. For example, educated parents are more successful in finding scarce university places for their sons and daughters than those who are not educated.[68] The transmission of wealth through inheritance will give their children an enormous advantage in a poor society. Also, it is likely that departicipation will secure political control by the present leadership and thus contribute to the closure of the urban middle class.

Urban workers also fail to fit neatly into a class analysis. Though skilled laborers have been called the "proletariat proper of tropical Africa,"[69] the applicability of this European concept is not so clear. Their incomes are several times that of rural farmers, though wage workers form a small minority of every African population. Though not at the top, they are firmly ensconced in the privileged sector. Nevertheless, their commitment to life-careers as workers has not been established. The more highly paid an urban worker in Nairobi, the more likely he is to maintain a close relationship with his rural home.[70] Less than one-quarter of these urban workers say they would prefer to stay in the city when they grow old. More poorly paid urban workers cannot afford to visit their families or bring them to the city and might be considered more likely proletarians. But they are more dependent on the income produced by their families in the countryside. Thus, "the men who are the most natural candidates to constitute a true proletariat are those whose families are of necessity most closely bound to the land."[71]

68. J. E. Goldthorpe, *An African Elite: Makerere College Students 1922-1960* (London: Oxford University Press, 1965), pp. 30-48; Pierre van den Berghe, "An African Elite Revisited," *Mawazo* (Kampala) 1, no. 4 (December 1968): 60-61; and William John Hanna, "Students," in *Political Parties and National Integration,* ed. Coleman and Rosberg, Jr., p. 442.

69. Arrighi and Saul, "Socialism and Economic Development in Africa," p. 149.

70. Ross, "Politics and Urbanization," pp. 73-74, 45, and 68, cited in Leys, "Politics in Kenya," p. 315.

71. Leys, "Politics in Kenya," p. 316. See also note 38 above.

The urban unemployed and those working intermittently or illegally would seem to be subject to the same constraints. It is not clear that this aggregate should be considered as a single class, even though its members occupy similar objective economic positions. Marxist writers often distinguish between the *lumpenproletariat*, those in illegal or casual employment, whom they regard as supporters of a conservative order, and the hard-core unemployed, the reservoir of revolutionary consciousness.[72] Whether or not this distinction is useful in African cases, studies that often note the desperation of members of both segments rarely demonstrate their common class consciousness.

For these reasons the notion of class must be applied carefully. If differences in objective economic and social opportunities are taken as the defining characteristics of class, there are classes in urban Africa. The existence of class consciousness, solidarity, and finally political mobilization, however, does not necessarily follow as a matter of course. Thus far in postindependence black Africa, the political consequences of class action have seldom been significant. The better approach is to assume that "class and class consciousness have a partial manifestation that may be activated in certain conditions and in certain measure."[73] The task of the researcher is to discover when and where economic grievance becomes political participation.

Class as a conceptual tool is no easier to apply in the countryside. However, since over four-fifths of the population lives in rural areas, class analysis will not prove to be very useful if it cannot be applied here. Inequalities certainly exist between subsistence cultivators and successful peasants who have mastered the intricacies of growing and processing cash crops.[74] In

---

72. Drawing from Frantz Fanon and Amilcar Cabral, Peter Worsley argues that the African lumpenproletariat has revolutionary potential. "Frantz Fanon and the Lumpenproletariat," in *The Socialist Register 1972,* ed. Ralph Miliband and John Savile (London: The Merlin Press, 1972).

73. Robin Cohen, "Class in Africa: Analytical Problems and Perspectives," in *The Socialist Register 1972,* ed. Miliband and Savile, pp. 243 and 250.

74. Calling African farmers "peasants" has provoked a debate. Lloyd A. Fallers argues that in the precolonial period rural Africans formed "semi-autonomous local communities" both politically and economically but did not have "semi-autonomous cultures" (particularly because of the absence of a literary tradition). Thus, he

fact, successful farmers (or merely somewhat better educated rural dwellers) have often taken advantage of their greater knowledge to enrich themselves at the expense of their more naive fellows.[75] It is possible to argue that class formation is a widespread phenomenon in rural areas, just as it is in the cities. After World War II the process of class formation, particularly in East Africa, was masked by the coincidence of racial and economic stratification. Upward social mobility in the country-side meant displacing Asians and other outsiders in collecting and processing cash crops. A further source of inequality has been the growth in the number of landless laborers as larger farms are formed by more successful peasants or taken over (often from departing white settlers) by those with political influence. This social change, particularly apparent in Ghana and Kenya, suggests the possibility of a rural proletariat[76] — but not its necessity.

In Kenya, for instance, Leys has closely analyzed the efforts of British officials to develop a rural status hierarchy capped by a class of "yeoman" farmers by providing farms of differing sizes.[77] In Central Province a land consolidation scheme was

thought they were "ready," but not quite peasants. "Are African Cultivators to be Called 'Peasants'?" *Current Anthropology* 2, no. 2 (April 1961). As Fallers suggests, the widespread acceptance of the value of Western education during the colonial period provided a high culture which is unattainable by the vast majority and which converts traditional cultivators into peasants. Ken Post offers a more elaborate definition of peasants incorporating Fallers's argument in " 'Peasantization' and Rural Political Movements," pp. 226-227 and 233.

75. Contrary to Fanon's argument that "it is clear that in the colonial countries the peasants alone are revolutionary, for they have nothing to lose and everything to gain." *Wretched of the Earth,* p. 61.

Cooperatives, rural lending agencies, and tractor hire services are often fertile fields for sudden financial success for the unscrupulous through embezzlement and unfair allocation of government resources. Again, class formation may occur through the provision of a government service supposedly intended to reduce private enterprise (e.g., by giving a monopoly on processing to cooperatives when it was previously handled by the private sector). See John Saul, "Marketing Co-operatives in a Developing Country: The Tanzanian Case," *Taamuli* 1, no. 2 (March 1971): 31-35 and 39-45.

76. See Leys, "Politics in Kenya," p. 314, and Polly Hill, *The Migrant Cocoa Farmers of Southern Ghana: A Study in Rural Capitalism* (Cambridge: Cambridge University Press, 1963), pp. 187-190 and 213-214.

77. "Politics in Kenya," esp. pp. 316-329. The remainder of this paragraph summarizes Leys's argument. One difficulty with Leys's use of "peasants" to describe rural society is the problem of handling landless laborers. Leys does not offer a satisfactory solution. Ibid., pp. 314-315.

initiated to increase farming efficiency and to develop a rural group that would oppose the Mau Mau fighters. Shortly before independence a second project, the Million Acres settlement scheme, was developed to provide farms of specific sizes for Africans in the "White Highlands." Contrary to official expectation, in both cases the average size of the farming unit has more closely approximated subsistence holdings (through de facto unregistered subdivision) than the minimum felt necessary for effective cash cropping.

This process will continue, at least until the land frontier is closed (only half the area formerly owned by European settlers has been taken over thus far), because the growth of the rural population is outstripping the increase in wage employment.

> The point is, then, that the numbers of the peasantry are expanding at a rate that far exceeds the capacity of the industrial sector to absorb them; and that the historical device that exists in Kenya for dealing with this problem is *internal migration* into the former enclave of capitalist farming. This in turn implies a geographical extension of peasant society, not just an increase in the demographic dominance of peasants; *and at the expense* of the capitalist sector.[78]

In other words, contrary to the anticipated historical development of capitalism with its antagonistic classes, Kenya is experiencing the *growth* in the number of peasants who spurn the lure of permanent urban employment in favor of acquiring land in plots too small to generate the production of wealth.

Thus, factors generally associated with modernization, particularly Western education (through the cleavage opened between those of high and low status) and cash crops (through the incentive provided to shift from subsistence cultivation), have made unequivocal the existence of a rural peasantry and have introduced new differentiations in objective economic position which must be considered when analyzing rural dwellers. The creation of the peasantry, then, is a consequence of colonialism. But the predominance of peasants in rural life should not be overemphasized. Acceptance of Western education and cash crops occurs unevenly through the countryside. If traditional

78. Ibid., p. 326. Italics in original.

loyalties continue to shape aspirations anywhere, they have their strongest hold in rural areas.

Just as with urbanites, the issue is whether rich or poor peasants or landless agricultural laborers can form sufficient bonds on the basis of their economic activities to participate in political action. Over one hundred years ago Karl Marx wrestled with the same question when he attempted to explain the support of French peasants for Louis Napoleon's coup d'etat. Their isolation and self-sufficiency, he suggests, gives them a local orientation which "begets no community, no national bond and no political organization among them, they do not form a class."[79]

The same point can be made for African peasants in most cases. It is precisely their semiautonomous status that makes class consciousness the exception rather than the rule. Caught up in local relationships resulting from cultural attachments and government-organized crop marketing arrangements and cut off by their ignorance of the social and political processes of the new state, peasants are unlikely to participate in political protest extending beyond the confines of neighboring villages unless they receive — and accept — outside leadership.[80] Their semiautonomous economic status also shields them from class consciousness, since they grow their own subsistence crops and thus are not entirely dependent on the market. Also, peasant political consciousness is likely to grow when land is scarce and rents are high. But in most parts of black Africa, land is still abundant, and landlords are less likely to provoke political opposition because cultivated areas are generally held on customary tenure without the obligation to pay more than a nominal rent.[81]

If peasants are politically conscious of their class interests, it should be evident when they are mobilized in protest move-

79. *The Eighteenth Brumaire of Louis Bonaparte* (New York: International Publishers, 1963), p. 124.

80. Danus Skene, "The Peasant Factor in the Modern Politics of Eastern Africa" (M.A. diss., Department of Political Science, University of Chicago, May 1970), pp. 10-11, and Post, " 'Peasantization' and Rural Political Movements," p. 241.

81. W. Arthur Lewis, *Politics in West Africa* (New York: Oxford University Press, 1965), p. 18. However, contradictions between communal ownership and individual land use are growing in West Africa. Post, " 'Peasantization' and Rural Political Movements," p. 227.

ments. There is little to indicate peasant consciousness of peasant goals, however. Examination of African rural protest inevitably focuses on preindependence economic boycotts and both peaceful and violent nationalist movements. Resistance both to the establishment of colonial rule and to measures requiring the cultivation of *new* cash crops must be excluded by definition since none of the participants were peasants at that stage. The boycotts seem to have remained relatively local affairs. The independence movements, on the other hand, did become truly national, but with leaders from outside the peasantry. In those cases where the peasantry was mobilized, urban and Western educated leaders transformed rural grievances into support for their own goals.[82] The striking paucity of postindependence cases – aside from the widespread protests in eastern Zaire in the mid-1960s, where central government authority was virtually nonexistent, and in Western Nigeria – is evidence of departicipation as well as lack of peasant class consciousness.

Poorer peasants and those entirely within the subsistence sector are even less likely to develop class consciousness. Whether landless laborers are sufficiently alienated to think in terms of class action rather than a private plot for themselves is not clear, though the availability of land and the thrust of Leys's argument suggest the latter. The most potentially explosive of the demands made by the Mau Mau leadership in Kenya may have been their call of land for the landless.

In both city and countryside, then, class analysis can carry only part of the burden of explaining political participation. Motivations other than the attempt to acquire and preserve economic interests are often primary. A patron, an ethnic unit, security (rather than investment) in land may be more important in specific situations (though not in every one) than efforts to control the means of production. As in political life in other parts of the world, "neither ethnic nor class factors are constants; on the contrary, both are variables."[83] There are likely to be situations in which economic interests and ethnicity are both important factors – either reinforcing or conflicting

82. Skene, "The Peasant Factor," pp. 15-57, 83-92; and Post, " 'Peasantization' and Rural Political Movements," pp. 242-250.

83. Robert A. Dahl, *Who Governs? Democracy and Power in An American City* (New Haven: Yale University Press, 1961), p. 58.

with each other. In other cases, possibly involving the same individuals, one or the other may be the sole significant consideration. Any one of these four possibilities may be relevant to a particular case.[84]

The problem with the radical view of ethnicity is that it imposes a false dichotomy on events and forces the analyst to choose between class and ethnicity. In Mafeje's discussion, for example, ethnicity is restricted to either the defense of "traditional integrity and autonomy" or the protection of "a power position, not in the tribal area, but in the modern capital city . . . [to] exploit the supposed tribesmen."[85] Any adherence to ethnic sentiment by peasants who have moved beyond the small, self-sufficient, and isolated rural unit is "false consciousness." However, rural dwellers are obviously prepared to make use of ethnicity to achieve *new* economic and social goals that they choose for themselves, as the preceding section of this chapter suggests. If they are successful, they may increase their "material base" and their control over it. But even if they are mistaken about their "true" interests and possessed by "false consciousness," ethnicity remains an important political factor which cannot be analyzed by ignoring their noneconomic motives.

Furthermore, given the low levels of class consciousness discussed above, how could leaders arouse followers without making use of the solidarity created by traditional ties – historical or fictional? Elites cannot exist without masses. If this solidarity exists, it remains an empirical question to determine who benefits from their linkage. The variation is far more complex than radical analysts suggest. Leaders and followers are likely to make different sorts of demands, reflecting the differences in their social positions. Parkin found that socioeconomic status in Kampala was inversely related to ethnic consciousness – except in crisis, when men of high status also urged ethnic solidarity.[86] In Western Nigeria the leaders of political parties pressing ethnic goals were less apt to accept the moral concerns of the tradi-

---

84. Although I have approached the relationship between ethnicity and class from an inquiry into ethnicity, Robin Cohen reaches precisely the same set of possibilities from an inquiry into class. "Class in Africa," pp. 244-252, esp. 250-251.

85. "The Ideology of 'Tribalism,' " p. 258.

86. "Tribe as Fact and Fiction," pp. 285 and 293-294.

tional order than were their followers.[87]   But these different interests may reinforce one another. Rural Baganda peasants and the political elite did not share common motives in Kabaka Yekka (KY), the political movement they both supported. In fact the motives of the elite who founded it formed a tangled and conflicting web.[88]

Conversely, it may be the "leaders" who race after their supposed followers in order to gain their loyalty. Shortly before the formation of KY, some low-level Baganda politicians fashioned a wildcat boycott of Asian traders called the Uganda National Movement (UNM). Though embarassed and surprised by its loss of initiative, the Kabaka's government could not condemn the UNM when requested to do so by Protectorate authorities for fear of losing the alliance it had constructed with the Baganda masses.[89]   The Rwenzururu movement in western Uganda threw up a bewildering plethora of leaders who claimed to be able to control its direction. But in the first few years these leaders were unable to turn the Bakonzo and the Baamba from their desired goal of a district entirely separate from the Toro kingdom toward a solution that the Ugandan government might accept.

In both the Buganda and the Rwenzururu situations, leaders were able to pursue personal aims only by following mass sentiment once it was aroused. This situation was not stable, since mass sentiment could not be maintained at a steady pitch. For considerable periods of time, however, the nature of these movements was defined in ethnic terms by the goals of the followers, and not by those of would-be leaders.

87. Richard L. Sklar, "The Contribution of Tribalism to Nationalism in Western Nigeria," in *Social Change,* ed. Wallerstein, pp. 296-297. He describes a case in Lagos in which poor members of one subunit of the Yoruba suspended their rivalry with another by accepting the middle-class leadership, drawn from the second subunit, in pursuit of a joint ethnic goal – a consolidated Yoruba ethnic unit in Nigerian politics. Ibid., pp. 291-292.

88. Many of the strands are untangled in Ian Hancock, "Patriotism and Neo-Traditionalism in Buganda: The Kabaka Yekka ('The King Alone' Movement, 1961-1962)," *The Journal of African History* 11, no. 3 (1970). Both the Kabaka Yekka and the Rwenzururu movement are described briefly in chapter five.

89. Consider the Kabaka's analysis of this incident: "The Lukiiko [the Buganda parliament] and I were in a difficult position, not wishing to attack the boycott publicly. . . . Under some pressure, I made a speech with a discouraging reference, but it was not thought strong enough by the Governor." *Desecration of My Kingdom* (London: Constable, 1967), pp. 154-155.

The variance in motives between leaders and followers in the same ethnic movement suggests that some may have economic motives while others have ethnic interests closer to heart. It is not possible to predict in advance which motive will be more important to leaders and which to followers. Although it is conventionally argued that leaders will be pursuing their economic interests and followers their ethnic interests, both may be using ethnicity to cover very different sorts of economic demands, or both may greatly fear a threat to their very survival which they may define in ethnic terms. Or leaders may — in all sincerity — initiate pursuit of ethnic interests. During the prelude to the Nigerian conflict, it was the more educated and more prosperous Ibo, returning from the North, who in response to ethnically directed attacks perceived the threat as an ethnic conflict and then rallied rural dwellers in the East to regard their "Ibo-ness" as their primary identity. Given the complexity of motives uniting leaders and followers, it generally makes little sense to restrict ethnicity to a strategy of "embourgeoisement" by elites.

Ethnicity reinforces class interests on many occasions. In some cases occupational stratification has been defined in ethnic terms. A study of Livingstone, a town in Zambia, found that skilled and better-paid jobs were held by members of specific ethnic units. "There was a tendency, in other words, for economic class to correspond with tribal group."[90] In West Africa certain occupations tend to be reserved for certain ethnic groups, partly because of the use of cultural ties to obtain jobs and develop new skills.[91] In such cases ethnicity may be used to develop a tight political organization to keep exclusive control over entry by competitors.[92]

Ethnic distribution of job opportunities, particularly in

90. Merran McCulloch, *A Social Survey of the African Population of Livingstone,* The Rhodes-Livingstone Institute, paper no. 26 (Manchester: Manchester University Press, 1956), p. 67, quoted in J. Clyde Mitchell, *The Kalela Dance,* The Rhodes-Livingstone Institute, paper no. 27 (Manchester: Manchester University Press, 1956), p. 16.

91. Wallerstein, "Ethnicity and National Integration," pp. 479-480. In Kampala, "for instance, food supply and town-to-home taxi services were most efficiently ethnocentric." Parkin, "Tribe as Fact and Fiction," p. 282. But see n. 8 above.

92. Abner Cohen, *Custom and Politics in Urban Africa: A Study of Hausa Migrants in Yoruba Towns* (London: Routledge & Kegan Paul, 1969), pp. 184 and 190. He discusses the ability of the Sabo Hausa to control the kola-nut trade in the Yoruba town of Ibadan.

scarce labor markets, is likely to result in the coincidence of
class and ethnic hostility. A comparison of Hausa-Fulani, Ibo,
and Yoruba in the 1920s shows the early lead of the Yoruba in
the professions. By the 1950s the Ibo had made rapid advances,
but the Hausa-Fulani remained far behind both units.[93] This
change in stratification is central to the political situation that
led to the civil war. The coincidence of ethnic and economic
identification of both Hausa-Fulani and Ibo in the North meant
that "conflict of any sort — whether over jobs or markets or
political office — threatened an all-out communal struggle."[94]
The Fanti in Ghana, the Baganda in Uganda, and the Chagga
and Bahaya in Tanzania also found themselves in ethnically
defined leading economic positions by virtue of early and rapid
modernization. They held the highest-salaried positions or became the most successful cash-crop farmers. Ethnic political
participation by the less fortunate was often the response in the
preindependence period. For example, the NLM united Ashanti
cocoa growers, both rich and poor, into a single political movement seeking both ethnic and economic protection in Ghana.

Ethnicity and economic interests may also work against each
other. One factor may override the other, or they may each be
the cementing force of opposing factions. Finally, the same
individuals may switch from their identity as members of an
ethnic unit to an identity as part of an economic aggregate or
the reverse, depending on the situation. One case in which
ethnic concerns block economic advantage is the total refusal of
Luo and Baganda in Kampala to merge and form businesses
together, even when economic benefits have been perceived and
discussed by potential partners.[95]

People can, however, attempt to avoid opprobrious class
distinctions by insisting on the higher priority of a nonstratifi-
able ethnic identification.[96] For example, Banyarwanda migrants to Buganda attempt to become identified as Baganda in

93. Coleman, *Nigeria*, pp. 142-143.

94. Melson and Wolpe, "Modernization and the Politics of Communalism," p.
1116.

95. Parkin, "Tribe as Fact and Fiction," pp. 282-283. Baganda and Luo, according to Parkin, are also reluctant to marry each other.

96. Michael Moerman, "Being Lue: Uses and Abuses of Ethnic Identification,"
Essays on the Problem of Tribe, ed. Helm, p. 162.

order to escape from a status system in which they are con-
signed to an inferior class position. Ethnicity may also be a
useful tool for those who assert their original ethnic identity
but attempt to improve their status by raising the position of
their unit in the stratification system. Individuals who feel
helpless acting alone can gain support through the efforts of
their ethnic unit. The assistance that Ibo have given one another
in business and education is an example. As Wallerstein points
out, this consequence of ethnicity contributes to a more fluid
class system.[97]

Perhaps the most vigorous controversy over the relationship
of economic and ethnic considerations concerns urban workers.
The question of which factor predominates often turns out to
be closely related to the situation being analyzed. Urban sociol-
ogists working in the Copperbelt of Zambia before independence argued that "trade unions transcend tribes," but more
recently other writers have shown that ethnicity may actually
reinforce vested interests when the economic privileges of an
ethnic unit are under attack.[98] In other words, the situation in
which workers find themselves may dictate which interests are
uppermost to them and thus which aggregates they will join for
the moment.

Even within trade union activity, motivation still must be
sorted out in terms of differing situations. It has often been
remarked that workers will join together regardless of ethnic
affiliation to present a grievance to management when the latter
is composed of Europeans, while they will often split along
ethnic lines in determining internal union policy.[99] The same
shift in identities has been noted in the success of the 1964
general strike in Nigeria and the failure, soon thereafter, of
trade union leaders to convince their men to vote for labor
candidates rather than ethnic representatives in the general
elections. "The moment the strike was concluded, the lines of
political cleavage within the nation were redrawn, socio-eco-

97. "Ethnicity and National Integration," pp. 479-480.

98. Parkin, "Tribe as Fact and Fiction," pp. 274 and 292. See also Abner Cohen,
Custom and Politics in Urban Africa, and note 27 above.

99. A. L. Epstein, *Politics in an Urban African Community,* pp. 235-238; and
Roger Scott, "Trade Unions and Ethnicity in Uganda," *Mawazo* (Kampala) 1, no. 3
(June 1968).

nomic identities once again being subordinated to the communal identities of region and nationality." [100]

Political party conflict can also sharpen the conflict between economic interests and ethnicity, as the following two Nigerian cases illustrate. [101] In the early 1950s in Benin (Nigeria), the local Edo elite formed a branch of the *Ogboni* Fraternity and later affiliated with the Action Group, well known to be under Yoruba control. An opposition party called Otu Edo was formed on the basis of Edo tradition, though its leaders were also progressive and nationalistic. The ethnically oriented party swept the class-based party from office in 1951 and later joined the NCNC. At about the same time Ibadan municipal politics presented a similar dispute between Ijebu and Ibadan, two rival subunits in the larger Yoruba aggregate. The Ijebu, who were recent settlers in the city and members of the rising middle class, declared their loyalty to the AG. The Ibadan, who were sons of the soil, responded by forming an ethnic party called Mabolaje ("Do not reduce the dignity of chiefs"), which easily defeated its rival and which affiliated with the NCNC.

In one case the elite was indigenous; in the other it was not. In both, "communal partisanship emerged as a reaction to the political drives of a rising class." [102] Ethnicity and economic interests became the organizing principles of opposing factions. The consequence in both cases, however, was to accept elitist leadership at the national level, since each local party was quick

100. Melson and Wolpe, "Modernization and the Politics of Communalism," p. 1127. It is inappropriate to argue, as Melson and Wolpe do, that a situational analysis can "explain" shifts in identity from pocketbook to ethnicity. Situations are merely the contexts in which the causes of changes must be discovered. Otherwise the explanation turns out to be a tautology, since all behavior necessarily occurs in "situations."

101. Sklar, "The Contribution of Tribalism to Nationalism," pp. 293-296. Sklar notes that in both cases chiefs dropped out of the ethnic parties but were unable to sway the masses to change their political loyalties. This is a further illustration that the relationship between tradition and ethnicity is variable – that the two terms cannot be equated.

The issue of settlers versus sons of the soil also added a dimension of ethnic conflict to political disputes in the Nigerian Coal Miners' Union. See David Smock, *Conflict and Control in an African Trade Union* (Stanford: Hoover Institute Press, 1969).

102. Sklar, "The Contribution of Tribalism to Nationalism," p. 296.

to affiliate with a national political organization. As Sklar points out, the "historic significance" of ethnic partisanship was to draw millions of tradition-oriented people into political participation.[103]

4. CONCLUSION

The main point of this chapter has been to rescue ethnicity from the challenge to its significance for African politics posed by the conventional wisdom of both modernization and class theory. Many analysts of modernization overlook the range of variation that can characterize the relationship between tradition and ethnicity. At times tradition greatly influences the form and the demands of ethnic movements. On other occasions the sheerest fiction, born of entirely new and externally inspired demands, becomes the ideology of an ethnic unit. Thus, the strategic use of tradition becomes an important weapon in the African political arena. Through ethnic learning other units can become similarly armed.

Given this variation between tradition and ethnicity, modernization and ethnicity will also vary in complex fashion. Ethnicity may reinforce the will to modernize of people who did not receive the original social and economic benefits of colonialism. Modernization may reinforce or stimulate the creation of entirely new ethnic units in both the city and the countryside. Consequently, the view that ethnicity is becoming outmoded in Africa as modernization advances is entirely inadequate.

Modernization theory, or at least the variant which emerged from the ideas of Max Weber and Talcott Parsons, has been rejected by class analysts. They accept that ethnicity can be used as a strategy but unnecessarily restrict its importance to the class-based actions of the bourgeoisie. In doing so they often assume that differences in wealth and education will necessarily lead to class consciousness and consequently to political participation. The nature of consciousness in African cities and countryside is likely to be far more uneven and intermittent and to depend upon particular situational "trig-

103. Ibid., p. 298.

gers." The relationship between consciousness and political action introduces further questions. Ethnicity is not the monopoly of the elite, since it may be used by nonelites as well — sometimes to manipulate their leaders. Economic interests and ethnicity interrelate in subtle ways, sometimes to sharpen political demands by reinforcing each other and sometimes to alter political formations by crosscutting each other. To expect, therefore, that when workers in the city and peasants in the countryside become more sharply aware of their economic position they will abandon ethnic concern is to engage in wishful thinking.

In a sense the inadequacies of the modernization perspective on ethnicity are complemented by those of the class perspective. Conventional modernization theorists stress the objective nature of ethnicity, locate it among the masses, and regard it as the product of deeply held values that shape one's psychic identity. Radical analysts, on the other hand, insist that ethnicity is subjective, consider it a tool used by the elite, and argue that it is rationally chosen to exploit others. The questions raised for research by either theoretical stance will obviously differ. Although it necessarily increases the complexity of the research task, regarding all three of these themes as empirically variable dimensions is more realistic than automatically accepting the assumptions of either theory. The definition and behavior of virtually every ethnic unit involves to some degree *both* objective and subjective features, *both* the mass and the elite, and *both* rationally calculated strategies and fundamental values. Differences along these lines among ethnic units in Uganda are discussed in chapters four, five, and six.

One other problem may be troubling readers at this point. If ethnicity is so much a feature of contemporary politics in Africa despite the challenges mounted by class and modernization theorists, if the seemingly inexorable advance of new social and economic influences on Africans seems to increase their reliance on ethnic identity and its political organization, how is it possible to use a departication strategy successfully to remove ethnicity from the political arena? Have I argued such a good case for ethnicity that I have necessarily disproved my major hypothesis? I do not think so.

In the first section of this chapter, the fluid nature of ethnicity in African politics was considered. Both ethnic units and the intensity of demands of their members are subject to sudden and surprising changes. The variability of both follows from a notion of ethnicity which emphasizes its situational nature. Within limits, political leaders can attempt to restructure the rules of the game in order to de-emphasize ethnicity, just as colonial officials established some of these rules to emphasize ethnicity. The condition of fluidity, which brought some success to the efforts of colonial administrators, permits current rulers to introduce the reverse policy. By the same token it seems unlikely that they can make this sort of change permanent. The Ugandan political situation since the Amin coup provides us with a case in point. Departicipation, then, is a potential strategy, a form of political engineering, available to African leaders who are intent on reducing the uncertainties they face and redirecting the political energies of the people they rule.

PART II
ETHNIC POLITICAL PARTICIPATION IN UGANDA: GROWTH AND CONTRACTION

NOTE: An earlier version of parts of chapters four, five, seven, and eight appeared in my article "Cultural Sub-Nationalism in Uganda," in *The Politics of Cultural Sub-Nationalism in Africa,* ed. Victor A. Olorunsola (Garden City, N.Y.: Doubleday, 1972).

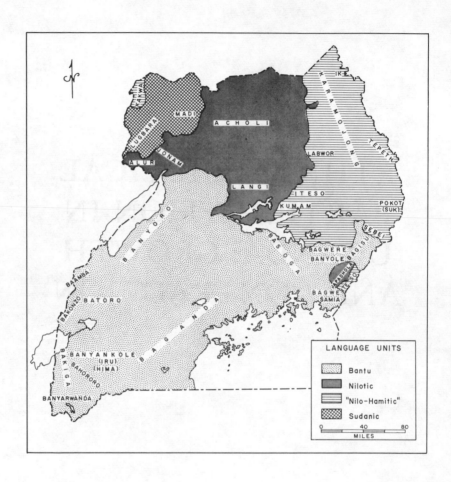

Map 1. Objective ethnic and language units in Uganda (source: Department of Geography, Makerere University).

Map 2. Districts and district capitals of Uganda, 1967–1971 (source: Department of Geography, Makerere University).

FOUR

◇

GROWTH OF ETHNIC POLITICAL PARTICIPATION

Why did ethnicity become so important in Ugandan politics? The first step in understanding the government's later policy of ethnic departicipation is to consider the structural factors in Ugandan politics that intensified the entry of ethnic units. In discussing Indian political development, Lloyd and Susanne Rudolph argue that "the 'entry' of any particular caste into the political arena and the strategies it pursues there are affected by the circumstances it confronts in the environment and by its inner life and state of development."[1] The same considerations affect Ugandan ethnic units.

Many of the factors that led to expanded ethnic units with a new political consciousness – to their more complex "state of development" – have been suggested in chapter three. Just as the Bagisu attempted to match cultural, linguistic, territorial, and administrative boundaries in order to strengthen their claim to consideration as an ethnic unit,[2] so have many other enterprising Ugandans to a greater or lesser degree. Several examples are briefly described in chapter five.

Here, however, I want to focus on what the Rudolphs call the "environment" or the "situation" – that is, the forces shaping political response in terms of ethnic definition. These include the colonial rules of the game, the advantages of an earlier start in the race for economic and educational benefits, and fears of what independence might mean without an impartial referee. Together these led to the formation of ethnic political units

1. *The Modernity of Tradition: Political Development in India* (Chicago: University of Chicago Press, 1967) p. 28.
2. J. S. La Fontaine, "Tribalism among the Gisu: An Anthropological Approach," in *Tradition and Transition in East Africa: Studies of the Tribal Element in the Modern Era,* ed. P. H. Gulliver (London: Routledge & Kegan Paul, 1969), p. 186.

and, through the ensuing competition, to widening political participation.

Before we can examine the seven propositions offered to explain why ethnic political participation grew in intensity through the early years of independence, we need to keep three caveats in mind. First, I shall refer to units that Ugandans generally perceived to be ethnic groups. Their perceptions, however recent many of them are, have helped to create these groups. On the other hand, Ugandans, as well as administrators and researchers, have sometimes endowed these aggregates with false concreteness. They have interpreted as coherent groups what are often merely fluid, loosely joined units, if that. The use of the ancestral name of an ethnic unit does not necessarily imply a coherent group continuously poised for political action.

Second, there is the Rudolphs' reference to the "inner life" of the unit. To speak of ethnic units should not blind us to the existence of conflicts within them or differences among them. Smaller aggregates within ethnic units can also be defined in ethnic terms of more restricted compass. The fluidity of ethnicity in Uganda is such that ethnic movements are often little more than coalitions of an incredible variety of even smaller groups.

The jostling of interests in the Kabaka Yekka movement, for example, is suggested in chapter five. In Ankole, memories of precolonial kingdoms now provoke rivalries among counties. At the same time Ankole has been deeply split by ethnic rivalry between the Bairu (agriculturalists) and the Bahima (pastoralists) scattered among those counties.[3] In Teso a dispute over local appointments between the northern and southern areas of the district led to the breakdown of local government.[4] Acholi has been the scene of geographical and clan rivalries.[5] The petty kingdoms amalgamated into the district of Busoga have con-

3. See Martin Doornbos, "Kumanyana and Rwenzururu: Two Responses to Ethnic Inequality," in *Protest and Power in Black Africa,* ed. Robert I. Rotberg and Ali A. Mazrui (New York: Oxford University Press, 1970), pp. 1088-1136. In addition to these ethnic considerations, intense political and religious conflicts further fragmented politics in Ankole.

4. Fred Burke, *Local Government and Politics in Uganda* (Syracuse: Syracuse University Press, 1964), pp. 149-151.

5. See Colin Leys, *Politicians and Policies: An Essay on Politics in Acholi, Uganda 1962-65* (Nairobi: East African Publishing House, 1967), pp. 15-21.

tinued their competition, as the dispute over the Kyabazinga-ship (kingship) demonstrates.[6] In districts with several ethnic aggregates, such as Bukedi, Kigezi, and West Nile, relatively sophisticated ethnic arithmetic in allocating district political and administrative posts was necessary to maintain a minimal level of unity. During those periods when one ethnic unit monopolized the posts, the severe resentment of other units tended to fuel ethnic political participation. Many more examples could be given, but it should be clear that one of the factors moderating the intensity of ethnicity at the level of the larger unit is the difficulty of coordinating these small entities for any length of time.

In addition the "inner life" of ethnic units will not be identical from one politically engaged group to another because the objective characteristics that become the basis for ethnic response will differ — as the conception worked out in chapter two contemplates. Ethnicity in one case will be built upon a strong identification with a local region; in another, upon a common language or a particular political structure; in a third, upon some combination of these. In general, a claim to a distinctive and shared traditional past will be invoked to rationalize the assertion of a closed group identity. But ethnic participation resulting from these claims will vary. This point is taken up in chapter five.

The third caveat is that singling out ethnic political participation magnifies its role in national and local politics at the expense of several other kinds of participation. Politics in Uganda has been extraordinarily complex. Sharp discord has arisen over land ownership, religious competition, wealth, economic ideology, and race.[7] However, since the government chose to respond separately to ethnic political participation by attempting to reverse it, we ought to take a close look at the political dynamics of ethnicity.

6. See Emanuel Hansen, "Busoga," in the Uganda District Handbook, stenciled (Kampala: Institute of Public Administration, n.d.).

7. See F. B. Welbourn, Religion and Politics in Uganda: 1952-62 (Nairobi: East African Publishing House, 1965); D. A. Low, Political Parties in Uganda, 1949-62 (London: Athlone Press, 1962); and S. Griffith, "Local Politicians and National Policies: The Secretaries-General of Uganda" (B. Phil. diss., University of Oxford, 1969).

No discussion of the structure of politics in Uganda can penetrate very deeply without considering the role of Buganda. The boundaries of the Buganda kingdom, fixed by the Protectorate authorities and dismantled by Obote, enclosed approximately one-fourth of Uganda. On the basis of cultural criteria the Baganda are the largest potential ethnic group, amounting to about one-sixth of Uganda's population. They were the first colonized and hence have an historical advantage over others. They were themselves colonizers, since the British used Baganda agents to govern other areas of the country in the first two decades of the twentieth century. The capital of the country, and thus the focal point of national politics, lies in their heartland. Forced to confront the success of the Baganda as an *ethnically defined* aggregate, people in other parts of Uganda came to participate in politics on the same basis.[8] Opposition to Buganda often became a common ground for politicians elsewhere, but one which reinforced the political significance of ethnic consciousness.

The 1900 Agreement with Buganda that made Uganda a protectorate instead of a crown colony initiated the development of this state of affairs.[9] The Baganda came to regard themselves as equals with the British in governing Buganda. As time passed, they demanded more autonomy in various spheres of government. Their success led others to demand similar privileges based on ethnic criteria. A striking example of the kind of locally oriented politics this competitive pattern produced was the decision of a prominent politician, William W. Nadiope, to give up a national ministry in 1962 and become Kyabazinga (king) of Busoga, a district at that time attempting to gain federal status. Three years later he persuaded the Busoga

8. In several cases this confrontation was direct, rather than by example. The use of Baganda agents in the eastern region of Uganda, for example, stimulated the use of ethnic definition by those ruled. In that case active resentment against the rapacious conduct of these agents, fear of their potential acquisition in freehold of land traditionally belonging to those administered, and the introduction of a more precise notion of the concept of "tribe" through history books and administrative control resulted in the revival of traditional rituals and the broadening of ethnic consciousness. Michael Twaddle, " 'Tribalism' in Eastern Uganda," in *Tradition and Transition in East Africa,* ed. Gulliver.

9. The Buganda Agreement of 1900 was signed prior to British occupation of all Uganda. Agreements were later signed with certain other chiefs, and these are reflected in the semifederal status given Ankole, Bunyoro, Toro (and indirectly Busoga) in the 1962 constitution.

district council to make him ruler for life, like the Kabaka of Buganda, rather than for a fixed term.[10]

Seven interrelated propositions help to explain the marked increase in ethnic political participation that developed during the colonial and independence period until the confrontation between the central government and the Baganda took place in 1966.

1. Precolonial migrations and military conflicts created rivalries that are reflected in contemporary politics.
2. The British colonial policy of indirect rule tended to increase ethnic identification.
3. Colonial administrative techniques often strengthened ethnic identities.
4. The introduction of local government based on districts and kingdoms increased competitive ethnic political participation.
5. The consequences of differential modernization, particularly in Buganda, aroused frustrations and consequently intensified feelings of ethnic deprivation.
6. The development of nationalist parties as coalitions of district political notables stimulated ethnic political competition.
7. The fear among smaller ethnic units that the departure of the British would leave them unprotected caused them to enter the political arena just before independence.

The cumulative effect of the factors represented in these propositions was to connect political prize with ethnic protest and organization. The entry of ethnic units into the political arena seemed a useful technique to gain advantages previously monopolized by others. "All Uganda," declared one parliamentarian, "is advocating parochial institutions."[11]

1. PRECOLONIAL MIGRATIONS AND MILITARY CONFLICTS CREATED RIVALRIES THAT ARE REFLECTED IN CONTEMPORARY POLITICS

Just as traditional customs are sometimes the basis for the definition of contemporary ethnic units, memories of hostilities

10. The Ministry of Regional Administrations, however, invalidated this decision. Griffith, "Local Politicians and National Policies," p. 58. See also Dan Mudoola, "The 'Upicification' (U.P.C.) of Kyabazingaship," *Research Abstracts and Newsletter* (Makerere Institute of Social Research, Kampala) 1, no. 3 (July 1973).

11. "Proceedings of the Legislative Council, 34th Session, 6th Meeting, February 17, 1955," p. 131, quoted in David Apter, *The Political Kingdom in Uganda: A Study of Bureaucratic Nationalism* (Princeton: Princeton University Press, 1967), p. 39.

in the precolonial period are sometimes important in creating competitive ethnic politics in postindependence Uganda. Current ethnic units in Uganda often attribute precolonial grievances to the acts of members of some other "tribe." The Baganda, for example, are remembered for their policy of military imperialism. When European explorers first entered the Lake Victoria area, forces led by Mutesa I, the Kabaka of Buganda, were expanding Buganda's hegemony at the expense of the empire of Bunyoro-Kitara. Baganda were also devastating parts of Busoga. About 1830 a prince broke away from Bunyoro-Kitara and set up a new kingdom in part of what is now Toro district. His descendants asserted hegemony over areas occupied by Bakonzo and Baamba. Insisting that their ancestors had preceded the Batoro, ethnic movements of Bakonzo and Baamba demanded their own district in the early 1960s.

The migration of Nilotic-speaking peoples that passed from the north through eastern Uganda left people in the area around Mount Elgon among Bantu-speaking traditional groups who practiced different customs. This led to intermittent warfare suppressed under British rule but not forgotten. Boundary disputes often arose between groups — for example, the Acholi and Langi. When the Protectorate officials decided not to insist on maintenance of the peace in Karamoja, cattle raiding intensified, "resharpening the edge of tribal rivalry."[12]

2. BRITISH COLONIAL POLICY OF INDIRECT RULE INCREASED ETHNIC IDENTIFICATION

With the arrival of colonial authority, ethnic boundaries were either frozen to better maintain law and order or changed to reward one ethnic aggregate at the expense of another. Indirect rule was justified mainly by the argument that it would be cheaper to permit traditional authorities to carry out administrative tasks under British supervision than to have British officers do so themselves. Reliance on traditional authorities

---

12. James D. Barber, *Imperial Frontier: A Study of Relationships between the British and the Pastoral Tribes of North East Uganda* (Nairobi: East African Publishing House, 1968), p. 218.

meant organizing administrative units in traditional or, as the British perceived them, tribal terms.[13]

In Buganda the British found a well-organized traditional state on a relatively large scale. Having allied with the Baganda in the military expeditions against the Banyoro and having deported one Kabaka and installed an infant in his place, they found a treaty negotiated with important Baganda chiefs the most expedient basis for securing the British presence in this traditional kingdom. This treaty, the Buganda Agreement of 1900, rewarded the chiefs with grants of freehold land (contrary to traditional custom) and rewarded the Baganda generally by giving them administrative control over large areas of land taken from the defeated Banyoro. The agreement guaranteed the position of the Kabaka and introduced a modified version of the traditional Baganda hierarchy of chiefs, acting under the supervision of British officers. This treaty has been central to the development of Baganda separatism, since it gave traditional chiefs an important administrative role, which in practice resulted in a delegation of considerable autonomy. Lord Lugard regarded Buganda as a good example of successful indirect rule.[14] Since the Baganda, on the other hand, regarded the agreement as a contract between equals, they believed it could be terminated by either party. The contradiction in these views

13. The most revealing rationale of this colonial policy can be found in the speech by Sir Hugh Clifford to the Nigerian Council on 29 December 1920: "It is the consistent policy of the Government of Nigeria to maintain and to support the local tribal institutions and the indigenous froms of Government ... which are to be regarded as the natural expressions of [African] political genius. ... I am entirely convinced of the right, for example, of the people of Egbaland, ... of any of the great Emirates of the North, ... to maintain that each one of them is, in a very real sense, a nation. ... It is the task of the Government of Nigeria to build up and to fortify these national institutions." Quoted in James S. Coleman, *Nigeria: The Background to Nationalism* (Berkeley and Los Angeles: University of California Press, 1958), p. 194.

14. R. Cranford Pratt, "The Politics of Indirect Rule: Uganda, 1900-1955," in D. Anthony Low and Pratt, *Buganda and British Overrule, 1900-1955: Two Studies* (Oxford: Oxford University Press, 1960), p. 178. Lucy Mair, on the other hand, argues that the introduction of freehold land and the division of the office of Katikiro into prime minister, treasurer, and chief justice makes the use of the term "indirect rule" for the Buganda case "singularly inappropriate." "Busoga Local Government," *Journal of Commonwealth Political Studies* 5, no. 2 (July 1967): 92-93.

did not become fully apparent until Uganda gained its independence.

The British next set out to introduce a pattern of rule over what they perceived as the rest of the tribes of Uganda, and that rule reflected aspects of their relationship with the Baganda. Three other kingdoms (Ankole, Bunyoro, and Toro) were recognized — a move that meant reconstructing them. The original kingdom of Ankole was expanded to include some smaller kingdoms to the west. Toro was also expanded as a buffer to Bunyoro. The latter was reduced in size in consequence of its rebellion. Since Buganda's boundaries were also expanded, *none* of the kingdoms corresponded exactly to the areas under their influence in the precolonial period.

Semei Kakunguru, an important Muganda chief, was sent to Busoga to "weld scattered chiefships into a tribal organisation"[15] and also to Teso and Bukedi. Baganda agents were sent to Lango and Kigezi as well. Each of these areas was separately administered on the assumption that indirect rule required a tribal unit governed by traditional authorities.

In practice there were several difficulties with this assumption. First, many Ugandan cultural or linguistic aggregates were too small to warrant a separate district and thus were gathered together for administrative purposes. In these districts counties were often demarcated along cultural lines and given the name that the people gave themselves. Second, in some cases the kingdoms asserted sovereignty over culturally dissimilar people — Buganda over Banyoro in the "Lost Counties" (the territory ceded in the 1900 Agreement) and Toro over Baamba and Bakonzo. Third, Baganda agents were sent out to establish hierarchical chiefly rule in many areas which had no tradition of hierarchy (Teso, Kigezi). Fourth, the introduction of a bureaucratic style of administration — standing orders, salaries, and transfer — further vitiated whatever traditional obligations of loyalty remained. Outside Buganda and, to some extent, the other kingdoms, indirect rule meant little more than direct rule by Africans rather than Europeans.

The Ugandan version of indirect rule made several contributions to the growth of ethnic identification. Most important, it sanctioned the notion that the existence of an ethnic unit was a

15. H. B. Thomas, "Capax Imperii: The Story of Semei Kakunguru," *Uganda Journal* (1939), quoted in Mair, "Busoga Local Government," p. 93.

valid basis for an administrative unit. Indirect rule thus provided an institutional expression for political unity on the basis of cultural symbols. This was most obvious in Buganda, where top local government officers were ever-watchful for encroachment by British authorities. In all four kingdoms the traditional identification between chiefs and people was strengthened beyond precolonial levels by British policy, though economically the two were becoming more stratified. Greater coherence within the ethnic unit identified with the rulers in Ankole and Toro became possible because the British refused to tolerate armed struggles between rival factions for the throne. Ethnic identity was also increased by the establishment of clear territorial boundaries among cultural and linguistic aggregates, which eliminated the fluid situation typical of the earlier period. At the same time British policy increased the frustration of ethnic units which in accepting the equation between cultural unity and administrative boundaries felt that they had lost territory rightfully theirs.

Indirect rule enhanced the position of local rulers as the focus of cultural identity. This was immediately true in the four kingdoms, and later in many of the districts as well. As Milton Obote has commented, the doctrine of prohibiting a commoner to hold a position above the king "enriched indirect rule and the operations of separate development."[16] Finally, by using Baganda agents and by giving Buganda a degree of self-government denied all other kingdoms and districts, the British contributed to the sense of resentment other peoples felt for the Baganda and to their growing awareness that only by demonstrating a cultural unity approximating that of the Baganda could other ethnic units wring similar concessions from the British.

3. COLONIAL ADMINISTRATIVE TECHNIQUES OFTEN STRENGTHENED ETHNIC IDENTITIES

Because they were understaffed and poorly informed about the people they were governing, particularly in the early part of the century, Protectorate officials gravitated toward the administrative use of ethnic criteria on the assumption that these de-

16. "The Footsteps of Uganda's Revolution," *East Africa Journal* 5, no. 10 (October 1968): 9.

scribed real social distinctions. This policy was bound to affect those administered. One important reason for drawing district and county boundaries in accordance with cultural and linguistic aggregates was to simplify the task of keeping order for colonial officers. Application forms for government employment included a question on the "tribe" of the prospective job seeker. Census forms requested similar information. The African court system constructed under colonial rule consisted largely of " 'tribal courts,' because they were principally composed of the local elders or chiefs of the tribe and their jurisdiction was restricted to Africans."[17]   Administrators — particularly when the rationale of indirect rule was the basis of policy — put heavy emphasis on the role of customary law in settling disputes. The colonial education system also emphasized ethnic affiliation. [18] By giving administrative sanction to the collection of information about ethnic affiliation, by institutionalizing traditional legal practices, and by using ethnicity as an organizational factor in the schools, the legitimacy of ethnic identity was strengthened. In short, colonial prestige sanctioned ethnic self-definition by Ugandans.

In encouraging development, colonial officers often emphasized ethnic identity in an explicit effort to build a greater sense of collective participation. Thus, the Iteso were urged to grow more cotton and collect more taxes so as not to fall behind the Langi.[19]   Even the reverse policy maintained high levels of ethnic affiliation. During much of the colonial period, development in Karamoja was sacrificed for a minimal level of order through a policy of benign neglect. The decision not to bring in

17. Eugene Cotran, "Tribal Factors in the Establishment of the East African Legal Systems," in *Tradition and Transition in East Africa,* ed. Gulliver, p. 131; and Burke, *Local Government and Politics,* p. 218.

18. J. W. Tyler, "Education and National Identity," in *Tradition and Transition in East Africa,* ed. Gulliver, p. 170. The organization of discipline at Tabora secondary school in Tanganyika illuminates the conceptions of ethnicity held by British colonial school officials in the 1920s and 1930s: "Discipline at Tabora, adapted for African conditions, was maintained by a tribal system. Travers Lacey organised the boys into tribes corresponding roughly to the districts from which they came. Each tribe elected a chief and one or more subchiefs who, subject to the headmaster's veto, were responsible for the discipline and general behaviour of their tribe." Judith Listowel, *The Making of Tanganyika* (London: Chatto and Windus, 1965), pp. 90-91.

19. Burke, *Local Government and Politics,* p. 59.

administrators, technical officers, and schools followed the murder in 1923 of a chief appointed by the British. Not until the 1950s were developmental resources invested in Karamoja, and then only because the inhabitants drew attention to themselves through cattle raiding.[20] The result has been the close identification of tradition and ethnicity within each rival unit in Karamoja, but with little emphasis on ethnic political participation in national affairs.

4. INTRODUCTION OF LOCAL GOVERNMENT BASED ON DISTRICTS AND KINGDOMS INCREASED COMPETITIVE ETHNIC POLITICAL PARTICIPATION

As conceptions of indirect rule gave way to preparation for self-government after World War II, the Protectorate authorities began to emphasize the development of local government as a training ground in democracy and administration. National self-government, even in the early 1950s, was felt to be decades away. Educated Africans were encouraged to seek work in a district government and leave central administration to British officers. Thus local government became a focus of loyalty and African participation, while the central government remained distant and aloof.

The 1949 Local Government Ordinance and its successors determined that the district (or kingdom) would be the basic local government unit. This meant that power was shifted slowly from chiefs to democratically elected representatives, but without disturbing the ethnic basis of rule. Introduction of the electoral principle in these circumstances tended to exacerbate ethnic feelings.

Once again Buganda led the way. In the 1955 Agreement (which replaced the 1900 treaty and paved the way for the Kabaka's return from exile), the central government's control over the Buganda government was greatly reduced. Buganda gained the right to select its chiefs and other officers through its own Appointments Board. It was also permitted to introduce government by ministers on the pattern of English national government rather than English local authority. Baganda civil servants who had been posted to other districts returned to take up newly created positions in the Kabaka's government. "Trib-

20. Barber, *Imperial Frontier,* pp. 201-221.

alism and local service appointment were brought together as never before."[21]

The other kingdoms and districts were anxious to acquire the same governmental structure and autonomy: "Both the colonial administration and non-Ganda political leaders [saw] political development in terms of building up the other kingdom and district administrations to a comparable level of competence and vigour."[22]   Since competition with Buganda was by definition ethnic, the rivalry stimulated ethnic entry into politics.

The struggle of the districts to achieve "federal status" and a "constitutional head" illustrates this desire to emulate Buganda.[23] Under the 1962 constitution, districts and kingdoms had three different kinds of relationships to the central government. Only Buganda had a truly federal relationship implying separate spheres of autonomous power. The three western kingdoms of Ankole, Bunyoro, and Toro had also signed agreements with Britain but gained far less autonomy. The three kingdoms had demanded full federal status in discussions on local government in 1953. This issue increased in intensity as independence approached. But they ultimately settled for a semifederal status, which offered less independent political power than Buganda had but gave them strong protection for their traditional customs and their king and provided the trappings of local government — "ministers" and the like — rather than local administration.

Busoga, a collection of petty kinglets unified only under British colonial rule, insisted on a similar federal position. In 1961 its local councillors made their preferences clear by speaking "of the division of 'states in Uganda' into federal, semifederal, and 'others, the despicable unitary.' "[24] Busoga also managed to achieve semifederal status under the independence constitution.

The remaining areas — "mere" districts (except Karamoja, a "Special District" more closely administered by the central

21. Apter, *Political Kingdom,* p. 362.

22. Leys, *Politicians and Policies,* pp. 9-10.

23. See Donald Rothchild and Michael Rogin, "Uganda," in *National Unity and Regionalism in Eight African States,* ed. Gwendolen M. Carter (Ithaca, N.Y.: Cornell University Press, 1966), pp. 348-351.

24. Quoted from district council minutes in Mair, "Busoga Local Government," p. 99.

government) — were concerned by their lack of status for reasons of prestige and because the example of Buganda suggested that greater autonomy meant greater power and more economic rewards. They could not, however, point to a traditional unity either because there were members of several ethnic units in the district, or, if there were only one ethnic unit, because it was not united under a single traditional authority before the arrival of the British.

These complications, however, did not prevent them from agitating for constitutional heads for their districts. As Leys puts it, these were to be "Kabaka-substitutes."[25] Finally in 1963 an act was passed giving district councils the right to establish the position of constitutional head and to elect its occupant for a term of five years.[26] The Acholi, who traditionally possess a political system without a supreme authority figure, chose a Laloyo Maber ("Good Ruler") as their constitutional head. Councillors in Bukedi district also installed a constitutional head as their "traditional ruler," even though the occupant had to represent seven widely varying traditional cultures.[27] Everyone else either imitated the Buganda example or at least discussed doing so.

In what might be termed the high-water mark of legal recognition of ethnicity as a basis for politics in Uganda, the first amendment to the 1962 constitution limited the choice of president and vice-president of Uganda to "the Rulers of the

25. *Politicians and Policies*, p. 10.

26. Constitutional Heads (Elections) Act, no. 66 of 1963.

27. Oddly enough, there were *colonial* precedents, even if there were no traditional justification. Up to 1900, British officials toyed with the idea of instituting a "Kabaka" in each district to clothe British rule with what they thought was traditional legitimacy. Recognition was officially given to a "Kabaka" of Bukedi, and proposals for a "Kabaka" of Acholi were put forward. D. A. Low, "The Anatomy of Administrative Origins: Uganda 1890-1920" (paper delivered to the East African Institute of Social Research Conference, Kampala, January 1958), pp. 19-20.

Demands for a "Paramount Chief" or king on the model of the Kabaka were made throughout the colonial period. The Kyabazingaship was established in Busoga in 1919. Langi chiefs called for a Won Nyaci in the mid-1940s. In 1949 the district commissioner in Acholi declared that "it will not be permitted to try and make a sort of hereditary king whose family would become rulers." "Minutes of Acholi District Council, 12 April 1949," Entebbe Archives, ADM 21/A. The information in this paragraph is taken from Cherry Gertzel, *Party and Locality in Northern Uganda, 1945-62* (London: Athlone Press, 1974). I am grateful to Professor Gertzel for permission to see the manuscript prior to publication.

Federal States and the constitutional heads of the Districts." [28]
The rules of the game thus put a premium on competition
among districts and kingdoms for important political prizes —
competition which was limited to officials whose positions were
justified by ethnic criteria. Nowhere else does Lloyd Fallers's
prediction that all over Africa "*administrative* units are, in the
period of independence, coming to function primarily as *political* units"[29] apply more directly than to Uganda.

For those districts that acquired a pseudotraditional monarch, the next logical step, which several took, was to agitate for
federal status. Thus, in the first four years of independence,
Uganda experienced growing ethnic nationalism, often totally
unrelated to any long-standing customs but clothed in traditional garb. Ethnic learning led to competitive political participation.

5. CONSEQUENCES OF DIFFERENTIAL MODERNIZATION, PARTICULARLY IN BUGANDA, AROUSED FRUSTRATIONS AND CONSEQUENTLY INTENSIFIED FEELINGS OF ETHNIC DEPRIVATION

In Uganda, as in many other African countries, the spread of
new social and economic influences radiates out from the capital city.[30] Kampala (and Entebbe) was the focus of colonial
influence, since it was the point at which Captain (later Lord)
Lugard established the first permanent military presence. The
piecemeal acquisition of territory under the British flag thereafter is not unrelated to the degree of modernization enjoyed
today. Most Ugandans are deeply aware that the Baganda to a
large extent owe their preeminent position to this fortuitous
historical event.[31]

28. Paragraph 8, Constitution of Uganda (First Amendment), Act no. 61 of
1963. Edward Mutesa, Kabaka of Buganda, and William W. Nadiope, Kyabazinga of
Busoga, were elected president and vice-president, respectively.

29. "Political Sociology and the Anthropological Study of African Polities,"
Archives Européenes de Sociologie 4, no. 2 (1963): 329. Italics in the original.

30. The historical pattern of establishing post offices provides some confirming
evidence — the nearer a location is to Kampala, the higher the probability of its
obtaining a new postal agency. Burton O. Witthuhn, "The Spatial Integration of
Uganda as Shown by the Diffusion of Postal Agencies, 1900-1965," *The East Lakes
Geographer* 4 (December 1968): 15.

31. The connection is neatly captured by the title of a pamphlet written by
M. B. Wamala discussing the history of a Buganda Cooperative: *Where Does Uganda's
Wealth Come From? From the 1900 Agreement* (Kampala: Uganda Growers Cooperative Union Ltd., n.d.). Non-Baganda, of course, would greatly resent the suggestion
that the wealth of Uganda stemmed from an agreement covering Buganda only.

The optimal combination of factors creating modernization is a subject of much debate, though the availability of new techniques and traditional receptivity to using them are both felt to be important. Thus, David Apter's argument that the rapid Baganda acceptance of Western religions, education, and cash incomes resulted from the essentially secular character of their traditional value system integrated by an hierarchical pattern of authority[32] cannot be proved or disproved by psychological or historical evidence. The Baganda may have been motivated by their culture, by their advantageous relationship to the colonial rulers (buttressed by the favorable treaty signed in 1900), or by both. Whether or not the argument can be resolved, overcoming, or at least equaling, the educational and economic advantages of the Baganda has become a potent political goal for other Ugandans.

Several external influences gave the Baganda a one-to-two generations' head start on the rest of the country. Missionaries, responding to Henry Morton Stanley's appeal, came first to Buganda. Later, rivalry between Catholics and Protestants ensured that mission work would be well established in Buganda before other regions were penetrated.[33] The schools and hospitals built by missionaries were thus disproportionately available to Baganda. Today the best-equipped hospitals in the country are in Kampala.

In a country with an enormous income gap between peasant farmer and civil servant, the importance of gaining a place in secondary school and in university can scarcely be underestimated. Up to independence, the Baganda filled a disproportionate number of secondary school places. As table 2 indicates, in 1960 the Baganda had slightly less than twice as many school places (based on Education Department figures) in comparison with their share of the country's population. However, visible discrimination in favor of the Baganda probably was felt to be much higher, since they occupied three out of every ten places.

But disproportion in secondary school places is not a sufficient explanation of the resentment of Baganda felt by other Ugandans. For example, it is less well known, perhaps, that the Acholi were also overrepresented by only a slightly smaller

32. *The Politics of Modernization* (Chicago: University of Chicago Press, 1965), pp. 81-122.
33. Welbourn, *Religion and Politics in Uganda,* pp. 4-15.

proportion relative to their share of the population. The Samia, surprisingly, were more overrepresented than any other ethnic group. The Banyoro, Batoro, Iteso, Kumam, and Langi were also slightly overrepresented. If the secondary school population is divided into major language groups and compared with the general population, the factor of overrepresentation virtually disappears, as the index of dissimilarity indicates. (See table 2.)

At this time more secondary schools were located in Buganda than anywhere else (though the situation has changed considerably since independence). This factor worked in favor of secondary school entry of Baganda slightly less qualified than members of other aggregates. Although students are admitted primarily on the basis of a Primary Leaving Examination (formerly called the Junior Secondary Leaving Examination), headmasters have some discretion and often tend to choose the pupil living nearer the school. Thus, in 1961 "more than half the boys who entered senior secondary school from junior secondary schools in Buganda had JSLE marks of less than 168, as compared with less than a quarter of the boys from junior secondary schools in other districts."[34]

Baganda overrepresentation at Makerere University College, the only university in East Africa during the colonial period, has been far more striking. Considering that university degrees were the gateway to the most powerful positions and greatest economic opportunities, the fact that 40 percent of the 1,698 persons who entered Makerere before 1954 from all parts of East Africa were Baganda explains much of their predominance today.[35] Although Baganda overrepresentation at Makerere has fallen (and continues to fall), they still provided over 50 percent of the Ugandan entrants as late as 1950-1953.

Based on data taken from the college's nominal roll (for which entering students were asked to state their "tribe"), table 2 presents the students from each ethnic unit figured as a percentage of all Ugandan African students attending Makerere in 1959/1960. The Baganda possessed a higher disproportion of university places (to population) in comparison to the dispro-

34. H. C. A. Somerset, *Predicting Success in School Certificate: A Uganda Case Study* (Nairobi: East African Publishing House, 1968), pp. 18-19.

35. J. E. Goldthorpe, *An African Elite: Makerere College Students 1922-1960* (London: Oxford University Press, 1965), pp. 24 and 28.

portion in secondary school places they held in the same year. This comparison suggests (as table 5 demonstrates) that their university percentage would fall during the 1960s, as the changes in ethnic composition in secondary schools were reflected in university attendance. The Baganda percentage of Ugandans at Makerere in 1959/1960 was almost three times their percentage of the general population and amounted to only slightly less than half of the total Ugandan contingent in the college. All other ethnic aggregates, with the exception of the Bagwere, Banyole, Banyoro, Jonam, Kumam, and Samia, were underrepresented. If ethnic units are amalgamated into linguistic aggregates, which are sometimes claimed to be politically potent, the Bantu-speakers held four-fifths of the places while they accounted for two-thirds of the general population; and the Nilotic, "Nilo-Hamitic," and Sudanic aggregates were significantly underrepresented in varying degrees.

In addition to those in higher studies in Ugandan secondary schools and Makerere, an increasing percentage of students have gone overseas for training. Although no breakdown by ethnic units exists for those abroad, the Baganda probably have had a disproportionate share of these opportunities also. Of Ugandan students abroad in the last quarter of 1960, 143 were sponsored by the Kabaka's government, as compared with only 106 sponsored by all the rest of the districts and kingdoms.[36] Of the 103 students sponsored by the Ugandan and foreign governments and the 124 students studying on private resources, the Baganda also probably took more places than their numbers alone would warrant.

Ugandan parents who have gone to school demand similar privileges for their children. There is a strong and growing tendency for Makerere students to have educated parents, brothers, and sisters.[37] Built into the early and unequal provision of education to Baganda, therefore, is a demand for its continuation.

In economic development and patterns of consumption, the Baganda also forged ahead of their neighbors. The Baganda were

36. Compiled from data in the *Annual Report of the Education Department: 1960* (Entebbe: Government Printer, 1961), p. 46.

37. Goldthorpe, *An African Elite,* pp. 30-48, and Pierre van den Berghe, "An African Elite Revisited," *Mawazo* (Kampala) 1, no. 4 (December 1968): 60-61.

given cottonseed in 1904 to encourage them to grow cash crops to generate funds for the payment of the poll tax. Farmers elsewhere received seed later. The first Ugandan cooperative union was begun by Baganda in 1923. Later, the first ginnery to be turned over to Africans was run by this union.

The existence of freehold land in Buganda (there is very little in other districts) also gave some Baganda disproportionate opportunities to grow wealthy.[38]   Large plots were given to chiefs to persuade them to sign the 1900 Agreement. The rental income was sufficient to provide school fees for their children and money for investment in trade. Chiefs sometimes sold their land to peasants who had become wealthy growing cotton or coffee.

TABLE 1
AFRICAN EMPLOYEES BY REGION, 1967

Region	Private industry	Public services	Total
Buganda	75,000	34,800	109,800
Eastern	34,000	27,700	58,800 [sic]
Western	31,800	21,600	53,300 [sic]
Northern	9,300	10,700	20,000

Source: *Enumeration of Employees: June 1967* (Entebbe: Statistics Division, Ministry of Planning and Economic Development, August 1968) p. 1.

When the capital city, Kampala — already offering many central government jobs — attracted industry, the Baganda were more available to take up wage employment. They continue to get the higher-paying jobs because they are better educated. They also can commute to work and still grow their own food on plots near Kampala. Thus, they tend to be more stable employees and advance more rapidly into skilled positions. [39]

38. Later discussion of the possibility of introducing freehold tenure in other districts was resisted not only for fear that Europeans would gain ownership, but also because Baganda who had already grown wealthy would be in a better position to acquire property than the local people. For example, an assistant district commissioner in Lango reported both fears, commenting that the "stronger and more general apprehension was that the new system would enable other African tribes to secure land rights in Lango." *Lango District Archives*, ADM 9/6 (January-February 1956), quoted in Gertzel, *Party and Locality in Northern Uganda*, p. 40.

39. Lloyd A. Fallers, "The Modernization of Social Stratification," in *The King's Men: Leadership and Status in Buganda on the Eve of Independence*, ed. Fallers (London: Oxford University Press, 1964), p. 148.

The inequality in wage opportunities favoring the former Buganda region is now quite pronounced, though a large number of these jobs are held by non-Baganda. (See table 1.)

Consequently, a market catering to fairly sophisticated tastes has developed in Buganda, but not elsewhere. As Walter Elkan puts it: "Everybody [in Uganda] needs money to pay their poll tax, and in most areas there is a sale for cloth, cigarettes, soap and bicycles. In Buganda there is also a sale for refrigerators, motor cars and dinner jackets."[40]

Members of other ethnic groups became acutely conscious that they had to become strangers in the home of the Baganda to earn high incomes. They resented the fact that the development of their schools and hospitals lagged behind those of Buganda. They watched the Baganda consolidate their numerical advantage by becoming the educational and economic elite as well. By demanding a share of the benefits of development equal to that of the Baganda, the disadvantaged necessarily intensified the ethnic basis of Ugandan politics.

One important exception to the pattern of economic opportunities favoring the Baganda was recruitment into the police and army. The British set a height requirement which tended to discriminate against the shorter Bantu aggregates. They also recruited more vigorously in the northern parts of the country among ethnic groups possessing a reputation for martial skills and few other economic opportunities.

The data presented in table 2 (taken from Police Departments statistics) confirm the widespread belief that the Acholi (at least in 1960) occupied a disproportionate share of positions among the nongazetted ranks in the police force. They were the largest group in absolute numbers and one of the largest in comparison with their share of the general population.[41] The Alur, Japadhola, Iteso, Jonam, Kakwa, Kumam, and Madi were also heavily overrepresented. Contrary to general belief, the Langi produced only a few more policemen than their percentage of the population would have suggested. The Baganda were severely under-

40. *The Economic Development of Uganda* (London: Oxford University Press, 1961), p. 13.

41. The Samia and the Luo were more heavily represented by comparison with their *Ugandan* population than were the Acholi. However, it is likely that a large number of each of these groups were Kenyans. In September 1964 there were 488 Kenyans serving in the Uganda Police Force. Grace Ibingira, minister of state, *Parliamentary Debates,* vol. 34 (Entebbe: Government Printer, 1964), p. xv.

TABLE 2

ETHNIC DISTRIBUTION IN SECONDARY SCHOOLS, MAKERERE AND THE POLICE FORCE IN THE LATE COLONIAL PERIOD

Ethnic census unit	Population 1959 %[a]	Secondary school places 1960 %[b]	Ugandan African Makerere students 1959/1960 %[c]	Police force 1961 %[d]
Baganda	16.3	29.0	46.6	3.8
Iteso	8.1	10.6	6.1	15.2
Banyankole	8.1	6.5	6.1	2.6
Basoga	7.8	6.1	6.1	4.2
Bakiga/Bahororo	7.1	5.5	6.4	2.7
Banyarwanda	5.9	2.6	1.8	1.2
Langi	5.6	6.5	1.8	7.5
Bagisu	5.1	4.6	3.6	4.0
Acholi	4.4	7.1	4.3	15.5
Lugbara	3.7	2.6	0.4	4.5
Batoro	3.2	3.7	1.8	0.7
Banyoro	2.9	3.5	3.6	2.6
Rundi	2.2	–	0.0	–
Karamojong	2.0	–	0.4	0.5
Alur	1.9	1.2	0.4	3.5
Bagwere	1.7	1.7	2.1	1.3
Bakonjo	1.7	–	0.7	–
Japadhola (Badama)	1.6	1.4	1.4	2.2
Banyole	1.4	1.3	1.4	–
Madi	1.2	1.1	0.7	3.8
Kumam	1.0	1.2	1.4	3.7
Samia	0.7	1.8	0.7	3.1
Kakwa	0.6	0.5	0.0	1.6
Sebei	0.6	–	0.0	0.2
Bagwe	0.6	–	0.4	–
Luo	0.6	–	0.0	3.4
Baamba	0.5	–	0.0	–
Jonam	0.4	0.4	1.4	2.6
Suk (Pokot)	0.3	–	0.0	0.1
Baluhyia	n.e.s.[e]	–	0.4	3.1
Bachope	n.e.s.	–	0.0	0.1
Bukusu (Kitosh)	n.e.s.	–	0.0	0.3
Nubian	n.e.s.	–	0.0	0.5
Okebo	n.e.s.	–	0.4	–
Other ethnic units[f]	3.1	1.1	0.0	5.3
Total ...	100.0 (N = 6,449,558)	100.0 (N = 3,586)	100.8 (N = 281)	99.8 (N = 4,804)
Index of dissimilarity		Δ[g] = 21.4	Δ = 33.1	Δ = 43.3

TABLE 2 (Continued)

Ethnic census units aggregated into language units	Population 1959	Secondary school places 1960	Ugandan African Makerere students 1959/1960	Police force 1961
	%	%	%	%
Bantu	65.7	66.3	81.5	29.8
Nilotic	14.5	16.6	9.3	34.8
"Nilo-Hamitic"[h]	12.7	12.3	7.8	21.4
Sudanic	5.0	3.7	1.4	8.8
Others	2.1	1.1	0.0	5.3
Total ...	100.0	100.0	100.0	100.1
Index of dissimilarity		$\Delta = 2.7$	$\Delta = 15.8$	$\Delta = 36.0$

[a]*Uganda Census 1959: African Population* (Statistics Branch, Ministry of Economic Affairs), 1961, p. 18. The percentages are based on the population of Ugandan Africans only.

[b]Compiled from *Annual Report of the Education Department: 1960* (Entebbe: Government Printer, 1961) pp. 27-28. The percentages are based on Ugandan Africans in the first through the fourth year of secondary school only. The report omits all ethnic units with a total of ten or fewer pupils.

[c]Compiled from *Makerere University College Nominal Roll of Students, 1959/1960.* The percentages are based on the population of Ugandan Africans only.

[d]Compiled from *Annual Report of the Uganda Police: 1961* (Entebbe: Government Printer, 1962) p. 4. The percentages include all nongazetted African ranks, except for 253 Africans whose ethnic breakdown was not given. The table also omits the 59 African gazetted officers, who occupied 22.3 percent of the gazetted posts.

[e]n.e.s. – not enumerated separately.

[f]This category includes a different segment of the population in each column. Since there are both secondary school students (40) and police (253) who are not broken down into ethnic units, it would be incorrect to assume that units for which there is no entry in these columns had no members in secondary schools or the police in 1961.

[g]Δ is the index of dissimilarity and is used here to measure the sum of the deviations of ethnic representation in each institution from that unit's percentage of the general population. A perfect fit ($\Delta = 0$) would result if the institutional percentage distribution were identical to the ethnic distribution of the general population. The result indicating the poorest fit would have a value of $\Delta = 100$. Note that for secondary schools and the police the values of Δ are approximate, because the identities of the ethnic units making up the residual category are not available. I wish to thank Stephen Taber for bringing this index to my attention.

[h]Linguists differ over whether there is an independent category of "Nilo-Hamitic" languages, or whether it is a branch of the Nilotic family. For the latter view see J. H. Greenberg, "Nilotic, 'Nilo-Hamitic', and Hamito-Semitic. A Reply," *Africa* 27, no. 4 (October 1957).

represented.[42]   As a whole, the Bantu-speakers provided less than half the number of policemen that one would have predicted on the basis of their share of the population. The Nilotics, "Nilo-Hamitics," and Sudanic-speakers were correspondingly overrepresented.

By comparing the data for secondary schools, university, and police with population in a given year, the wide ethnic variations become readily apparent. The only groups which were overrepresented in all three institutions were the Acholi and the Kumam. A comparison of the indices of dissimilarity shows that in the late colonial period secondary school places were more representatively allocated in ethnic terms than were university places. The police had the worst "fit" and were more than twice as unrepresentative as the secondary schools. The dissimilarity of the three institutions is even more marked when the major language aggregates are compared with their percentages of the general population. It should be kept firmly in mind, however, that the identifications in each column may have been based on a different criterion of ethnicity and in any case are subject to all the conceptual problems discussed in chapter two.

Even though Buganda's greater wealth created frustration everywhere else, the same differential modernization process also created resentment on a smaller scale within several of the districts and kingdoms. Rural social structure has been changing all over Uganda, though at varying rates of speed, as new educational and economic opportunities become available. In Toro, for example, Bakonzo and Baamba found themselves at a disadvantage in the number of school places, medical dispensaries, and positions in the district administration in comparison with the Batoro. In Sebei district Bagisu moved from the more densely populated lowlands into territory that the Sebei traditionally had regarded as their own. By 1962 they were producing twice as much of the coffee marketed in Sebei as the Sebei themselves.[43] The ethnic movements for separate

42. There are some indications that Baganda do not apply for positions in the police force in very large numbers. In 1967 only 104 Baganda applied to the police training school out of 47,975 applicants. Of these, 13 were accepted. In 1968, 217 Baganda applied out of 24,534; and 63 Baganda were accepted. These figures may be influenced by the Baganda reaction to the events of 1966. They were stated in parliament by Basil Bataringaya, minister of internal affairs, *Uganda Argus,* 22 February 1969, p. 3.

43. Twaddle, " 'Tribalism' in Eastern Uganda," p. 345.

districts in both cases were strengthened by the economic inequality Bakonzo, Baamba, and Sebei observed at home.

Differential modernization might not have had such serious ethnic consequences if colonial policies of indirect rule, education, courts, and local government had not conditioned Ugandans to think in ethnic terms. However, given the structure of resource allocation developed under colonial rule, it is not surprising that inequalities in education and economic development reinforced perceived distinctions among ethnic units. Feelings of ethnic deprivation became a potent source of political participation.

6. DEVELOPMENT OF NATIONALIST PARTIES AS COALITIONS OF DISTRICT POLITICAL NOTABLES STIMULATED ETHNIC POLITICAL COMPETITION

Wallerstein argues that "the most important mechanism to reduce the conflict between ethnicity and national integration is the nationalist party."[44] Ugandan political parties, however, exacerbated ethnic political participation up to 1966. None of them developed centralized national organizations. Instead they were oriented toward district politics and vulnerable to the appeals of ethnic movements. The national organization of the Uganda People's Congress (UPC) controlled neither nominations of candidates for the National Assembly nor policy statements of district branches.[45] Nearly all of its local party officers were stationed in the areas of the ethnic units to which they belonged.[46] The former UPC secretary general John Kakonge commented that "the basic forces in the formation of the U.P.C. were tribal and personal, and its structure was based on a conglomeration of tribes."[47] The Democratic Party (DP) also showed few signs of centralization and found it extremely difficult to impose a single approach to strategy, policy, or

44. "Ethnicity and National Integration," p. 138.

45. Cherry Gertzel, "Report from Kampala," *Africa Report* 9, no. 9 (October 1964): 7; and Rothchild and Rogin, "Uganda," pp. 394-395.

46. Joseph S. Nye, Jr., "TANU and UPC: The Impact of Independence on Two African Nationalist Parties," in *Boston University Papers on Africa: Transition in African Politics,* ed. Jeffrey Butler and A. A. Castagno (New York: Praeger, 1967), p. 231.

47. "The Political Party, Its Structure, Organization, and Its Members," in *The Challenge of Independence* (Kampala: The Milton Obote Foundation, 1966), p. 3.

candidate nominations on branches or members.[48]   KY, as discussed in chapter five, was an ethnic movement and only in the broadest sense a party at all.

The Uganda National Congress (UNC), the predecessor to the UPC and the first popular Ugandan party, made headway only where it was able to take advantage of local issues.[49]   It never developed a specifically national appeal. The Lango branch of the UNC, for example, was run by local notables rather than by the national party officers. The party had relatively little organization and few dues-payers, though district leaders had an effective rural following based on informal contact. Because its national leaders were Baganda commoners, it reaped a full harvest of mistrust from the Buganda government, to which it posed a fundamental challenge, and to a lesser extent from other Ugandans, who feared Baganda domination. Furthermore, the UNC itself temporarily abandoned its efforts to gain a nationwide following when its leaders felt the integrity of Buganda threatened during the crisis over the exile of the Kabaka in 1953.

A number of factors contributed to the failure of Ugandan parties to develop strong national organizations. In the early 1950s the colonial policy of thinking in terms of tribes led Governor Cohen to suggest that African members of the Legislative Council should be elected by district councils because "abler representatives would be likely chosen, since it is the district which is the natural unit of public life everywhere outside Buganda; here tribal loyalty and cohesion is strong. . . ."[50]   In 1958 the district was made the constituency in those areas in which representatives were to be elected. By necessity, then, the district also became the "natural unit" for organization of the party. Benedicto Kiwanuka, leader of the

48. Rothchild and Rogin, "Uganda," pp. 390-391.

49. Apter, *The Political Kingdom,* pp. 326-328; and Richards, "Epilogue," in *The King's Men,* ed. Fallers, p. 379. For Lango see Gertzel, *Party and Locality in Northern Uganda.*

50. *Correspondence Relating to the Composition of the Legislative Council in Uganda* (Entebbe: Government Printer, 1953), p. 3, quoted in Apter, *The Political Kingdom,* p. 272.

DP, claimed that the voters in the 1958 elections — the first direct election to the Legislative Council — chose primarily on "tribal" grounds.[51]

Low offers several additional reasons for the inability of any party to develop an effective central executive. The most important are (1) the lack of urgency in the nationalist struggle (from the middle 1950s no one doubted that independence ultimately would be granted); (2) the small number of elections; (3) the inability of parties to find popular issues due to the vigorous reforms undertaken by the colonial government in the 1950s; (4) the absence of a dynamic or charismatic leader; and (5) the attack on all political parties by Baganda neotraditionalists, who feared that the Kabaka and chiefs would necessarily lose power to commoners if elections were held.[52] Weaknesses in central party structure meant growing reliance on local coalition — often rationalized through ethnic unity. These coalitions became an additional focus for political participation.

After the 1961 elections (won by the DP on a fluke growing out of a boycott of the election by most Baganda), the DP and UPC struggled to achieve an absolute majority in the National Assembly elections of 1962 since the winning party would form the first independent government. They were both forced to take up local grievances and accept deviations from the national party line. Thus, for example, both parties felt constrained to support the demands of Ankole, Bunyoro, Toro, and Busoga for full federal status.[53] Benedicto Kiwanuka, then the prime minister, agreed that the Sebei should have their own district and managed to give the same impression to the Baamba and Bakonzo without actually saying so. The result was further to legitimize ethnic political participation within the national arena, since the UPC had to respond in kind.

The party candidates selected for the 1961 elections demon-

51. George Bennett, "Tribalism in Politics," in *Tradition and Transition in East Africa,* ed. Gulliver, p. 64. Bennett adds that "indeed, a pattern was beginning whereby the members elected to the Legislative Council appeared as tribal spokesmen or 'ambassadors.' " Ibid.

52. *Political Parties in Uganda,* pp. 7-43.

53. Ibid., p. 56.

strate the importance placed on local factors by politicians. [54] Only 9 out of 185 African candidates were born outside the district in which their constituencies were located. Only 18 out of 175 candidates in nonurban constituencies were identified with an ethnic unit other than the largest one in their constituencies. Most of these came from the second-largest ethnic unit. Seventy-five percent of the winners and 49 percent of the losers were born in their home constituencies. Rothchild and Rogin conclude that "ethnic and religious politics . . . dominate Uganda's voting patterns," with "tribalism" becoming even more important in the 1962 elections. [55]

As Godfrey Binaisa, the UPC attorney general, dolefully remarked six months after independence, "We are not a mass party because most of our MPs are here for tribal merits." [56] The UPC's victory in 1962 dislodged the DP from national office but left the structure of ethnic political participation intact.

7. FEAR AMONG SMALLER ETHNIC UNITS THAT THE DEPARTURE OF THE BRITISH WOULD LEAVE THEM UNPROTECTED CAUSED THEM TO ENTER THE POLITICAL ARENA JUST BEFORE INDEPENDENCE

Independence, it is popularly assumed, increases national integration because an alien colonial administration is replaced with a local indigenous government. But the coming of independence can also arouse fears of future ill-treatment and an upsurge of political activity by those who were formerly quiescent. The British had established a reputation as relatively impartial umpires who would protect the rights of groups under their jurisdiction. Would an African regime do the same?

In addition, the departure of the alien government tended to remove one force for unity within the national state. With the British present, Ugandans could unite against the common enemy. With the British absent, they would have to allocate resources among themselves. One result in Uganda was an increased willingness to regard ministers and senior civil servants

54. Robert O. Byrd, "A Portrait of Leadership in a New Nation: The Case of Uganda," *Queens' Quarterly* 69, no. 4 (1963): 524 and 531. Byrd notes that the UPC was slightly more willing than the DP to nominate candidates outside their districts of birth. Ibid., pp. 532-533.

55. "Uganda," p. 384.

56. Nye, "TANU and UPC," p. 231.

"as representatives of their respective tribes, whose function in government was to safeguard and plead tribal interests in matters of appointments, distribution of development projects and social services."[57]

Another consequence was the initiation or intensification of secessionist movements and demands for separate districts all over Uganda. The "Lost Counties" issue, which concerned whether the area surrendered by Bunyoro to Buganda at the beginning of the century should be returned, produced agitated pronouncements and desperate maneuvers that resulted in violence and arson. And at one point, the Lukiiko declared that Buganda itself was leaving Uganda. Sebei nationalists organized their followers behind the demand for a separate district. Baamba and Bakonzo leaders began to demand entrenched constitutional protection from the Batoro; and when they failed to get it, they converted the cultural thrust of the Rwenzururu movement into a political weapon. In October 1963 a motion for a separate district in East Acholi was proposed but defeated.[58] The Bahororo living in Ankole and the Iteso of Bukedi also demanded separate districts.[59] Perhaps an indication of events to come could have been seen in the increasing demand for creation of new districts. In the short run, ethnic political participation seemed to provide some protection against an uncertain future.

8. CONCLUSION

Several factors contributed to a situation in which ethnic identification became a pertinent response in Ugandan politics. The most important were memories of precolonial migrations and military conflicts; indirect rule; certain colonial administrative techniques; the introduction of local government on the basis of districts and kingdoms; frustrations resulting from differential modernization; the development of nationalist parties as coalitions of district notables; and fears of loss of protection and a fair share of future resources upon the departure of the British. These factors prepared the way for the formation of ethnic

57. Obote, "Uganda's Revolution," p. 7.
58. Leys, *Politicians and Policies,* n. 6, p. 19. But see p. 154 below.
59. Rothchild and Rogin, "Uganda," p. 413.

units predisposed to seek their goals through political participation. However, the political impact of ethnicity must not be magnified out of proportion — it is only one among many cleavages and concerns that shaped political life in the preindependence period.

Ethnicity might have been less important had there not been a sharp increase in political participation in preparation for independence. The sudden reversal of British imperial policy contributed significantly to an environment predisposed to the entry of ethnic units into politics. In the early 1950s Ugandan sovereignty was thought to be a problem for the next generation; by the end of the decade everyone knew it was imminent. Consequently, there were frantic efforts (at least in comparison with the more leisurely pace of the past) to expand existing political structures and introduce new ones.

Even the original stage-by-stage approach to the expansion of participation worked to reinforce ethnicity. Ugandans were supposed to learn about politics in the arenas of their local districts and kingdoms before being permitted to enter national politics. The sudden abandonment of this strategy left Ugandans with incipient district organizations to cope with competition from all over the country. Since districts and kingdoms were equated with ethnic units in the minds of both people and rulers, the short-range future of ethnic policial participation was assured.

FIVE

◇

SIX CASE STUDIES IN ETHNIC POLITICAL PARTICIPATION

A closer look at some of the ethnic disputes that aroused intense passion helps explain the politics of ethnic involvement in Uganda. The six case studies discussed in this chapter include three movements, two controversies (based on somewhat less organized opposing movements), and the supposed confrontation between linguistic "coalitions." These examples are the Kabaka Yekka movement, which attempted to preserve Buganda's autonomy at independence; the Sebei movement for a separate district; the Rwenzururu secessionist movement; the "Lost Counties" dispute between Buganda and Bunyoro; the Mbale dispute between the Bagisu and the inhabitants of Bukedi; and the asserted opposition between the Bantu and Nilotic "blocs," which many claim to have dominated Ugandan politics from independence until 1966.

These cases were highly salient for their participants, aroused the most public concern in Uganda, and involved a considerable portion of the energies of the central government in coping with them. There were, of course, many others. A brief description of each of the six provides a sense of what motivates people to join such movements, how movements respond to their organizational problems, and how the government handles the controversies they create. Ethnic political involvement is anything but uniform, as the discussion of the components of participation in these movements indicates.

1. KABAKA YEKKA

KY presents a case in which ethnicity defined — for a short time — the scope of political participation for most Baganda. It dominated the loyalties of the overwhelming majority of Baganda and bridged conflicts over religion, class, ideology, and

119

acceptance of Western influences. Radical left-wing educated nationalists clasped hands with conservative neotraditionalists. KY drew enormous support from the traditional beliefs of Baganda, as the name, "Kabaka Only," indicates. It had elements of a mass movement and yet was most effective when supported by the organizational resources of the Buganda government.

Although KY was founded in June 1961, only a little more than a year before independence, its roots were much older. KY descended from a series of sharply conflicting political organizations which pitted peasants against chiefs within Buganda. It gained its extraordinary power by uniting these opposed factions in a burst of popular enthusiasm, but it was unable to sustain a consensus among leaders for very long.

The split in Buganda's political life developed out of a basic change in its traditional political system. Several hundred years ago the Bataka, or heads of clans, probably occupied the positions of greatest power within Buganda. This meant that the political system was far more decentralized and perhaps more egalitarian than it was in the 1860s, when the first Europeans visited. By then the Kabaka had established his preeminent position as Sabataka, head of all the clans, *and* as head of a separate administrative hierarchy. In his latter capacity he received the personal loyalty of chiefs whom he appointed. As tax collectors, military leaders, and road builders, these chiefs became far more important than the clan heads, who retained responsibilities over land and ancestor worship. In certain cases the Kabaka was required by tradition to appoint a clan head as county chief. In addition, the Kabaka came to have the power to appoint other individuals at his personal discretion to administer royal estates scattered throughout the kingdom. Basically, however, there were two systems of authority, and they were united in the person of the Kabaka.

When the British agreed in 1900 that the Kabaka and his higher-ranking chiefs should receive freehold land, the Bataka lost their rights over these areas. They put themselves forward as the protectors of ancient traditional customs of the people against the chiefs, who were attacked as opportunists. The Bataka first raised the issue of land rights in 1922 and directed their appeal against the chiefs to the Kabaka.[1] With support from both traditional custom and peasants paying rent, the Bataka movement introduced an important populist element into Baganda politics and left open the possibility for a future Kabaka to lead it.

From 1938 through 1949 the Sons of Kintu (organized by Ignatius Musazi) and the Bataka Party represented these feelings. They attacked the Kabaka's government — that is, the chiefs — and appealed to the Kabaka to dismiss them.[2] The riots of 1945 and 1949 were inflamed by the activities of these politicians. They advocated a combination of traditionalism and democracy in the Lukiiko (the Buganda parliament), then dominated by appointed chiefs. After the Bataka Party was proscribed by the Protectorate government, Musazi and Abu Mayanja formed the Uganda National Congress in 1952 to bring Uganda to independence. But, as mentioned above, the UNC tended to revert to a "Buganda-first" party whenever its members felt Buganda's institutions were threatened.

The position of Edward Mutesa, the Kabaka, remained uncertain during this period. He was not personally popular and tended to rely on the advice of his appointed chiefs and ministers. Many nationalist Baganda politicians regarded him as little more than a British agent. However, the crisis of 1953 wrought a major change in the structure of authority in Buganda. Old fears over possible federation of the three East African territories were stirred by a speech given by the secretary of state for the colonies. Unsatisfied by the governor's reassurance that federation would not be imposed, the Kabaka refused to recommend to the Lukiiko the Protectorate government's proposals for a new constitution. The government responded by withdrawing recognition and deporting him. One of his minis-

1. David Apter, *The Political Kingdom in Uganda: A Study of Bureaucratic Nationalism* (Princeton: Princeton University Press, 1967), pp. 141-146.

2. Ibid., pp. 203-204, 226-229, 259-260. There are striking parallels between the career of Musazi and that of Herbert Macauley, the "father" of Nigerian nationalism. Both were highly educated and had elite occupations. Both thrived on political agitation. Macauley led the Nigerian National Democratic Party, which remained exclusively a Lagos organization, though it attempted to form branches in other parts of the country. He was preoccupied with the defense of the House of Docemo, and

ters thought that if his deportation had been delayed a few months, the Kabaka would have been deposed.[3]

Instead he became a hero to his people. "The identification of the Kabaka with Buganda nationalism was immediately and clearly displayed."[4] Traditional religious ceremonies were performed and ancient praise-names for the Kabaka were printed by the vernacular press. Upon his return groups vied to give him presents and demonstrate their loyalty. Mutesa thus became the focus of mass support that made him for the first time an extremely powerful figure in his own right, as well as the fundamental symbol of Baganda tradition.

The civil service chiefs who formed the Kabaka's government at Mengo, the capital of Buganda, received high income from rents on official lands which went with their positions, and they were heartily disliked for it. However, as KY later demonstrated, the chiefs still held enormous influence among the peasants. The Mengo government had long taken special pains to preserve Buganda's privileges and autonomy. Since 1921 leaders of the Buganda Lukiiko had consistently attempted to reduce the Protectorate government's supervisory role and opposed East African federation and Buganda's participation in the Legislative Council. Joining a larger political unit, it was feared, would mean that the Baganda no longer controlled their own destiny. They were even willing to forego independence for Uganda in order to protect their ethnic autonomy. "Buganda," they said, "can not sell all her heritage for the purchase of Uganda's independence."[5]

The Lukiiko also opposed direct elections in 1958 and 1961,

---

this impeded the expansion of the NNDP, just as Musazi and the UNC never really transcended Baganda politics. For a sketch of Macauley's career see James S. Coleman, *Nigeria: The Background to Nationalism* (Berkeley and Los Angeles: University of California Press, 1958), pp. 197-199.

3. F. B. Welbourn, *Religion and Politics in Uganda: 1952-62* (Nairobi: East African Publishing House, 1965), p. 26; and Apter, *The Political Kingdom,* p. 279.

4. Audrey I. Richards, "Traditional Values and Current Political Behaviour," in *The King's Men: Leadership and Status in Buganda on the Eve of Independence,* ed. Lloyd A. Fallers (London: Oxford University Press, 1964), p. 323. See also Welbourn, *Religion and Politics in Uganda,* pp. 42-44; and Apter, *The Political Kingdom,* p. 372.

5. "Termination of British Protection: A Memorandum to Her Majesty Queen Elizabeth II Submitted by Members of the Lukiiko of the Kingdom of Buganda," reproduced in Apter, *The Political Kingdom,* p. 488.

since participation meant acceptance of the Legislative Council (and, of course, of political parties that were likely to attack the Mengo government). The 1955 Agreement, in which the Kabaka became a constitutional monarch and Mengo received virtual autonomy in domestic affairs, represents the high-water mark in the preservation of Buganda's special position. It strengthened Buganda's hand at the independence conferences in 1961 and was a major factor leading to federal status for Buganda.

As independence approached and Baganda became more concerned over the protection of their unique status, these two groups — chiefs and politicians — began to draw closer together. The Uganda National Movement (UNM) sprang up in 1959 to fight for independence (though it had little support outside Buganda), to oppose the Wild Committee, and to boycott shops and bus companies run by non-Africans. It was directed by populist-minded Baganda politicians but also appeared to have the reluctant backing of the Kabaka's ministers. The UNM sponsored a parade of protestors dressed in barkcloth, the symbol of Buganda nationalism. It was declared illegal after a few months.[6]

At the end of 1960 the Lukiiko declared that Buganda had decided to terminate its agreement with Great Britain and thus was independent. Though highly symbolic of Baganda desires, the gesture turned out to be an idle threat. In March 1961 the Kabaka's government called for a boycott of the national elections. It was over 97 percent effective in Buganda, demonstrating a near-universal response. Refusal to participate was the chosen tool of ethnic political action on this occasion. However, the twenty thousand people who cast their votes managed to elect Democratic Party candidates in twenty out of twenty-one constituencies. As a result Benedicto Kiwanuka, a Catholic Muganda commoner, became Uganda's first prime minister. To many Baganda he appeared to have a more important position than the Kabaka, which, given the popularity and traditional status of the latter, was unthinkable. Furthermore, as a Catholic he was unacceptable to the Protestant establishment that ran the Mengo government.

In this atmosphere KY held its first meeting in June 1961. Most of the men who founded it were wealthy Protestants with

6. Audrey I. Richards, "Epilogue," in *The King's Men,* ed. Fallers, pp. 371-372.

close informal ties to the Kabaka. It met with an immediate enthusiastic response far beyond the expectations of its sponsors. Politicians of all ideologies, conservative and radical, quickly joined the bandwagon, and in November it received the open support of Mengo government officials.[7] It grew rapidly throughout Buganda.

KY leaders denied that it was a political party, but it acted as one to contest the Lukiiko elections of February 1962. The electoral machinery of the party consisted mainly of the chiefly hierarchy,[8] completing at least a formal rapprochement between chiefs and politicians. These elections were of particular importance, since the Lukiiko was to choose Buganda's representatives for the National Assembly (another concession to Buganda not shared by the rest of the country). On the basis of an unexpected political bargain with KY that created a coalition at the national level, the UPC agreed to run no candidates in the Lukiiko races. Thus, the battle for the Lukiiko was fought by KY and DP, with control of the national government the ultimate prize.

The frankly ethnic appeal with overtones of traditional obligation was overwhelming. The Kabaka was made the focus for the uncertainties of Buganda's survival after independence. Without him there could be no kingdom, it was argued; and without the kingdom, there could no longer be any Baganda, since the political structure and the culture were perceived to be inextricably related. In a political pamphlet one of the founders of KY stated its central theme: "That the Kabaka shall never be preceded by anybody else on the entire soil of Buganda. KABAKA YEKKA."[9] The party symbol was a chair that could easily be interpreted as a throne. An explicit ideology that rested unmistakably upon ethnic identification and called as well for a massive popular response was thus forged.

7. Ian R. Hancock, "Patriotism and Neo-Traditionalism in Buganda: The Kabaka Yekka ('The King Alone') Movement, 1961-1962," *Journal of African History* 11, no. 3 (1970): 423-427. See also Cherry Gertzel, "How Kabaka Yekka Came To Be," *Africa Report* 9, no. 9 (October 1964).

8. Hancock, "Patriotism and Neo-Traditionalism," pp. 430-431. KY candidates had to get the Kabaka's approval as well. Welbourn, *Religion and Politics in Uganda*, p. 32.

9. Hancock, "Patriotism and Neo-Traditionalism," pp. 425-426 and 431-432. The overwhelming electoral defeat of the DP demonstrated that ethnicity exerted a stronger pull than religion for Catholic Baganda.

Even though KY candidates were certain winners almost everywhere, in two-thirds of the constituencies over 90 percent of the registered voters cast a ballot. Only 9.8 percent of those who voted (mainly Banyoro in the "Lost Counties") resisted this ethnic appeal, while over 90 percent voted for KY. Of the sixty-eight seats, all except three in the "Lost Counties" went to KY candidates. Voting percentages of this magnitude are unusual in contested elections anywhere, and turnouts this high are particularly surprising in Africa. They attest to an intense mobilization of political participation in response to fears of interference with the privileges, the status, and above all the autonomy of the Baganda.

However, KY was not a political machine, and its victory at the polls removed the common goal that had cemented all factions. The Kabaka's senior ministers feared that the popular support generated by the movement might be turned against them. They moved to prevent elected members or progressives from taking control. To achieve this end, Michael Kintu, the Katikiro (prime minister) of Buganda, was elected head of KY's executive committee. The chiefly hierarchy won all battles against reform. Most important KY decisions were made after discussion with Kintu and the Kabaka. The progressive and educated politicians who had joined KY began to resign, and in 1963 nine KY members of the National Assembly crossed the aisle to the UPC, claiming that this was the best way to protect Buganda's traditions.[10]

As an ethnic movement KY briefly achieved a unity that had eluded Buganda for at least the past hundred years. For a short time it united populist democrats and bureaucratic officials, poor peasants and successful professionals, by drawing on the new popularity of the Kabaka. It was a mass movement appealing to a deep level of personal identity during a critical time for the Baganda. It combined traditional symbols and customs centering on the Kabaka with the political goal of ethnic autonomy for the Baganda. "Kabaka Yekka became a movement of Buganda against the world."[11]

For various reasons, however, it was not to survive for long. Part of its success was due to the fact that it employed a

10. Gertzel, "Kabaka Yekka," pp. 10 and 13. I am indebted to conversations with Ian Hancock for several points made in this paragraph.
11. Richards, "Epilogue," pp. 384 and 385.

formidable organization — the Kabaka's governmental machinery and particularly the chiefly hierarchy — to direct and control the popular enthusiasm aroused by the movement. This was a case of the state's taking over the party, rather than the other way around. Nevertheless, KY possessed little in the way of party machinery, and what it did have was beset by splits and disputes. "The simple objectives had become overlaid with personal ambitions and factionalism."[12] No one in the elite had been able to resist KY *when it had been focused on a particular issue* — the threat to the Kabakaship in the situation created by the Lukiiko elections. In that situation ethnicity ruled all motives. But in the long run KY's future was doomed by its lack of organizational coherence. " 'Kabaka Yekka' was a powerful slogan in Buganda, but as an organization it carried no political weight."[13] Vested interest and ethnicity were intertwined, but the combination proved unstable. The defections of KY members of parliament to the UPC and subsequent harassment by the central government also contributed to its loss of influence. Crippled by national legislation declaring that the use of the title of any constitutional head to "raise discontent" was sedition, KY ceased to be an effective participatory structure, though several of its organizers remained active in local areas until the military confrontation of May 1966. Ethnicity remained important to the Baganda, but they have discovered no more successful vessel.

2. SEBEI

Politicization of ethnicity in Sebei may have reached the same level of intensity as KY for a short period but was less involved with protection of traditional values and authority patterns and more with elimination of Bagisu overrule and faster economic and social development.[14] The movement was based on a single

12. Hancock, "Patriotism and Neo-Traditionalism," p. 431 *et passim.*
13. Ian R. Hancock, "The Buganda Crisis of 1964," *African Affairs* 69, no. 275 (April 1970): 116.
14. This section is based on M. Crawford Young, "Sebei," in the Uganda District Handbook, stenciled (Kampala: Institute of Public Administration, n.d.). See also Donald Rothchild and Michael Rogin, "Uganda," in *National Unity and Regionalism in Eight African States,* ed. Gwendolen M. Carter (Ithaca, N.Y.: Cornell University Press, 1966), pp. 412-413.

ethnic unit easily distinguishable from its neighbors by language and customs.

The Sebei are few in number — 35,000 compared with the 275,000 Bagisu living in Bugisu district in 1959 — and live on Mount Elgon and the nearby plains close to Uganda's border with Kenya. Their traditional political organization was decentralized. No individual could command obedience from all Sebei. The present district was a backwater county of Bugisu during the colonial period and shared in policies producing modernization only to a small extent until a road was built across the mountain in the late 1940s. There were few missions, few schools, and few means of earning a cash income. Meanwhile their neighbors, the Bagisu, had several schools and grew high-quality arabica coffee in a scheme introduced by the colonial government. In addition, Bagisu were steadily migrating to Sebei areas to grow coffee. The majority of teachers in Sebei primary schools were Bagisu.

Sebei political consciousness began in the 1950s and quickly intensified in response to the introduction of the Bugisu district council in 1956. Sebei political leaders felt that the interests of their people were being neglected by Bagisu, who controlled the council, and that independence would only make matters worse. They complained that few Sebei were employed by the district administration or the cooperative union. When the central government insisted on reduction of services to Bugisu to cut down a deficit created by a district council resolution to lower tax assessments but not social services, Sebei county lost an expected ambulance and a new road. The Sebei felt they were being "punished" for the Bagisu councillors' mistakes.

A branch of the UNC was formed in 1956, but the ethnic movement did not take root until 1960, when Y. K. Chemonges became its leader. He had served for fifteen years with the Kenya police and was well known in the district. Through his flamboyant behavior and his ability to articulate Sebei grievances, Chemonges became a charismatic leader unifying the Sebei for the first time.

Toward the end of 1960 Chemonges set up a roadblock and stopped the car of an assistant district commissioner. Standing on top of the car with a spear and shield, he demanded a separate district for his people. His subsequent arrest and fine aroused the Sebei. The Sebei leaders then announced that no further taxes would be paid to Bugisu district but would be collected by the county council. No Bagisu officials were permitted to enter the county. Bagisu primary school teachers were driven out. The Bugisu district council responded by suspending all services to the county in April 1961.

The dispute was then transferred to the national arena. Chemonges was elected to the Legislative Council in 1961 as a UPC candidate. However, the DP government under Kiwanuka agreed to make Sebei a separate district in late 1961 and Chemonges won the 1962 election as a member of the DP. [15] Young points out that the nearly identical vote totals for Chemonges and his two Bagisu opponents in the two elections, in spite of changing party labels, indicate that politics in the district revolved around the separate district issue. When the UPC/KY coalition took power, Chemonges crossed the aisle again and campaigned for the UPC candidates in the district council elections of 1963.

Sebei's ethnic demands were officially consolidated when its district council created the position of constitutional head, called "Kingoo." Chemonges was the unanimous choice to fill this position and received three votes in the election for the presidency of Uganda. The fruits of district status came to Sebei in the form of a new hospital and a senior secondary school. Chemonges had sufficient influence to gain government approval for the creation of the Sebei Elgon Cooperative union, which was carved out of the Bugisu union. Not surprisingly, there was intimidation of Bagisu farmers living in the district who refused to join the new union. Many took refuge in Bugisu. In 1967 the cooperative officer reported to the Sebei district team that because of heavy transportation expenses, the Sebei alone could not produce sufficient coffee to permit the union

15. Before independence a district could be formed by administrative fiat (as has again become the case since the Amin coup). Partly as a result of Sebei's having succeeded with little justification on the grounds of size, population, or wealth (it is the smallest and least populous of Uganda's districts, and among the poorest), the 1962 constitution made it virtually impossible to alter district boundaries. However, exceptions for Mbale and the "Lost Counties" were made.

to break even. Nevertheless, members of the union were not prepared to accept the larger Bugisu cooperative union's offer to amalgamate and give ten administrative posts to Sebei union members.[16] In addition to increased ethnic prestige, these new projects and the staffing of the new district administration meant many jobs for the men of Sebei.

Achievement of a separate district meant satisfaction of the major goal of Sebei subnationalism. Though there were continuing ethnic troubles with the large (25 percent) minority of Bagisu living in the district, the movement lost much of its raison d'être a few years after it was founded.

The creation of Madi district on the Sudanese border in northwestern Uganda provides a useful comparison with the establishment of Sebei, because it is an example of a different pattern which hardly qualifies as ethnic political participation of any sort.[17] For many years the colonial government attached Madi first to Acholi and then to West Nile district on the grounds that it was not large enough nor sufficiently well developed to justify district status. But its lines of communication with the headquarters of both districts were poor. Thus, it was convenient to make Madi a separate subdistrict. Later a district commissioner was posted there, partly because a senior administrator was needed on the border following the Equatoria Corps revolt in 1955 and full Sudanese independence in 1956. The West Nile district council obliged the Madi — after complaints had been voiced — by electing a Madi as the West Nile and Madi representative in the Legislative Council. Moreover, West Nile did not oppose the desire of the Madi for a separate administrative identity, as Bugisu had resisted the demands of Sebei. However, even during the last years of colonial rule, no political movement formed to fight for Madi's autonomy and to demonstrate its cultural integrity. On 9 October 1962 Madi officially became a separate district and showed few further traces of ethnic organization in its political activities.

16. "Minutes of the District Team, Sebei, 10 May 1967." p. 2.
17. See Emory Bundy, "Madi," in the Uganda District Handbook, stenciled (Kampala: Institute of Public Administration, n.d.); and personal communication from Michael Davies, formerly assistant district commissioner in West Nile and later in Acholi.

3. RWENZURURU

The Rwenzururu movement is in many ways the most spectacular example of Ugandan ethnic political participation.[18] Mobilizing people almost exclusively on the basis of ethnic identity, it involved the entire range of types of participation, from discussion to pitched battles and secession. Although it began shortly after the Sebei movement and for largely the same reasons, it did not result in a separate district. Frustration of its demands created splits within the movement. One faction rebelled and declared Rwenzururu an independent state. For over a decade, this faction has collected taxes, run schools, organized an army, trained government officials, and met a government payroll, though the area it controls has steadily diminished since 1966.

Rwenzururu is the vernacular equivalent of *Ruwenzori* and refers to the mountains in which the Bakonzo live and the surrounding plains inhabited by both Bakonzo and Baamba. Through the mountains runs the boundary between Uganda and Zaire, which divides families and clans of both ethnic units. The Batoro, a breakaway Banyoro ethnic unit, exercised control over the area as part of Toro district, formerly Toro kingdom. However, the mountains have never been brought under effective administrative control, and Bwamba county (home of the Baamba) was not opened up until a road was completed through the foothills in 1938.

Both groups have a vivid sense of a traditional period free from Batoro overrule, though the Baamba were in closer contact with the Batoro because they paid tribute and later worked as laborers on farms run by Batoro. Many Bakonzo living in the mountains have never experienced the sovereignty of any outsiders, not even colonial authorities. Both Bakonzo and Baamba traditional political systems are decentralized, in contrast with that of the Batoro, which resembles in general outline the

18. This account is based on my field research and on Martin Doornbos, "Kumanyana and Rwenzururu: Two Responses to Ethnic Inequality," in *Protest and Power in Black Africa*, ed. Robert I. Rotberg and Ali A. Mazrui (New York: Oxford University Press, 1970). See also Kirsten Alnaes, "Songs of the Rwenzururu Rebellion: The Konzo Revolt against the Toro in Western Uganda," in *Tradition and Transition in East Africa: Studies of the Tribal Element in the Modern Era*, ed. P. H. Gulliver (London: Routledge & Kegan Paul, 1969); and Nelson Kasfir, "Toro Society and Politics," *Mawazo* (Kampala) 2 no. 3 (June 1970).

traditional kingdom of Buganda. The 1959 census reported 104,000 Bakonzo, 33,000 Baamba, and 183,000 Batoro living in Toro kingdom.[19] The Baamba and Bakonzo amount to about 40 percent of the population of the district. However, the two ethnic units have traditionally regarded each other as inferior. There is virtually no intermarriage between them. The Baamba rarely venture into the mountains and the Bakonzo have only come down to the plains during the past two generations.

Like the Sebei, the Baamba and Bakonzo have suffered discrimination in the provision of education. However, figures collected by a commission of inquiry indicate that the Toro government had made an effort to develop schools in areas in which Baamba and Bakonzo predominate. At the same time the commission felt there had been discrimination favoring Batoro in the award of bursaries and scholarships.[20]

Few Baamba and Bakonzo had been appointed chiefs at the subcounty level (six of thirty-eight in 1963) and none at the county level, even though they amounted to a sizable proportion of the population. They felt that they were given inferior medical treatment and often forced to wait until Batoro were examined by the Batoro medical staff in rural dispensaries. They were aggrieved by the requirement that they use Lutoro, the language of the Batoro, rather than their own. However, the most serious complaint underlying all others concerned the contemptuous attitude with which Batoro regarded the other two groups. The Batoro considered them primitive and found it inconceivable that they should share political power with them. This attitude was reinforced by their struggle for full federal status. To make their point convincingly to the central government, the Batoro had to insist on the preeminence of their Omukama (king) and the unity, under a single (pseudo-) ethnic mantle, of all inhabitants of the district.

Unlike the Sebei, the Baamba and Bakonzo were both a populous minority and the chief source of wealth and taxes in the district. The mountain areas are suitable for coffee; the

19. *1968 Statistical Abstract* (Entebbe: Government Printer, 1969), p. 11.
20. *Report of the Commission of Inquiry into the Recent Disturbances Amongst the Baamba and Bakonjo People of Toro* (Entebbe: Government Printer, 1962), pp. 6-11.

plains on the southeast side of the mountain for cotton; and the rich volcanic soil of Bwamba for coffee, rice, sugarcane, and cocoa. There is a salt industry and a copper mine in this part of the district. The rest of Toro is not so blessed. As a result, the potential for conflict between growing Baamba and Bakonzo wealth and Batoro political control rapidly increased. Batoro resistance to separatist demands could be expected to be more severe than that of the Bagisu and certainly more than that of West Nile inhabitants.

Baamba political and cultural societies were started in the 1940s by members of the tiny educated elite. Their discussions centered primarily on how to get better jobs within the Toro district administration. Later, more progressive groups began covertly to attack Batoro domination. The Bakonzo participated in an abortive rebellion against the Omukama in 1919, for which three men were publicly hanged. The memory of this event suddenly came to the fore in the 1960s and is now cited with pride by Rwenzururu leaders. Bakonzo associational activity began in the 1950s with attempts to record the history and customs of the Bakonzo people. After the visit of a British journalist, these inquiries were formalized in an organization called the Bakonjo Life History Research Society. Its president was Isaya Mukirane, a primary school teacher, who organized branches of the society to investigate customs and later instill political consciousness by inveighing against the wrongs committed by the Batoro.

The grant of separate district status to Sebei, as well as agitation by Banyoro for the return of the "Lost Counties," had its effect on Baamba and Bakonzo leaders. In February 1962, after getting two places on the Toro constitutional committee (originally denied them), they demanded that the constitution for the kingdom officially recognize that all three ethnic units were "tribes" in Toro. When the Batoro refused, they walked out. The following month most Baamba and Bakonzo representatives walked out of the Rukurato (the district parliament) after a disagreement about the same point, and the leaders escalated their demands by announcing that they would accept nothing less than a separate district. The Toro government struck back by arresting Mukirane and two Baamba leaders (Yeremiya Kawamara and Petero Mupalya) on charges of violating customary law by insulting the Omukama.

Baamba and Bakonzo refused en masse to pay taxes and license fees to the Toro government and threatened Batoro living near the mountains. In August 1962 spontaneous incidents broke out when Batoro chiefs attempted to collect taxes. Meanwhile the three leaders were in Kampala waiting for their appeal to be heard and petitioning the Uganda government to create a separate district. Following arguments over tactics and leadership, Mukirane broke with the other two and headed for the mountains. From this time there was only the loosest connection between Baamba and Bakonzo in the movement, though in their documents they invariably purported to represent all members of both ethnic units, and both claimed the name Rwenzururu.

While this meant separate and largely uncoordinated activity, it did not spell the end of the movement for either Baamba or Bakonzo. Many Baamba continued to recognize Kawamara and Mupalya as their leaders and paid taxes directly to the Ugandan government. However, some Baamba also organized a guerrilla movement, operating at night, that attacked Batoro who refused to leave Bwamba county and Baamba who collaborated with the Toro government and its chiefs.

Under Mukirane's leadership an independent Rwenzururu government claiming full sovereignty was set up by Bakonzo in the mountains. It was based on the branches of the Bakonjo Life History Research Society. To support itself, it collected "contributions," which later became taxes. Mukirane soon had himself appointed king of Rwenzururu. During the early period Bakonzo support for the movement was virtually unanimous. However, the people living on the plains found themselves in a difficult and insecure situation when the Ugandan government announced that it would not grant a separate district. They were expected by both Uganda and Rwenzururu to pay taxes and give undivided loyalty. Some of the more highly educated community leaders in lowland areas, most of whom had been members or chairmen of Bakonjo Life History Research Society branches, began to lose enthusiasm for a movement that intended to secede from Uganda and set up an independent nation with little trained manpower. They remained adamantly opposed to the Toro government but were ready to accept either a separate district or direct rule by the Ugandan central government.

For many the declaration of an independent nation was simply a ploy to engage the attention of the Ugandan government. Mukirane, however, may have been ready to go it alone on the theory that the rewards flowing from separate district status were apt to be multiplied by United Nations membership and the possibilities of foreign aid that might follow (several applications for membership were sent to the UN). An attempt was made to enlist the Banande (Zairean Bakonzo) and to include a large portion of Kivu Province, Zaire, in the Rwenzururu kingdom. This met with virtually no response, since the Banande were represented in the Zairean parliament and had never experienced discrimination at the hands of the Batoro, who live only in Uganda.

In early 1963 the central government introduced another possibility by taking over the administration of services in the Toro counties in which the disturbance was then active. They also appointed agents, many of whom had been involved in Rwenzururu activities, to carry out the functions of the chiefs. At first this policy had little effect, and the agents had their homes burned and lives threatened. After a while, however, larger numbers of people tiring of the constant dangers rallied to the agents. The promise of a 100-bed hospital in Bwamba and the grant of an amnesty by President Obote in late 1965 weakened the secessionist movement. Passage of the 1967 constitution, which abolished the Toro Omukama along with all other kings in Uganda, also advanced reconciliation.

The Baamba appear to have had less heart for rebellion, less encouragement for secession from their leaders, and a far more exposed position, since they live entirely on the plains. Their resistance became increasingly disorganized and ineffectual. Some Bakonzo, on the other hand, with intimate knowledge of the mountain paths — no roads exist in the mountains, with the exception of one security track built after the troubles began — and the sanctuary afforded by the Zairean border, were still holding out in 1974.

Once the Batoro had been removed from Bakonzo areas,

though, the fury of the movement turned on Bakonzo who, because of their exposed position on the plains, had refused to cooperate with the mountain government. Lowlanders, often with the help of Ugandan security forces, responded by organizing forays into the mountains to burn and loot. The Rwenzururu government retaliated in kind. By 1969 Uganda had achieved peace and order in the lowlands and lower mountain spurs by stationing security forces throughout villages in the southernmost mountains.

Of all the organizations claiming the name Rwenzururu, the kingdom government has been the best organized and has demonstrated the greatest concern with developing the national consciousness and culture of the people (conveniently limited to members of one ethnic unit, the Bakonzo)[21] by removing all contaminating Batoro influences. Much effort has been expended in returning Lunyarwenzururu (Lukonzo, language of the Bakonzo) to its pristine state. The language is the required medium for teaching purposes in lower primary grades in Rwenzururu schools, churches, and official government communications. The history of the Bakonzo people is taught as a required subject in the schools. Aside from the change in language of instruction and the addition of a local (Rwenzururu) history subject, the Ugandan curriculum is followed. To celebrate independence day each year, a program of traditional songs and dances is performed. The kingdom government sees itself as fulfilling the historical mission of the Bakonzo.

The kingdom government illustrates the ambivalence between traditional rationale and new political goals and techniques that must be resolved, or at least coped with, by all ethnic movements (see the discussion in chapter three). The justification for the movement is cast in traditional terms and based on rights presumed once to have been possessed by the "tribe." However, the methods used to dramatize the movement's demands and to organize the members of the movement would be familiar tactics in Western countries today. For example, there has been no effort to set up the Rwenzururu kingdom government on the

21. After the official stamp was changed from "Rwenzururu – Bakonjo Bamba" to "Rwenzururu Kingdom Government" in September 1967, the awkward absence of participation by Baamba in the government of the kingdom could conveniently be ignored.

basis of traditional Bakonzo political organization. Nor has there been any return to ascriptive standards of recruitment.

The government is consciously modeled on the most up-to-date political organizations available for imitation – those of Toro and Uganda. Few older men have served in the government. Almost all of the officeholders have been educated young men in their twenties. The major exceptions were Mukirane, who died in 1966, and his prime minister. Traditional positions of authority or prestige count for little, though the leading clans contribute most of the officeholders. Also, the charismatic appeal with which Mukirane held the government together seems to have been based mainly on the fact that he had more Western education and had previously held a more highly skilled position (headmaster of a primary school) than any other member of his government. Even Mukirane's creation of the position of king to head the government was intended more for tactical and ego-gratifying reasons than as a response to tradition. The Bakonzo are accustomed to local hereditary chiefs who regard themselves as kings, but these are mainly ceremonial figures who have little power to command anyone. Mukirane argued that the Rwenzururu government "needed an Omukama to fight an Omukama" and thus that the existence of a king would give the government greater legitimacy in the eyes of the people in its struggle against the Batoro.[22] As king, however, Mukirane behaved as much as possible as if he were an executive president in a present-day Western government.

4. "LOST COUNTIES" CONTROVERSY

In December 1893 British and Baganda forces entered and soon overran Bunyoro and drove out the Omukama, Kabarega.[23]

22. Many of the officeholders in Mukirane's government were distinctly unhappy about being led by a king but felt they could do nothing about it without seriously weakening the movement.

23. This account is taken primarily from John Beattie, *The Nyoro State* (London: Oxford University Press, 1971), pp. 74-94; and Fred Burke, *Local Government and Politics in Uganda* (Syracuse: Syracuse University Press, 1964), pp. 77-85. For the response of the Baganda, particularly in the Lukiiko, see Hancock, "The Buganda Crisis of 1964," pp. 113-114 and 118-120. See also Rothchild and Rogin, "Uganda," pp. 415-418; and G. F. Engholm and Ali A. Mazrui, "Violent Constitutionalism in Uganda," *Government and Opposition* 2, no. 4 (July-October 1967): 587-589.

Bunyoro had been the ancient enemy of Buganda, and during the latter's religious struggles a few years earlier had given shelter to many dissident Baganda preparing for another attack on the ruling faction. But the alliance between the British and this faction proved overwhelming. As a reward to their Baganda partners, the British agreed that Buganda should receive all Bunyoro land south of the Kafu River. A provision to this effect was included in the 1900 Agreement. A considerable amount of territory was involved, amounting to all counties in Mubende district and parts of Singo, Bulemezi, and Bugerere counties. About 40 percent of the Banyoro live in this area. The graves of the Banyoro Omukamas and important shrines are located here. In two of these counties the Banyoro form an overwhelming majority of the population, while in the remainder they are a small minority.

The question of the return of this land has dominated politics for the Banyoro ever since. In 1901 the successor to Kabarega resigned as Omukama over the "persecution" of Banyoro in the "lost" counties.[24] In 1921 a political organization, the Mubende-Banyoro Committee, was formed to agitate for return of the land. Its campaign was carried out primarily through formal appeals and petitions to various British authorities during the colonial period.

As independence approached, the Banyoro became fearful that an independent African government would be heavily dependent upon Baganda support and would refuse to entertain any notions of changing the boundaries. A commission appointed to consider issues that had to be resolved in Uganda's independence constitution proposed that a referendum be held to determine the wishes of the residents, at least in those counties populated primarily by Banyoro. Another commission recommended that these two counties be transferred to Bunyoro before independence and that Mubende town, which contained certain shrines, be declared a municipality and thus be placed under the central government's, rather than Buganda's, jurisdiction. Both Banyoro and Baganda were intransigent in their rejection of any compromise.

24. This, at least, has been the Banyoro belief. The British view is that the youth showed little promise as a potential ruler. Beattie, *The Nyoro State*, p. 79.

During the early 1960s, violence supplanted petitions, perhaps partly as a way for both sides to demonstrate the depth of their feelings to the various commissions of inquiry. Over two hundred incidents involving crop slashing, arson, and threats of assault against Baganda occurred in the two counties in which Banyoro formed a majority. When neither side would agree to any solution before independence, the secretary of state for the colonies decided to put the matter into the hands of an independent Ugandan government by leaving the decision on a referendum to the National Assembly but delaying the possibility of holding it until two years had passed. During that period Buganda was to share administration with the central government.

Rioting and disorder continued through 1962 but gave way to more ominous developments in 1963. The Kabaka established a new lodge at Ndaiga on Lake Albert in one of the counties in which the referendum was to be held and invited Baganda ex-servicemen to take up residence there to increase the pro-Buganda vote.[25] Bunyoro reacted by gathering and arming its ex-servicemen in Hoima, its capital. Fortunately conflict was avoided.

The national situation was sufficiently fluid to encourage desperate tactics, because the UPC had been able to form a government after the 1962 elections only through alliance with KY. This meant that the prime minister had to take a cautious position on the referendum. At the same time, however, several MPs were leaving their parties to join the UPC. When the UPC achieved an absolute majority of MPs, it decided to press ahead with the referendum. This decision caused KY to withdraw from the governing coalition in August 1964 and set the stage for the 1966 confrontation.

In the referendum the government decided to deny the vote to the Baganda ex-servicemen who had recently moved into the area on the grounds that they were not on the 1962 voting registers in the "Lost Counties." The vote in both counties was strongly in favor of rejoining Bunyoro. The Buganda govern-

25. The "Ndaiga scheme," on which the Kabaka's government spent an extremely large amount of money, was also intended to develop the two "Lost Counties" subject to the referendum. Hancock, "The Buganda Crisis of 1964," p. 113.

ment promptly attacked the results of the referendum in court, claiming that the exclusion of its ex-servicemen from voting was invalid. Its case was dismissed on appeal and Buganda's battle with the central government moved on to other fronts.

What is striking about ethnic political participation in Buganda and Bunyoro in this dispute is the intransigence of both sides. The issue was defined in ethnic terms and reached a high level of intensity because it was successful in evoking traditional affiliation as a moral obligation. Richards reports that she "met no Muganda, educated or uneducated, who was willing even to consider Bunyoro's case.... It is a matter of prestige." [26] Indeed, Michael Kintu, the Kabaka's own choice for Katikiro, was mobbed by Baganda and forced to resign when the results were reported. On the other side, Beattie notes that "I discussed the 'Lost Counties' with very many Banyoro, and I was left in no doubt of the strength of Nyoro feelings on the issue." [27]

Given too free a rein, the dispute over the "Lost Counties" could have resulted in serious internal warfare, which in turn might have stimulated other ethnic units to adopt similar methods in equally intensely felt disputes. It is also significant that an issue creating such concern could disappear so rapidly without raising an outcry in Buganda for the recovery of territory it has now "lost." However, the resolution of the controversy undoubtedly contributed to the anxiety of Baganda, who saw their worst fears being realized. They were demonstrating their inability to control their own destiny in an independent Uganda.

5. MBALE CONTROVERSY

The bitter controversy over the "ownership" of Mbale illustrates the different varieties of ethnicity that can become intertwined in a single dispute. [28] Though the area around the present town of Mbale at the foot of Mount Elgon in eastern Uganda was once the scene of traditional rivalry between Bagisu

---

26. "Epilogue," p. 387.
27. *The Nyoro State*, p. 84.
28. This section is based on Michael Twaddle, " 'Tribalism' in Eastern Uganda," in *Tradition and Transition in East Africa*, ed. Gulliver, pp. 341-342; and Burke, *Local Government and Politics*, pp. 204-208.

and Bagwere, the later controversy also pitted — in ethnic guise — the districts of Bugisu and Bukedi against each other.

The district boundaries of Bugisu and Bukedi have been altered several times. At one point there were three districts called Bugwere, Bugisu, and Budama. In 1937 Bugwere and Bugisu were amalgamated, only to be split apart in 1954, when Bugisu was made a separate district in recognition of its greater ethnic homogeneity (only two ethnic units, including the Sebei) and its political and economic progress. Bugwere was then rejoined to Budama to form Bukedi district. During these changes Mbale town remained the common administrative capital, though in 1954 it became a separate "Territory" belonging to neither district.

The Bagwere resented the intrusion of Bagisu into Mbale and felt humiliated by the necessity to cross a thin strip of land belonging to Bugisu district in order to enter the town. The crusade for the "return of Mbale," however, became one of the few instances in which the Bagwere were supported by the other six ethnic units in Bukedi. The Bagisu, on the other hand, "wished to make Mbale their town much as independent African states wish to establish their own university, as a symbol, as much as for its own sake."[29]

The demands of each faction that Mbale be amalgamated with its district became the focus for intense emotions exacerbated by the fact that the two district administrations were housed in different wings of the same building. Tempers flared in September 1962, when the car of the Bukedi secretary-general was stopped by Bagisu adherents and he was forced to flee for his life. As in the other cases examined above, an urgent fear of all participants that they might fare less favorably at the hands of an independent government caused the issue to take on greater political significance. The controversy has also deepened interest in ethnic history and culture, at least among the Bagisu. A research society was formed in the 1950s to collect traditions and to oversee efforts to standardize the language. Bagisu students at Makerere published a magazine concentrating on ethnic matters.

29. J. S. La Fontaine, "Tribalism among the Gisu: An Anthropological Approach," in *Tradition and Transition in East Africa,* ed. Gulliver, p. 185.

A commission of inquiry suggested a compromise altering the boundaries to give the inhabitants of Bukedi direct access to Mbale while giving nominal title to the town to Bugisu. Under this scheme Bukedi's district administration would be moved to Tororo, which is within the district. A solution was explicitly postponed by the authors of the 1962 constitution, which established for Mbale an exception to the rigid provisions preventing most boundary changes. The exception was limited to the first two years following independence. However, no decision was made. The Ugandan government finally took action in 1967, when the new constitution left Mbale and the strip of land surrounding it in Bugisu. The Bukedi district administration was then transferred to Tororo. Characteristic of the new political situation in Uganda after the 1966 changes (discussed in chapter eight), the decision did not spark off a resurgence of ethnic political participation.

6. ANTI-BAGANDA COALITIONS AND BANTU AND NILOTIC "BLOCS"

In addition, there are the various coalitions of political forces in Uganda which have been interpreted as ethnic groupings. At first these were presumed to have formed as a negative reaction to Buganda's efforts to gain greater privileges and autonomy. Later they were seen as groupings formed on linguistic lines which appeared to parallel economic position (the richer south versus the disadvantaged north). For the most part these groupings have consisted of little more than a few politicians seeking tactical advantage in a fluid situation. Few, if any, cultural ties exist that would permit publicists to create for these aggregates more than a fleeting semblance of coherence.

For the variety of reasons discussed earlier, members of other ethnic units have tended to resent Buganda's special position and have feared its dominance. Although this resentment was felt generally, it did not achieve political form until 1958. Before that year Baganda had been influential in the organization of all political parties. Following the 1958 elections to the Legislative Council, seven members, representing seven districts, formed the Uganda People's Union (UPU). The UPU attempted to channel dislike of Baganda into a political party. One specific event that gave impetus to the formation of this party was hostility outside Buganda over statements in the Buganda Lukiiko that the Kabaka should be made king of a self-governing Uganda.[30] Another was the resistance of non-Baganda areas to Buganda's campaign against a strong unitary central government. However, the party never achieved an organization outside of the Legislative Council. It remained a collection of the personal followings in each district of the politicians who formed it.[31] In March 1960 it merged with the Obote faction of the Uganda National Congress to become the UPC.

Two years after independence factional struggle in the cabinet gave rise to rumors that developing Bantu and Nilotic blocs within the UPC were each seeking to control the state. The ideological positions of leaders in each bloc seemed to be opposed. The Nilotic group was presumed to be "pro-East" in international affairs and in favor of more radical social policies, while the Bantu politicians seemed to favor more conservative social policies, particularly with regard to kingship, and a "pro-West" international stance. Obote's arrest and detention in February 1966 of five ministers who came from areas in which Bantu languages predominate appeared to indicate the formation of two broad ethnic blocs.

If the confrontation of 1966 had not occurred, such blocs might possibly have solidified into serious ethnic movements. Clifford Geertz has pointed out that postindependence struggles can result in a transfer of loyalties to larger groups as local issues are resolved in a national arena and groups seek allies to secure their positions.[32] In Uganda, however, this has not happened. Both Bantu and Nilotic areas have been marked more by conflict than by political, let alone social, solidarity. [33] Other Bantu areas, especially Bunyoro, did not overcome their suspicion of Buganda, and many were badly divided internally, particularly Kigezi, Ankole, and Toro. The Nilotic-speaking ethnic units were also suspicious of one another. The Alur were

30. D. A. Low, *Political Parties in Uganda: 1949-62* (London: Athlone Press, 1962), pp. 29-30 and 43.
31. Rothchild and Rogin, "Uganda," p. 395; and Apter, *The Political Kingdom,* pp. 346-347.
32. "The Integrative Revolution: Primordial Sentiments and Civil Politics in the New States," in *Old Societies and New States,* ed. Geertz (New York: Free Press, 1963), pp. 153-154.
33. M. Crawford Young, "The Obote Revolution," *Africa Report* 11, no. 6 (June 1966): 11-12.

not on good terms with the Lugbara (Sudanic-speaking), nor were the Acholi and Langi. Neither bloc was sufficiently coherent to overcome the pervasive factionalism that marked the politics of Uganda before 1966.

7. COMPONENTS OF ETHNIC POLITICAL PARTICIPATION

The accounts on which these case studies are based do not provide sufficient evidence to permit precise analysis using the different components of participation discussed in chapter one. A brief discussion of participation, however, can bring out some of their similarities and differences.

Five of the six cases discussed, leaving aside the largely fictitious Nilotic and Bantu "blocs," illustrate the extraordinary importance placed on ethnic concerns by both leaders and followers. In each case a territory presumed to belong to particular people by virtue of their objective ethnic characteristics galvanized subjective perception of membership in an ethnic group. A cultural rationale was simultaneously developed. The Baganda and, to a lesser extent, the Banyoro shaped theirs over years of battle with Protectorate officials, while most of the others discovered a new rationale with new political implications as the colonial era was ending.

The Baganda focused heavily on the political symbols of ethnicity — their king and his government. The Bakonzo and Baamba, on the other hand, began with linguistic and cultural features perceived as "destroyed" by the actions of contemptuous outsiders also linked by their ethnic identity. In every one of these cases, however, the presence of additional objective characteristics was soon cited to help substantiate the group's political brief and to persuade other potential members to enter the fray.

Ethnic identification, however, does not necessarily result in political participation. For example, among the Karamojong, Jie, Dodoth, and Suk in northeastern Uganda, tradition and ethnicity still coincide to a great degree. Their members seem to prefer passivity to political struggle in the national arena.

Since ethnic identity was put forward as the justification for political action, the personae in each of the five cases were limited to those who could objectively claim membership, with the exception of a few mavericks. These numbers varied greatly

— from one million Baganda to thirty-five thousand Sebei. [34] The Banyoro, amounting to perhaps a fifth of the number of the Baganda and possessing far fewer economic resources, had to involve the central government in order to make their participation in the "Lost Counties" dispute effective. But when this issue was restructured in a constitutional conference as a plebescite in two of the counties, the Banyoro suddenly gained the upper hand in terms of the personae defined as relevant to the dispute. The Buganda government responded unsuccessfully by attempting to import Baganda ex-servicemen whose ethnic loyalty was overt and thus to increase its own electoral support. Similarly, in the Mbale dispute the Bagwere, who are far fewer than the Bagisu, sought additional allies by promoting a spurious ethnic identity that was districtwide.

Census figures at best can only tell us what are the potential limits of support for an ethnic group. Not everyone who possesses the appropriate characteristics will choose to participate on a given issue or to lend more than symbolic support. However, aside from the Mbale dispute, each of these movements seems to have resulted in virtually universal and highly intense participation, though for short periods of time only.

An interesting question, then, is to try to follow the changes in personae over time. Those who founded KY were members of the Protestant elite — unlike the small traders (loosely organized by Augustine Kamya, a Catholic) who founded the UNM two years earlier. After achieving its widest number of adherents the following year, KY declined in numbers of active supporters. Those who became disenchanted with KY appear to have been its more progressive members. Similarly, educated Bakonzo and Baamba began the Rwenzururu movement. It suddenly expanded as its leaders campaigned for seats in the Rukurato and grew even further as the pressures to oust Batoro living near the mountains increased. By the end of 1962 it would have been hard to find anyone objectively identified as a Mukonzo or a Mwamba who was not at least a sympathizer. But

---

34. Use of census categories introduces additional difficulties into the determination of members of ethnic units. However, the categories are generally accepted in Uganda as reasonable approximations. The difficulties are discussed in greater detail on pp. 175 and 178.

by 1967 there were many Bakonzo and Baamba who actively opposed the movement. Those who left Rwenzururu appear to have been those who lived in lowland areas and who were better educated and somewhat wealthier than those who fought on.

The original proponents of Bukedi's right to Mbale seem to have been local notables who felt that better jobs and more development projects were likely to result from raising the prestige of their district. They were able to mobilize many Bagwere by framing the issue in terms of loss of territory. But they could count on the support of a smaller proportion of the rest of the "Bakedi"[35] than the proportion that was available in the other disputes. What is clear in all these cases is that the personae participating in each ethnic movement were never constant and often fluctuated with startling rapidity.

The scope of participation in each of these cases turned on the general issue of protection or promotion of the ethnic group. But several significant differences are apparent. KY and the "Bakedi" were fighting defensive battles in their efforts to hold on to territory and privileges. The Sebei, Baamba, Bakonzo, Bagisu, and Banyoro, on the other hand, were attempting to gain new status with the coming of independence.

Scope also differed because tradition played varying roles in the claims made by these movements. The privileges the Baganda enjoyed during the colonial period helped them to maintain the illusion that their precolonial independence continued intact. Consequently, postindependence readjustments were defined as a direct attack on their core values. The revival of traditions was the original basis of the Rwenzururu movement, but its leaders quickly switched to political claims and a political organization more suitable to the battles of the day than any based on the customs of the past. Where subunits of the ethnic movement held radically different traditional values or had been rivals in the precolonial period, the problem of maintaining a solid front became difficult. The "Bakedi" were particularly

35. The "Bakedi" are residents of Bukedi district and are members of the seven ethnic units found there. They represent "district nationalism" even though they attempted to portray themselves as a single ethnic group for political purposes. In terms of the definition of politicized ethnicity in chapter two, they lack social solidarity in spite of their taking common political action to a limited extent in certain instances.

afflicted by this problem, and so were the Bakonzo and Baamba.

Whether or not a single traditional heritage was central to the
demands of these ethnic groups, the nature of their appeals
differed considerably. The solidarity that binds members of an
ethnic unit into a group may be based on a set of absolute
moral principles or on a calculation of the strategic value of an
ethnic stance in gaining greater material rewards for the group
or individuals. District "nationalism," in which different ethnic
units allied themselves in making demands on the central
government, was often a conscious strategy for material gain
before 1966. The "Bakedi" are a typical example. Demands for
constitutional heads which had no traditional justification and
demands for development projects where ethnically defined
rivals appeared to have received more benefits are examples of
the political use of ethnicity based on rational calculations of
group interests.

The power of the moral imperative of loyalty to the Kabaka,
on the other hand, was central to KY's campaign in the elections to the Lukiiko. This consequence, as Ian Hancock points
out,

> was largely . . . the effect of simplifying the issue into
> a choice between "Ben" (Benedicto Kiwanuka
> [leader of the DP]) and the Kabaka.
>
> In posing the choice in this way, Kabaka Yekka
> was presented as the defender of the faith, the party
> which was for Buganda and the throne. The Demo-
> cratic Party had no counter to this sort of propagan-
> da.[36]

The "Lost Counties" issue raised moral principles based on
ethnic prestige for both Baganda and Banyoro. Calmer spokesmen who argued that a campaign by Buganda to prevent or win
the referendum was both expensive and futile were waved
aside.[37] Both Rwenzururu and Sebei began by demanding that
group interests must be protected. The Sebei movement succeeded, and its members ceased active mass participation. The

36. "Patriotism and Neo-Traditionalism," p. 432.
37. Hancock, "The Buganda Crisis of 1964," pp. 118-120.

Rwenzururu movement failed, and its remaining leaders became advocates of absolute moral principles.[38]

Although one type of appeal was dominant in each case, both moral principles and calculations of group interests were present in all. There were, nevertheless, important differences between leaders and followers. Also, the leaders themselves were often in conflict over the nature of the appeal, as the cases of KY and Rwenzururu demonstrate. The nature of the appeal in some cases changed dramatically when new categories of people began to participate or when the government reacted in a threatening manner. The escalation to moral principles was rarely of long duration, however. People could stand the insecurity of coffee trees slashed, houses burned, and relatives killed only so long. The Rwenzururu movement outlived the others, but lost its moral salience for most of its original supporters.

The bases of participation also varied greatly. Financial resources played an important role in sustaining and increasing the volume of participation. KY had more access to financial resources than did any of the other ethnic organizations. Far more Baganda had entered occupations providing them with a cash income, partly because many of them had easy access to jobs in Kampala and partly because various colonial policies favored their economic development. In addition, Indian and Pakistani traders, who remembered the effectiveness of the 1959 boycott, were ready to contribute to KY's campaign chest.[39] Paradoxically, the fact that Rwenzururu leaders had to raise their money through many small contributions (and later taxes) because their followers had much lower cash incomes may have increased the level of sustained mass commitment beyond that received by KY.

One exceptionally important base of participation for the Baganda was their control over a local government and its chiefly hierarchy. Because the Kabaka's government was relatively independent of the central government, KY officials

38. That is, the section of the movement representing Bakonzo in the mountains, which effectively seceded from Uganda, refused to consider the issue in cost-benefit terms. Other sections of the original movement did and found a modus vivendi with the central government – though not a particularly satisfactory one from their point of view.

39. Hancock, "Patriotism and Neo-Traditionalism," p. 428.

could use its revenue (in the "Lost Counties" campaign) and its chiefs (in the Lukiiko elections) to increase the volume of participation. The Bakonzo, Baamba, and Sebei began their activities without this resource. After the Sebei acquired their own district, they reduced their participation, since this resource was also their main goal. The Rwenzururu kingdom government, on the other hand, was constructed by a segment of the Bakonzo to fill this void. The Banyoro, the Bagisu, and the "Bakedi" could turn to local governments for personnel and money for some activities, but to a more limited degree than the Baganda. And they were further hampered by the central government's control over the actions district administrators could take.

By far the most important organizational resource, however, was the degree of coherence within formal structures representing each ethnic group. Virtually every Ugandan movement had to cope with the problem of part-time leaders who refused to act together. Perhaps the most disciplined ethnic organization has been the Rwenzururu kingdom government, though one reason for its formation was the inability of Mukirane, its first leader, to cooperate with anyone else unless his primacy was accepted. However, it was relatively free from conflicts until he died and had the benefit of attention to its problems from full-time officials. As a result it has operated continuously for a longer period of time (though in a diminishing area) than any other Ugandan movement.

KY can be found at the other end of the spectrum. It lost its coherence after its original purpose, winning the Lukiiko elections, was achieved. The county chiefs and the Kabaka's intimate advisers were suspicious of any organization that might be turned into a political party and therefore maneuvered to bring KY under their control. The politicians who originally hoped to lead it included traditionalists and modernizers, progressive small traders and conservative landowners, as well as many ambitious opportunists.

Thus, ethnic movements vary in the degree to which organizational resources are monopolized by one leader or divided among many. Ethnic organizations in which resources are not centralized are generally plagued by intermittent operation and lower capacity to work effectively after the original burst of enthusiasm fades. Although the Rwenzururu kingdom government operated with fewer educated personnel and less financial assistance than KY, it possessed far more organizational coherence.

The weight of participation in these cases covered the full range of types of involvement, though in different mixes in each one. Electoral activities were important in several of the cases, particularly KY. There was violence or threat of violence in each instance. The Rwenzururu movement was the most extreme, since it engaged in armed attacks. The tendency toward violence began relatively early when those identified as Batoro were defined as enemies and driven out. The Sebei followed the same pattern in chasing out Bagisu who had settled in what was then Sebei county. Violence was, however, directed as much against those who were objectively within the same ethnic unit as it was against the "enemy." In KY and Rwenzururu in particular, the level of coerced participation was relatively high.

Just as personae change over time, so does the weight of participation. After succeding at the constitutional conferences as well as participating in the national government through a coalition, the Baganda turned unsuccessfully to the courts when the central government took steps against their interests and in 1964 made the coalition untenable. The Banyoro moved from petitions to burning the homes and destroying the crops of Baganda in the "Lost Counties." Many Bakonzo moved from requests made to government officials for changes in policy to electoral politics to violence and then to secession. The Baamba and some Bakonzo moved as far as participation through violence but then reduced the weight of their involvement by limiting their participation to village councils established by the national government.

The amount of opposition to ethnic demands was an important factor in determining the level of involvement on which they were pressed. To a large extent, opposition confirmed the fears of ethnic participants, particularly when it could be identified as coming from another mobilized ethnic group. The Madi encountered little opposition to their demands for a separate district from the people of West Nile, who come from several ethnic backgrounds. The Sebei encountered more from the Bagisu, and the Bakonzo and the Baamba were met with intense, unyielding opposition from the Batoro. Few signs of ethnic political mobilization appeared in Madi, but an organized movement arose in Sebei, only to become quiescent after the Bagisu were unable to resist the creation of a separate district by the national government. The Bakonzo in the mountains responded to the national government's constant refusals to create another district by establishing a separate state. Banyoro and Baganda fed each other's stubbornness by contemplating ever more threatening actions.

Calculations made by each participant of the likely benefits and the expected costs of involvement could have been tested through a survey if one had been attempted at the time. However, two general factors are likely to have increased the propensity to participate in all cases. First, fears that life under an independent government would be far more uncertain than under British rule grew sharply as the colonial period came to an end. Second, as it became increasingly clear that the Protectorate administration and the Colonial Office were prepared to entertain changes in existing relationships, flamboyant campaigns were mounted to gain autonomy and win privileges that might otherwise be awarded to rivals. To no one's surprise, ethnic claims of all sorts were put forward, particularly over "control" of territory (that is, the creation of new districts), since district boundaries would not be easy to change later.

In examining the impact of participation on government policy, it is clear that KY was successful at first, since it managed to control its national MPs by sweeping the elections to the Lukiiko. Its leaders found themselves in the pivotal position between the two "national" parties, the DP and the UPC, and reaped the rewards. By pressing its advantage in its early successes, however, KY did nothing to allay fears of Baganda domination, and this failure contributed to its ultimate downfall. The Sebei movement started soon enough to become a prize in the electoral competition between the DP and the UPC. It received its district as part of the DP's desperate bid to outmaneuver the UPC and KY and returned the favor by delivering the vote of its followers. The Baamba and the Bakonzo started too late to achieve the same goal before the independence constitution made the creation of districts virtually impossible. The Banyoro had been considerably worried by the coalition between KY and UPC, but their leaders could guess that it was only a matter of time before that unlikely marriage dissolved and they would be called upon to support the UPC in return for a government decision to hold a referendum in the "Lost Counties."[40] Their contribution to ensuring this result was to hold the government's attention by participating in activities that underlined the intensity of their feelings.

8. CONCLUSION

In these disputes Ugandans were mobilized for political action as Baganda, Baamba, Bakonzo, Sebei, Bagisu, Banyoro, and even, to some extent, as "Bakedi." Language, traditional customs, and territory became the most salient dimensions of identity. In the ensuing struggles ethnic *groups* emerged and played prominent political roles without, however, becoming monolithic. In terms of the three themes of ethnicity discussed in chapter three, each ethnic group − during the period in which it became a distinct political force − embodied subjective perceptions of objective ethnic characteristics (usually by both members and outsiders), a mixture of rational calculations and deep-seated fundamental values, and the interplay of mass and elite interests.

Similar in some characteristics, components of ethnic political participation vary in others, as the comparison of different Ugandan cases illustrates. The volume of participation achieved by each movement is not the end of the matter, however, since the movements must also link themselves effectively to the government in order to succeed. Several structural factors external to the ethnic unit lie behind the choice of different participatory strategies adopted by leaders and followers in these movements. The government also has a range of potential roles from which it can choose its response. These are taken up in the next chapter.

The government could also take into account another characteristic of each of these cases. Ethnicity was never a con-

40. See G. S. K. Ibingira, *The Forging of an African Nation: The Political and Constitutional Evolution of Uganda from Colonial Rule to Independence, 1894-1962* (New York: The Viking Press, 1973), p. 273.

tinuous concern. Certain situations made possible the evocation of intense ethnic response. The resolution of the situation, even if it was unfavorable, often caused the ethnic group to evaporate, at least as a political force. New situations might again call forth similar feelings and similar participation. Consequently, it is possible for national political leaders to try to manage affairs so that situations which are ethnically loaded do not arise. In part this sort of political engineering required a change in the Ugandan "environment," which – up to 1966 – had encouraged ethnic political participation. And in part it depended upon adroit political maneuvers.

A comparison of the ethnic strategies of the Obote and Amin regimes (discussed in chapter eight) is instructive in this regard. Obote attempted a strategy of ethnic departicipation, but Amin's policy has been more ambiguous, and to a great extent he has aroused the very ethnic fears that Obote tried to dampen.

VARIATIONS IN ETHNIC POLITICAL LINKAGE TO GOVERNMENT

Although political participation is not always directed toward government,[1] a very large portion is involved in competing for greater social and economic benefits, convincing national officials to give more autonomy to the activities of a group, or insisting that protection be given against oppression threatened by some other group. In each case, once the ethnic group is mobilized, someone must find some method to link it to the government at either the local or central level.

Linkages may be established through existing participatory structures or through new informal channels to top leaders. They may be continuous or intermittent. The elements of linkage include individuals or groups possessing a political prob-

1. What might be called "lateral" ethnic participation (or side-linkages) could be the basis of a most interesting study. The reasons why members of different ethnic units attempted to ally with one another (ranging from distant tactical understandings to incorporation) and the resistance these efforts sometimes engendered would illuminate important aspects of politics in Uganda. For a general discussion of incorporation in postindependence Africa, see Ronald Cohen and John Middleton, "Introduction," in *From Tribe to Nation in Africa: Studies in Incorporation Processes,* ed. Cohen and Middleton (Scranton, Pa.: Chandler, 1970), pp. 24-30. For a specific traditional case of an ethnic unit in Uganda, focusing mainly on the precolonial period, see Aidan Southall, "Ethnic Incorporation among the Alur," in ibid.

Baganda leaders attempted to form side-linkages with various notables from other kingdoms. Such contacts were probably part of the maneuvering that led to the confrontation in 1966 and were almost certainly the only solid basis for the rumors of Bantu and Nilotic "blocs." An intriguing resolution of the Toro district parliament condemned Kabaka Yekka activities in Toro for creating tension, especially in the disturbed areas, by promising Baamba and Bakonzo a separate district. "Minutes of the Toro Rukurato, 16 December 1965", Min. 23/65. Assuming there was a basis in fact for this accusation, it suggests that some sort of KY organization was being revived, possibly to fight the expected elections (which were later postponed) on a broad interdistrict front. I have also been told of KY recruitment and rallies outside Buganda in districts as far away as Kigezi and Bugisu.

lem, the government, and a middleman (either an organization or an individual) who brings them together.

Linkages are the connective tissue between government and people. For example, when the West Nile district council proposed that their district should have a cabinet representative, since that was the only way they could be assured of receiving tractors and industries,[2] they were trying to solve a linkage problem. Similarly, when the Acholi district council sent what was regarded by the central government as an "ethnic" delegation to request that a spinning mill ultimately built in Lango district be placed in their area,[3] they were following a well-worn Ugandan path linking the center to local groups.

Establishing that path had been the goal of ethnic political participation before 1966 and may have become so again in the early stages of the Amin government. Campaigning for a separate district was an important tactic. Thus, the Madi and the Sebei were able to open an official channel linking them to the center when they acquired districts and could thus ensure that ethnic leaders could represent them in day-to-day dealings with central government administrators. In 1971 the East Acholi also were granted a separate district.[4] They had campaigned unsuccessfully for one almost a decade earlier. On occasion the center resisted demands for this sort of linkage. The Baamba and many lowland Bakonzo reluctantly accepted a more restricted channel based on county councils. Bakonzo who lived in, or fled to, the mountains and were frustrated by their failure to gain a separate district repudiated the very notion of linkage when they set up an independent state.

An increase in political involvement often contributes to the formation of an ethnic group and thus to the establishment of ethnic linkage, though it is worth remembering that this sort of linkage accounts for only a fraction of the process of participation in Uganda. The pattern of ethnic linkage that is established

2. "Minutes of West Nile District Council, 28 August 1965," Min. 72/65, cited in Apolo Nsibambi, "Increased Government Control of Buganda's Financial Sinews since the Revolution of 1966," *Journal of Administration Overseas* 10, no. 2 (April 1971): 100.

3. This incident is discussed in greater detail in chapter eight below.

4. In 1974 the government began to implement a policy to reorganize local administration which involved considerable changes in district boundaries. The implications of these changes are not yet clear, but see note 65, chapter eight below.

will depend upon three factors: (1) structural variations influencing ethnic political participation, (2) variations in the response of government, and (3) differences among the middlemen who make the connections.

1. STRUCTURAL VARIATIONS INFLUENCING ETHNIC POLITICAL PARTICIPATION

Out of a multitude of possible influences, three considerations external to a particular ethnic group seem especially important. These are size (relative and absolute), arena (national or local), and degree of value congruence between members of the ethnic group and the central government. The specific combination of these variables sets parameters determining the pattern of linkage of an ethnic group with the center.

a. Size

Size is a significant consideration in determining the seriousness with which ethnic demands are treated. The larger the ethnic group, the more impact it can make. In part this is a matter of absolute size — both in making credible threats and in raising sufficient resources to force the center to negotiate. However, size relative to other potential ethnic groups may provide a more accurate assessment of the success of participation on behalf of a group. Clifford Geertz suggests a typology to compare states in terms of the relative size of their ethnic units. With some changes in the African examples, his categories are the following:

1. A majority set against a single large minority (Rwanda [with the Watutsi making up in influence for their limited numbers], Cyprus, and Ceylon)
2. One central unit opposed to several medium-sized peripheral units (Uganda and perhaps Ghana and Indonesia)
3. Two evenly balanced major units (Kenya and Lebanon)
4. A gradation of units from large ones to small ones (Zaire, India, and the Philippines)
5. Multiple small units (Tanzania)[5]

5. "The Integrative Revolution: Primordial Sentiments and Civil Politics in the New States," in *Old Societies and New States,* ed. Geertz (New York: Free Press, 1963), pp. 117-118.

Geertz ignores the fact that not all those possessing the objective characteristics of an ethnic unit will choose to participate in the activities of the mobilized ethnic group. There is no reason to assume that all leaders will rally all followers all of the time. To make use of this typology, then, we must consider whether rates of political mobilization will vary. This, as suggested in chapter one, is a question of personae. But the size of potential groups does make a difference, since it affects the estimates made by actors (both insiders and outsiders) of the probability that a particular demand will be successful.

Ethnic political participation is likely to vary in states in one category by comparison with those in another. For this reason Uganda, Kenya, and Tanzania represent three types of ethnic linkage. This typology also suggests differences *within* countries. In Uganda relative size affects the linkage opportunities of different ethnic movements. Kabaka Yekka (KY) could confront the central government in situations that were out of the question for the Sebei movement, Rwenzururu, or the Mubende-Banyoro Committee. The government could contain the threats (even of secession) of the latter, but its own survival might have been in doubt if it did not handle Baganda demands skillfully. The Baganda possessed resources of location, long-standing unification on the basis of traditional values, a history of autonomy from the central government, and comparatively developed skills in communications and publicity to augment their numbers. The others were far weaker in these respects. Although the Rwenzururu kingdom government did secede (de facto), smaller movements with fewer resources (for example, the Baamba, the Sebei, and the Banyoro) usually depended on the central government to help them win their battles against local opponents.

Exceptionally large size, based on numbers and resources, may lead to efforts by ethnic groups to capture the government — to become the center. Belief in the capture theory is widely held in Uganda.[6] Linkage suggests distance between

6. I am grateful to Frank Holmquist for suggesting some of the implications of this point. He discovered that notables in Kisii district, Kenya, could name *every* Kisii man of consequence in the central government and that they would assume that these officials would have an ethnic bias. Personal communication, October 1971. On the other hand, one of the conclusions of a 1966 survey carried out in and near Nairobi indicated that "spokesmen of tribal interests" were more aroused by this

group and center; the capture theory, however, assumes a merger, or at least a wide degree of overlap. If the latter theory is accurate, linkage becomes far less pertinent. Members of smaller ethnic units possessing fewer resources may act on this theory by promoting greater representation of fellow members in government. A basic assumption of this view is that ethnic membership will be crucial in shaping the decisions of government because it will control the administrative response of government officers.[7]

Although ethnic considerations are undoubtedly an important calculation in government decisions, the capture theory has several weaknesses. First, instead of leaving the importance of ethnicity to empirical evaluation, it presumes that it will be both a continuous influence and the central motivation of political actors. By considering participation in terms of linkage, however, it is possible to discover ethnic ties operating in certain situations and not in others. Second, in arguing that ethnic groups act to place their members in government positions, the capture theory lays too much emphasis on the continuity and organizational capacity of ethnic groups. Third, a breakdown of the Ugandan public service by ethnic unit (based on census definitions) indicates that during the 1960s the service became more representative of the general population. Figures for secondary school and university places suggest that the trend will continue if future entry into the public service is not manipulated.[8] These data suggest (though without proving) that, as a whole, the public service has been insulated from ethnic pressures. Fourth, although capture of the government or part of it may be the intention of those who assess their influence by counting their "ambassadors" in the public service,

issue than were their followers. Donald Rothchild, "Ethnic Inequalities in Kenya," *The Journal of Modern African Studies* 7 no. 4 (1969): 698-699.

A similar argument identifying ethnic units and regional governments in precoup Nigeria is often put forward. See Robert Melson and Howard Wolpe, "Modernization and the Politics of Communalism: A Theoretical Perspective," *The American Political Science Review* 64, no. 4 (December 1970): 1121.

7. A few years ago those Bété in the Ivory Coast who had school problems serious enough to bring them to Abidjan did not see the minister of education, who came from a different ethnic unit, but went to the minister of agriculture, who was also a Bété. Aristide Zolberg, "Patterns of National Integration," in *Governing in Black Africa: Perspectives on New States,* ed. Marion E. Doro and Newell M. Stultz (Englewood Cliffs, N.J.: Prentice-Hall, 1970), p. 182.

8. See table 2 in chapter four and tables 4 and 5 in chapter seven.

it does not follow that officials are either completely free to assist their "brothers" or always desire to do so. In other words, the constraints of bureaucratic rationality and the wider horizons that knowledge of government policy affords are likely to restrict the extent to which public servants can or want to act as "messengers."

b. Arena

Donald Horowitz suggests that ethnic politics (and consequently linkages between ethnic groups and the central government) will follow different patterns depending on whether the locus for political interaction falls primarily in a local or a national arena.[9] The basic difference lies in the degree to which the center is isolated from the conflict itself. If the center is directly challenged, it cannot play the role of neutral arbiter, cannot deal with each conflict at times of its own choosing, and cannot build interethnic coalitions.

The problem in applying this distinction to Uganda is that the central government was simultaneously faced with both sorts of conflicts.[10] Buganda posed a direct threat to the full exercise of sovereignty by the center, while a variety of smaller ethnic groups simultaneously put forward challenges which may have involved the center, but not its right to rule. The size of a group, the importance of its resources in comparison to those of the center, and the number of large mobilized groups in the system help to establish the arena in which the political struggle will take place, as well as to shape the pattern of linkage.

Another consideration in regard to the arena is that the center may be concerned about the "demonstration effect" of giving a reward to one ethnic group while denying it to others

9. "Three Dimensions of Ethnic Politics," *World Politics* 23, no. 2 (1971): 237-240. For a related discussion of how local integration and national integration can affect each other (with examples from Uganda), see Martin Doornbos, "Kumanyana and Rwenzururu: Two Responses to Ethnic Inequality," in *Protest and Power in Black Africa,* ed. Robert I. Rotberg and Ali A. Mazrui (New York: Oxford University Press, 1970), pp. 1130-1136.

10. Horowitz recognizes this problem, though he does not specify which pattern of ethnic politics one should expect in the intermediate case. "Three Dimensions of Ethnic Politics," p. 240.

who might then mobilize and make similar demands. This worried the Ugandan government. Giving a separate district to the Sebei and to the Madi made it that much more difficult to deny one to the Baamba and the Bakonzo.

c. Value Congruence

A third major factor differentiating ethnic political activity is the extent of value congruence between the ethnic group and the central government to which it turns for satisfaction of its demands. The *interests* of the ethnic group clearly are incongruent with those of the government, or the group would not have entered politics. However, values common to its members, or its leaders, may vary slightly or greatly from those of the government.[11] Since national leaders themselves have only recently arrived from the district, they have not yet developed an elite subculture which differentiates them from leaders of most ethnic movements.

However, some movements are far more concerned than others with the preservation of traditional values. Paradoxically, the Baganda, who have undergone the most extensive social change in Uganda, have made the greatest effort to maintain certain traditional customs, those surrounding the Kabakaship. The less authentic the customs espoused, the easier it is for the central government to deal with the leaders of the movement through bargaining. Few Ugandan political movements have made traditional values their central concern — as opposed to their grounds for justification. Most ethnic movements are more concerned with new goals — jobs, schools, and social benefits — which are seen to flow from greater political autonomy.

To make this point, though, is not to reject the possibility that traditional values may play an important role in shaping involvement in ethnic group political behavior. Responses to many new social and economic situations may be explained in

11. See F. G. Bailey's use of the notion of "encapsulation" to refer to divergences in normative orders between peasant villagers and national administrators. Where rational calculations of group interest are predominant, there is far less likelihood of a clash in *values.* See his *Stratagems and Spoils: A Social Anthropology of Politics* (Oxford: Blackwell, 1969), pp. 146-155.

part by important traditional values. It is possible that some traditional value patterns create a greater propensity to organize in these situations than do others.[12]

For example, traditional customs may determine whether strong urban ethnic associations capable of providing leadership and support for ethnic political action can be formed. In some cases traditional criteria of leadership permit a man to stay away for a number of years without losing his position in his home in the countryside. Thus, urban associations are likely to be more vigorous where rural community status is automatically determined on the basis of age, sex, or descent and weaker where rural status flows from cultivation of patron-client ties and community service. In the latter cases, urban migrants often have to return home too soon to build a successful organization in the city.[13]

2. VARIATIONS IN THE RESPONSE OF THE CENTER

The central government is not merely a dependent variable responding to the different pressures thrust upon it by ethnic demands. Within limits it can shape its response in an effort better to achieve its own goals. In addition, it can actively pursue an ethnic policy of its own, which ethnic movements will have to take into account. The basic possibilities revolve around the degree of tolerance the center intends to adopt on the whole issue of ethnic politics. Fundamentally, there are two positions it can take: (1) explicitly to open the political process to ethnic claims (among others) or (2) to close it in the hope of ultimately destroying ethnicity as a political factor.

If the latter position becomes the stance of the center, as it did in Uganda under Obote, the government will still have to

---

12. See Aidan Southall, "The Concept of Elites and Their Formation in Uganda," in *The New Elites of Tropical Africa,* ed. Peter Lloyd (London: Oxford University Press, 1966), p. 357; Lloyd A. Fallers, *Bantu Bureaucracy: A Century of Political Evolution among the Basoga of Uganda* (Chicago: University of Chicago Press, 1965), pp. 238-247; and Raymond Apthorpe, "The Introduction of Bureaucracy into African Polities," in *Readings in Comparative Public Administration,* ed. Nimrod Raphaeli, (Boston: Allyn and Bacon, 1967), pp. 277-280.

13. Peter Lloyd, "Introduction: The Study of the Elite," in *The New Elites,* ed. Lloyd, p. 32. Two other factors affecting the vigor of urban ethnic associations are the presence of such alternative sources of social security as large companies and the distance between the town and the rural home.

respond to ethnic demands, at least in the short run. Linkages already established cannot be easily dismantled, and movements based on ethnicity will not promptly disappear in response to a government pronouncement. There is the further problem of overcoming the unequal pattern of economic development that is often one of the original causes of the rise of ethnicity. For example, to deprive Buganda of new projects and to reduce its share of positions in the national bureaucracy and among university students is to accept ethnicity as a basis for achieving central government goals.[14]

The Obote government tried to meet this problem by stressing the use of equality and rationality (themselves often contradictory principles of allocation) in determining project locations and technical criteria in making civil service appointments. At the same time the distress of the government over suggestions of continuing ethnic concern (see chapter eight) indicated that constant attention had to be paid to ethnic considerations in private, while attempts to dampen them were made in public.

By comparison, Julius Nyerere, president of Tanzania, took a forthright position on this issue. Recognizing in a public speech that members of three ethnic units had gained a head start in the modernization process as a result of early missionary activity, he made it clear that the government intended to rectify this situation gradually.[15] Thus, in both countries the flexibility of the government is restricted by its long-range policy on ethnicity and the difficulties in implementing it.

Often the strategy of the Ugandan government was to involve itself in issues to *prevent* mass ethnic movements from developing. As prime minister and as president, Obote often intervened in district politics to strengthen the faction more closely allied with the UPC or more favorable to the policies of the central government. Because of such interference, ethnic unity within the district became far more difficult to achieve.[16]

14. In fact, the percentage of Baganda in the public service and in the university is lower than is popularly assumed and has fallen as opportunities widened. See tables 4 and 5, chapter seven.

15. "No Room for Racialism," *The Standard* (Tanzania), 10 December 1968, p. 2.

16. For descriptions of direct interventions in Bunyoro, Kigezi, Toro, and Ankole, see Stephen Griffith, "Local Politicians and National Policies: The Secretaries-General of Uganda" (B. Phil. diss., University of Oxford, 1969), pp. 64-73.

Within general government policy, the center can respond to ethnic demands by taking the role of arbiter, bargainer, unilateral actor, or capitulator. Each role dictates a different pattern of linkage.

a. Neutral Arbiter

This posture is almost always the center's public perception of itself, but it was rarely employed effectively in Uganda because of the instability of the center. The implications of the struggle to overcome the DP and later the Ibingira faction of the UPC made this role a difficult one to utilize. The stance was used most effectively in dealing with interethnic conflict within a single district in which the national government took the same risks in favoring either side. The conflict between the Batoro and the Bakonzo and Baamba in Toro is a typical example.

The linkage strategy that the center was likely to follow, when it depended on this approach, was to rely on the Ministry of Regional Administrations to establish links with formal and informal leaders of the various ethnic groups and factions involved. To the extent that any ethnic leaders could force the dispute out of the ministry and into the president's office, they probably transformed the center's role by making it a political participant.

b. Bargainer

The center may choose to bargain in the hopes of reaching a satisfactory compromise, in an effort to build its national coalition, or in an attempt to split the ethnic group and thus reduce its threat. Bargaining means that both parties are willing to enter into transactions to maximize their own interests. This has been characteristic of many new states and Uganda in particular.

However, "in pluralistic societies bargaining is severely restricted by the weakness of moral links tying all groups together."[17] In Uganda this framework of national identity was always fragile. Bargaining was less stable because it was seldom reinforced by acceptance of the "higher" value of national

17. Donald Rothchild, "Ethnicity and Conflict Resolution," *World Politics* 22, no. 4 (July 1970): 615-616; see also pp. 602-606.

unity or of the rules of the game. Still, where the interests of each bargainer differed, mutually beneficial arrangements were sometimes negotiated. For example, the DP promised a separate district to the Sebei in exchange for electoral support and implied much the same to the Baamba and Bakonzo. The "Lost Counties" issue, however, was beyond political bargaining because both claimants insisted on exactly the same prize — "sovereignty" over the disputed territory.

Bargaining with the leader of one faction in order to divide a mobilized ethnic group was also a prevalent strategy in Uganda. Thus, the center backed one or another UPC faction in various district councils. The Obote government appeared to have deliberately left undecided the question of whether the district commissioner or the secretary-general (the highest local political appointee) was the more important link between the center and the district. This calculated ambiguity enabled the national government to force issues up to central officials for decision.[18]

At other times the government was careful not to press its full legal advantage in order to avoid making too many enemies. For example, in 1963 the minister of regional administrations was given a say in the appointment of all top district officials because of factionalism in the local councils. However, the power was used sparingly (until 1968), and only a few changes were made.[19]

This situation should be distinguished from the one in which the center is actively looking for local leaders with whom to bargain but cannot find anyone likely to be effective because the local groups are too fragmented. The number of competing politicians within many Ugandan ethnic movements — each purporting or bidding to lead the whole unit (or prepared to dispense with their loyalty to the larger movement in return for an important position) — created both problems and opportunities for the central government. On the one hand, national officials could pick and choose those with whom they wanted to negotiate. On the other, they had no guarantee that bargains struck would not come unstuck. Thus, the problem that caused

18. The fact that legislation to solve this ambiguity was prepared but then quashed suggests that it was a conscious strategy of the center. Griffith, "Local Politicians and National Policies," pp. 105-106.

19. Ibid., pp. 47-49.

the greatest delay in settlement among the Baamba was less a matter of principled opposition than identification of leaders who could provide important links. Everyone may be interested in bargaining in this situation, but it cannot be done successfully. In the case of pseudotraditional movements organized on the basis of districts — Bukedi, West Nile, and Toro (for the Batoro) — leaders were more easily identified because they were usually the top officers in the district administration.

Those who bargained were either local middlemen or central officials acting in a political rather than an administrative capacity (that is, outside their formal responsibilities). To the degree that the center attempts to maintain its hold on the country by building a political machine, a bargaining stance toward ethnic groups is likely.[20]

c. Unilateral Actor

The center is likely to respond with the strategy of a unilateral actor either when it feels threatened, as it did in the 1966 Buganda situation, or when it cannot come into contact with a mobilized ethnic group through normal political channels. In responding to the Rwenzururu situation, the government took a number of steps on its own in an effort to alter fundamentally the situation without enraging either of the local sets of disputants. It eliminated the Toro kingship (symbol of oppression), promised (and built) a new 100-bed hospital, gave a 100 percent loan to a local cooperative to purchase a cotton ginnery, and announced an amnesty to those who deserted the movement. At the same time it mounted security operations in the mountain areas and refused to consider the possibility of a separate district.

Earlier, to the great disappointment of the Batoro, the center took over direct administration of the disturbed areas of the district. However, in 1970 it returned control to the Toro district administration. The center attempted (with as much success as could be expected) to maintain a neutral position, but through active intervention, not through mediation. To the

20. See Henry Bienen, "One-Party Systems in Africa," in *Authoritarian Politics in Modern Society,* ed. Samuel P. Huntington and Clement Moore (New York: Basic Books, 1970), pp. 113-122.

extent that the unilateral actor uses force or nonnegotiated rewards, there is, by definition, no linkage.

d. Capitulator

The center could choose to appease the ethnic group and accept all their demands. This is obviously a risky strategy in countries where the vulnerability of national political structures is becoming increasingly apparent. However, there is an interesting use of this technique in dealing with ethnic units. If demands are granted before they are intensely felt, a widespread ethnic movement may not arise at all. Linkage with the central government in this situation shifts to the local arena, as "messengers" establish bonds with the center by posing demands which are accepted without negotiation.[21]

3. POLITICAL MIDDLEMEN AND THE LINKAGE ROLE

"Interaction between those involved in different social forms [here the center and ethnic movements]," Martin Staniland remarks, "will bring into play interstitial or intercalary roles."[22] The question of what social positions will yield those who can play interstitial roles must await further research. However, the different roles that such interstitial behavior might fill can be delineated. Here, the concept of the political middleman is especially useful.

The middleman pursues a specialized political activity growing out of the divergent interests and values of center and periphery. He is "the man who interrelates and articulates the needs, aspirations, resources, and traditions of his local village or tribe to the corresponding demands, supplies, resources and jural order of the province and the nation."[23] Bailey observes that "the essence of the role is to keep a foot in both

21. "Messenger" is Bailey's word for one who cannot bargain but merely delivers the terms. *Stratagems and Spoils,* p. 170.

22. 'The Rhetoric of Centre-Periphery Relations," *The Journal of Modern African Studies* 8, no. 4 (1970): 625.

23. Marc J. Swartz, "The Middleman," in *Local-Level Politics: Social and Cultural Perspectives,* ed. Swartz (Chicago: Aldine Press, 1968), pp. 199-200. See also Joan Vincent, *African Elite: The Big Men of a Small Town* (New York: Columbia University Press, 1971), pp. 254-255 and 273-274.

camps."[24]   Where there is ethnic political participation, his task is to forge links between center and ethnic group.

Variations in the middleman role can be arranged along a continuum based on the dimension of autonomy of the individual (or organization) that links the center with the ethnic group. The types range from messenger to opportunist to broker to boss. The messenger has no freedom and is merely a delegate come to deliver the demands of his ethnic group or, alternatively, the demands of the center. The opportunist is looking for an ethnic constituency that will accept his leadership. The broker is the negotiator who may or may not be able to convince his followers to accept the agreement he makes with the center. Finally, the boss is the ethnic leader who can "deliver" his group. The personal motivations of the middleman increase in importance as the pattern of linkage shifts across this continuum.

Patron-client relations, based on reciprocity and personal contact, provide one variant of linkage based on the "boss" type.[25]   More influential patrons may have lesser patrons as their clients. This possibility suggests that the middleman role may actually be played by a number of persons who are hierarchically linked themselves. More than one type of middleman may be involved. For example, patronage based on personal contact may be more important at the village level, while brokers may aggregate patrons in mobilizing a unified group.

In Uganda, Isaya Mukirane provides an excellent example of a boss (though not of a patron). He was in a position to insist that the followers of the Rwenzururu kingdom government

24. *Stratagems and Spoils,* p. 167. Bailey focuses on communication as the essence of the middleman's role (to overcome incongruent political cultures), but this seems unnecessarily restrictive. Absence of communication is one of the reasons for the development of middlemen, but it is not the only one. Policy conflicts are likely to be more important. Indeed, Bailey himself calls attention to the use of deceit on both sides as a possible strategy of middlemen. Ibid., pp. 167-176 and n. 18, p. 184.

25. See generally Rene Lemarchand, "Political Clientelism and Ethnicity in Tropical Africa: Competing Solidarities in Nation-Building," *The American Political Science Review* 66, no. 1 (March 1972); and John Duncan Powell, "Peasant Society and Clientelist Politics," *The American Political Science Review* 64, no. 2 (June 1970), esp. pp. 413-415.

This subvariant has also been called "vertical mobilization." See Lloyd I. and Susanne Hoeber Rudolph, *The Modernity of Tradition: Political Development in India* (Chicago: University of Chicago Press, 1967), pp. 24-25.

accept his decisions. Following secession, he managed to keep control of his faction even after rejecting center proposals that many of his lieutenants regarded as reasonable bases for negotiation. At the other end of the continuum, Michael Kintu, prime minister of Buganda, was forced to take a role as messenger in the "Lost Counties" affair. Unable to suggest a realistic course of action without bringing down his government, he was finally forced to resign to save his life when Buganda lost the referendum. Almost as unhappy was the life of the KY MPs. When they agreed with the central government that Buganda could not receive a greater financial grant than the constitution specified, several of them were called on the carpet by irate members of the Lukiiko for not adequately representing Buganda. Later, however, after 1966, when there were public cries of betrayal against those who had become UPC ministers, many Baganda quietly told them not to resign, since they had become the most important links between the Baganda and the center.[26]

Creation of the coalition between the UPC and KY is an excellent example of the operation of brokers. About March 1961 Ibingira broached the idea of an alliance to Obote, whose first response was to reject the idea.[27] Ibingira had then to convince his own party officials before he could enter negotiations with leaders of the Kabaka's government. In late May the UPC Elected Members gave Obote and Ibingira a mandate to proceed. Ibingira and B. K. Kirya then persuaded the reluctant Mutesa and Kintu of the political advantages of this sort of linkage. An understanding was reached by early September 1961. At this point the linkage existed between a local government (the Kabaka's) and a party. Later it temporarily became the bridge between Baganda ethnicity and the central government.

Middlemen also vary in the mix of personal motivations that fuel their careers. Just as ethnic groups enter politics to gain

26. Personal communication from Joshua Zake, August 1973.
27. This account is a summary of G. S. K. Ibingira, *The Forging of an African Nation: The Political and Constitutional Evolution of Uganda from Colonial Rule to Independence, 1894-1962* (New York: The Viking Press, 1973), pp. 201-205. Ibingira says he was ready to organize an attempt to remove Obote from the UPC presidency (until Obote, for independent reasons, changed his mind about the coalition) and had even approached W. W. Nadiope as his successor.

either moral or material rewards, so do the middlemen who purport to represent them. When a former policeman, or coffee trader, or primary school teacher promotes ethnic demands, he may regard promotion of the fortunes of his ethnic group as inextricably bound up with his own success in breaking out of the local arena, with its limited influence and limited rewards. In addition, to gain influence at the center, a middleman must demonstrate his rural support. [28] Indeed, to view middlemen as always performing a linkage function would be misleading, since they may also exacerbate relations between center and periphery.

To take one example, Y. K. Chemonges, in spite of serving for fifteen years in the Kenya police, was able to monopolize leadership of the Sebei movement in Uganda. He dramatized Sebei grievances with Bagisu, partly through flamboyant personal behavior, and convinced the center to create a separate district in which he was the unchallenged leader. Though he switched from the UPC to the DP and back to the UPC, he was able to maintain his good standing with the center. His ability to carry his voters with him from one party to the other gave him added negotiating strength. He was a boss who could deliver.

Determination of Chemonges's motivation would require more information, but it seems unlikely that he was opposed to the salary and prestige that came with being both MP and "Kingoo." Some middlemen are attracted to the role because of the profit to be acquired, and some because of the chance to serve. For example, some educated Bakonzo sided with the center against the Rwenzururu kingdom government with no hope of personal reward and great personal insecurity. The calculation of the rewards that tempt individuals to become middlemen may permit some assessment of the likelihood that they will either exploit the differences between their ethnic group and the center or assist in resolving them.

The resources a middleman brings to his position may determine his effectiveness. In a country as poor as Uganda, mundane advantages may dictate which individuals will play the

28. Ernest Gellner illustrates this point in discussing linkage in Morocco. "Patterns of Rural Rebellion in Morocco: Tribes as Minorities," *Archives Européenes de Sociologie* 3, no. 2 (1962): 309.

critical role linking center and ethnic group. In identifying Eric Lakidi as the "active and effective intermediary" between Kampala and Gulu (the capital of what was then Acholi district), Colin Leys notes that he had "ready access to ministers in Kampala and Entebbe, a voice in parliament, a car and adequate travelling allowances . . . [as well as] some independent income." [29]

Holding a government position may be an ambiguous resource. Although the colonial district commissioner has generally been viewed as an agent of the center, it has sometimes been more realistic to see him as acting on behalf of an ethnic group. In Tanzania area and regional commissioners occasionally became agents for local interests and ceased to function "as an arm of the center." [30] The outbreak of hostilities in the Rwenzururu crisis was marked by moderately successful efforts by the Bakonzo and Baamba to convert the district commissioner into a sympathetic broker with special links to the center. [31] For this reason it is not easy to predict whether the appointment of a local leader of an ethnic movement to a national position will "buy him off" or give him access to added resources to promote his cause and secure his position as head of it.

Officials who try to perform linkage roles can be cast into a dilemma by the conflicting demands of the center. One of the minor dramas of the last few years of UPC government was the unsuccessful struggle of the secretaries-general (politicians appointed by the Ministry of Regional Administrations) to remain somewhat free from central control. They hoped to become brokers, or even bosses, while the center conceived of them predominantly as messengers. The center's response to the

29. *Politicians and Policies: An Essay on Politics in Acholi, Uganda, 1962-65* (Nairobi: East African Publishing House, 1967), p. 94.

30. Henry Bienen, *Tanzania: Party Transformation and Economic Development* (Princeton: Princeton University Press, 1967), p. 146.

Max Gluckman argues that this reversal of loyalty sometimes occurred even in the unlikely cases of Northern Rhodesia and Zululand in South Africa. "Inter-hierarchical Roles: Professional and Party Ethics in the Tribal Areas of South and Central Africa," in *Local-Level Politics,* ed. Swartz, pp. 69-93.

31. Shortly thereafter the central government declared the counties in which the Bakonzo and Baamba lived "disturbed areas" and appointed the district commissioner to administer them directly and separately from the rest of Toro.

Acholi-Lango factory dispute made it clear that secretaries-general had to follow government policy. Yet, they were still expected to "serve the people."[32] Their role as middlemen was greatly reduced in importance as a result.

Often the primary difficulty in considering the role of middlemen outside governmental structures is to identify the incumbents. The best clue, as Aristide Zolberg suggests, is probably to look for those individuals who hold dual leadership roles in the wage-earning and "residual" sectors of society.[33] Where ethnic movements do not incorporate local administrative structures, these individuals are the most likely candidates to forge patterns of linkage.

The interconnections between rural and urban life suggest linkage possibilities. There is a tendency for individuals who achieve status in the cities to adopt a new life-style but to continue to observe obligations to kin who follow older customs. This "asymmetrical structure"[34] of the new elite provides social bonds out of which political linkage can easily grow. Wealthy professionals who often return to rural areas to procure symbols of prestige and traditional leadership positions are typical examples. In the cities one man's acquisition of leadership positions in several organizations can also open up intercalary roles. In some cases leaders of ethnic associations have been able to take important positions in political parties.[35]

But linkage specialists are also vulnerable to criticism from all sides. It is unlikely that they will be able to satisfy everyone for long. Janus-faced, the middleman role is inherently unstable. A middleman who does not hold a government position will

32. This dilemma was posed sharply by the Mwangu contretemps in Busoga, where the central government insisted upon appointing a manifestly unpopular official as the secretary-general. For the problems that conflicts between government policies and popular preferences created in other parts of Uganda, see Griffith, "Local Politicians and National Policies," pp. 89-90.

33. *Creating Political Order: The Party-States of West Africa* (Chicago: Rand McNally, 1966), p. 130.

34. Martin Kilson, "African Political Change and the Modernisation Process," *The Journal of Modern African Studies* 1, no. 3 (1963): 437.

35. See Paul Mercier, "On the Meaning of 'Tribalism' in Black Africa," in *Africa: Problems of Change and Conflict,* ed. Pierre van den Berghe (San Francisco: Chandler, 1965), p. 500.

probably be "a political variety of the socially and culturally 'marginal man' "[36] – linking both camps while belonging fully to neither.

4. CONCLUSION

Ethnic political participation converts disparate collections of people possessing objective ethnic characteristics in common into ethnic groups mobilized behind demands for protection, autonomy, or economic benefits. Differences in their political behavior and the success of their demands are products of the pattern of linkage they are able to establish with the central government, as several Ugandan cases demonstrate.

Comparatively large size, financial backing, and an extremely intense sense of moral obligation based on traditional unity facilitated Baganda confrontation with the central government in the national arena, but the lack of organizational coherence in KY after the Lukiiko elections of 1962 weakened their effectiveness. At first the central government attempted to bargain. When its position became stronger, it acted unilaterally in holding the "Lost Counties" referendum in 1964 and in its military attack on the Kabaka's palace in 1966. The role of neutral arbiter was not possible, and the Baganda seemed to be prepared to accept nothing less than the capitulation of the center. In this context middlemen could only be messengers (or bosses, the position the Kabaka might have occupied if he had played a more active role). The lack of organizational unity in KY after 1962 meant that a number of opportunists sought to become middlemen.

The Rwenzururu movement provides an interesting comparison. Small, far from the center, poor in financial resources, though possessing moral appeal equal in intensity to that of KY, this movement was contained in the local arena at first. It offered a direct challenge to the center when violence broke out and secession took place, but in spite of the organizational coherence of one faction, the Rwenzururu kingdom government, it never managed to force the center out of its role as

36. Swartz, "The Political Middleman," p. 203.

neutral arbiter, though several unilateral attempts to end the problem were made. Rather, the problem in resolving the dispute was to find brokers who could negotiate a settlement acceptable to all sides. However, the presence of a boss who refused to compromise and the obstruction of the Batoro, whose feelings of moral principle were equally intense, made bargaining virtually impossible. As a result the problem, though reduced in importance, has continued up to the present.

The mobilization of the inhabitants of Bukedi district in the Mbale dispute provided a pattern of linkage that differed significantly from KY or Rwenzururu. As a potential group of moderate size at best, it could not mount a fundamental challenge to the center. Based on a fictitious traditional unity symbolized by a "Kabaka-substitute," it was technically not even an ethnic group. Its appeal was basically a rational calculation of benefits that could be brought to the district. The district council and administration provided the organizational fulcrum for the movement, and their top officials acted as middlemen. As a result the central government could respond through established government channels as a neutral arbiter in judging the claims to Mbale put forward by Bukedi and Bugisu officials.

The Sebei, Banyoro, and Bagisu movements, among others, offer further variations on these three patterns. However, the situation changed considerably with the central government's policy of ethnic departication after 1966. The earlier patterns of concatenation discussed here became considerably muted, and middlemen had to find a new rationale or cease to operate. This did not mean that linkage disappeared, though its importance was reduced considerably. The Obote government and the military regime which followed it continued to search for ways to articulate center and periphery, though they always insisted that the former dominate the latter. The price of this insistence has been departication, not only in matters of ethnicity, but in political life generally.

SEVEN

◇

ETHNIC CRITERIA IN THE SELECTION OF LEADERS

Few issues are more sensitive than the role of ethnicity in recruitment into the political elite in Uganda and most other African countries. In this area the government faces the most important test of its credibility. If top government positions are believed to be monopolized by individuals identified with a particular ethnic unit, as suggested by the capture theory discussed in chapter six, ethnic political participation is likely to increase. There is a dilemma, however, confronting leaders who want to promote ethnic departicipation. Policies that aim to increase the representativeness of government in ethnic terms may satisfy some claimants, but only at the expense of putting greater emphasis on ethnicity as a political criterion. The result may be an increase in ethnic competition for elite positions. Yet policies that ignore the presumed ethnic membership of officials may only exacerbate imbalance where members of one or more ethnic units have educational and economic advantages due to differential modernization.

This dilemma is part of the larger question of demands for professionalization as opposed to demands for representation in government. Recruitment patterns are often related to political policies,[1] though governments generally have less ability to make major changes than they might prefer. The argument in favor of professionalization rests on maintenance of the effectiveness of government programs. The principle of representa-

1. W. H. Morris-Jones, "Political Recruitment and Political Development," in *Politics and Change in Developing Countries: Studies in the Theory and Practice of Development,* ed. Colin Leys (Cambridge: Cambridge University Press, 1969), pp. 113-114.

tion is often justified in terms of the security of the elite. [2] Although a degree of representation is probably necessary to prevent disaffection, official emphasis on this principle is likely to *reduce* stability by introducing a civil service or armed forces "issue" into politics. "Tribalism," James O'Connell observes, "can be seen as the competitive struggle for modernisation between the elite members of different ethnic groups. It tends to be expressed in the scramble for jobs in the bureaucracy." [3] In Nigeria, for example, ethnic favoritism has been the common explanation for failure to receive a job. [4]

Consequently, governments may find it in their interest to insulate aspects of recruitment — a form of political participation — from direct political influence. Ugandan leaders face this problem. There is widespread belief among Ugandans (and scholars who have written about Uganda) that Bantu-speakers and particularly Baganda dominate the civilian bureaucracy. Since the Amin coup there have been allegations that Langi were given many of the important positions during Obote's years in power. [5] Both of these charges are inaccurate. Instead, the behavior of the government during the 1960s amounted to a

2. See Lester G. Seligman, "Elite Recruitment and Political Development," in *Political Development and Social Change,* ed. Jason L. Finkle and Richard W. Gable (New York: John Wiley & Sons, 1966), p. 335. See also Colin Legum, "Tribal Survival in the Modern African Political System," *Journal of Asian and African Studies* 5, nos. 1-2 (January-April 1970): 107. Social justice or patronage are alternative rationales of this position.

3. "The Inevitability of Instability," *The Journal of Modern African Studies* 5, no. 2 (1967): 185.

4. P. C. Lloyd, "The Ethnic Background to the Nigerian Crisis," in *Nigerian Politics and Military Rule: Prelude to the Civil War,* ed. S. K. Panter-Brick (London: Athlone Press, 1970), pp. 7 and 10. At the University of Ibadan, Lloyd adds, "control of the University Council became an ethnic/political issue and almost every professorial appointment (or delayed appointment) was seen as a move in the struggle for dominance between the rival ethnic groups." Ibid., p. 10.

See also the Nigerian government's defense of its recruitment policies in *Unity in Diversity* (Lagos: Federal Ministry of Information, 1967).

5. At the same time it is believed that Nilotic-speakers and particularly Acholi and Langi dominated the army and police before the Amin coup. In fact, there was strong, though not overwhelming, representation of Acholi, and slight overrepresentation of the Langi, in the police at independence. Together Acholi and Langi amounted to less than one-quarter of the police. See table 1, chapter four. Information for an ethnic analysis of the security services after independence is not available. However, the massacres of soldiers after the Amin coup have presumably virtually eliminated those identified as Acholi and Langi in the army.

policy of insulating the civilian bureaucracy against ethnic political considerations, while ministerial posts, on the other hand, were spread as widely as possible.

University students, who will compose the leadership in the next generation, form an important recruitment channel into the elite. Charges of favoritism just after independence led to the establishment of a scholarships committee by the cabinet. An analysis of students indicates that the government did not manipulate their entry on an ethnic basis. In other words, instead of promoting ethnic departicipation, the government has acted to prevent ethnicity from entering politics in sectors of elite recruitment where merit, as opposed to political accessibility, could be the basic criterion.

By examining ethnic representation at various times from the late colonial period until after the confrontation of 1966, it is possible to demonstrate that these propositions describe government policy. A survey of university students projects the analysis into the future by indicating whether the pool of public service candidates is likely to favor any ethnic unit. Although a complete ethnic analysis would require an examination of the police and army, particularly since Amin's coup (and presumably the General Service unit during the Obote government), much can be learned about the government's attitude toward ethnic participation by looking at the political, administrative, and educational sectors.

The data presented are derived from the determination of objective characteristics of ministers, deputy ministers, public servants, and university students that most Ugandans would use to assign an individual to a particular ethnic unit. The number or percentage in each category can be compared to the percentage of the Ugandan African population that was found to be in the same ethnic unit in the *Uganda Census* of 1959.[6] The comparison permits a determination of over- or underrepresentation.

Use of census data presents certain difficulties. First, we cannot be sure that ethnic categories employed by census enumerators were based on precisely the same boundaries as those used in tables 3-5 to designate the ethnic membership of in-

6. The 1969 census eliminated the question on ethnic unit.

TABLE 3

Ethnic Distribution of Ministers and Deputy Ministers

(Including parliamentary secretaries and the director of planning)

Ethnic census unit	1959 Population %	Sept. 1959 Executive Council	Dec. 1961 DP	July 1963 UPC/KY	August 1965 UPC	March 1967 UPC
Baganda	16.3	3	7	11	7	7
Iteso	8.1	0	0	1	2	3
Banyankole	8.1	1	2	2	3	2
Basoga	7.8	1	1	2	2	1
Bakiga/ Bahororo	7.1	1	1	1	1	1
Langi	5.6	0	1	2	2	2
Bagisu	5.1	0	0	1	1	1
Acholi	4.4	0	1	1	2	2
Lugbara	3.7	0	1	0	1	1
Batoro	3.2	0	1	1	3	3
Banyoro	2.9	0	0	2	2	1
Karamojong	2.0	0	0	1	1	1
Alur	1.9	0	0	0	1	1
Bagwere	1.7	0	0	1	1	1
Bakonjo	1.7	0	0	1	1	0
Japadhola (Badama)	1.6	0	1	0	1	1

Madi	1.2	0	0	0	1	1
Samia	0.7	0	0	0	1	1
Others[a]	16.9	0	0	0	0	0
Total	100.0	6	16	30	34	31
Language unit						
Bantu	65.7	6 (100%)	12 (75%)	24 (80%)	23 (68%)	19 (61%)
Nilotic	14.5	0 (0%)	3 (19%)	3 (10%)	6 (18%)	6 (19%)
"Nilo-Hamitic"[b]	12.7	0 (0%)	0 (0%)	2 (7%)	3 (9%)	4 (13%)
Sudanic	5.0	0 (0%)	1 (6%)	1 (3%)	2 (6%)	2 (6%)
Others	2.1	0	0	0	0	0
Racial unit						
Africans	98.7	6	16	30	34	31
Europeans	0.2	6	4	0	0	0
Asians	1.1	1	2	0	0	0
Total	100.0	13	22	30	34	31

SOURCE: *Central Government Organization* and *Government Directory*, nos. 12, 19, 23, 27, and 29 (Entebbe: Government Printer).

[a] Including Banyarwanda, Rundi, Banyole, Kumam, Kakwa, Sebei, Bagwe, Luo, Baamba, Jonam, Bakenyi, Suk, Labwor, and Lendu.

[b] As mentioned in table 2, chapter four, there is controversy over whether "Nilo-Hamitic" languages belong in the Nilotic category. The reader can easily combine the two categories in tables 3–5 if he is so inclined.

dividuals in elite positions. Indeed, even the census enumerators made arbitrary distinctions on occasion.[7] Second, different cultural aggregates may have different birth and death rates. A comparison of the 1948 and 1959 censuses reveals that the increase by ethnic unit ranged from 13 (Iteso) to 37 percent (Langi), excluding cases where the ethnic designation itself was changed.[8] To some degree the 1959 census may be more accurate than the earlier one in 1948, but the figure for an ethnic unit's percentage of the total population may also be different in 1967 from what it was in 1959 because of differences in longevity and reproduction. This would alter some of the findings of over- and underrepresentation.

A further qualification that must be kept in mind is that individuals in the political elite who are assigned to a particular ethnic unit do not necessarily regard this identification as important for any purpose. Finally, the tabulations presented below are subject to many of the criticisms regarding inadequate ethnic definitions discussed in chapter two. The tabulations, to be precise, are based on generally accepted *beliefs* that possession of certain objective characteristics determines the ethnic group to which an individual belongs. Nevertheless, since widespread beliefs about the "domination" or lack of influence of ethnic groups have political relevance, it is important to compare them with data on ethnic representation.

1. MINISTERS AND DEPUTY MINISTERS

Two studies show that Baganda dominated the top positions within political parties during the last years of colonial rule. A questionnaire administered in 1956 to forty branch chairmen of the Uganda National Congress (UNC) indicated that 50 percent were Baganda, 11 percent were from Lango, 9 percent from Acholi, and 7 percent from Busoga and Teso. The central committee of the UNC contained seventeen Baganda, one Mun-

7. For example, Joan Vincent reports that there was a spate of correspondence between Teso district officers and the census statisticians on this point. Since the Pagero were not "recognized" in the census as a possible ethnic unit, people claiming this designation were sometimes listed as Banyoro. *African Elite: The Big Men of a Small Town* (New York: Columbia University Press, 1971), pp. 25 and n. 2, p. 295.

8. *Uganda Census 1959: African Population* (Entebbe: Statistics Branch, Ministry of Economic Affairs, 1961), p. 19.

yoro, one Musoga, and one man with a Seychellese father and a Muganda mother.[9] A second study examined the top leadership positions of the major parties active in 1958. Out of thirty persons whose ethnic orgin could be identified (using local district in certain cases), twenty-five were Baganda; two were from Acholi; and one each came from Busoga, Lango, and Toro.[10]

When elections were held in most parts of Uganda for the National Assembly, control of branch leadership of the parties tended to become localized. A parallel trend resulted in most candidates for the National Assembly running in areas in which their own ethnic unit predominated.[11] The most flamboyant exception was Daudi Ocheng, an Acholi, who became a land-owner in Buganda, joined the KY, and defended Baganda interests in parliament (though as a nominated, not a popularly elected, member). A few other MPs represented urban constituencies in which their ethnic unit was not in the majority.

Out of the ethnically well-distributed MPs, Obote chose his ministers and deputy ministers. There is wide-spread agreement on the ethnic identity of each of them.[12] Their distribution has been tabulated in table 3. Parliamentary secretaries and colonial civil servants holding ministerial positions are also included for comparison. The table demonstrates the extent to which the

9. David Apter, *The Political Kingdom in Uganda: A Study of Bureaucratic Nationalism* (Princeton: Princeton University Press, 1967), pp. 318 and 322-323. The basis on which the sample of branch chairmen was selected is not given. Nor is it clear whether the ethnic identity of the branch chairmen refers to their ethnic unit or to the district in which they live. District residence is sometimes a poor guide to the identification of a person's likely ethnic designation because many districts contain several ethnic units. However, Lango, Acholi, Teso, and Busoga are each almost wholly populated by what is generally regarded to be a single ethnic unit.

10. David A. Gugin, "Africanization of the Ugandan Public Service" (Ph.D. diss. University of Wisconsin, 1967), p. 127. Included for examination were officeholders in the Progressive Party, the Uganda National Congress, the Democratic Party, and the United Congress Party.

11. See the discussion of Robert Byrd's findings in chapter four, section 6.

12. The data in table 3 are confirmed in an analysis of ethnic representation of Obote's 1971 cabinet which was published in Tanzania shortly after Amin's coup. This article was written to refute allegations that Obote had practiced "tribalism." The only deviations from table 3 are the inclusion of one fewer Muganda and the substitution of one "Kwaka" (Kakwa?) and the labeling of the Musamia in the table as a Muluhyia (a different name referring to the same Ugandans). "Where Was Tribalism in Uganda?" *The Standard* (Tanzania), 12 February 1971, p. 4.

most important and most prestigious political offices have been spread among all important ethnic units. Of all twenty units containing 1 percent of the population or more, only one fairly populous unit (Banyarwanda) and one small one (Banyole) have never had representation at the ministerial level. Thus it is also not surprising to discover that the number of ministerial positions during the Obote period increased until it included about one-half the UPC members in the National Assembly.

Second, the Baganda — even after the 1966 crisis — have always been overrepresented on the basis of their share of the population. However, their overrepresentation has been declining since 1963, when the KY was allied with the UPC in the government. In 1967 the Baganda held a proportion of ministerial positions smaller than their share of places in the higher civil service or in Makerere University College (see tables 4 and 5). The most overrepresented unit in the 1967 ministerial ranks was the Batoro.

Third, if ethnic units are combined into four main language units in Uganda, their representation has been roughly equivalent to their share of the population since 1963. The representation of Bantu-speakers among ministers and deputy ministers fell below their population percentage for the first time following the arrest and detention of five of their number in February 1966. Neither the Acholi, Langi, nor the Nilotic unit as a whole, often reputed to have consolidated the top positions, are significantly overrepresented.

Finally, UPC leaders followed the practice of replacing ministers who resigned with members from the same ethnic units. Between April and July 1967, C. Obwangor (Itesot), A. Nekyon (Langi), and G. Binaisa (Muganda) resigned. Since then J. Anyoti (Kumam, an ethnic unit closely related to the Iteso) and J. Okae (Langi) have been the only new recruits to ministerial positions in the Obote government. When Amin took office, he reduced the number of ministers. But in spite of his emphasis on a technocratic rather than a political image, he followed Obote's practice and appointed eighteen representatives from more than ten different ethnic units, including Acholi and Langi. Contrary to popular expectations, he included fewer Baganda in his first cabinet than Obote had. Thus, in both postindependence governments there has been heavy reliance on ethnicity in recruiting the top political officers.[13]

2. PUBLIC SERVANTS

The higher public service plays just as important a role in guiding government business as top politicians do. Permanent secretaries and district commissioners receive high salaries and much deference. It is not surprising that fears of ethnic domination in the bureaucracy have been raised from time to time. Different members of parliament have claimed either that there is a calculated policy of "northernizing" the civil service or, on the contrary, that there is increasing Baganda domination. These accusations have been refuted in parliament, and the data presented in table 4 support the refutations.[14]

The higher public service is made up of appointed officials who formulate and implement government policies. The criterion for inclusion in table 4 was either a listing in the *Government Directory* (excluding personal secretaries and jobholders in the office of the National Assembly) or a position of district commissioner or assistant district commissioner. The positions analyzed focus on the administrative cadre and exclude most technical officers.

The determination of each officer's ethnic unit was made by analyzing his name. However, since many ethnic units use the same names, an attempt was made to confirm the identity of each person by asking someone who knew him. The Ugandan

13. An ethnic breakdown of Kampala municipal councillors for 1967 and 1970 reveals a similar emphasis on ethnicity. Of the thirty-one councillors in 1967, there were eight Asians, six Baganda, six Acholi, and one or two from nine other Ugandan ethnic units. By 1970 the council had been increased to thirty-eight members, of which there were twelve Baganda, four Bakiga, four Acholi, three Langi, three Basoga, and one or two from eight other Ugandan ethnic units, plus one Asian. The major shift is the *increase* in Baganda during the late Obote period at the expense of the Asians. Since the councillors were appointed, rather than elected, during this period, the ethnic distribution probably tells us more about UPC patronage than about power. I am grateful to Michael Lee for permission to take these figures from his paper, "The Structure of Local Government," delivered to the Seminar on African Politics, Institute of Commonwealth Studies, University of London, November 1973. (Stenciled.)

14. The attack on these allegations was presented by Felix Onama, then minister for internal affairs. *Parliamentary Debates* (Uganda), vol. 36 (1964), pp. 104-111.

bureaucratic elite is still sufficiently small that almost every person could be positively identified in this manner. All public servants in the population under examination have been accounted for.

The data must be approached with some caution, however. First, no attempt has been made to give additional weight to the more important or more sensitive posts, some of which are not even included in the *Government Directory*. Knowing the holders of these positions is likely to give either more comfort or more anxiety to those believing in an "ethnic capture" theory of Ugandan politics. Second, the security forces, in which members of non-Bantu-speaking ethnic units predominate, and the public corporations have not been considered, since no recent listings are available. Consequently, the findings of this analysis cannot be taken as describing the ethnic profile of the whole government.

Third, the listing of posts in the *Government Directory* has changed over the past ten years, so a somewhat different set of positions is included in each column. However, there is no evidence that the changes in listing posts have been influenced by ethnic considerations. Fourth, the percentages for the early years (1959 and 1961) are somewhat misleading, since the total number of African officials was so small. Thus, both percentages and absolute numbers are given in the table.

Table 4 indicates that the Baganda were overrepresented in the higher public service by a factor fluctuating between two and three times their population percentage during the period between 1959 and 1967. They represented as much as 46.9 percent in 1961, during the first frantic years of Africanization, and then fell steadily to 35.6 percent in 1967.[15] However, a comparison of the changes in the Baganda percentage of representation with the changes in their absolute numbers reveals that while their proportion of higher civil servants fell by more than 10 percent, the actual number of Baganda in this sector of the bureaucracy increased from 11 to 105.

15. Information presented by Onama on the ethnic composition of 151 officers paid at superscale rates in 1964 (a different population from the one I have used) tends to confirm the figures of table 4. He found a somewhat higher percentage of Baganda (44.4 percent) and Iteso (9.3 percent). The differences may reflect differences in the two populations. Ibid., p. 108.

These simultaneous changes in opposite directions helped to keep the civil service insulated from the imposition of ethnic criteria. The imbalance caused by the headstart of the Baganda in modernization (see section 5 in chapter four) has not been as difficult to handle as observers predicted. In this way Uganda's sudden late start on Africanization has paid an unexpected political dividend. The Baganda cannot make much of a claim that they are being discriminated against, and others can take satisfaction in the rising percentage of higher public servants from their respective ethnic units.

None of the "northern" units have ever been significantly overrepresented except the Acholi, who were somewhat so in 1965. The Langi, contrary to the claims of critics of Obote, have always been somewhat underrepresented. Aside from the Baganda, in 1967 the Iteso, Batoro, Banyoro, Japadhola, Banyole, Samia, and Kakwa were the only units to have achieved parity or better in comparison with their share of the general population. Apart from the Rundi, no ethnic aggregate with more than 1 percent of the population has been totally unrepresented in the higher public service.

The sharp fall in Δ indicates that the ethnic profile of the higher public service was coming to resemble more closely the distribution of the general population by 1963. Since that time the degree of dissimilarity appears to have stabilized, though the percentages of higher civil servants from various ethnic units have fluctuated. Changes in ethnic composition of secondary schools and Makerere may alter these percentages in the next few years.

If Ugandan ethnic aggregates are categorized in terms of the major language divisions, the arguments about Nilotic or Bantu domination are further weakened. By 1967 Nilotic- and "Nilo-

---

Gugin also examined the ethnic composition of the higher public service. His figures for Baganda overrepresentation are consistently higher than mine, reaching a level of 66.7 percent of African bureaucrats listed in the *Government Directory* in 1962 and 50.1 percent of those listed in 1964. "Africanization of the Ugandan Public Service," pp. 135-136. However, in both cases he collected data on only two-thirds of the bureaucrats listed and tended to assign them to ethnic categories on the basis of the district in which they were born. It is likely that both of these considerations inflated the Baganda contribution. Only 55 percent of the inhabitants of the former Buganda region are Baganda.

Hamitic"-speakers were very slightly underrepresented, though Sudanic-speakers were more so. Without the Baganda the other Bantu ethnic units are also underrepresented and have been over the entire eight-year period. With the Baganda added in, the overrepresentation is relatively mild. In terms of language units the higher public service was slightly less than twice as representative of the general population by 1967 as it was in 1959.

For comparison a racial breakdown of the higher public service during the years examined is included. There has been a rapid rate of Africanization (from 10.2 percent to 67.9 percent), reflecting Uganda's late start. The number of European members of the bureaucracy has slipped from 84.2 percent to 18.7 percent during the same period. Much more surprising has been the steady increase in Asians (Indians and Pakistanis) from 5.7 percent to 13.4 percent. The extreme dissimilarity between the racial composition in the bureaucracy and in the general population has been moderated somewhat but remained quite high in 1967. However, the 1972 expulsion of noncitizen Asians and the departure of many European expatriates has considerably reduced this dissimilarity.

Further support for the conclusions reached in table 4 is provided in an ethnic breakdown of the top layer of the Ugandan elite published in 1971.[16] Ethnic information is provided for the highest levels of the public service, diplomats, judges, heads of public corporations and state-owned companies (those nationalized in May 1970), leading Makerere officials and academics, and important administrators in the East African Community. The public servants analyzed are limited to permanent secretaries and heads of departments and amount to fifty-one of the highest bureaucratic officials. Of these, 35 percent

16. *The Standard* (Tanzania), 12 February 1971, p. 4. This article was almost certainly prepared by Ugandans who had fled after the coup, and possibly by Obote himself. Thus, there are obviously questions about the reliability of the data. Incumbents of positions that should have been included may have been left out by accident or by intention. In particular the results would "look better" if several Langi were left out. On the other hand, both names and positions are given for top officials in public organizations, state-owned companies, Makerere, and the East African Community. The inclusion of misleading information in these cases would be so obvious to many Ugandans that it would defeat the purposes of the writer. As I mentioned in note 12, the ministerial and deputy ministerial ethnic designations agree with mine, with one exception.

(eighteen officers) are described as Baganda. This is almost exactly the same as the total Baganda percentage of the larger set of officials reported for March 1967 in Table 4.

The next largest set of top public servants are the Acholi with 10 percent (five officers) and the Basoga with 8 percent (four men). No other ethnic unit has more than three representatives (6 percent). The Samia (listed as Baluhyia) and Japadhola are the most overrepresented (about four times their population percentage, though the numbers are too small to permit satisfying comparisons). The Acholi and the Baganda are somewhat more than twice as numerous as their percentage of the population would warrant. The Langi, Batoro, Banyoro, and Banyole were slightly overrepresented. These conclusions (with the possible exception of the Acholi) also parallel the data presented in table 4.

In this analysis the entire set of elite officials counted occupy 132 positions (five men were counted twice because they hold 2 positions). Of these, Baganda again compose 35 percent (forty-six officials) — a little more than double their percentage of the population. The Acholi (9 percent — twelve officials) are over-represented to about the same degree. Only two other units (the Iteso and the Basoga) have representatives amounting to as much as 7 percent (nine men). They are slightly under-represented. Once again the Samia and the Japadhola are the most overrepresented ethnic units. The Langi (6 percent — eight men) are only slightly overrepresented according to this study, contrary to the charges of the military leaders after the coup. The 1971 report is silent, however, about Langi representation in the army and in the General Service unit, Obote's intelligence and "private" military wing.[17] Overall, the 1971 study suggests that the ethnic breakdown of the top level of the political elite closely resembles the higher public service. It also confirms that changes in ethnic distribution have proceeded rather slowly

17. In 1968 Obote stated that "as everyone who wants to assess the position will find out, the number of my tribesmen in the Police and in the Army is negligible." "Myths and Realities," *The People* (Supplement), 29 August 1970, p. iv. However, during his last year in office, fears were expressed within the army that Obote was preparing the way for a few Langi officers to take positions of command. A. G. G. Gingyera-Pinycwa, "A. M. Obote, the Baganda and the Uganda Army," *Mawazo* (Kampala) 3, no. 2 (December 1971): 42. These fears were an important factor in causing the coup.

TABLE 4
ETHNIC DISTRIBUTION OF THE HIGHER PUBLIC SERVICE[a]

Ethnic census unit	1959 population %	September 1959 % (N)	December 1961 % (N)	July 1963 % (N)	August 1965 % (N)	March 1967 % (N)
Baganda	16.3	40.7 (11)	46.9 (23)	38.1 (51)	37.3 (87)	35.6 (105)
Iteso	8.1	3.7 (1)	2.0 (1)	5.2 (7)	4.7 (11)	8.1 (24)
Banyankole	8.1	0.0 (0)	4.1 (2)	7.5 (10)	6.9 (16)	6.8 (20)
Basoga	7.8	7.4 (2)	4.1 (2)	9.0 (12)	6.0 (14)	3.4 (10)
Bakiga/Bahororo	7.1	3.7 (1)	10.2 (5)	6.0 (8)	5.2 (12)	4.7 (14)
Banyarwanda	5.9	11.1 (3)	4.1 (2)	3.7 (5)	4.7 (11)	4.4 (13)
Langi	5.6	3.7 (1)	2.0 (1)	1.5 (2)	3.0 (7)	4.1 (12)
Bagisu	5.1	0.0 (0)	4.1 (2)	4.5 (6)	3.0 (7)	2.7 (8)
Acholi	4.4	7.4 (2)	4.1 (2)	6.7 (9)	7.3 (17)	4.4 (13)
Lugbara	3.7	0.0 (0)	2.0 (1)	1.5 (2)	1.3 (3)	1.4 (4)
Batoro	3.2	7.4 (2)	6.1 (3)	3.0 (4)	3.4 (8)	7.1 (21)
Banyoro	2.9	7.4 (2)	6.1 (3)	5.2 (7)	6.0 (14)	5.1 (15)
Karamojong	2.0	0.0 (0)	0.0 (0)	0.7 (1)	0.9 (2)	0.7 (2)
Alur	1.9	0.0 (0)	0.0 (0)	0.7 (1)	0.9 (2)	0.7 (2)
Bagwere	1.7	0.0 (0)	0.0 (0)	0.0 (0)	0.4 (1)	0.3 (1)
Bakonjo	1.7	0.0 (0)	0.0 (0)	0.0 (0)	0.4 (1)	0.3 (1)
Japadhola (Badama)	1.6	0.0 (0)	2.0 (1)	2.2 (3)	0.9 (2)	4.1 (12)
Banyole	1.4	3.7 (1)	0.0 (0)	0.7 (1)	1.7 (4)	1.4 (4)
Madi	1.2	3.7 (1)	2.0 (1)	1.5 (2)	0.9 (2)	0.3 (1)
Kumam	1.0	0.0 (0)	0.0 (0)	0.0 (0)	0.9 (2)	0.7 (2)
Samia	0.7	0.0 (0)	0.0 (0)	0.7 (1)	3.0 (7)	2.4 (6)

	General population					
Kakwa	0.6	0.0 (0)	0.0 (0)	0.7 (1)	0.9 (2)	1.4 (4)
Sebei	0.6	0.0 (0)	0.0 (0)	0.0 (0)	0.0 (0)	0.3 (1)
Jonam	0.4	0.0 (0)	0.0 (0)	0.7 (1)	0.4 (1)	0.0 (0)
Other[b]	7.0	0.0 (0)	0.0 (0)	0.0 (0)	0.0 (0)	0.0 (0)
Total . . .	100.0	99.9 (27)	99.8 (49)	99.8 (134)	100.1 (233)	100.4 (295)
Index of dissimilarity		$\Delta^c = 46.2$	$\Delta = 41.1$	$\Delta = 29.0$	$\Delta = 30.0$	$\Delta = 30.2$
Language unit						
Bantu	65.7	81.5 (22)	85.7 (42)	78.4 (105)	78.1 (182)	73.9 (218)
Nilotic	14.5	11.1 (3)	8.2 (4)	11.9 (16)	12.4 (29)	13.2 (39)
"Nilo-Hamitic"	12.7	3.7 (1)	2.0 (1)	6.7 (9)	7.3 (17)	11.2 (33)
Sudanic	5.0	3.7 (1)	4.1 (2)	2.9 (4)	2.1 (5)	1.7 (5)
Other	2.1	0.0 (0)	0.0 (0)	0.0 (0)	0.0 (0)	0.0 (0)
Total . . .	100.0	100.0 (27)	100.0 (49)	99.9 (134)	99.9 (233)	100.0 (295)
Index of dissimilarity		$\Delta = 15.8$	$\Delta = 20.0$	$\Delta = 12.8$	$\Delta = 12.5$	$\Delta = 8.2$
Racial unit						
Africans	98.7	10.2 (27)	19.0 (49)	45.6 (134)	66.8 (233)	67.9 (295)
Europeans	0.2	84.2 (223)	73.6 (190)	46.3 (136)	24.1 (84)	18.7 (81)
Asians	1.1	5.7 (15)	7.4 (19)	8.2 (24)	9.2 (32)	13.4 (58)
Total . . .	100.0	100.1 (265)	100.0 (258)	100.1 (294)	100.1 (349)	100.0 (434)
Index of dissimilarity		$\Delta = 88.6$	$\Delta = 79.7$	$\Delta = 53.2$	$\Delta = 32.0$	$\Delta = 30.8$

[a] Complied from *Central Government Organisation* and *Government Directory*, nos. 12, 19, 27, and 29 (Entebbe: Government Printer) and from *Staff Lists*, 1959, 1961, 1963, 1965, and 1967 (Entebbe: Government Printer).

[b] Including Bagwe, Baamba, Luo, Suk, Labwor, Rundi, Bakenyi, and Lendu.

[c] Δ measures the degree of dissimilarity by comparison with the ethnic distribution of the general population. See the explanation on p. 111.

since the completion of the first burst of Africanization in 1963.

In contrast to some other African countries, notably Nigeria, Uganda has managed to avoid heavy political pressures to distribute bureaucratic positions on the basis of ethnic representation. As a northern Ugandan asked, "Why should we leave [out] capable Baganda, who can render service to the nation . . . are they not part of Uganda?"[18] In Nigeria many posts in the federal bureaucracy were either left vacant or filled under contract by expatriates "because of the understandable desire to hold a proportion of posts open until northerners are available to fill them."[19] Both of these divergent policies attempted to rectify imbalances in the public service caused by differential modernization. But in Nigeria – in contrast to Uganda – the result was much less insulation of government officers from ethnic political participation.

3. UNIVERSITY STUDENTS

Receiving a university degree automatically secures one's entry into the upper reaches of the small Ugandan elite. It is thus a matter of intense concern to all parents that their children survive the competition for secondary school places and enter Makerere University or go abroad for further studies. There is, however, surprisingly little public discussion of the allocation of places at Makerere. It is generally assumed that merit alone is the criterion for entry, though the differential location of secondary schools and missions does give advantages to certain ethnic units, as suggested in chapter four.

University students of today are likely to be the top civil servants – and perhaps politicians – of tomorrow. Consequently, an examination of trends in the ethnic composition of Makerere yields a prediction about the likely profile of the higher public service in the late 1970s.

The data on representation of ethnic units at Makerere was

18. Onama, *Parliamentary Debates,* vol. 36, p. 109.
19. J. Donald Kingsley, "Bureaucracy and Political Development, with Particular Reference to Nigeria," in *Bureaucracy and Political Development,* ed. Joseph LaPalombara (Princeton: Princeton University Press, 1963), pp. 304-305.

compiled from the *Nominal Roll* for four different years. Since Makerere offers a three-year degree program, an overlap of students was avoided by choosing every fourth year from 1959/1960 to 1968/1969. Each student's ethnic unit is listed (on the basis of information provided by the student), so it is possible to make an accurate determination of the numbers representing each unit. The sudden increase in foreign scholarships just before independence explains why Makerere attendance fell between 1959/1960 and 1962/1963. Since a large number of Ugandan students take their degrees abroad, these figures may be a somewhat inaccurate measure of the entire category. [20]

Once again the Baganda are heavily overrepresented, though their percentage steadily falls from 46.6 percent to 33.6 percent over the ten-year period. Although the Baganda took more than two of every five places held by Ugandan Africans in 1959/1960, or almost three times their percentage of the general population, they now occupy one place in three, or double their expected share. As in the case of the higher public service, the absolute number of Baganda at Makerere has rapidly risen, while their percentage has fallen. The rapid expansion of the university from 873 to 2,011 students and the increasing share of the places held by Ugandan Africans has made this possible. Thus, there has been little reason to complain of discrimination.

The most overrepresented ethnic unit in 1968/1969 was the Samia, who were present in almost triple the proportion they are found in Uganda's population. The Acholi, Batoro, Banyoro, Bagwere, and Madi were slightly overrepresented in 1968/1969. The rest were underrepresented. However, it is clear that most ethnic units, even the smallest ones, have had some members who have attended the university. The degree to which the ethnic composition of Makerere has reflected the distribution of the general population has steadily risen.

20. A supplementary scheme was instituted in 1961 to increase the number of foreign scholarships from 49 to 300. Not all of these were filled that year, however. *Annual Report of the Department of Education: 1961* (Entebbe: Government Printer, 1962), p. 8. In 1967/1968, 2,500 students were studying abroad, including 345 working for bachelor's degrees. *Education Statistics: 1967* (Kampala: Ministry of Education, 1967), section F, table 1.

TABLE 5
ETHNIC DISTRIBUTION OF UGANDAN MAKERERE STUDENTS[a]

Ethnic census unit	1959 population %	1959/1960 % (N)	1962/1963 % (N)	1965/1966 % (N)	1968/1969 % (N)
Baganda	16.3	46.6 (131)	42.5 (102)	36.9 (206)	33.6 (377)
Iteso	8.1	6.1 (17)	5.0 (12)	5.9 (33)	7.8 (88)
Banyankole	8.1	6.1 (17)	8.8 (21)	7.5 (42)	6.2 (69)
Basoga	7.8	6.1 (17)	7.1 (17)	7.3 (41)	6.4 (72)
Bakiga/	7.1	5.3 (15)	7.5 (18)	7.2 (40)	6.5 (73)
Bahoro		1.1 (3)	1.7 (4)	0.9 (5)	0.4 (5)
Banyarwanda	5.9	1.8 (5)	2.5 (6)	2.0 (11)	2.9 (33)
Langi	5.6	1.8 (5)	3.8 (9)	4.8 (27)	5.2 (58)
Bagisu	5.1	3.6 (10)	2.5 (6)	2.9 (16)	2.9 (33)
Acholi	4.4	4.3 (12)	4.2 (10)	7.0 (39)	5.4 (61)
Lugbara	3.7	0.4 (1)	0.8 (2)	1.6 (9)	2.2 (25)
Batoro	3.2	1.8 (5)	1.3 (3)	2.5 (14)	4.1 (46)
Banyoro	2.9	3.6 (10)	2.1 (5)	4.3 (24)	4.5 (50)
Karamojong	2.0	0.4 (1)	0.0 (0)	0.0 (0)	0.2 (2)
Alur	1.9	0.4 (1)	0.4 (1)	0.9 (5)	1.4 (16)
Bagwere	1.7	2.1 (6)	1.3 (3)	1.4 (8)	1.9 (21)
Bakonjo	1.7	0.7 (2)	0.4 (1)	0.2 (1)	0.3 (3)
Japadhola (Badama)	1.6	1.4 (4)	1.7 (4)	1.6 (9)	1.1 (12)
Banyole	1.4	1.4 (4)	0.8 (2)	0.5 (3)	0.8 (9)
Madi	1.2	0.7 (2)	0.4 (1)	1.3 (7)	1.9 (21)
Kumam	1.0	1.4 (4)	1.3 (3)	0.9 (5)	0.7 (8)
Samia	0.7	0.7 (2)	2.1 (5)	1.4 (8)	1.9 (21)
Kakwa	0.6	0.0 (0)	0.0 (0)	0.2 (1)	0.3 (3)
Sebei	0.6	0.0 (0)	0.0 (0)	0.2 (1)	0.1 (1)
Bagwe	0.6	0.4 (1)	0.0 (0)	0.0 (0)	0.2 (2)

		(281)	(240)	(558)	(1,121)
Baamba	0.5	0.0 (0)	0.0 (0)	0.4 (2)	0.2 (2)
Jonam	0.4	1.4 (4)	2.1 (5)	0.0 (0)	0.5 (6)
Labwor	0.1	0.0 (0)	0.0 (0)	0.0 (0)	0.1 (1)
Okebo	—	0.4 (1)	0.0 (0)	0.0 (0)	0.0 (0)
Baluhyia	—	0.4 (1)	0.0 (0)	0.0 (0)	0.1 (1)
Bari	—	0.0 (0)	0.0 (0)	0.2 (1)	0.0 (0)
Nubian	—	0.0 (0)	0.0 (0)	0.0 (0)	0.2 (2)
Other[b]	5.9	0.0 (0)	0.0 (0)	0.0 (0)	0.0 (0)
Total	100.0	100.4 (281)	100.3 (240)	100.0 (558)	100.0 (1,121)
Ugandan Africans Index of dissimilarity		Δ[c] = 33.1	Δ = 32.4	Δ = 26.6	Δ = 23.3
Language unit					
Bantu	65.7	81.5 (229)	80.4 (193)	75.4 (421)	72.9 (817)
Nilotic	14.5	9.3 (26)	12.1 (29)	14.3 (80)	13.6 (153)
"Nilo-Hamitic"	12.7	7.8 (22)	6.3 (15)	7.3 (41)	9.2 (103)
Sudanic	5.0	1.4 (4)	1.3 (3)	2.9 (16)	4.3 (48)
Other	2.1	0.0 (0)	0.0 (0)	0.0 (0)	0.0 (0)
Total	100.0	100.0 (281)	100.1 (240)	99.9 (558)	100.0 (1,121)
Ugandan Africans Index of dissimilarity		Δ = 15.8	Δ = 14.7	Δ = 9.8	Δ = 7.2
Total number of Makerere students[d]		873	763	1,158	2,011

[a] Compiled from *Makerere University College Nominal Roll.*
[b] Including Rundi, Luo, Bakenyi, Suk, and Lendu.
[c] Δ measures the degree of dissimilarity by comparison to the distribution of the general population. See explanation on p. 127.
[d] Including non-African Ugandans and non-Ugandans.

The major language aggregates also became represented more equitably at Makerere as the decade passed. The Bantu-speakers remained somewhat overrepresented, though without the Baganda the remaining Bantu-speakers always were underrepresented. The Nilotic, "Nilo-Hamitic," and Sudanic units remained slightly underrepresented. In terms of language units Makerere was twice as representative of the general population in 1968/1969 as it had been in 1959/1960.

If we ask which Makerere students are most likely to become high-level public servants, we should examine more closely the Arts and Social Science faculties. To the extent that the British tradition of "generalists" remains an important norm of recruitment into the Ugandan public service, the administrative cadre is more likely to include men and women with degrees in political science, economics, English, and the like than those taking more technical subjects.[21]

In general, the percentages of ethnic distribution of students in arts and social science subjects hover around the respective percentages of students in the university as a whole. The Baganda composed slightly over half (51.2 percent) of arts and social science students in 1959/1960 but now include about one-third (34.6 percent). Most ethnic units have not been represented at a level consistently above or below their percentage in Makerere. The ethnic profile in these faculties is currently only very slightly more dissimilar to the ethnic distribution of the population ($\Delta = 25.6$) than is the profile of the university as a whole. In terms of language aggregates, for the ten-year period there has been in the two faculties slightly higher overrepresentation of Bantu-speakers at the expense of all other units than that which existed in the university as a whole.

In summary there appears to be a trend in the ethnic profile of Makerere and the higher civil service toward a closer approximation of that of the general population. Ethnic representation

21. Oddly, considering the current demands for technically skilled personnel, the percentage of Ugandan African Makerere students in the Arts and Social Science facilities rose over the ten-year period from 27.8 percent to 52.6 percent. This trend is to be reversed during the third five-year plan period, and the total numbers in the arts and social sciences are to be cut by almost one-half. See *Uganda's Plan III: Third Five-Year Development Plan, 1971/2-1975/6* (Entebbe: Government Printer, 1972), pp. 347-348.

at Makerere in 1968/1969 has almost achieved the degree of similarity found in secondary schools in 1960.[22] Thus, even though the ethnic profile of the higher public service has remained at the same cumulative level of dissimilarity from the ethnic distribution of the general population since 1963, the Makerere figures suggest that it will become more representative during the 1970s.

4. CONCLUSION

Ethnic criteria have played an important role in the selection of top politicians — parliamentary candidates, ministers, and deputy ministers. However, high-level positions in the public service and places at the university have been generally insulated from ethnic calculations despite accusations to the contrary. Both of the latter structures have slowly grown to resemble more closely the ethnic distribution of the general population. However, this trend has not occurred at a sufficiently rapid rate to suggest that ethnic representation has been a policy that the Obote government was actively pursuing. It is simpler to explain these findings on the assumption of random distribution of leadership capabilities throughout the population and as the natural consequence of more evenly distributed opportunities for secondary schooling.

Imbalance in university places and civil service positions resulting from differential modernization has stimulated some ethnic political participation in Uganda, as it has elsewhere. It poses a serious challenge to governments attempting to use merit as the basic criterion in selection for government and university. Both Kenya and Tanzania have also had to grapple with this problem.[23] Uganda has been fortunate in having an "expanding pie" to distribute during the first decade of inde-

22. The policy of building many new secondary schools in outlying areas during the 1960s is likely to contribute further to the representativeness of Makerere and the higher public service during the 1970s.

23. See Donald Rothchild, "Ethnic Inequalities in Kenya," *The Journal of Modern African Studies* 7, no. 4 (1969): 705; and the reply of Rashidi Kawawa (the prime minister of Tanzania) to a charge of "tribalism in employment in our government." *Parliamentary Debates* (Tanzania), 9 July 1968, cols. 1530-1532. I am grateful to J. Harris Proctor for pointing out this statement to me. Both countries appear to be depending on provision of more evenly distributed secondary school opportunities (which raises its own problems for ethnic political participation) to solve ethnic imbalance in the civil service in the long run.

pendence. Africanization has resulted in an extremely rapid expansion of available public service posts. The increased number of places in secondary schools and the university have permitted members of every ethnic unit to increase their share of new benefits. At the same time the percentage of overrepresentation by the Baganda among top politicians, bureaucrats, and university students has declined, even though their absolute numbers have increased. Thus, grievances that might have led to intense ethnic political participation have not been prominent.

Opportunities in education and the public service are likely to expand much more slowly in the future. However, the governments of both Amin and Obote have made efforts to open up to Africans a wide variety of positions in commerce and industry previously monopolized by Indians and Europeans — as have the governments of Kenya and Tanzania. While Obote was president, a trade licensing act, new requirements for work permits, and nationalization measures presented new opportunities for Africans. Amin has maintained the government's part ownership of companies nationalized by Obote, though at a reduced percentage. His decision in August 1972 to expel noncitizen Indians and Pakistanis dramatically increased the possibilities for Africans to enter the commercial sector.

For the time being, therefore, access is relatively open, and the issues that might have sparked ethnic political competition remain in the background. Overall, however, Uganda's resources are severly limited and are not growing much faster than its population. Now that Ugandan Africans have added control over their domestic economy to their monopoly over political and administrative positions, the growing pie has been replaced by a fixed pie — a zero-sum resources situation. But to some extent ethnic political participation may be less intense because the government has already corrected some of the ethnic imbalances inherited from the colonial period.

EIGHT

◇

GOVERNMENT POLICIES TOWARD ETHNICITY: OBOTE AND AMIN

Faced with intermittently intense ethnic political involvement, postindependence Ugandan governments have adopted a variety of strategies. To some extent these resulted from the political difficulties in which each leader found himself. In all three governments the leaders were willing to accept ethnicity as a legitimate basis for political participation at the outset of their terms in office. The DP, which formed the first African government (before independence), ruled for too short a time and was under too heavy a set of electoral pressures to abandon reliance on bargains with ethnic middlemen and appeals to ethnic movements. The UPC came into office with only a little more popular support than the DP and was assured of power only because of its parliamentary coalition with an avowed ethnic movement – KY. From 1962 until 1964 the UPC accepted much ethnic political participation, not only by KY but also by other groups imitating KY.

The announcement of the referendum on the "Lost Counties," which occurred when the UPC gained an absolute majority in the National Assembly as a result of aisle crossing, signaled the end of the coalition with KY. Obote's insistence on following the constitutional requirement for holding a referendum marked an early stage in his willingness to introduce a policy of ethnic departicipation. The confrontations of 1966 crystallized this policy and tied Obote's personal political fortunes to its continuation. The Amin government has continued this policy in its broad outlines but was forced by its immediate legitimacy requirements to alter it virtually beyond recognition.

A policy of ethnic departicipation can alter political involvement because ethnicity is fluid and evoked in certain situations only. But it does not necessarily mean that people cease to act

195

upon ethnic political calculations, nor is such a policy likely to achieve much success in the short run. What did happen in Uganda was the elimination (during the Obote period) of public assertions of ethnicity in political life. It is likely that some ethnic linkage continued to occur in private. However, a new political situation was created, to which Ugandans might, over time, have learned to respond without resorting to ethnicity. Nevertheless, Obote's policy was seriously flawed because it reinforced the ethnic identity of Baganda. The reaction to the coup and the new policies of the Amin government demonstrate that many Baganda, as well as other Ugandans, still regard their ethnic identities as important for political purposes. In addition, the contrast between the approaches of Obote and Amin illustrates how important government policy can be in shaping situations either to enhance or to de-emphasize ethnicity.

1. ETHNIC DEPARTICIPATION UNDER THE OBOTE GOVERNMENT

Obote's battle for political survival in 1966 led directly to the introduction of several government measures to reduce the political use of ethnicity. The battle culminated in two major confrontations — with Obote's opponents in the cabinet in February and with Baganda mobilized to defend their Kabaka in May. He came very close to losing the first. The steps he took to stay in power made the policy of ethnic departicipation possible. But its implementation over the following five years left the Baganda with a heightened sense of their own ethnicity. Whether this was a necessary cost that Obote had to pay or poor statesmanship is a difficult issue to resolve.

With hindsight, it is possible to see that at the time of independence, the national leadership of the UPC was somewhat more committed to the reduction of ethnic political participation than was the DP and certainly more so than was KY. In 1960, the year the UPC was formed out of Obote's wing of the UNC and the anti-Buganda Uganda People's Union (UPU), Obote asserted that "African nationalism hates small states."[1] In March 1963, he stated that the "tribe" has "served

1. *Uganda Argus,* 3 February 1960, quoted in Ali A. Mazrui, "Violent Contiguity and the Politics of Retribalization in Africa," *Journal of International Affairs* 23, no. 1 (1969): 101.

our people as a basic political unit very well in the past. [But now] the problem of people putting the tribe above national consciousness is a problem that we must face, and an issue we must destroy."[2]

In spite of its coalition with KY, between 1962 and 1964 the UPC took a number of steps to counter ethnic politics — many of which were perceived to be carried out at the expense of the Baganda. A number of the demands of the Buganda government for *ebbyaffe* ("our things") were rejected by the center, whose position was sustained by the courts. The UPC refused to concede Buganda to KY and began organizing party branches there in 1963.[3] In spite of its sympathy for the Baamba and Bakonzo, the central government steadfastly refused to grant their demands for a separate district.

Before 1966, however, Obote was far too weak to insist upon changes in the political process that might have resulted in ethnic departicipation. Indeed, several ethnic political initiatives were taken by the UPC leadership, particularly in the preindependence period. In 1961, for example, the UPC members of the Legislative Council pressed the governor to grant many of Buganda's demands.[4] Their speeches were public signals demonstrating their good faith in the negotiations then being carried out with the Kabaka's government. The alliance with Buganda ensured that the independence constitution would have several federal features. Furthermore, the UPC attempted to strengthen its position in the 1962 elections by calling upon the secretary of state for the colonies to negotiate federal status for Busoga and the three western kingdoms. Thus, the UPC helped to reinforce some of the bases of ethnic political participation.

Obote was also hampered by a variety of overlapping factional disputes within the UPC in spite of the majority the party held in parliament and in district councils by the end of 1964. In a bitter fight for the position of UPC secretary-general, John Kakonge, the candidate of radicals calling for national mobiliza-

2. Quoted in Donald Rothchild and Michael Rogin, "Uganda," in *National Unity and Regionalism in Eight African States,* ed. Gwendolen M. Carter (Ithaca, N.Y.: Cornell University Press, 1966), p. 418.

3. Cherry Gertzel, "How Kabaka Yekka Came To Be," *Africa Report* 9, no. 9 (October 1964): 12.

4. G. S. K. Ibingira, *The Forging of an African Nation: The Political and Constitutional Evolution of Uganda from Colonial Rule to Independence, 1894-1962* (New York: The Viking Press, 1973), pp. 204, 243, and 221.

tion, lost by only two votes to Grace Ibingira, a representative of more conservative local notables with close links to the Kabaka's government.

A year later the struggle for control of the UPC and the government (which was serious enough to produce rumors of a coup on independence day, 1965) brought Ibingira and his followers into direct rivalry with Obote in the cabinet and party ranks.[5] The crisis came to a head on 4 February 1966, while Obote was out of Kampala on tour in the north. In his absence the cabinet – many of whose members were out of town – suddenly reversed an earlier decision and scheduled immediate debate on a motion brought by Daudi Ocheng, born an Acholi but nonetheless a parliamentary member of KY. Ocheng's motion called for a commission of inquiry to investigate charges of corruption against the second-ranking army officer, Colonel Idi Amin. The charges, which grew out of alleged gold smuggling across the Zairean border, implicated the prime minister and two other members of the cabinet – Obote's cousin Adoko Nekyon and the minister of defense, Felix Onama.

Only half of the members of the cabinet came to the debate, but most of these spoke in favor of the inquiry. The motion passed overwhelmingly. On 13 February a new election was held for a UPC branch chairmanship in Buganda. Godfrey Binaisa, the attorney general and a supporter of Obote, was defeated by another Muganda, Dr. E. Lumu, a close associate of Ibingira. On 14 February the cabinet decided to establish an independent commission to inquire into the charges of corruption. Obote's control of the government and the UPC seemed to have ebbed away to the point where he was virtually isolated.[6]

5. Andre de la Rue (pseud.), "The Rise and Fall of Grace Ibingira," *The New African* 5, no. 10 (December 1966). On the political conflict in the UPC during 1965-1966, see also M. Crawford Young, "The Obote Revolution," *Africa Report* 11, no. 6 (June 1966); Emory Bundy, "Uganda's New Constitution," *East Africa Journal* 3, no. 4 (June 1966); G. F. Engholm, "Buganda's Struggle for Power," *New Society*, 2 June 1966. For accounts of these events by Obote, see "The Footsteps of Uganda's Revolution," *East Africa Journal* 5, no. 10 (October 1968): 12-13, and "Myths and Realities," *The People* (Supplement), 29 August 1970, pp. iii-iv. The last account was prepared by mid-November 1968.

6. In fact, matters reached the point where, Obote says, two units of troops were ordered "to start shelling Kampala" and the parliament building while he was in the north on 7 February 1966, but they refused to obey orders. Another platoon was then sent on the same day to arrest him. 'Myths and Realities," p. iv. The Kabaka

During this time, however, he quietly and carefully consolidated his support among strategic political and military figures. On 22 February he struck back by having five ministers, including Ibingira and Lumu, arrested during a cabinet meeting and by temporarily taking over all powers of the government. Two days later Obote announced that the constitution was suspended. About this time the commander of the army, Brigadier Shaban Opolot visited Edward Mutesa, the president and the Kabaka. An attempt to rally troops against Obote failed. On 2 March Obote assumed full executive authority with the advice and consent of the cabinet. This action effectively abolished the offices of the president and the vice-president. Obote accused Mutesa of approaching foreign powers and discussing possible military intervention. The Kabaka admitted raising the question with the British high commissioner.[7]

In March a commission of inquiry deliberately composed of respected jurists from outside Uganda was appointed to look into Ocheng's charges. Little substantial evidence was brought forward, though testimony did indicate an enormous increase in Colonel Amin's personal bank account. Obote testified that the money was intended for the purpose of buying supplies for Congolese rebel forces, though he conceded that it was unwise for Amin to use his personal account for this purpose.[8] The case against the accused government officials seemed to collapse.

The impact of the impartial public hearings of the commission, the admissions of the Kabaka, the lack of public support for the arrested ministers, and the surprisingly calm atmosphere in which government officers carried out their normal duties helped to swing public opinion behind Obote once again. On 15 April the National Assembly was suddenly convened, and a new

claims that Obote was requested to return by the cabinet and that the brigadier (Shaban Opolot) sent "a guard to escort Obote to Kampala, as it seemed possible that he would need one." *Desecration of My Kingdom* (London: Constable, 1967), p. 186.

7. Kabaka, *Desecration of My Kingdom*, p. 186.

8. The report of the commission was not published until after Amin's coup. See *Evidence and Findings of the Commission of Enquiry into Allegations Made by the Late Daudi Ocheng on 4th February 1966* (Kampala: Uganda Publishing House, 1971).

constitution was presented to the members for immediate action, with no opportunity for debate. The opposition and four government members walked out. The "revolutionary" constitution was enacted by fifty-five votes to four.[9]

The 1966 constitution kept many of the articles of its predecessor but removed several of the legal provisions that encouraged ethnic participation. Among the three major changes was the virtual elimination of autonomous powers of districts and federal kingdoms. The finances of district councils were to be more carefully supervised by the central government. The councils lost the power to appoint local civil servants. Second, the Buganda government lost a number of prerogatives, including its entrenched privilege of indirectly electing its members to the National Assembly, and the right to give official lands to chiefs and Buganda ministers as perquisites of office. The Kabaka (as well as other kingdom rulers) was reduced to a ceremonial position on the same level as constitutional heads in the districts. Henceforth Buganda was to be treated as a district no different from any of the others. By severely weakening the position of civil service chiefs as well as the Mengo government's control over them, the 1966 constitution crippled the organizational framework that had given the KY its overwhelming success in rural areas.

A third important change was a significant enlargement of the powers of the head of government — as much a result of the way the constitution was amended as it was a result of the new provisions themselves. The largely ceremonial presidency was merged with the office of the prime minister. Most of the formal powers of the new office had existed in the 1962 constitution, however. These three changes — elimination of the independent powers of the districts and kingdoms, removal of Buganda's special privileges, and creation of a new and more powerful presidency — provided a new legal framework that was instrumental in ethnic departicipation.

Most Baganda (particularly those under the sway of the

9. The 1962 constitution was quite difficult to amend. It required a two-thirds vote in the National Assembly and concurrence by all federal assemblies for some of the changes included in the 1966 document. Obote was not likely to achieve a two-thirds majority for sweeping changes with five UPC members detained and with DP and KY members in opposition. In addition, the Buganda Lukiiko would certainly have rejected any proposal that Obote placed before them at this time.

traditionalists) reacted angrily to this sudden attack on their prerogatives. The Lukiiko rejected the new constitution and on 20 May ordered the central government to withdraw from Buganda. Three Buganda county chiefs and Amos Sempa, an important member of the Baganda elite and former Ugandan minister of finance, were arrested by central government police two days later.

Baganda interpreted the arrests as a move against the Kabaka, since those arrested had little personal popularity and were unlikely to pose a threat to the central government.[10] They responded with the most violent forms of ethnic political participation employed by Baganda since independence. They rioted, blocked roads, burned bridges, and attacked police stations. Baganda ex-servicemen went to the Kabaka's palace, the Lubiri, which was later surrounded by Uganda army and Special Force units. After brief but fierce fighting on 24 May the central government captured the palace, and the Kabaka escaped to England, where he resided until his death in 1969. Whether leaders on either side intended to precipitate a decisive military encounter is unclear.[11] The result, however, was a symbol of Buganda's subordinate position and the end of federalism in Uganda. From this time forward Obote's government explicitly stressed a policy of ethnic departicipation.

The new constitution was intended to be no more than an interim document, since it specifically provided for the establishment of a constituent assembly at some future time. However, the government did not act until after the 1966 constitution had been tested in the Uganda High Court. In overruling the habeas corpus plea of a former Buganda county chief, the court found that a revolution had taken place "that destroyed the entire legal order and was superseded by a new Constitution, and by effective government. . . ."[12] For these reasons the 1966 constitution was deemed legally valid.

10. Personal communication from Joshua L. Zake, January 1972.
11. Both Obote and Mutesa deny that they intended one. Mutesa regards the central government's intrusion as an inept but intentional military attack. *Desecration of My Kingdom,* pp. 9-14. Obote claims that the army unit was sent to investigate stores of arms. "Myths and Realities," p. i. The first unit sent was small (forty men) and easily repulsed.
12. Uganda v. Commissioner of Prisons, *ex parte* Matovu, *Eastern Africa Law Reports* (1966), p. 515.

With the court decision legitimating the "revolutionary" constitution, the government began to formulate the 1967 "republican" constitution. The approach it took was quite different from the swiftly imposed solution of 1966. The proposed document was issued in June 1967 and subjected to intensive and relatively free debate for over a month by a constituent assembly (made up of members of parliament).[13]   In direct response to the debate, the government amended certain of its proposals, and after brief further discussion, the constitution was adopted on 8 September. Considering the factional struggles in the country only one year before, the performance was deeply impressive. As the president said, "Uganda was probably making history in Africa by having its proposals debated so openly."[14]   The very fact that the central government and the UPC felt sufficiently secure to permit open debate on the fundamental political structure of Uganda was an indication of the degree to which the events of 1966 had shifted political power from district and ethnically oriented groups to those supporting the policies of the national government. More recent events, however, indicate that deep feelings of resentment among the Baganda had not vanished.

The 1967 constitution carried the changes of the previous year another step forward in a careful effort to create conditions that would reduce ethnic participation. First, and of great symbolic importance, the kingdoms were abolished, and the kings (with the exception of the Kabaka) were given pensions. Constitutional heads were also eliminated. Second, Buganda was divided into four districts subject to the minister of regional administrations on the same basis as all other districts.

Third, central government control over district administration was further tightened by giving the National Assembly the power to determine the form district administration should take and the right to provide for appointment rather than election of members of district councils. Fourth, the requirement that boundaries of constituencies of MPs be limited by district

13. Views expressed in the debate are briefly summarized in Nelson Kasfir, "The 1967 Uganda Constituent Assembly Debate," *Transition* 7, no. 2 (October-November 1967).

14. *East African Standard* (Nairobi), 5 August 1967.

boundaries was eliminated — another indication that the role of districts was to be reduced in the future.

The attack on ethnic politics was also extended by the central government's clarification of its policy toward the districts in the wake of the Acholi-Lango factory dispute six months later. Acholi and Lango are neighboring districts populated almost entirely by those possessing the objective characteristics of Acholi and Langi, respectively. The boundary between them has been disputed for many years. The issue remained a live one and was debated in the Acholi district council in 1967.[15] One of the first demands of Langi nationalists was to call for replacement of Acholi as the language of instruction in Lango primary schools.[16]

In February 1968 the Acholi district council, employing a typical pre-1966 pattern of linkage, sent a delegation containing UPC (and one DP) members to Kampala to complain about unfair distribution of industry between the two districts. [17] Their principal complaint was that a textile factory that they claimed had been intended for an Acholi site was now to be placed in Lango. At the same time the DP introduced a motion in parliament asking the government to support an existing proposal to build it in Gulu, the capital of Acholi. The issue was especially sensitive, since Obote comes from Lango.

The textile factory was to be run by the Uganda Development Corporation and was one of the largest projects the UDC had ever undertaken. The Soviet Union had agreed in 1964 to lend £3 million to help build the factory.[18] On at least two occasions, Soviet experts carried out feasibility studies on possible sites. The government made an early decision that the project should be located in the north as part of its strategy to decentralize industry in order to promote even economic devel-

15. See the discussion in *Parliamentary Debates* (Uganda), vol. 46 (Entebbe: Government Printer, 1965), pp. 1948-1949; and *The People,* 13 April 1968, p. 11.

16. Young, "The Obote Revolution," p. 12.

17. This account is based primarily on the debate in the National Assembly. *Parliamentary Debates,* 2d series, vol. 81, 15-21 February 1968. See also reports in *Uganda Argus* and *The People* from the middle of February through the middle of April 1968. I am also grateful to Garth Glentworth for information relating to the role of the Uganda Development Corporation (UDC) in this dispute.

18. The UDC had to put up the remainder. Rising costs have greatly increased its share.

opment throughout the country. Several sites in both Acholi and Lango — the major cotton-growing areas in the north — were under consideration. The government had also hoped to put the project into a rural area, but the total absence of any supporting facilities made that too costly.

After the Soviet experts completed their second study, a Soviet economic adviser announced that the factory would be located close to Gulu.[19] In the parliamentary debate five months later, however, the government claimed that no final decision had been made, since certain proposed facilities had not been costed and since the USSR would not release its study until Uganda paid £50,000. As a matter of fact, though, the government had decided the previous November that the project would be located in Lango, either at Lira, the district capital, or Atura Ferry.[20] Lira was ultimately chosen.

In the debate J. M. Okae, the minister of planning and economic development (and an MP from Lango), admitted that there were difficulties with all the potential sites, particularly concerning adequate water, but stressed that Lango produces more cotton than Acholi and is more centrally located among cotton-growing areas.[21] The government was particularly irked by the Acholi demands, since Acholi district had already received a far greater share of development benefits than Lango. "If there is any district which has got nothing so far from this Independence," complained Okae, "it is only Lango."[22]

At the same time other UPC speakers attacked the opposition for suggesting that an MP might demand that a project be placed in his constituency. "If we are going to stop this tribalism there is need for ruthlessness," Onama threatened.[23] The government also took the position that the bipartisan character of the district council delegation indicated that its members

19. *Uganda Argus,* 21 September 1967, p. 4.

20. UDC, "Development Committee Memorandum," no. 49/67, 30 November 1967.

21. Work on expansion of the Lira water supply was still continuing in early 1974. *Voice of Uganda,* 25 January 1974, p. 9. From 1960 through 1964 Lango produced an average of three bales of cotton for every two grown in Acholi. *Annual Report for the Department of Agriculture for the Year Ended 31st December 1964* (Entebbe: Government Printer, n.d.).

22. *Parliamentary Debates,* vol. 81, p. 2998.

23. *Parliamentary Debates,* vol. 81, p. 3094.

were coming as representatives of the Acholi "tribe," not as members of a political party. In doing so the district secretary-general and his assistant had violated party policy. As a result they were dismissed and replaced by the leaders of the other Acholi UPC faction. In a long article in the party newspaper, the allegations put forward by the Acholi district council were also attacked. The government argued that the district council and MPs had no business discussing a matter to be decided upon by experts in the Ministry of Planning in consultation with the Russian foreign aid team.

The minister of regional administrations, James Ochola, explained that the districts had to carry out central government policy and could not formulate policies of their own. "It was the Government's aim," he added a few months later, "to guide and advise administrations to make the best use of their resources and to direct the Government's policies to the benefit of various areas and of the country as a whole."[24]

However, no matter how pure the government's original motives may have been, the UPC leadership created a dilemma by simultaneously insisting that public policies eschew ethnicity and directing that the project be located in the home district of Obote, Okae, and Nekyon — and this in spite of at least one contrary report by outside experts. This dilemma undoubtedly weakened popular acceptance of the government's policy of ethnic departicipation. A year later many Acholi district councillors were still refusing to cooperate with their new secretary-general, whom they had previously repudiated when he had held the job several years earlier.[25] And when the coup occurred, the soldiers were quick to call attention to the "Russian textile factory to be situated in Lango."[26]

In spite of this sort of reaction, the UPC leaders, having chosen this rationale, firmly committed themselves to pursuing its implications for the three years in office remaining to them. The UPC overhauled its party structure in June 1968 in an

24. *Uganda Argus,* 11 July 1968, p. 6.
25. *Uganda Argus,* 13 January 1969, p. 6; and *Uganda Argus,* 25 January 1969, p. 5.
26. *The People,* 27 January 1971, p. 3. The "18 points" that constituted the manifesto of the coup also suggested that the Obote government had decided "that nothing of importance must be done for other districts especially Acholi District." Ibid., p. 1.

effort to eliminate its earlier tendencies toward ethnic factionalism. The new structure maintained a dual hierarchy of conference and executive at three of its four levels — the parish, parliamentary constituency, and national.[27] However, the district level was frozen out both by the absence of a district conference and by the maintenance of direct communication between the constituency executives and the national executive. The new "system was intended to abolish regionalism which was encouraging differences in the party."[28] Thus, the district party organization, an important focus of ethnic participation in past years, was eliminated. Party membership was specifically restricted to Ugandan citizens who did "not support tribalism and parochialism. . . ."[29]

The decision to hold national elections in 1971 provided a major, though abortive, test for the government's policy of ethnic departicipation. Elections mean participation, and participation is likely to lead to ethnic mobilization. Discussing electoral strategy in 1964, Ibingira, then minister of state, had reminded elected members of the UPC that "all politicians, even members of Parliament or of District Councils, will be forced, in order to get votes from the common man, since they have to speak the language he understands, to speak in terms of tribe or religion no matter how much, when we go to higher places, we may wish to deny that this is a fact."[30]

Although Ibingira had been thinking in terms of multiparty competition, the issue worried Obote six years later, even though the UPC was to be the only party permitted to participate in the 1971 elections.

The 1970 elections of chairmen of UPC party branch and

27. *Constitution of the Uganda People's Congress: Adopted by the Fourth National Delegates Conference 11th June 1968* (Kampala: UPC National Headquarters Secretariat, n.d.), pp. 12-25. See also Michael Davies, "Structure of the Government Party: The Uganda People's Congress, and its Potential as a Means of Communication," stenciled (Kampala: Uganda Institute of Public Administration, June 1968).

28. Felix Onama (then secretary-general of the UPC) in *Uganda Argus,* 28 April 1969, p. 2.

29. *Constitution of the Uganda People's Congress,* p. 11.

30. "The State of the UPC in the Kingdoms and Districts," letter to the prime minister, all ministers, parliamentary secretaries, and UPC back-benchers, 7 March 1964.

constituency organizations tended to support Ibingira's argument. The conflicts that surfaced during these elections showed that it would take time for the new policy to take root. In Jinja, in Kampala, and in rural constituencies in Busoga, Buganda, and Kigezi, ethnic considerations played an important and sometimes decisive role.[31] Obote himself was under no illusions that government measures promoting ethnic departicipation between 1966 and 1970 had eliminated ethnicity as a political force. He warned that

> if the pull of the tribal force is allowed to develop, the unity of the country will be endangered. To reduce it to its crudest form, the pull of the tribal force does not accept Uganda as one country, does not accept the people of Uganda as belonging to one country, does not accept the National Assembly as a national institution but as an assembly of peace conference delegates and tribal diplomatic and legislative functionaries, and looks at the Government of Uganda as a body of umpires or referees in some curious game of "Tribal Development Monopoly."[32]

The electoral solution he proposed to meet this dilemma was most ingenious.

Instead of the conventional system of having each candidate run in a single constituency, he proposed that all candidates should run simultaneously in four constituencies, each in a different region.[33] One of these constituencies, would be the "basic" constituency with which a successful candidate would be associated in parliament, while the remaining three would be his "national" constituencies. Thus, the two or three candidates

31. D. L. Cohen and J. Parson, "The Uganda People's Congress Branch and Constituency Elections of 1970," *Journal of Commonwealth Political Studies* 11, no. 1 (March 1973): 58-60.

32. *Proposals for New Methods of Election of Representatives of the People to Parliament: Document No. 5 on the Move to the Left* (Kampala: Milton Obote Foundation, 1970), pp. 6-7.

33. Ibid., pp. 18-24. For a discussion of problems raised by the proposals, see Selwyn Ryan, "Electoral Engineering in Uganda," *Mawazo* (Kampala) 2, no. 4 (December 1970): 3-8. Following the Tanzanian model, the proposals were based on the assumption of a single-party system in which competing candidates would be nominated through the party organization.

for each basic constituency would have to carry their campaign to three additional areas, a requirement which — given the ethnic distribution of Ugandans — would necessarily force them to appeal to voters of at least four different ethnic units. [34] Ethnically oriented promises or attacks by a candidate in one constituency would be quickly communicated to voters in another by his opponent.

Presumably this would deter ethnic politics and promote the success of candidates with a national orientation. In addition, the system insured that "leaders [will] be conversant with the problems and issues, as well as what goes on, throughout Uganda." [35] The proposal underlined the determination of the government to introduce elections which would not reverse its policy of ethnic departication, but Amin's coup interrupted this experiment before it could be carried out.

UPC leaders made additional decisions to place ethnic appeals outside the rules of the political game. The question on "tribe" was quietly dropped from the 1969 census form. County chiefs in multiethnic districts were, for the first time since the Baganda agents had departed, transferred out of the counties in which they shared the objective ethnic characteristics of most of the inhabitants. [36] Also, when UPC party elections were held in 1970, the supervisors were drawn from all over the country and posted to areas outside their home district. [37] Top political leaders and the party newspaper were emphatic in their condemnations of all appeals to "tribalism." [38]

After Amin's coup, Obote summarized the basic approach his government took toward ethnic departication. He felt that

> we did not have any special formular for dealing with
> cultural subnationalism. In a few cases we used both

34.   Side-linkages (see note 1, chapter six) or alliances were rumored to have sprung up among aspirants in different areas. These would have had to be extraordinarily complex, since each set of four constituencies might have been different from each additional set. See Ryan, "Electoral Engineering in Uganda," n. 12, p. 7.

35.   Obote, *Proposals for New Methods of Election,* p. 12.

36.   *Uganda Argus,* 23 January 1968, p. 3.

37.   Cohen and Parson, "The Uganda People's Congress Branch and Constituency Elections of 1970," p. 55.

38.   For statements by Obote see *His Excellency The President's Communication from the Chair of the National Assembly on 11th February 1969* (Entebbe: Government Printer, 1969); and A. Milton Obote, *The Common Man's Charter* (Entebbe: Government Printer, 1970).

the letter and the spirit of the Constitution. Such cases include the Lost Counties, the Mbale Territory and Lango/Acholi border. In Districts with more than one Community (tribe) we adopted the policy of Chiefs being posted to areas other than those of their communities. The basic policy, however, was to reduce the importance of the District Councils and District Administrations. This had some demerits but it was being compensated by the other side of the basic policy, the projection of the centre — the National Government and the National Assembly — as the most important institutions. The compensation was that more and more attention was being paid to the centre. In the Party, we made the once powerful District Committee (Executive) to be consultative and provided for direct dealings between the Constituency Executive Committee and the Party Headquarters.

These experiments have been disturbed. . . .[39]

Two sorts of questions can be raised in assessing the implementation of this policy by the UPC. First, how did the government respond when the goal of removing ethnicity conflicted with another goal considered equally important? Second, could this policy have been carried out more successfully?

Choosing languages for broadcasting on the government radio illustrates the problem of conflict between goals. Full implementation of ethnic departicipation necessarily contradicts another important policy, effective communication between the center and the periphery. Unlike Kenya and Tanzania, Uganda has no language that is understood throughout the country. The introduction of any language besides the vernacular in a local area has caused political problems in the past.[40] Although communication in the vernacular permits effective understanding, it may also serve as a focus for ethnic political participation. Rivalries over the use of scarce air time are likely to bring the language issue into politics.

39. Personal communication, August 1971.

40. W. H. Whiteley gives several examples. "Language Choice and Language Planning in East Africa," in *Tradition and Transition in East Africa: Studies of the Tribal Element in the Modern Era,* ed. P. H. Gulliver (London: Routledge & Kegan Paul, 1969), p. 120.

The Obote government decided to increase the number of languages instead of following a policy of departicipation, and for three years the Amin regime did likewise. At independence, broadcasts were made in five languages. The number increased to fourteen by 1967, eighteen by 1969, and twenty-one by July 1972.[41] Political pressure led to the addition of some languages.[42] But Obote was quick to point to other reasons as well:

> We want to inform the people of Uganda. We find it exceedingly difficult to inform the Karamojong in Luganda or in any other language except their own, so we have Karamojong broadcast on the Radio. Then we use the Radio for educational purposes and we find that to assist those who never went to school at all, we must broadcast in their own mother tongues.[43]

Additional languages mean higher financial costs, especially for staff, and greater repetition of the same information, which leads to bored listeners.[44] More difficult to resolve, perhaps, is the conflict with a policy of de-emphasizing ethnicity.

The conflict between other goals and ethnic departicipation reflects a fundamental paradox in the development process. The

41. A. Milton Obote, "Language and National Identification," *East Africa Journal* 4, no. 1 (April 1967): 5; Apolo Nsibambi, "Language Policy in Uganda: An Investigation into Costs and Politics," *African Affairs* 70, n. 278 (January 1971): 62; and *Uganda Argus,* 3-8 July 1972. The languages used in July 1972 were Lwo, Ateso, Kiswahili, Luganda, Lugbara, Karamojong, Kakwa, Madi, Alur, Runyankore/Rukiga, Lusoga, Rukonzo, Runyoro/Rutoro, Kupsabiny, Lunyole/Lusamia/Lugwe, Lumasaba, Kumam, Dhopadhola, English, French, and Arabic. Hindustani had been dropped. Amin added Rukonzo, Kiswahili, Arabic, and French.

At the end of 1973 a government spokesman announced that the number of languages was to be cut to eleven (retaining French, Arabic, English, Kiswahili, and seven vernaculars) from 1 January 1974. *Voice of Uganda,* 20 December 1973, p. 6.

42. The Kakwa were insulted by the suggestion that they knew Lugbara and thus did not need to request that their own language be put on the air. "Soon Kakwa was accepted on Radio Uganda." Nsibambi, "Language Policy in Uganda," p. 64. The addition of Rukonzo to Radio Uganda was a long-standing demand of many Rwenzururu partisans. Amin finally obliged them in March 1972. *Uganda Argus,* 13 March 1972, p. 5.

43. "Language and National Identification," p. 6.

44. Nsibambi, "Language Policy in Uganda," pp. 64-65. Complaints rose after the addition of French and Arabic, which are understood by almost nobody in Uganda. *Uganda Argus,* 7 July 1972, p. 1.

UPC government, like most others in Africa, was anxious to increase the growth of the economy as rapidly as possible. But it had to take into account that existing levels of education and employment were differentiated along lines often perceived as ethnic. The location of any new factory raised questions among those who failed to benefit. "A leader," Obote pointed out, "who is a fanatic of tribal hegemony will see any project outside his tribal area as having been sited purely on tribal grounds."[45]

The same problem arose in filling new employment opportunities. To take the best-qualified individual for a job aroused resentment from those denied opportunities for preparation. But to push ahead those from relatively underprivileged areas further embittered those who had acquired higher levels of skill. An official in a public corporation admitted that if two applicants had the same qualifications, his organization would take the non-Muganda.[46] Whichever decision was made, however, distrust would be fueled by increased ethnic suspicion and rivalry. Spurring development heightens ethnic concern.

To some extent the Obote government was able to avoid the problem by greatly expanding the resources available for distribution. By 1971 the total number of government hospital beds had increased 70 percent over the 1966 figure.[47] The number of secondary school enrollments tripled between 1961 and 1966 and almost doubled again by 1971.[48] University places increased by two and a half times from 1966 to 1971. Thus, in these areas, as in the civil service and more recently in the commercial sector, the government has been able to reduce feelings of deprivation by enlarging the pie.

However, even a growing pie can exacerbate ethnicity, since the government cannot simultaneously put equivalent projects in all areas. To avoid accusations of favoritism, the government sometimes stressed that new projects were located on the basis

45. Obote, *Proposals for New Methods of Election*, p. 7. The vehemence of his statement suggests that in 1971 he still felt under considerable pressure from ethnic middlemen pressing for new industries.

46. Conversation, March 1969.

47. *Uganda's Plan III: Third Five-Year Development Plan 1971/2-1975/6* (Entebbe: Government Printer, 1972), p. 308.

48. *Work for Progress: Uganda's Second Five-Year Plan, 1966-1971* (Entebbe: Government Printer, 1966), p. 137; and *Uganda's Plan III*, pp. 335 and 346.

of technical criteria and sometimes insisted that services were distributed equally.[49]   Thus, the third five-year plan argues that "the requirements of national cohesion dictate that the various regions of the country should enjoy comparable standards of living."[50]

These constraints — generated by conflict among desirable goals — left little room for maneuvering and required delicate choices by the government. The basic strategy of the UPC was to press for equal development. However, controversies like the one over the textile factory that ended up in Lango marred its image and raised questions about the impartiality of its leaders. To promote an ethnic departicipation policy in this context could only undercut its very goals.

All policies exact their own price — in this case exacerbation of the tendency toward ethnic definition by the losers. The UPC's approach to ethnic departicipation was aggravated further, however, because it rested on a direct confrontation with the members of a unit that the government, as well as those affected, persisted in treating as Baganda. Once again Obote was presented with a virtually intractable paradox. The issue, then, is whether he could have handled it better.

The bitterness of the Baganda over the sudden withdrawal of their special status ran deep. Much of what the government accomplished in its attack on ethnic politics was seen to take place at their expense. While agreeing with much in the 1967 constitutional proposals, E. M. K. Mulira, a progressive nationalist from Buganda, conceded that "I cannot however sign a death warrant for kingship, because it would be tantamount to writing one's own obituary."[51]   Baganda of high and low status, from farmers to university students, displayed intense grief when they heard about the death of the Kabaka, a refugee in London, in late 1969. The extraordinary enthusiasm they showed for Amin's coup — far more than was observed elsewhere in Ugan-

49. Occasionally the government manages to bring these often contradictory principles of allocation together in justifying a project. For example, the twenty-two new rural hospitals "are being sited in places where hospital services are most needed, with an even distribution between regions." *Work for Progress,* p. 151.

50. *Uganda's Plan III,* p. 5. The planners' solution is to create more rapid growth in poorer areas. Amin has called for "the even distribution of industries throughout Uganda." *Uganda Argus,* 15 December 1971, p. 1.

51. *Uganda Argus,* 1 July 1967.

da — also demonstrates their alienation from the Obote government.

If ethnic departicipation succeeded temporarily in Buganda, it was at the cost of disaffection that must have intensified feelings of ethnic identity. Obote was partly responsible because he destroyed many of the symbols of Buganda and consequently evoked a situation in which people felt themselves under attack *as Baganda.* The central government permitted the Kabaka's palace in Kampala to be turned into an army barracks and the Bulange, home of the Lukiiko, to become an office building for the Ministry of Defense. [52] The official name of the road between these two buildings was changed from Kabaka Anjagala ("The Kabaka loves me") to Republic Avenue. In addition, the boundaries of Kampala were extended, with the effect of removing the separate identity of Mengo, the municipal seat of the former Kabaka's government. Among the former rulers only the Kabaka was not offered a pension following the introduction of the 1967 constitution. Finally, the UPC government refused permission to bring the Kabaka's body back for burial at home.

These moves served as continuous reminders to Baganda of their defeat on the field of battle. For the most part the Baganda retreated into political passivity for the rest of Obote's period of office. [53] On occasion, however, disaffection burst into violent participation. More than one attempt was made on Obote's life. He was wounded in an attempted assassination in December 1969. Several Baganda were arrested (and later released by Amin, who claimed that they were not involved).

Obote could not avoid the paradox that the pursuit of ethnic departicipation would kindle ethnic feelings among those whose privileges were removed. But he could have made greater efforts to conciliate the Baganda and to persuade them to consider new forms of identity. To do so would have meant avoiding measures that singled out Baganda by destroying their symbols. The

52. The central government did pay the four new districts created out of Buganda for the building.

53. There were relatively few violent incidents and virtually no demonstrations of the sort that followed the exile of the Kabaka in 1953. Conversations with central government staff posted to the new districts in the former Buganda kingdom indicated that opposition to the government remained widespread in 1970, however.

political calculus that led him to exacerbate feelings of ethnicity in this fashion remains puzzling, though some of the factors that may have contributed can be identified.

Obote was heavily dependent on maintaining good relations with important figures in the army, as their shadowy role in the 1966 confrontations suggests. These men may have insisted that the historic reversal of status they perceived as the outcome of the events of 1966 be celebrated symbolically. In addition, UPC leaders may have felt that the complete elimination of the symbols of ethnicity might be necessary before those possessing the objective characteristics of Baganda would come to regard themselves otherwise. And Obote may have felt that the resentment that people elsewhere in Uganda bore toward Baganda was a useful political resource – one that could be employed to increase support outside Buganda for a policy of ethnic departicipation, in spite of its consequences for the victims.

The combination of political fortune and personal values caused the UPC government to oppose public assertion of ethnicity for political reward. To a large degree, the success of this policy was restricted by the pattern of uneven development inherited from the past and the requirements of other important but conflicting policies. Within those limits, however, the government could have done better. Its statesmanship was flawed by its handling of the symbols of Baganda ethnicity and by its insistence on promoting that policy in a public debate on a development project in which its intentions were suspect. All the same, a relatively consistent policy had emerged and – given sufficient time to mature – might have greatly reduced the emphasis placed on ethnicity by eliminating many situations within which popular ethnic response would have been likely to occur.

2. EXPERIMENTS DISTURBED: AMIN'S APPROACH
TO ETHNICITY

Explanations of the actions of Amin and his government must be considered with much caution because his policies seem to change from day to day. His approach to ethnic departicipation seems to retain the central principle of Obote's stand against ethnicity while reversing most major details. Departicipation, of course, is more complete than before.

"We want," said Amin a month after taking power, "to build

our country as a single united and strong nation, and not as a federation of petty and powerless tribes that are jealous of one another."[54]   On various occasions Amin has reiterated his opposition to "tribalism" and his insistence that "kingdoms will not be re-introduced."[55]   To this extent the Obote policy continues to guide the country.

However, Amin has wavered on the point of kingship and has not followed his own pronouncement opposing "tribalism." The contrast with Obote could hardly be more vivid. The reasons for the contradiction in Amin's approach grow out of three problems that he had to face when he carried out his coup. First, he had to explain why he intervened (or, in his version, why the "soldiers" intervened and then insisted he accept office). Second, he had to adopt measures that would immediately increase his legitimacy; and, finally, he had to cope with the ethnic problems which remained subterranean factors in Ugandan politics. In each case he laid stress on ethnicity in explaining political behavior.

Amin's difficulty in justifying the coup was a consequence of the awkward fact that he took power without the support of a large segment of the army.[56]   His explanation presumed that his opponents were guided primarily by ethnicity. He contended that he was forced to act because "Acholi and Langi" soldiers attempted to disarm soldiers of other "tribes" on Obote's orders. He then stepped in to prevent a "mutiny."[57]   There is

54. "Speech to the Nation by His Excellency Major-General Idi Amin Dada," *The Uganda Gazette* 64, no. 8 (26 February 1971): 79.

55. *Uganda Argus,* 2 February 1971, p. 1; *The People,* 11 February 1971, p. 1; *The People,* 15 February 1971, p. 1; *Uganda Argus,* 11 October 1971, p. 1; and *Uganda Argus,* 26 January 1972, p. 5.

56. The split in the army between those who supported Amin and those who remained loyal to Obote accounts for Amin's constant references throughout much of 1971 to "guerrillas" attacking Uganda and for the massacres of soldiers and officers which came to public attention in June and July 1971. See Colin Legum's report in *The Observer* (London), 25 July 1971, p. 5; and Obote's analysis in *The Standard* (Tanzania), 15 February 1971, p. 3. Amin deplored the fighting in the barracks in a speech to a police unit. *Uganda Argus,* 17 August 1971, p. 1. This split makes it impossible to attribute much weight to economic "class" as a corporate motivation for the military intervention, as suggested in Michael F. Lofchie, "The Uganda Coup – Class Action by the Military," *The Journal of Modern African Studies* 10, no. 1 (May 1972): *passim.*

57. *The People,* 27 January 1971, p. 1. The author of the "18 points" avoided this political error and took care to point out "Acholi" grievances against Obote. See the quotation cited in note 26 above.

no conclusive evidence yet to establish whether the loyalty of part of the army to Obote was based on ethnic identity or whether Amin chose to interpret it in that fashion to obscure the limits of support within the army for his coup. By casting political action in ethnic terms, however, he immediately created a threatening situation for people — both inside and outside the army — who were easily identified as Acholi and Langi. From the start, therefore, he reversed Obote's policy of avoiding all public reference to ethnic units as political actors.

The rationale for intervention set the tone for Amin's remarks for several months. The new government claimed that Obote had been "picking out his own tribesmen and putting them in key positions in the Army and everywhere."[58] In March it published a "document" labeled the "Lango Development Master Plan," which had been mentioned in the "18 points" originally advanced to explain the coup.[59] It turned out to be a crude letter (possibly a forgery) written *to* Obote in 1967 explaining how he could remain in power for fifty years by appointing Langi to high places and siting new industries in certain districts. Its contents do not suggest that it had a discernible impact on Obote's policies. These charges against the Langi also sought to play upon fears of the General Service intelligence unit, which was directed by Akena-Adoko, a Langi and Obote's cousin.

One of the most productive techniques employed by Amin's government to gain legitimacy in its first few months of rule was to offer ethnic concessions to those hurt most by Obote's policies. The Baganda were the main recipients. The major tactic adopted by the government was to offer them symbolic rewards which had the effect of reinforcing their ethnic identity. Releasing fifty-five of ninety-two detainees, many of whom were publicly recognized as prominent Baganda, lifting the state of emergency, and, most important, holding a state funeral for the Kabaka were significant gestures by the regime.[60] In what appears to have been a compromise, certain

58. *The People,* 27 January 1971, p. 1.
59. *Uganda Argus,* 5 March 1971, pp. 1, 4, and 7.
60. *The People,* 29 January 1971, p. 1; "Speech to the Nation by Amin," p. 80; *The People,* 5 April 1971, p. 1; and "Out of Africa," *Africa Report* 16, no. 6 (June 1971): 6.

ceremonies were held at Bamunanika, one of the former Kabaka's palaces, to give his son Ronald Mutebi some of the
indicia of the Kabakaship without actually making him Kabaka.
The names of East and West Mengo districts were changed to
East and West Buganda, thus restoring the name *Buganda* to a
sort of official status. The Baganda were genuinely enthusiastic
about the coup as well as these government actions.[61]

Other moves had symbolic significance to previously mobilized ethnic groups in other parts of the country. Amin went
out of his way to consult the former kings and constitutional
heads and even released one from prison.[62] The first new
districts to be created since independence were introduced by
dividing Acholi and Karamoja.[63] Baamba and Bakonzo middlemen immediately demanded that Amin consider their claim for
separation from Toro district. Amin's approach in this case was
to arrange a meeting with several of the old and discredited
leaders on both sides.[64] As a result they gained a quasi-legiti-
mate standing to pursue ethnic demands. Having resurrected the
dispute, Amin left it suspended by referring it to a commission
of inquiry that never met. Both Baamba and Bakonzo finally
received two new districts, however, in the sweeping administrative reorganization of the whole country that Amin announced
in August 1972.[65]

61. They were not, however, instrumental in the coup itself. A. G. G. Gingyera-
Pinycwa, "A. M. Obote, the Baganda, and the Uganda Army," *Mawazo* (Kampala) 3,
no. 2 (December 1971): 44.

62. *The People,* 17 February 1971, p. 1, and 18 February 1971, p. 1. Amin said
that it was wrong of Obote to treat "these people as enemies," and thus he was
calling them to meet him — presumably to rectify that "error." "Speech to the
Nation by Amin," p. 79.

63. *The People,* 22 March 1971, p. 1, and 9 April 1971, p. 1. East Acholi
notables had made several previous attempts to gain their own district.

64. *The People,* 4-6 May 1971. The Rwenzururu kingdom government rejected
the possibility of a separate district as a derogation of its independent status.

65. *Uganda Argus,* 30 August 1972, p. 2. The changes were put into effect in
early 1974. However, the boundaries of the ten new provinces and thirty-eight new
districts functioning in April 1974 were strikingly different from those announced in
August 1972. It is significant that even by the later date the government did not
regard these boundaries as final. Furthermore, in several cases the April 1974
boundaries reflected ethnic quarrels of the late colonial period. Both the nature of
the changes between 1972 and 1974 and the hesitation of the government to confirm
them strongly suggest that at least a low volume of ethnic political participation —
which revived dormant feelings of ethnicity — occurred under military rule.

218 ETHNIC POLITICAL PARTICIPATION IN UGANDA

As his position became consolidated, Amin introduced new structures to take the place of the district councils he had dissolved. These were councils of "elders," consisting of local notables usually chosen by the district commissioner.[66] The format is strongly reminiscent of colonial efforts to establish indirect rule by building up pseudo- or quasi-traditional structures.[67] The councils of elders are often discussed as if they are based on traditional customs and represent an ethnic unit rather than an administrative area. Who or what they represent, what they do, whether their membership is fixed, and whether their position has been formalized has never been made clear.

They appear to be a forum as much to legitimize government actions as to carry the grievances of the people to the center. In other words, they channel both material and symbolic participation. In some cases it appears that after the government has made a decision, it praises elders who had "previously" submitted memoranda calling for that action. For example, "General Amin again thanked the Elders of Koboko for their advice as how to handle the Church leaders from Namirembe and West Buganda Dioceses."[68] In another case an attempted coup was "revealed" to the government in a "memorandum" submitted by "Alur and Jonam elders."[69]

On the other hand, the Baamba and Bakonzo elders, the Kigezi elders, and the Baganda elders, among others, have made some demands on the government. The Baamba and Bakonzo elders submitted several memoranda requesting a separate district. The Kigezi elders apparently asked for a variety of projects, including a new police post and aid to private schools.[70]

66. Conversation with a Ugandan civil servant, October 1971.

67. The use of councils of elders as participatory structures provides one confirmation of Edward Feit's prediction that "the system that will prevail [in African governments of the future] will, most likely, be an adaptation of administrative and traditional rule along the lines of former colonial government. . . ." "Military Coups and Political Development: Some Lessons from Ghana and Nigeria," in *Governing in Black Africa: Perspectives on New States,* ed. Marion E. Doro and Newell M. Stultz (Englewood Cliffs, N.J.: Prentice-Hall, 1970), p. 232.

68. *Uganda Argus,* 14 December 1971, p. 5. Koboko is in West Nile, and it is unlikely that the Alur elders there were closely acquainted with the religious conflicts within the Protestant establishment in Buganda that were troubling Amin at the time.

69. *Uganda Argus,* 14 October 1971, p. 1.

70. Amin announced that the government had provided solutions to some of the problems these elders had raised. *Uganda Argus,* 21 August 1972, p. 8.

Amin invited 1,200 Baganda elders to discuss their grievances at a meeting in August 1971. They demanded the restoration of the Kabakaship.[71] Perhaps taken by surprise, Amin wavered on his antikingship stand and announced that he would appoint a committee to look into the question and then asked the elders in other districts for their opinions. Two weeks later, statements were sent from several councils of elders announcing that they did not want their constitutional heads back and advising against the restoration of the Kabakaship.[72] They offered virtually the identical reasons that Amin had raised in his discussion with the Baganda elders — financial implications and the rekindling of politics. Whether these messages were actually written by officials from the center or expressed the spontaneous response of anti-Baganda feeling in the districts is impossible to state on the basis of present evidence. At any rate, in his next meeting with the Baganda elders, Amin warned them not to raise the issue of restoration.[73]

In his speeches Amin tends to discuss people as if their ethnic identity were the most salient feature of their personality. In doing so he reinforces ethnic self-definition much as the colonial, DP, and UPC governments did before 1966. For example, he referred to the Obote partisans undergoing military training in Tanzania as mainly "Alur, Acholis [sic], and Bagisu. . . . According to the latest information, Lango [sic] are no longer in the majority. . . . Alurs and Jonams were being smuggled out of the country to Tanzania. . . ."[74] When prisoners were given amnesty in anticipation of the first anniversary of the coup, the number from each ethnic unit was published. In discussing rumors of another coup, Amin said, "Last year there was confusion among the Alur people, then among the Jonams and now it is the Lugbara."

Whether the staffing and operation of the government depends as much on ethnic considerations as these pronouncements by Amin might suggest is extremely hard to discover at

71. *The People*, 6 and 7 August 1971, p. 1.
72. See *Uganda Argus*, 23 August 1971, p. 1 (Lango elders); 25 August 1971, p. 1 (Ankole elders, including the former Omugabe [king]); and 27 August 1971, p. 5 (Madi elders).
73. *Uganda Argus*, 1 October 1971, p. 7.
74. *Uganda Argus*, 14 October 1971, p. 1; 19 January 1972, p. 1; and 8 July 1972, p. 1.

this time. However, the Nubians have become an important political factor since the 1971 coup. They now hold many important positions at the top levels of both the government and the army and seem to have received many of the businesses reallocated by the government after the expulsion of the Indians and Pakistanis. Nubians are particularly interesting for a study of ethnicity because they illustrate the fluidity of ethnic identity. An unusually large proportion of them were born into other ethnic units. They became Nubians by adopting Islam, learning to speak Nubi (an Africanized form of Arabic), and adopting certain Nubi customs.[75] The number of Ugandans engaged in this conversion process is likely to have greatly accelerated since the coup.

Amin's actions and speeches have certainly increased the relevance of ethnicity for Ugandans, both in categorizing people and in explaining their conduct. If he shows signs of losing control, this situation might result in greater ethnic political participation, particularly in the army. Could Amin then prevent ethnic middlemen from mobilizing their followers without losing what little popular support he retains? To prevent that would require extraordinarily subtle political skills of the sort in which Amin — together with military men around the world — has on several occasions pronounced himself deficient.[76]

3. CONCLUSION

Both Obote and Amin saw political advantages in supporting certain ethnic demands when they first became national leaders. Later they both vigorously asserted that national unity meant that ethnicity should be kept out of politics. The difference

75. D. R. Pain, "Ethnicity in a Small Town" (paper delivered to the East African Universities Social Science Council Conference, Nairobi, December 1972), pp. 8-9. Members of this ethnic unit have lived in what is now Uganda for over a hundred years. They even include people who can trace their ancestors back to Northern Nigerians who settled in the Sudan on their way back from Mecca. Nubians were among the "Sudanese soldiers" recruited by the British for the conquest of Bunyoro in the 1890s and later taken into the King's African Rifles. They have only the most doubtful link to the Nubians of the northern Sudan.

76. "I am not a politician, but I am a professional soldier." The People, 27 January 1971, p. 8.

between them is that Obote consistently implemented a government policy that avoided ethnicity, particularly in public, but Amin has barely paid lipservice to ethnic departicipation.

These divergent approaches toward ethnicity suggest the role governments play in shaping situations that can affect ethnic participation. In formulating their policy, UPC leaders were most directly concerned to contract the scope of participation by removing ethnicity from public discourse. The attacks on "tribalism" in speeches by public officials, the removal of the question on "tribe" from the census, and the plan for the new electoral system are illustrations. However, reducing scope without attending to the bases, weight, and personae of ethnic participation would have been futile. For this reason, among others, they eliminated the autonomy, financial powers, and independent electoral bases of Buganda officials and district councillors. In addition they reduced the importance of the district in party structure and arranged for better insulation of top party officials from ethnic demands by having them appointed rather than elected. Near the end of their rule they banned opposition parties, a move that eliminated the possibility of using that channel for ethnic pressures.

Obote's government also tried to reduce ethnic rivalry in the competition over new development projects by prohibiting discussions in the National Assembly and district councils of the ethnic implications of the sites selected. In taking these measures the government significantly diminished the weight of participation of those most likely to organize or respond to popular ethnic demands. The same actions deprived ethnic middlemen of the opportunities to accumulate financial and organizational resources with which they might have been able to force UPC leaders to accept ethnic linkages.

The strategy of the government was flawed, however, because it could not avoid dilemmas growing out of the uneven pattern of modernization, and because it chose policies that kept Baganda ethnicity alive and intense. And the UPC government never freed itself from the suspicion that it was covertly employing ethnic criteria in guiding the process of development. Amin manipulated these resentments to legitimize his coup — and in so doing made ethnicity politically vital once more.

Even under the most favorable conditions, ethnic responses

are not so flexible that a government policy will necessarily make an immediate impact on habits of several years' duration. A "before-and-after" survey in Ankole found that the events of 1966 and the new constitution of 1967 had virtually no impact on the identity processes of people living in Ankole.[77] The most popular response to the question "Who are you?" was "Munyankore" in both 1965 and 1967.

One of the false hopes of African independence was the expectation that ethnicity would suddenly disappear. Gone and forgotten are predictions like Sekou Toure's statement that "in three or four years, no one will remember the tribal, ethnic or religious rivalries which in the recent past caused so much damage to our country and its populations."[78] Within the realm of possibility, however, is the longer-term prediction of Joshua Zake, formerly Uganda's minister of education: "The death of the thing called tribe has started. No-one will regret the death of the tribe. The death of the tribe is a function of conditions under which we live now. Another two generations and the thing will be dead anyway."[79]

Nevertheless, twentieth-century experience in North America and Europe, in communist and noncommunist countries, lends little support to any suggestion that ethnicity will totally disappear in the near future. However, because ethnicity is a social force, it is subject to social conditioning. Through the attitudes and policies of leaders, governments in all parts of the world can choose to influence their citizens to give less attention to ethnic interpretations of political issues.

Ethnicity is only one of the problems facing African governments. Departicipation is one approach to that problem, but it has also been employed as a weapon against many other difficulties facing African leaders. When Obote explained that the attack on ethnicity may have produced some problems, he

77. Marshall H. Segall, Martin Doornbos, and Clive Davis, *Patterns of Self-Identification among the Banyankole in Uganda* (forthcoming). However, the number who predicted that there would be "better days" without the Omugabe (king) went up from 5 percent to 35 percent.

78. *Towards Full Re-Africanization* (Paris: Presence Africaine, 1959), p. 34, quoted in Rupert Emerson, "Nation-Building in Africa," in *Nation-Building,* ed. Karl Deutsch and William Foltz (New York: Atherton, 1963), p. 106.

79. *Uganda Argus,* 11 July 1968, p. 3.

added that these were "compensated by the other side of the basic policy, the projection of the centre. . . ."[80]   In reshaping the political structures with which Uganda entered independence, he was following a pattern of political activity with several African precedents. Amin has carried it much further by making virtually any form of civilian political participation a hazardous activity.

Elsewhere in Africa leaders have also taken steps to reduce popular involvement in politics. They have focused on building both the authority of their national governments and the security of their own rule. With only a few significant exceptions, the first fifteen years of African independence have been characterized by the progressive elimination of political structures through which voluntary participation might take place.

80. Personal communication, August 1971.

PART III
DEPARTING POLITICS
IN AFRICA

◇

NINE

PERVASIVE SPREAD OF DEPARTICIPATION

Departication is the most striking feature of postindependence political change in black Africa. It occurs in a wide range of situations beyond its application to the dampening of ethnic politics. Just as the reasons why people participate in politics are various, so are the strategies used by leaders to promote departication. But the general trend is clear. All over tropical Africa political structures which markedly increased participation were hastily installed in the last hectic years of colonial rule. Since independence they have been unceremoniously dismantled with the same alacrity.

Although some participation can be found in every country, it is often supported by little more than rhetorical commitment. Many African leaders act as if participation by anyone other than their intimates or administrators were detrimental to national development. Even seeming exceptions, such as Tanzania, serve to underline this basic political change. The script established by Ghana seems to remain the same; only the players change, as latecomers to independence pass through the same cyclic transformation. "The most significant variable may well be the passing of time. . . ."[1]

Contrary to the expectations at independence most single-party states have led to "a real decline in popular participation in the governmental process in the sense of the ability of individuals to affect the decisions of the state by communicating their point of view."[2] The tactics used by governments in

1. Aristide R. Zolberg, "The Structure of Political Conflict in the New States of Tropical Africa," *The American Political Science Review* 62, no. 1 (March 1968): 78. Zolberg is discussing coups in particular, but the sense of deja vu is far broader.

2. Immanuel Wallerstein, "The Decline of the Party in Single-Party African States," in *Political Parties and Political Development,* ed. Joseph LaPalombara and Myron Weiner (Princeton: Princeton University Press, 1966), p. 211.

five West African countries were listed by Zolberg several years ago.[3] They included growing executive control, co-optation, detention, and control of both local government and voluntary associations. The same techniques, it has since become clear, have been applied by governments in East Africa, Zambia, Malawi, and Lesotho.

In the debate over Uganda's 1967 constitution, Obote stressed that "there was no point in pretending that Uganda was at a stage where full Parliamentary democracy could obtain."[4] The new constitution significantly increased his powers, armed him with the right to ask the National Assembly to pass a preventive detention act (which was promptly enacted), and gave the government extensive control over local administration. And "Kenya," report Yash Ghai and J. P. W. B. McAuslan, "is becoming once again a bureaucratic state in which administrators, a term which here includes Ministers, take precedence over politicians, particularly MPs and local party officials."[5] The consequence is departicipation. As David Apter puts it, "The billiard game of politics is being played on a table that constantly grows smaller."[6]

In analyzing the specific changes which have taken place, it is important to remember that although most African countries possessed new and fragile participatory structures at independence, political involvement was enthusiastic. In the two popular elections in Ghana before independence, the combined opposition received 44.6 percent in 1954 and 43 percent in 1956, though it must be kept in mind that the personae involved

3. *Creating Political Order: The Party States of West Africa* (Chicago: Rand McNally, 1966). See also the even earlier treatment in Martin Kilson, "Authoritarian and Single-Party Tendencies in African Politics," *World Politics* 15, no. 2 (January 1963): 263.

4. *Uganda Argus,* 23 June 1967.

5. *Public Law and Political Change in Kenya: A Study of the Legal Framework of Government from Colonial Times to the Present* (Nairobi: Oxford University Press, 1970), p. 513.

6. "Ghana," in *Political Parties and National Integration in Tropical Africa,* ed. James S. Coleman and Carl G. Rosberg, Jr. (Berkeley and Los Angeles: University of California Press, 1964), p. 314. Apter's reference is intended to illustrate precoup politics in Ghana, though it can be applied more widely.

amounted to only 16 percent of the adult population.[7]   In both the 1961 and the 1962 national elections in Uganda, the DP and the UPC split the popular vote relatively evenly.[8] KY candidates together received far more votes in the Lukiiko elections of February 1962 than the UPC candidates did in the non-Buganda constituencies in the general election the following April.[9] Competition was widespread and elections closely fought throughout the country except in Buganda. "For those who remember the kind of enthusiasm that was shown by the masses, it appears as though the same will never be witnessed again," reports one local observer.[10]   Other opportunities to participate were available through relatively unrestricted debate in parliaments and local government councils, through voluntary associations, and through party activity.

Yet the destruction of such opportunities followed immediately upon this spasm of popular involvement. The causes were the new policies strengthening the central administration and the growing desuetude of participatory structures — particularly the manipulation of elections, the suppression of opposition parties, the decreased notice taken of legislatures, the decline of the government party, and the loss of autonomy of both local

7. Dennis Austin, *Politics in Ghana: 1946-1960* (London: Oxford University Press, 1964), pp. 243 and 347-354.

8. However, in both elections the UPC won slightly more than three seats for every two taken by the DP. R. C. Peagram, *A Report on the General Elections to the Legislative Council Held in March, 1961* (Entebbe: Government Printer, 1961), p. 17; and R. C. Peagram, *A Report on the General Elections to the National Assembly of Uganda Held on the 25th of April, 1962* (Entebbe: Government Printer, 1963), p. 6.

Because the UPC fell short of a majority in both cases, Buganda played a pivotal role in determining who would rule. The DP came to power in 1961 because a few of its supporters were willing to break the electoral boycott in Buganda. The UPC formed the government in 1962 because it made an alliance with KY.

9. And somewhat more than the DP received in both 1962 elections. In the Buganda elections KY candidates accumulated a total of 618,696 votes, and DP candidates received 103,180. As part of the agreement with KY, the UPC did not enter any candidates in these elections. In the general elections in the rest of the country, UPC candidates mustered a total of 537,598 votes, while DP standard-bearers acquired 474,256. See Peagram, *A Report on the General Elections of 1962*, pp. 6 and 23-33.

10. Tarcise Banyenzaki, "The Effects of the General and District Council Elections on Administrative Effectiveness in the Parishes of Katooma and Masheruka, Sheema County, Gombolola Kigarama, Ankole District" (B.A. diss., Makerere University College, 1969), p. 8.

government and voluntary associations. By comparing changes in political structures in Ghana with those in Kenya and Uganda, the well-known analysis of the earlier case can be extended to those who began the process later. There are such obvious similarities elsewhere in tropical Africa that it is hard to argue that these transformations of government and politics amount to anything less than a trend of continental proportions, even though local variations in the pattern need to be pointed out. By making this argument, we may then directly confront the Tanzanian case – on its face the most likely exception.

To demonstrate the removal or impotence of participatory structures, however, offers only a prima facie case of departicipation, though a strong one. Since total departicipation is impossible in an existing political system, it remains to fix some limits to this process of removing people from politics by destroying participatory structures. This qualification allows us also to consider the relatively low, but nonetheless significant, volumes of participation that continue to exist in both civilian and military regimes that have passed through this transformation.

1. STRENGTHENING CENTRAL ADMINISTRATION

The removal of colonially imposed fetters on the freedom of action of the executive has not been a consequence solely of the disappearance of participatory structures, but is also the result of "a steady drive to achieve greater centralization of authority in the hands of a very small number of men who occupy top offices in the party and the government, and even more in the hands of a single man at the apex of both institutions."[11] These two complementary trends reinforce each other, since the increased authority of national leaders has contributed to departicipation as well.

Changes in the constitutions of African states mark the growth of the executive and the accompanying disengagement of popular involvement. The first step taken in Ghana, Kenya,

11. Zolberg, *Creating Political Order,* p. 135. It is worth keeping in mind Zolberg's warning that increasing the authority of the executive over government structures does not necessarily increase the scope of issues over which it has power in the nation. Ibid., p. 134.

and Uganda was to reverse federal structures that provided part of the compromise of independence settlements. Regional assemblies, upper houses, and entrenched local control over particular sources of finance and social services were intended to permit minorities to protect themselves after independence and thus to ensure their participation in national affairs. These minorities, usually perceived in ethnic or regional terms, were unable to sustain their protecting structures, in part because they lacked adequate power once the colonial regime was no longer available to bargain for them.

In Ghana, CPP supporters filled the regional assemblies and then dissolved them as soon as an amendment to the constitution permitted.[12] The Kenya African National Union (KANU) considered regionalism (known as *majimbo*) a serious mistake and reversed it by delaying the constitutionally required transfer of services and full financial responsibility to the new regions. When enough opposition MPs had crossed the aisles, a new constitution was enacted in December 1964, a year after independence.[13] The changes in Uganda's constitutions of 1966 and 1967, discussed in chapter eight, removed the federal powers of Buganda and quasi-federal position of the other kingdoms and paved the way for tighter central control over the district governments.

A second significant constitutional change has been the growth in powers given to the president. The republican constitution (1961) in Ghana gave legislative powers to the president that permitted him to bypass the National Assembly whenever he considered it to be in the "national interest" to do so.[14] In 1964 a further amendment gave Nkrumah the power to dismiss

12. Henry L. Bretton, *The Rise and Fall of Kwame Nkrumah: A Study of Personal Rule in Africa* (London: Pall Mall Press, 1966), n. 13, p. 193.

13. Cherry Gertzel, *The Politics of Independent Kenya 1963-8* (Nairobi: East African Publishing House, 1970), pp. 33-34.

14. Article 55 (section 1). See Bretton, *The Rise and Fall of Kwame Nkrumah*, p. 50. In the view of one observer, the effect of this section derogated the importance of parliament to the point where "political sovereignty was pushed so far as to mean the sovereignty of one man." Yaw Twumasi, "Ghana's Draft Constitutional Proposals: An Aristotelian-Burkean Riposte to the Nkrumah Constitutionalists," *Transition* 7, no. 6 (October 1968): 44.

judges of the highest courts "at any time for reasons which to him appear sufficient."[15]

The powers given to the president in Kenya have also been considerably enlarged and now allow him wide executive powers, including the right to detain without trial and to issue restrictions on movement and the press.[16] There had been a safeguard for the first five years of independence, since the president was required to be an elected member of parliament and had to submit to a formal vote of no confidence.[17] However, in 1968 the president became more independent of parliament as a result of another constitutional amendment providing for his direct election by the people.

The Ugandan constitution of 1967 gave the president the right to nominate MPs to give him a safe majority and introduced some political controls over the previously independent inspector general of police, director of public prosecutions, and auditor general.[18] It also allowed the National Assembly to pass a preventive detention act and permitted the president to act by legislative instrument, though only when the National Assembly was not sitting.

Governments have taken advantage of their new authority and have enlarged the role played by central administration and particularly the office of the president.[19] In addition, the

15. Bretton, *The Rise and Fall of Kwame Nkrumah,* p. 61. This amendment was approved in a national referendum in 1964 (together with the proposal making the CPP the only legal party). It was introduced following the acquittal of former high-ranking Nkrumah aides on charges of treason.

16. Gertzel, *The Politics of Independent Kenya,* pp. 174-176; see also pp. 34 and 152. Ghai and McAuslan comment that "it is the Constitution which has adjusted to the administrative structure, and not, as was clearly envisaged [by the framers of the independence constitution] the other way round." *Public Law and Political Change in Kenya,* p. 514.

17. Gertzel, *The Politics of Independent Kenya,* pp. 34 and 154. The president had the right to dissolve the parliament at any time and hold elections.

18. *The Constitution of the Republic of Uganda* (Entebbe: Government Printer, 1967), Articles 40, 69 (sections 2 and 3), 71 (section 5), 70, 10 (section 1, subsection j), and 64, respectively.

As one exception to the general trend toward departication, it is interesting to note that the original constitutional proposals gave somewhat greater powers to the president. Perhaps these were modified as a result of the public debate that preceded their enactment. For a summary of these changes, see [Nelson Kasfir], *Transition* 7, no. 2 (October-November 1967): 43.

19. Conflicts engendered by this process may affect the administration adversely. Efforts by the president's office to extend its control over civil service activities are

position of district and provincial commissioners, which had been stripped of many duties by the transfer of powers to local government at independence, was progressively restored in several African states.

In Ghana an increasing variety of activities was directly supervised by Nkrumah. Control over the security services, the prisons, and the appointment, promotion, and dismissal of civil servants was vested in him.[20] Important portfolios such as finance, planning, the Volta River project, and industrial development were removed from ministerial control and placed in secretariats directly responsible to him. In the field political commissioners who reported directly to Nkrumah were put in charge of regions. A similar growth of central government authority can also be traced through the Second Republic.[21]

After reversing the devolution that marked the *majimbo* period in Kenya, Jomo Kenyatta made certain that the powers restored were assigned to provincial and district commissioners. They became his "major organ of control," and their duties were increased by adding tax collection responsibilities and the chairmanship of crucial committees. "As a result the Government had retained in their control much of the resources available at district level."[22]

In his last few years in office, Obote began to take policy initiatives without extensive consultation — even from within his own administration. Many of his ministers, for example, were caught by surprise when he publicly announced the major nationalization measures in May 1970.[23] After 1967 Ugandan district commissioners once again became "local giants" in their

---

apt to be resented. Thus, Bretton argues that it was only the "personal rule" of Nkrumah that was strengthened and not the administration as a whole. In his view "the fourth branch [of government] was not the CPP but the President's Office. It combined executive, legislative, and judicial functions." *The Rise and Fall of Kwame Nkrumah*, p. 97.

20. Bretton, *The Rise and Fall of Kwame Nkrumah*, pp. 50-51 and 59; Lionel Tiger, "Bureaucracy and Charisma in Ghana," *Journal of Asian and African Studies* 1, no. 1 (January 1966): 25; and Dennis L. Cohen, "The Convention People's Party of Ghana: Representational or Solidarity Party?" *Canadian Journal of African Studies* 4, no. 2 (Spring 1970): 180-181 and 194.

21. David Goldsworthy, "Ghana's Second Republic: A Post-Mortem," *African Affairs* 72, no. 286 (January 1973): 19-23.

22. Gertzel, *The Politics of Independent Kenya*, pp. 36, 166-167.

23. See Felix Onama's testimony to the commission of inquiry into the National Trading Corporation. *Uganda Argus*, 23 May 1972, p. 5.

districts.[24]   They countersigned all checks and vouchers of district administration, had full access to district records, and chaired joint central government-local administration committees.[25]

Military regimes, now the modal form of government in black Africa, bring the process of administrative centralization close to its logical conclusion by banning politics and removing any participatory structures that are still functioning. In a statement to the nation shortly after the Ugandan coup, the armed forces declared that "we are aware that Uganda's present difficulties and most of Africa's problems are caused by greedy and ambitious politicians."[26]   Some military leaders are not opposed to politics per se, though, as the discussion in the last section in this chapter suggests. By and large, however, the insistence of military leaders on administration organized on the basis of a command hierarchy carries forward the postindependence trend toward departicipation.

As rulers the military tend to work closely with the civilian bureaucracy, to put technocrats in charge of ministries and local administration, and to eliminate the autonomy of any organization whose members publicly differ with them. The National Liberation Council (NLC) in Ghana "was directly dependent upon the civil service, and especially the advice of senior civil servants."[27]   Robert Dowse argues that the association was even more intimate and characterizes the military regime as "a civil/ military bureaucratic coalition."[28]   The NLC reduced and ratio-

24. Apolo Nsibambi, "Some Aspects of Local Administration in Uganda Since the Revolution of 1966-68," typescript, n.d., p. 4. There were challenges from the secretaries-general to the primacy of the district commissioner until the former position was abolished by the Amin government in February 1971. However, since secretaries-general were also appointed by the president, they did not represent a challenge to the control of the central administration.

25. K. J. Davey, "Local Bureaucrats and Politicians in East Africa," *Journal of Administration Overseas* 10, no. 4 (October 1971): 270; and Nsibambi, "Some Aspects of Local Administration in Uganda," pp. 4-5.

26. "Declaration by the Officers and Men of the Uganda Army and Air Force Made to the Nation on the 20th February, 1971," *The Uganda Gazette* 64, no. 8 (26 February 1971): 78.

27. Jon Kraus, "Arms and Politics in Ghana," in *Soldier and State in Africa: A Comparative Analysis of Military Intervention and Political Change,* ed. Claude E. Welch, Jr. (Evanston, Ill.: Northwestern University Press, 1970), p. 189.

28. "The Military and Political Development," in *Politics and Change in Developing Countries: Studies in the Theory and Practice of Development,* ed. Colin Leys (Cambridge: Cambridge University Press, 1969), pp. 231 and 240; for his general argument on this point, see pp. 229-232.

nalized the maze of offices and boards erected by Nkrumah and put administrators in place of the politicians who previously ran the nine regions. Parliament and municipal councils were dissolved. "The immediate result [of the coup] was to eliminate completely from the political scene — assuming they were ever really on it — the masses whom Nkrumah was supposed to have mobilized."[29]   The return to democracy under the new prime minister, Kofi Busia, was interrupted by a second coup in January 1972. Another military regime took over and promptly removed the new participatory structures designed by the architects appointed by the leaders of the first coup.

After the coup in Uganda, parliament and district, municipal, and town councils were dissolved.[30] The new cabinet (originally called the Council of Ministers) consisted of two military officers, (including the president), a university professor, and civil servants. According to a pamphlet issued by the new government, "the reason for the appointment of this technocrat [sic] Cabinet is because the present Government believes in getting down to reorganisation of the Country without indulging in political extravagance."[31] With elections postponed up to five years and political parties banned, the elimination of non-administrative channels of participation was virtually complete (with the unimportant exceptions of the heavily controlled judiciary and the newly established councils of elders). One civil servant, who worked for the Protectorate and the postindependence governments, observed shortly after the coup that "the form of Government is settling reasonably well into one of civil service direction and, as you know, this is a relatively easy exercise for us since this was the form of Government we had for 60 years before Independence."[32]

Given its extraordinary political difficulties since the end of

29. Ibid., p. 241.
30. *Decrees*, nos. 1 and 2 of 1971 (Entebbe: Government Printer, 2 February 1971). The trend toward consolidation of power in the hands of the district commissioners has moved beyond local challenge, particularly in those districts, such as Lango, where military officers were given this administrative post. Most of the first batch of provincial governors came from the military, though they had to give up their positions in the armed forces, at least temporarily.
31. *The Birth of the Second Republic of Uganda* (Entebbe: Government Printer, 1971), pp. 29-30.
32. Personal communication, March 1971. He would certainly modify that judgment in light of the army's often uncontrolled participation in Ugandan politics that became apparent later. See section 4 in this chapter.

colonial rule, it is not surprising that Zaire has become an exemplar of the trend toward administrative centralization. Under the direction of General Mobutu Sese Seko, participatory structures have been dismantled and public debate has been suppressed.[33] More and more government functions have been placed in the hands of "experts" (mainly former university students) acting under the direct supervision of the president. The number of provinces has been reduced from twenty-one to eight, and Mobutu has brought them under the direct authority of the central government. Etienne Tshisekedi, the minister of internal affairs, summarizes this dramatic shift in powers: "Thus, one paradoxically comes back again to the administrative structures existing before June 30, 1960, that is, a central and strong authority basing itself on decentralized provincial administrations which realize through district commissioners and territorial administrators all the options of economic and social progress."[34] Mobutu's decision — following demonstrations — to draft all Zairean students at Kinshasa (formerly Lovanium) University into the army for a two-year period suggests how effectively potentially powerful interest groups can be removed from politics by administrative measures.[35]

33. Jean-Claude Willame, "Congo-Kinshasa: General Mobutu and Two Political Generations," trans. Claude E. Welch, Jr., in *Soldier and State in Africa*, ed. Welch, pp. 144-145. It remains to be seen whether Mobutu can at the same time turn the Mouvement Populaire de la Révolution (MPR) into a viable organ of participation.

Willame also notes the gradual displacement of politicians in the cabinet in favor of technicians. See also Thomas Turner, "Congo-Kinshasa," in *The Politics of Cultural Sub-Nationalism in Africa*, ed. Victor A. Olorunsola (Garden City, N.Y.: Doubleday, 1972), pp. 255-259.

34. *Congo 1966* (Brussels: CRISP, 1967), p. 239, quoted in Willame, "Congo-Kinshasa," p. 146.

35. *Uganda Argus*, 7 June 1971, p. 6. Of 3,007 Zairean students, 2,889 were enrolled. Those who failed to enroll were sentenced by court martial to ten years' imprisonment. *Uganda Argus*, 14 June 1971, p. 8. The army has been used in other places in Africa to punish attempts to participate. For example, several high school teachers who distributed a tract critical of the government were drafted into the armed forces for twenty-four days by Hubert Maga, then president of Dahomey. W. A. E. Skurnik, "The Military and Politics: Dahomey and Upper Volta," in *Soldier and State in Africa*, ed. Welch, p. 72. Amin insisted that the civilian ministers in his first cabinet join the army without even waiting for a hint of disagreement on their part.

In their efforts to control student participation, presidents in Tanzania and Ghana have intervened directly. In Ghana Nkrumah directly appointed certain professors of law and sent directives to the university demanding more conformity with CPP goals.

Thus, the increasing power of the central administration and particularly of its top official has been a continuing trend throughout the continent. One result of its growing strength is greater departicipation. Central governments may encounter many difficulties in penetrating all areas of their nations, but policies of departicipation have met few setbacks. Here governments have expended great resources and have been highly successful. The desirability of this change, which is difficult to evaluate, is taken up in the next chapter.

2. GROWING DESUETUDE OF PARTICIPATORY STRUCTURES

To some extent the disappearance of participation in structures designed to facilitate political involvement is the consequence of efforts of the central administration to arrogate more authority. In other cases participatory structures have lost many of their functions because they were unable to carry out their intended tasks. Of the examples discussed here, the manipulation of elections, the harassment of opposition parties, the decreasing importance of legislatures, and the loss of autonomy of important voluntary associations such as trade unions and cooperatives fall into the first category. The decline of the government party is a good illustration of the second category. The loss of functions, and ultimately of autonomy, of local government falls into both. However, there are important exceptions to this trend, since governments have also experimented with new structures that might permit some participation which cannot threaten the policies of the leaders.

Electoral participation was originally intended as the primary linkage between citizens and governments after independence. But by stratagems both blunt and subtle the weight of this type of participation — where it still exists — has been significantly

---

A number of party activists "invaded" the campus to underline this demand. Bretton, *The Rise and Fall of Kwame Nkrumah,* pp. 93 and 96. Julius Nyerere ordered the rustication of most of the students in the University of Dar es Salaam in October 1966, following their demonstrations against student involvement in the government's new program of national service. In discussing this incident and the complications resulting from the Kenyan government's refusal to permit Oginga Odinga, then head of the opposition Kenya People's Union (KPU), to speak to students at the University of Nairobi, the UPC party newspaper, *The People,* editorialized that "no Government in a developing country will allow any group of people, whatever label they attach to themselves, to challenge its authority." 29 January 1969, p. 2.

reduced. The use of a single constituency for the entire nation in Guinea, Ivory Coast, and later Senegal insured that all the seats went to the victorious party.[36]   After Ghana gained its independence, the CPP won a series of by-elections (the last one held in 1960) accompanied by harassment and detention of members of the opposition United Party (UP).[37]   Nkrumah won the election for president against J. B. Danquah by taking almost 90 percent of the vote in 1960. In the 1964 plebescite the government's position was supported by over 99.9 percent of the electorate, with five of the nine regions – including Ashanti the scene of vigorous opposition eight years earlier – failing to record a single negative vote. Following the establishment of a legal one-party state, all CPP candidates for the National Assembly (in 1965) were declared elected without bothering with the ballot box, since they were unopposed.

A similar situation occurred in the 1968 Kenyan local authority elections. *All* Kenya People's Union (KPU) candidates – about eighteen hundred – were disqualified on technical grounds by government election officials, and KANU candidates were returned automatically.[38]   The next year parliament was dissolved in preparation for national elections, but following disturbances during the visit of President Kenyatta to the town of Kisumu, a KPU stronghold, all KPU MPs and several party officials were detained and the party was banned. The elections were held, but they amounted to primaries, with KANU members opposing each other in each constituency. At this point KANU was the only existing political party in Kenya, but voters were not required to produce evidence of party membership. The primaries did not appear to be further manipulated, since five ministers and fourteen assistant ministers, were among the seventy-seven MPs who lost their seats.[39]   Thus, the Kenyan

36. Zolberg, *Creating Political Order,* pp. 79-81.

37. Apter, "Ghana," pp. 292 and 312; and Austin, *Politics in Ghana,* pp. 384-386. ". . . it became increasingly clear that the electoral process was no longer going to be of significance in Ghana. . . ." Cohen, "The Convention People's Party of Ghana," p. 177.

38. Gertzel, *The Politics of Independent Kenya,* p. 166. Contests for six seats were held in Lamu township, but these did not involve KPU candidates.

39. Out of the 143 members of the old parliament who sought reelection. Göran Hydén and Colin Leys, "Elections and Politics in Single-Party Systems: The Case of Kenya and Tanzania," *British Journal of Political Science* 2, no. 4 (October 1972):

government permitted electoral participation under controlled conditions.

Uganda has avoided difficulties with elections by the simple expedient of not having held any at the national level since independence. The elections required by 1967 were ignored in the wake of the troubles with Buganda, and the continuing state of emergency was used to justify their further postponement. By-elections to fill empty seats were not held even in areas that were not under emergency regulations. New powers were given to the minister for regional administrations to nominate persons to district councils in the event of vacancies. In the debate over nomination, M. O. K. Omadi, an MP from Bukedi North, asserted that "but for the Constitution, he would like to see nominations to the House. . . . The masses were not demanding elections. . . . . They were demanding service. . . . ."[40]

Shortly before the coup, however, Obote seemed to be moving toward an electoral system that would permit a limited measure of participation at several levels J. O. Anyoti, minister of state for national service, announced in May 1970 that at the lowest levels (*miluka* and *batongole*) chiefs were to be elected to their offices beginning in 1971.[41] This would have been a startling innovation, possibly initiating intense participation at the point of greatest concern for most Ugandans. Second, Obote announced a new plan for the election of MPs (discussed in chapter eight).

In preparation for new parliamentary elections, the UPC ordered its branch and constituency units to elect chairmen. At first (in 1969) these elections apparently attracted rather low levels of participation. But in 1970 larger numbers participated at both levels. Out of ninety-six constituencies, twenty-one had only 1 candidate for chairman, while the remaining seventy-five

396. This election bears some similarities to the Tanzanian model, as does the abortive 1970 plan for one in Uganda.

40. The legislation under consideration was the Local Administrations (Amendment) (no. 2) Bill, 1968. Omadi's remark was reported in *Uganda Argus*, 15 February 1969, p. 3.

41. *The People*, 26 May 1970, p. 1. A *muluka* chief exercises authority over a parish. A *mutongole* is his assistant. Soldiers presided over "elections" of new chiefs at all levels in Uganda in March 1973. If for no other reason, these were suspect because villagers sometimes "selected" young soldiers who came from parts of Uganda far from the village in which they were installed as chiefs. A few were put on trial several months later for brutal behavior toward their "subjects."

were contested by 163 candidates.[42] The cumulative total of voters in all but one of the contested elections amounted to 53,617 (an average of 725 per constituency) according to published figures. At the branch (equivalent to a *muluka,* or parish) level, between one hundred and twenty-five hundred voters were reported to have participated in each election. On this basis Cohen and Parson estimate that between a third and four-fifths of a million people were involved. In discussing why people participated, they suggest that

> the most likely explanation, and the one we believe fits the situation best, is that the elections provided an open arena for the discussion of possible solutions for local disputes and issues. For the first time since 1966 people were given an opportunity to discuss issues, personalities and the possibility of solving their problems through political rather than administrative channels. . . . This would have meant a relatively heated campaign and high turnout in the general election itself.[43]

Whether or not this would have been so, military intervention canceled planning for the election, and the general trend toward departicipation transformed this experiment into one of the hypotheticals of history.

In the process of manipulating elections, governments have ensured that opposition parties — once a channel for participation — have been severely restricted or destroyed altogether. "Extra-parliamentary or extra-legal restrictions against opposition parties have occurred at one time or another in all of the 19 African states where the single-party tendency is dominant."[44] Many opposition party officials have been intimidated and imprisoned.

42. D. L. Cohen and J. Parson, "The Uganda Peoples Congress Branch and Constituency Elections of 1970," *Journal of Commonwealth Political Studies* 11, no. 1 (March 1973): 54-55. Their figures for the number of voters must be treated with caution, since they are based on newspaper reports in a situation in which there was political incentive to increase participation totals to avoid embarrassing party officials.

43. Ibid., pp. 55-56.

44. Kilson, "Authoritarian and Single-Party Tendencies," p. 288.

The government in Kenya and in Uganda regularly denied permission for opposition figures to speak at party rallies and often extended this prohibition to MPs of the governing parties.[45] KANU officials used every opportunity — aside from the polls — to destroy KPU.[46] To the fourteen single-party states that had banned opposition parties by 1963[47] can now be added the formerly multiparty states of Uganda, Kenya, Tanzania, Sudan, and Zambia.

Legislatures, the most important channel of indirect participation, have not fared much better. "What is striking . . .is that these regimes [in West Africa] do not find it desirable to maintain even the public facade of debate."[48] When P. K. K. Quaidoo, then a minister in Nkrumah's government, observed that "whether by design or accident, the prestige of Parliament has been made to descend rather low, and at this time it behoves [sic] every member to uphold the authority of Parliament," he was forced to resign as minister and was detained.[49] In May 1965 Nkrumah sent to the National Assembly a message noting that "the central committe of the CPP will be empowered by law to unseat any MP who in their opinion has lost the confidence of the Party."[50]

45. Gertzel, *The Politics of Independent Kenya,* pp. 146-147; *Uganda Argus,* 1 June 1968, p. 1.

46. Susanne D. Mueller, "Statist Economies and the Elimination of the K.P.U.: A Critique of Political Party Analysis and the 'Center-Periphery' Argument" (paper delivered to the African Studies Association Conference, Philadelphia, November 1972).

47. Kilson, "Authoritarian and Single-Party Tendencies," pp. 289-290. In four of the five single-party states which Kilson cites as exceptions on this point, opposition parties have since been banned at one time or another.

48. Zolberg, *Creating Political Order,* p. 112. He notes that on occasion committees of national assemblies have delayed legislation. In Zaire, the National Assembly "can be called upon to collaborate — it cannot decide anymore." Willame, "Congo-Kinshasa," p. 144. The bill to change the name of Lovanium University to the University of Kinshasa was the first one reported to be sent by Mobutu to the National Assembly in eight months. *Uganda Argus,* 14 June 1971, p. 8.

49. Quoted from parliamentary debate (without source) in Twumasi, "Ghana's Draft Constitutional Proposals," p. 48.

50. *The Ghanaian Times,* 26 May 1965, quoted in Bretton, *The Rise and Fall of Kwame Nkrumah,* p. 123. However, Robert Pinkney notes that "politically sensitive issues," such as shortages, rising rents, and neglect of particular regions, were raised in parliament by MPs up to the coup. *Ghana under Military Rule: 1966-1969* (London: Methuen & Co., 1972), p. 79.

Testifying before a commission of inquiry set up after the coup in Uganda, a former MP, E. N. Bisamunyu, said that "if you protested vigorously, you would be in trouble. Speaking on an issue like this [corruption in the National Trading Corporation — a matter on which Obote was sensitive] in Parliament, . . .you would sign a death warrant for yourself." He added that "after the 1967 constitution [was passed], . . . Members of Parliament never even bothered to read bills. . . ."[51]

The Kenyan case is particularly interesting because it provides a limited exception to the pervasive reduction in the autonomy of African legislatures. Vigorous debate occurred on all major issues, usually before packed public galleries and with full coverage in newspaper and on radio. The participants were more likely to be KANU back-benchers than opposition MPs. They "refused to be a rubber stamp for the Executive" and often forced compromises on government legislation.[52] Their vocal opposition to legislation designed to repress KPU did not, however, deter them from voting for it.[53] "Parliament," Hydén and Leys conclude, "cannot be said by and large to play a very important role in the government of Kenya."[54]

Participation in voluntary associations has become less meaningful as these organizations lose their autonomy and submit to government control. When this happens, their members are less able to influence their government through direct public activities. Take, for example, the cases of trade unions and cooperatives.

"Almost everywhere in the continent, labor organizations were taken over by the governing parties, once independence was achieved."[55] The process involved positive and negative incentives — offers of new union buildings and government jobs and threats of imprisonment and government takeover of unions. The Ghana Trade Union Congress (TUC) resisted government control until 1958 and still managed to hold an important strike in 1962. Nevertheless, it became an instrument of

51. *Uganda Argus,* 3 May 1972, p. 5.
52. Gertzel, *The Politics of Independent Kenya,* pp. 39, 129, and 132.
53. Mueller, "Statist Economies and the Elimination of the K.P.U.," p. 24.
54. "Elections and Politics in Single-Party Systems," p. 398.
55. Elliot J. Berg and Jeffrey Butler, "Trade Unions," in *Political Parties and National Integration,* ed. Coleman and Rosberg, Jr., pp. 366 and 369; Apter, "Ghana," p. 298.

party policy. The act was repeated with a new cast of characters when Busia's Progress Party (PP) government passed legislation in September 1971 to break once again the power of TUC leaders.[56]

In 1965 the Kenyan government set up a new central organization (COTU), whose "constitution entrenched state supervision of the centre's internal affairs."[57] In Uganda the Trade Unions Act of 1965 increased the government's supervisory and regulatory powers, and in 1969 the government announced its intention to create a single national trade union on the Tanzanian model.[58] In terms of organizational autonomy, "clearly, trade unions possess less freedom today than under the colonial regime."[59]

Agricultural cooperatives have also lost much of their autonomy, but more because of financial scandal and production inefficiency than any government fear of opposition to official policies. Although they have been regarded as channels for peasant participation, the striking feature of rural cooperatives has been the rather low level of efforts (either issue-oriented or otherwise) by members to convert them into instruments of political participation.

The United Ghana Farmers' Council was directed from above. In 1960 it was made the sole purchasing agent for cocoa, and in 1964 it became responsible for all agricultural cooperatives.[60] Legal control over Kenyan cooperatives was tightened in 1966 in a reversal of the earlier philosophy of allowing greater autonomy so that officials could learn from their own mistakes. In many cases members had become disillusioned by financial reverses and had reduced their participation.[61] The

56. Goldsworthy, "Ghana's Second Republic," pp. 16-17. State controls on the TUC had been relaxed after the 1966 coup.

57. Richard Sandbrook, "The State and the Development of Trade Unionism," in *Development Administration: The Kenyan Experience,* ed. Göran Hydén, Robert Jackson, and John Okumu (Nairobi: Oxford University Press, 1970), p. 281.

58. Ibid., p. 292. The national trade union project seems to have been shelved since the coup.

59. Ibid., p. 294.

60. Cohen, "The Convention People's Party of Ghana," 178; Apter, "Ghana," p. 298.

61. Göran Hydén, "Government and Co-operatives," in *Development Administration,* ed. Hydén, Jackson, and Okumu, p. 300.

"government has invariably been more concerned with promoting efficiency and economy and its own general control over the
unions and societies" which have become "a hand-maiden of
the state."[62]

The situation is similar in Uganda, though the cooperatives
are somewhat stronger and the government has intervened less
often. Still, the government increased its share of finance for
capital expansion by cooperatives. It also made the cooperatives
responsible for processing coffee and cotton, the main export
crops. As a result the government was unwilling to allow the
cooperatives very much autonomy.[63]   In 1970 a new Co-operative Societies Act increased the government's power to supervise
and intervene.

Leaders of single-party states would be likely to accept much
of the analysis up to this point. They would claim that preventing other structures from being focuses of autonomous political
involvement permits better organization of participation
through the mass party. But where such a party grows weak in
spite of the imagery of mass mobilization, it infects those
organized beneath its wing with the same degree of infirmity.
Thus, the "trend. . . toward inanition"[64] of the party in most
single-party states has meant severe erosion in overall participation.

The most important reason in cases across the continent is
that leading party officials were given major government positions after independence.[65]   The work of the party tends to be
neglected. Few meetings are held at national or ward levels, and
party dues become difficult to collect. The remaining top party
officials are not consulted on major policy decisions and are
unable to exact compliance from lower-level party branches. [66]

62. Ibid., pp. 314 and 315.
63. Nelson Kasfir, "Organizational Analysis and Uganda Co-operative Unions," in
Co-operatives and Rural Development in East Africa, ed. Carl Gösta Widstrand (New
York: Africana Publishing Corporation, 1970), p. 193.
64. Wallerstein, "The Decline of the Party," p. 208.
65. Ibid., p. 208. For the cases of Ghana, Burundi, and Kenya, see Cohen, "The
Convention People's Party of Ghana," p. 187; René Lemarchand, "Social Change and
Political Modernisation in Burundi," The Journal of Modern African Studies 4, no. 4
(December 1966): 414; and Gertzel, The Politics of Independent Kenya, p. 58.
66. Wallerstein, "The Decline of the Party," p. 208; and Henry Bienen, "The
Ruling Party in the African One-Party State: Tanu in Tanzania," in Governing in
Black Africa: Perspectives on New States, ed. Marion E. Doro and Newell M. Stultz
(Englewood Cliffs, N.J.: Prentice-Hall, 1970), pp. 69-71.

Alternatively, in countries like the Ivory Coast, "the party has become bureaucratized as an agency of the centre at the expense of the independence of local *sous-sections . . .*" with a consequent shrinking of the personae involved in politics.[67]

The shift of the CPP from a party of representation to a party of solidarity made departicipation more likely, partly because it meant that political involvement through party channels carried less weight and partly because the CPP proved organizationally unequal to the task.[68] Internal factionalism consumed much of the energies of insecure party officials. In May 1964 an important government civil servant (D. K. Ntosuoh) was given the top administrative position in the party; earlier three senior civil servants had been placed on the CPP's central committee.[69] The fact that the party and the government were becoming indistinguishable is not surprising in a de jure one-party state. However, the party seemed to have become more an extension of the government than the other way around. Furthermore, in the countryside "the C.P.P. was a political chameleon taking on the coloration of any particular part of Ghana where it existed."[70] Its irrelevance to Ghanaian politics was underlined by its immediate and total disappearance upon the announcement of the coup in February 1966.

Gertzel's portrait of KANU is less surprising only because KANU made fewer claims: "Party machinery scarcely functioned. KANU headquarters in Nairobi remained empty except for the occasional minor official. The telephone was discon-

67. Martin Staniland, "Single-Party Regimes and Political Change: The P.D.C.I. and Ivory Coast Politics," in *Politics and Change in Developing Countries,* ed. Leys, p. 163. ". . . the PDCI [has] seriously declined as an organizational reality in the Ivory Coast." Richard E. Stryker, "A Local Perspective on Developmental Strategy in the Ivory Coast," in *The State of the Nations: Constraints on Development in Independent Africa,* ed. Michael F. Lofchie (Berkeley and Los Angeles: University of California Press, 1971), p. 136.

68. On the shift from the function of representation to that of solidarity, see Cohen, "The Convention People's Party of Ghana," p. 189 and *passim;* and Apter, "Ghana," pp. 292-308. Cohen argues that it is more useful to see the CPP as two parties with the solidarity "wing" slowly taking over than to regard the CPP as becoming progressively weaker. Apter stresses conflicts among branches, regions, and national headquarters on the one hand and between regional and functional groupings on the other. "Ghana," pp. 293 and 301. Apter's view suggests that there were somewhat greater possibilities for participation within the CPP than does Cohen's.

69. Cohen, "The Convention People's Party of Ghana," p. 184; and Wallerstein, "The Decline of the Party," p. 210.

70. Dowse, "The Military and Political Development," p. 238.

nected because the account was not paid. Party finances were said to be in disarray. At district level branches were equally lacking in formal organization and membership dues were not collected." [71]   Though KANU still possessed much popular loyalty as the party which had won national independence, it was the administrative officer and not the party official that linked the government and the people. [72]

The same description could be applied to the UPC. An early warning from Grace Ibingira, then minister of state, went unheeded:

> This momentum, this enthusiasm carried us through all the successive victories in District Elections and Kingdom Elections in 1961 and 1962 and even part of 1963. *But no one can today claim with honesty that enthusiasm, that degree of unity of purpose, still remains as it was then. . . .*
>
> I maintain that what has gone wrong in UPC is that we, its leaders, at every level have neglected its organisation. [73]

In the years following the confrontation with Buganda in 1966, many of the UPC's up-country offices could be found locked and empty. A carefully constructed two-stage survey carried out in Ankole district in 1965 and 1967 revealed not only the expected decline in support for the DP, but a decline as well for the UPC from 59 to 48 percent. [74]   In a conference held in 1968 to rectify party matters and chart new directions, a new party constitution was adopted. It deliberately reduced participation in the party by providing that the president of the party appoint the major party officials who previously had been elected by the delegates. [75]   Although party electoral activity

71. *The Politics of Independent Kenya,* p. 58.

72. Ibid., pp. 59 and 167.

73. "The State of UPC in the Kingdoms and Districts," letter to the prime minister, all ministers, parliamentary secretaries, and UPC back-benchers, 7 March 1964. Italics in the original. This letter may have been an early tactic in Ibingira's successful efforts to oust Kakonge, Obote's ally, from the position of UPC secretary-general.

74. Marshall H. Segall, Martin Doornbos, and Clive Davis, *Patterns of Self-Identification among the Banyankole in Uganda* (forthcoming).

75. Section 7(4), *Constitution of the Uganda People's Congress: Adopted by the Fourth National Delegates Conference 11th June 1968* (Kampala: UPC National Headquarters, n.d.).

began again in 1969 and 1970, Amin's coup dispatched the UPC at a time when it was in a rather uncertain state of health.

Thus, with the exception of Tanzania, governing parties have become increasingly irrelevant to the political process. "In effect," remarks Wallerstein, "the one-party state in Africa has become in many places the no-party state."[76] Instead of reinforcing political involvement, the consequence of assembling other participatory structures under the governing party's direction has increased the amount of departicipation.

Local government has also been transformed by the transfer of many of its functions to the central government and by a change from election to appointment of political representatives — where these have not been removed entirely. The change is symbolized by Uganda's insistence that "local governments" be referred to as "local administrations."[77] The shift contributes to departicipation, since district and municipal councils were originally intended as forums for voicing grievances and for training democrats. Their removal does not mean that political struggle at the local level has ceased. However, the dismantling of structures makes political involvement more difficult and thus tends to reduce the volume of participation.

In West Africa, Guinea returned to the colonial system in 1959 when it dropped elected mayors in favor of appointed officials.[78] The Ivory Coast suspended the mayor and replaced

76. "The Decline of the Party," p. 214. Bienen's demonstration that TANU is an exception to Wallerstein's statement (though only an "intermittent" one) hardly justifies his assertion that "the idea of the 'no-party state' is not a satisfactory tool for the analysis of African politics. . . ." As he points out himself, "We may have to hurry before we have no phenomenon [i.e., no single-party state] to study." "The Ruling Party in the African One-Party State," pp. 73, 72, and 82-83.

77. "District councils . . . [are no longer] local governments but local administrations and as such have to pursue the policies of the Government." S. E. Isiagi, deputy minister of regional administrations, speaking in parliamentary debate, quoted in *Uganda Argus,* 15 February 1969, p. 3.

No distinction can be drawn here between rural councils and the supposedly more "modern" councils in towns. A study of the Kampala Municipal Council demonstrated "a switch from political management through the council to an almost exclusively centrally controlled performance." Michael Lee, "The Structure of Local Government" (paper delivered to the African Politics Seminar, Institute of Commonwealth Studies, University of London, November 1973), p. 20. Lee adds that "the formal structure's similarity to the colonial system is obvious." Ibid., p. 27.

78. Zolberg, *Creating Political Order,* p. 118; and Richard E. Stryker, "Political and Administrative Linkage in the Ivory Coast," in *Ghana and the Ivory Coast: Perspectives on Modernization,* ed. Philip Foster and Aristide R. Zolberg (Chicago: University of Chicago Press, 1971), pp. 96-100.

the municipal council of its third-largest city with an appointed commission in 1960. Initiatives taken by the colonial government in the Ivory Coast to introduce elective rural councils with financial autonomy were replaced after 1967 with new councils consisting of appointed officials whose powers of consultation were limited to small sources of revenue collected locally. Even in Senegal, where independent communes have had a long history, several municipal councils were dissolved in 1963 and reorganized to strengthen central government control. No opposition candidates were permitted in the municipal elections of 1964.

The effect of Mobutu's reorganization of Zaire's provinces was to eliminate their political potential and to reduce them to "mere administrative entities again."[79]   A decree in January 1968 removed the autonomy of the self-governing urban communes, a step that made them administrative subdivisions of the central government. Future mayors will be appointed, not elected. Local authorities in Ghana were weakened by the arbitrary increase in their numbers during the early 1960s and by declining central government grants. [80]   They were further restricted by increasing statutory controls imposed by the central government and by direct party supervision. Only one local council seat was contested after 1960. Following the same pattern, the Busia government passed legislation empowering the prime minister to appoint chairmen of district and regional councils.[81]

In Kenya and Uganda local government was plagued by a loss of qualified staff to more lucrative positions in the central government during the first wave of Africanization and by an inadequate tax base for the functions they were expected to carry out. The Kenyan minister for local government explained the ensuing financial difficulties as the result of "incompetence, dereliction of duty, failure to collect revenue, failure to keep accounts, [and] failure to maintain financial control."[82]   In

79. Willame, "Congo-Kinshasa," p. 146; and "News in Brief," *Africa Report* 13, no. 3 (March 1968): 24.

80. Harriet B. Schiffer, "Local Administration and National Development: Fragmentation and Centralization in Ghana," *Canadian Journal of African Studies* 4, no. 1 (Winter 1970): 73-75.

81. Goldsworthy, "Ghana's Second Republic," p. 15.

82. Quoted in Thomas Mulusa, "Central Government and Local Authorities," in *Development Administration,* ed. Hydén, Jackson, and Okumu, p. 250; see also Gertzel, *The Politics of Independent Kenya,* p. 38.

Acholi district in Uganda "the financial situation of the ADA [Acholi District Administration] was fundamentally impossible. . . . The fact was that the ADA's responsibilities were larger than the resources allocated to it could sustain. . . ."[83]

When these factors are considered in conjunction with the nervousness of the central government in both countries over the expression of opposition, the dismantling of local government occasions little surprise. In 1969 primary education, health, secondary road maintenance, and the collection of graduated personal tax were transferred to Kenyan central government officials.[84] Consequently, local authorities could no longer debate alterations in the central government's policies for these services.

Transformation of local government in Uganda has been even more radical. By the time Colin Leys was predicting that "local government in Uganda was unusually strong, both constitutionally and psychologically," and thus "not likely to disappear completely or at once,"[85] the attack on it was already well advanced. The original strength of local government was an additional outcome of Buganda's relative political autonomy at independence. Under the 1962 constitution, Buganda was guaranteed several sources of revenue free from central control and, as it turned out, central supervision.[86] Various districts expended funds illegally or without authorization in amounts ranging up to £126,796 in Buganda in 1962 and £276,835 (or 25 percent of its total budget) in Busoga in 1963. "The weak central government could not politically and in some cases constitutionally exercise any meaningful control over Buganda's financial expenditure."[87]

83. Colin Leys, *Politicians and Policies: An Essay on Politics in Acholi, Uganda 1962-65* (Nairobi: East African Publishing House, 1967), p. 41.

84. Mulusa, "Central Government and Local Authorities," p. 251; and Davey, "Local Bureaucrats and Politicians in East Africa," p. 271.

85. *Politicians and Policies,* p. 9.

86. Apolo Nsibambi, "Increased Government Control of Buganda's Financial Sinews since the Revolution of 1966," *Journal of Administration Overseas* 10, no. 2 (April 1971): 101-102. These sources included graduated tax, assigned revenue from petrol and diesel duty, statutory contributions from general revenue, and stamp duty from transfers of mailo land.

87. Ibid., p. 103. "Too much had been lost or wasted," argued J. S. M. Ochola, the minister of regional administrations, "through financial irresponsibility, factional disputes, administrative inefficiency and tribal self-interest." *Uganda Argus,* 11 July 1968, p. 6. He was discussing local government everywhere in Uganda and not just in Buganda.

With an absolute majority in parliament in 1964 and the defeat of the ex-servicemen defending the Kabaka in 1966, the position was reversed. In the Acholi-Lango factory dispute, Felix Onama spoke for many African leaders in warning that the

> time will come when we will have to decide whether we should continue with the present set up in the District Administrations which is continuously bringing tribal friction. People have failed to administer services and they now want to divert the attention of the people whom they are serving away from pointing out their laziness to the centre, and I do not think we are going to sit idle and allow things to be directed to us when the fault is at the bottom. *We shall go to the bottom and eliminate it and put things right.*[88]

The time came sooner than anyone expected. Following the enactment of a new local administration law, districts were informed in advance of the grants the central government would give them, a tactic that ended the local councillors' use of deficit budgeting as a tool against the center.[89] Certain of these grants could be withheld if tax collections lagged. The minister of regional administrations acquired the power to nominate members of district and municipal councils. He could dissolve a council if he thought it was in the public interest to do so, and he decided what the councillors could discuss.

Realizing that they were nominated by a minister who could remove the council if they contradicted government policy, councillors restricted the scope of their participation in council debates. Political relations with the center, a favorite topic in the early 1960s, gave way after 1966 to discussions limited to specific issues such as schools and wells. However, as services

88. *Uganda Parliamentary Debates,* 2d series, vol. 81 (20 February 1968), p. 3094. Italics added.
89. Nsibambi, "Increased Government Control of Buganda's Financial Sinews," pp. 105-107 and 109; and Davey, "Local Bureaucrats and Politicians in East Africa," p. 270. When the Toro district council wanted to discuss the restoration of the disturbed areas to its administration (see the discussion of Rwenzururu in chapter five), the Ministry of Regional Administrations sent them a telegram refusing permission.

were removed from the control of the councils, they had less
and less to discuss. Before they were all finally dissolved by the
military government, councils came "to realise that their involvement in the discussion of the estimates was largely an
exercise in rubber-stamping. . . ." [90] Local budgets and thus
local political arenas have steadily diminished, as the payment
of salaries to primary school teachers, technical maintenance of
water supplies, and forestry, veterinary, and health services were
transferred to central government ministries.[91]

3. TANZANIA: THE DEVIANT CASE?

Tanzania is the one African country whose leadership has made
a serious and continuing commitment to encouraging political
participation. It has done so, however, on its own terms. A brief
examination of the ways in which Tanzania has *controlled*
participation — and thus restricted popular political involvement — underlines the general trend toward departicipation
elsewhere. Tanzania shares many of the problems that caused
other African countries to dismantle their participatory structures. In addition, its top leaders are firmly committed to a
socialist strategy of development. This means they are prepared
to compromise their actual (if not rhetorical) adherence to
participation in order to achieve other goals.

Although some outside observers regard Tanzania's one-party
state as just another variant of authoritarian rule, Tanzanians
and their academic enthusiasts claim that a one-party system
can be more democratic than a multiparty regime. A Tanzanian policy statement insists that the educational system
should not "produce robots," but rather citizens with "enquir-
ing minds" to whom the government and the party "must
always be responsible."[92] One observer suggests that "political

90. Nsibambi, "Increased Government Control of Buganda's Financial Sinews,"
p. 110.

91. Davey, "Local Bureaucrats and Politicians in East Africa," p. 270; *Uganda
Argus,* 6 July 1968, p. 1; *Uganda Argus,* 19 June 1971, p. 1. Amin has also
announced that "District Service Committees have been suspended for the time
being." *The People,* 18 October 1971, p. 1. Presumably the national public service
commission has taken over the task of appointing, promoting, and dismissing officers
in local administration.

92. Julius K. Nyerere, *Education for Self-Reliance* (Dar es Salaam: Government
Printer, 1967), p. 8. See also Julius Nyerere, "Democracy and the Party System," in
Freedom and Unity ed. Nyerere (London: Oxford University Press, 1967).

participation in the rural party is the implicit goal of TANU [Tanganyika African National Union]." He adds that "mass participation has occurred in voting, local government councils, marketing cooperatives, and self-held [sic] activities." [93]

An intermediate view stressing controlled participation seems to be more accurate than either extreme. Raymond Hopkins regards Tanzania as developing a "containment" style of politics, which is a compromise between an open style and one based on coercion. [94] Containment politics involves making major decisions in private and then calling on the nation to support them. The elite decides "what political conflicts may become public. . . ." [95] Hopkins cites the establishment of a national bank, the union with Zanzibar, the nationalization of major industries and banks, and the decision that Tanzania should become a de jure one-party state as significant decisions that the public and legislators were called upon to ratify, but not to decide.

In discussing the role of the electoral process where the leaders are more committed to socialism than the masses are, John Saul comes to a similar conclusion. Rather than stressing the achievement of democratic accountability, elections in Tanzania represented "a conscious attempt to strike a delicate balance between such *participation* on the one hand and *central political* control on the other." [96] As Rashidi Kawawa, the prime minister, puts it, "We wanted . . . a system of democracy which would avoid the divisive tendencies apparent in many established democratic systems." [97] Keeping in mind the fragile compromise this implies, we can consider the restricted opera-

93. Norman N. Miller, "The Rural African Party: Political Participation in Tanzania," *The American Political Science Review* 64, no. 2 (June 1970): 564 and 551.

94. *Political Roles in a New State: Tanzania's First Decade* (New Haven: Yale University Press, 1971), p. 243. My discussion is limited to the mainland. Since its revolution, the Zanzibar government, which has controlled its own domestic affairs, has permitted little political participation.

95. Ibid., pp. 39 and 34.

96. "The Nature of Tanzania's Political System: Issues Raised by the 1965 and 1970 Elections," Part I, *Journal of Commonwealth Political Studies* 10, no. 2 (July 1972): 114. Italics in original. Working from a third perspective, Henry Bienen also agrees. "Political Parties and Political Machines in Africa," in *The State of the Nations,* ed. Lofchie, p. 213.

97. "Foreword," in *One Party Democracy: The 1965 Tanzania General Elections,* ed. Lionel Cliffe (Nairobi: East African Publishing House, 1967), n.p.

tion of participatory structures in Tanzania. As in the other cases, this inquiry demands a brief examination of the powers of central administration, the loss of autonomy of local government and voluntary associations, the National Assembly, elections, and TANU.

Like other African countries, Tanzania has "broadened the power and scope of government and increased the authority of the executive." [98] The republican constitution of 1962, which has been altered only slightly gave wide-ranging powers to the president. Although he cannot legislate without the National Assembly, he has broad powers of preventive detention, appointment, and control of the security services. As Nyerere has commented, "I have sufficient powers under the constitution to be a dictator." [99]

Both local government and voluntary associations have lost their autonomy and thus have become less effective as participatory structures. At independence, district councils had less protection from the central government than was the case in Uganda. A law had been passed to introduce formal elections, but it was never put into effect. As a result the minister of local government had the right to appoint councillors, even if informal elections determined local choices. "Obviously, government wanted the Minister of Local Government to retain control." [100] Though all the councillors were TANU members, they occasionally refused to implement central government policy.

At independence, district councils in Tanzania faced more serious versions of the same difficulties confronting Uganda and Kenya. Less revenue was available, the very few qualified administrators were shifted to central government, and new councillors had little sense of realistic policymaking. Financial crises, insolvency, malpractices by employees, and irrational policies followed. [101] In one council the regional commissioner insisted that no further expenditures could be made without his ap-

98. Hopkins, *Political Roles in a New State*, p. 26.
99. *The Standard* (Tanzania), 22 January 1966, quoted in Hopkins, *Political Roles in a New State*, p. 27.
100. Henry Bienen, *Tanzania: Party Transformation and Economic Development* (Princeton: Princeton University Press, 1967), pp. 103, 106, and n. 49, p. 106.
101. Stanley Dryden, *Local Administration in Tanzania* (Nairobi: East African Publishing House, 1968), pp. 99-100.

proval. In another district the council was dissolved. The desire of councillors to increase educational facilities caused them to reduce budgets for other services below minimal requirements. Routine maintenance of all sorts was neglected. Some councils paid their employees out of central government grants intended for specific projects.[102]

The central government responded in various ways. In October 1966 the district chairman of TANU was appointed to chair the local council in his area. This move suggests the reluctance of the government to permit an elected representative to become a rival to the local party official.[103] An amendment to the Local Government Ordinance "deemed" every council to have delegated economic and social services to district development committees. Although the latter were committees of the council, they also contained the area commissioner (who served as chairman) and ten officials from central government ministries. In Stanley Dryden's view: "The dependence of rural local authorities upon the administrative support and assistance of the central government is an essential feature of the local government system at the present time. It is the prop which buttresses the entire edifice and without which the activities of many councils would surely grind to a halt."[104]

The loss of autonomy of trade unions and, to a large extent, of cooperatives as well has also followed the pattern of Uganda and Kenya. Although the Tanganyika Federation of Labour (TFL) supported TANU before independence, there was conflict between them over Africanization in industry and pressure for wage increases followed by a series of strikes. Legislation was passed in 1962 requiring all unions to join a government-designated (but not controlled) organization and to submit to arbitration before striking. Strikes in the next two years sometimes met with the rustication and detention of labor leaders. Disgruntled trade unionists were suspected of taking advantage

102. Ibid., p. 99; n. 8, p. 105; and p. 101; and William Tordoff, *Government and Politics in Tanzania: A Collection of Essays* (Nairobi: East African Publishing House, 1967), p. 116. The councils in which the central government intervened were Rungwe and North Mara.

103. Dryden, *Local Administration in Tanzania,* p. 147; and Davey, "Local Bureaucrats and Politicians in East Africa," pp. 270-271.

104. *Local Administration in Tanzania,* p. 111.

of the unsettled conditions during the army mutiny of January 1964. The next month the government enacted a new law establishing a government-controlled union (NUTA) with a general secretary and deputy appointed by Nyerere. The new union was affiliated with TANU and expected to promote party policies. [105] The Arusha Declaration may also have dampened the participation of workers, since their annual average wage increases between 1967 and 1969 declined from 13 to 5 percent.[106]

Cooperatives foundered on problems of corrupt employees and committee members. Many members lost interest when no bonuses were forthcoming. There was a "lack of *generalized mass peasant involvement* in what should, ostensibly, be their own cooperatives." [107] The government responded with more intervention, and in 1966 it took over direct control of sixteen unions involving hundreds of primary societies. "The fact is . . . that political leaders in Tanganyika think increasingly in mono-institutional terms, with TANU as the core of a national political movement to which both the trade union and cooperative movements are affiliated — as subordinate, rather than as equal or parallel, organs." [108] These structures, through which individuals might have participated in politics, have been removed from the political arena.

The Tanzanian National Assembly has also become less important in national politics. The commission considering the establishment of a one-party state observed that "with a few notable exceptions, debates in the National Assembly have tended to be lifeless and superficial." [109] In the first five years

105. This discussion of Tanzanian labor policy has been taken from Tordoff, *Government and Politics in Tanzania,* pp. 141-150. One of the government's arguments for setting up NUTA was that 94 percent of the total income of the constituent unions in the TFL in 1962 had been spent on administration. Dryden, *Local Administration in Tanzania,* p. 81.

106. Sandbrook, "The State and the Development of Trade Unions," p. 291.

107. John S. Saul, "Marketing Co-operatives in a Developing Country: The Tanzanian Case," *Taamuli* (Dar es Salaam) 1, no. 2 (March 1971): 43. Italics in original. See also p. 45.

108. Tordoff, *Government and Politics in Tanzania,* p. 154.

109. *Report of the Presidential Commission on the Establishment of a Democratic One Party State* (Dar es Salaam: Government Printer, 1965), p. 20; and Tordoff, *Government and Politics in Tanzania,* p. 15.

of independence, no major legislation was opposed. Although debate and criticism of the government increased somewhat after the 1965 elections, it was the national executive committee of TANU that vigorously — but secretly — debated policy. The government has induced popular local leaders to play a role in the National Assembly that subordinates their constituency interests to national government policies. [110] Thus, policy differences are resolved in the small and private arena of inner party circles.

A comparison of two of the three government bills that have been rejected by the MPs illustrates some of the limits on participatory activity. In July 1968 the National Assembly rejected a proposal to pay gratuities to ministers and regional and area commissioners. The government acquiesced in its defeat and the then vice-president, Rashidi Kawawa, declared, "Parliament is empowered to approve or reject any decision made by the Government." [111] Five years later MPs rejected an income tax bill proposed by the government. The following day Nyerere recalled parliament to debate the bill afresh. "I am not prepared," he said, "to accept that a Bill, beneficial to the majority, should be rejected simply because it is not liked by a minority." [112] Two weeks later the National Assembly reconvened and the proposal was passed unanimously through both readings in a thirty-minute session.

Looking at the two cases together suggests that the TANU leadership was prepared to tolerate defeat only when it was clear that greater equality consistent with building Tanzanian socialism would be achieved — in spite of the statement made

110. Raymond F. Hopkins, "Constituency Ties and Deviant Expectations among Tanzanian Legislators," *Comparative Political Studies* 4, no. 3 (October 1971): 322 and 326.

111. H. U. E. Thoden Van Velzen and J. J. Sterkenberg, "Stirrings in the Tanzanian National Assembly," in *Socialism in Tanzania: An Interdisciplinary Reader,* ed. Lionel Cliffe and John S. Saul, vol. 1 (Nairobi: East African Publishing House, 1972), p. 252.

112. The *Daily News* (Tanzania), 29 November 1973, p. 1. The bill was defeated (sixty-six to forty-six) on 27 November 1973 and then passed on 13 December. The TANU Study Group attacked the "irresponsibility" of the MPs who voted against the bill and said there was "a stratum of pro-capitalist elements" which would have to be confronted. *Daily News,* 4 December 1973, p. 1. The MPs got the point. It is worth remembering that only one-third of the MPs in 1973 had served in parliament when the gratuities bill was defeated in 1968.

by Kawawa in 1968. In the case of the 1973 bill, the MPs seemed to be voting for their own pocketbook, since passage of the bill meant that their own income taxes would be raised. Participation appeared to be valued by the top leaders, but not where it led to the protection of privilege. However, there were a number of ways of undoing a decision the top leadership believed to be a step in the wrong direction. Humiliation of MPs was likely to further restrict participation in the National Assembly to a form of symbolic involvement.

In discussing Tanzanian elections, it is important to recall that in all contests in which TANU nominated candidates, no other parties have managed to elect MPs. [113] Instead of running in competition, TANU was like the racer who runs against the clock — in this case to convince the British that the party had the support of the people. Unlike most other African nations, Tanzania became a one-party state *after* TANU monopolized political participation in open competition. However, there was some relatively ineffectual opposition from dissident TANU politicians who formed two rival parties. The successful efforts by TANU officials to crush these parties before the establishment of a one-party state are reminiscent of measures taken against opposition parties elsewhere. [114]

But since most TANU candidates ran unopposed by the time of independence, the party's very success worked against popular involvement. "By a paradox the more support the people have given T.A.N.U. as a party the more they have reduced their participation in the process of government." [115] To rectify this problem to some extent, a new type of electoral system was adopted in 1965, in which two candidates from TANU were selected to run against each other in every constituency. They were nominated by voting in lower-level party conferences that insured some local orientation, though the national executive

113. The only time a TANU candidate was defeated, he was beaten by another member of TANU who had run as an independent. J. A. Namata, *The Civil Service in Tanzania* (Dar es Salaam: Government Printer, 1967), p. 10.

114. Though the right to run candidates in local and national elections was not denied to these parties prior to 1964. On their harassment in the Sukuma area, see G. Andrew Maguire, *Toward 'Uhuru' in Tanzania: The Politics of Participation* (Cambridge: Cambridge University Press, 1969), pp. 349-360.

115. *Report of the Presidential Commission on the Establishment of a One Party State*, p. 14.

committee occasionally exercised its right to nominate a candidate who had not been one of the top two in popularity at the lower level. The president ran unopposed.

The elections resulted in a major change of parliamentary personnel, since seventeen MPs (including two ministers and six junior ministers) were defeated at the polls, while thirteen more (including three junior ministers) failed to gain party nomination. [116] In addition twenty-seven others did not stand. Thus, four-fifths of the MPs elected in 1965 were new to the Assembly. Nyerere received 95.6 percent "yes" votes, which represented 78.1 percent of registered voters and over half the eligible population. The importance of electoral participation as perceived by the people was indicated in a survey carried out in Bukoba district in 1965. Voting was considered by 57 percent of the sample as the most effective way to influence the government. [117]

A second one-party election was held in 1970. The population eligible to vote rose by 29 percent over the 1965 figure because of population increase and the reduction of the voting age to eighteen. [118] Of this larger total the national registration average went up from 63 percent in 1965 to 74 percent in 1970. Voter turnout also rose from 48 to 51 percent. Only sixty of the MPs in the 1965 parliament chose to run and survived the nomination process. Of these, twenty-one were defeated. As a result over two-thirds of the members of the 1970 parliament were new. Nyerere's share of "yes" votes remained about the same (94.7 percent).

116. Tordoff, *Government and Politics in Tanzania,* p. 39. On the elections generally see Cliffe, *One Party Democracy.*

117. Göran Hydén, *TANU Yajenga Nchi: Political Development in Rural Tanzania* (Lund: Uniskol Bokförlaget Universitet och Skola, 1968), p. 222. Writing letters to one's MP or district councillor was regarded as the second most important method of influence. Virtually everyone knew the name of the president, though many did not know the names of lower officials. Ibid., p. 224.

118. Materials on the 1970 election have been taken from the useful presentation in Helge Kjekshus, "Tanzania's General Elections, 1965 and 1970: Some Statistical and Cartographical Notes," Service Paper 72/2, Bureau of Resource Assessment and Land Use Planning, University of Dar es Salaam (September 1972); Hydén and Leys, "Elections and Politics in Single-Party Systems"; and *Statistical Abstract 1970* (Dar es Salaam: Government Printer, 1972). Unavailable at the time of writing, unfortunately, was the more comprehensive analysis in *Socialism and Participation: Tanzania's 1970 National Elections,* ed. The Election Study Commitee (Dar es Salaam: Tanzania Publishing House, 1974).

Thus, the two elections suggest growing levels of voter participation, high turnover of MPs, and — insofar as a "yes-no" vote on a single candidate carries weight — a very high level of approval for Nyerere. However, the limits of this participation were controlled by the leadership. Only TANU members who supported the government's policies could run, and the issues on which they campaigned were restricted. Administrative officials traveled with the candidates and heard their speeches. Candidates did not discuss any of the implications of building socialism, for example, because they regarded it as settled party policy. The electorate could select their representatives; but aside from being able to cast a negative vote in the presidential election, they were not permitted to register their feelings about fundamental objectives such as socialism. Thus, the personae involved went up substantially, while scope remained relatively restricted, and the bases for campaigning were kept mainly under party control. Given the relatively low level of importance of parliament in Tanzanian politics, the weight of voter participation was probably not very high. Both elections indicate a significant volume of participation, but not one that suggests that political involvement was an absolute value held by the Tanzanian leadership.

The central focus of participation in the country is TANU, and it is a major exception to the general decline of governing parties in Africa. The problems TANU faced at independence, like the problems of parties elsewhere, came from two opposite directions. It faced competition from the bureaucracy over staff and over control of policy. And it confronted a peasantry with severe limitations in consciousness, not to mention in acceptance of the goals that the party's leadership hoped to achieve.

Staffing the highest levels of governments depleted the ranks of the party's most capable officials, [119] but Tanzania's response to this crisis differed from that of other African countries. Shortly after independence Nyerere resigned as prime minister in order to devote himself for almost a year to reviving

119. Colin Leys, "Tanganyika: The Realities of Independence," in *Socialism in Tanzania,* ed. Cliffe and Saul, p. 191. Leys estimates that well over half of the party's district secretaries and all of its provincial secretaries had left party work by early 1962. Nyerere's resignation, however, was involved in disputes over policy as well. Ibid., pp. 191-193.

the party's organizational effectiveness. A process of self-renewal has continued over the years. TANU found a new role by taking on a variety of tasks that fell beyond the reach of government officials. An elaborate system of cells, each containing a cluster of ten houses, was gradually built. The party was merged into government, without, however, losing its identity. In addition it continuously carried forward a constructive ideological debate on social goals. On the other hand, its success in articulating national goals was matched by its inability to explain its ideology to rural villagers.[120]

One important reason for TANU's ability to establish a presence in the countryside was that villagers — whether or not they comprehended (or accepted) the ideology for development enunciated by party officials — identified themselves with the party. In a survey in one rural area (Buhaya) far from the capital, 69 percent of those questioned claimed party membership, and 92 percent living in an even more remote part of the country (Tabora) told another researcher that they belonged.[121]

One result of this high level of acceptance was a willingness to bring problems which would otherwise have been left to traditional authorities or government officials to local party leaders for resolution. In one rural area TANU officials were involved in family mediation, administration, police, and welfare activities. [122] TANU member also carried out government policies where officials were shorthanded. They manned road-blocks, checked individuals to see if they have paid their taxes, and even collected the taxes. "The party itself becomes a catch-all organization. . . ."[123] Abuses such as the use of coercion to force people to participate and the use of the party apparatus for personal gain have occurred but seem to be the exception rather than the rule.

More serious for TANU was its inability to carry out goals it

120. Miller, "The Rural African Party," p. 551.
121. Hydén, *TANU Yajenga Nchi*, p. 218; and Miller, "The Rural African Party," p. 557. Miller believes that actual party membership is somewhat lower.
122. Miller, "The Rural African Party," pp. 551-554 and 567. Over 70 percent of his respondents said they took their "political problems" to the chairman of their party cell or village branch. Ibid., p. 557. See also Bienen, *Tanzania,* p. 99; and Dryden, *Local Administration in Tanzania,* p. 68.
123. Miller, "The Rural African Party," pp. 551 and 554-556.

set for itself. Bienen argues that "the party does not provide an institution which can transform the economy and make itself more effective in the process; it is too weak and too loose and has too few material and human resources to tackle developmental problems." [124]   The national headquarters remained small. It had fewer than twenty-five full-time employees (by comparison the CPP had over two hundred in 1966). [125]   None of its other central bodies exercised continuous control over regional and district bodies. Instead there was intermittent contact and alteration of directives and ideas as they were passed down the line. Indeed, at the bottom, "the district-village tie is the weakest link in the party structure." [126]   Paradoxically, perhaps, participation may have been somewhat higher because TANU was able to kindle enthusiasm without possessing the capability of extensive control.

More recently the party tightened its membership qualifications. In part this was a consequence of the sharpening ideological debate that followed the Arusha Declaration in February 1967. Those who refused to give up outside sources of income could not continue as leaders. Several resigned their government positions, and others were expelled from the National Assembly and TANU. [127]   Ironically, perhaps, given its socialist ideology, "the party has now emerged as a more distinct unit from the masses." [128]   In addition, there was a noticeable increase in coercion. Many major political figures have been jailed, executed, or driven into exile. On balance, however, TANU has been a comparative success in sustaining an important level of material participation.

Even more impressive, however, has been the continuing nature of the Tanzanian leadership's experiments with new participatory structures. The expansion of the role of the central government that necessarily resulted from nationalization

124. *Tanzania,* p. 407. It should be kept in mind that Bienen's assessment predates the Arusha Declaration, the explicit commitment to socialist goals.

125. Ibid., pp. 411, 413-414; and Cohen, "The Convention People's Party of Ghana," p. 183.

126. Miller, "The Rural African Party," p. 562.

127. John S. Saul, "The Nature of Tanzania's Political System: Issues Raised by the 1965 and 1970 Elections," Part II, *Journal of Commonwealth Political Studies* 10, no. 3 (November 1972): 209-213.

128. Hopkins, *Political Roles in a New State,* pp. 37 and 243.

of industrial and financial enterprises and the new responsibilities given to public corporations after the Arusha Declaration has not diverted the attention of national leaders from the question of the impact of the growth of administration on participation. For example, the president issued a directive in 1970 for workers' councils to be established in all public corporations "to give practical effect to workers' representation and participation in planning, productivity, quality and marketing matters." [129]   In 1965 an ombudsman was established to handle complaints of citizens against government officials. This commission toured the country, held public meetings, and received sixteen hundred complaints in its first year and almost twenty-five hundred in the second. [130]   Both the complaints and the public meetings are important examples of political participation.

A major reorganization of central and local government powers begun in 1972 resulted in the transfer of control over some of the revenue allocated for development from central government ministries to new district development councils. [131] These councils comprised both elected and appointed members and were expected to make decisions without being required to consult with ministerial headquarters in the capital. The purpose of decentralizing control was to reduce delays in the implementation of projects and to encourage participation in decision making by more people — though within guidelines laid down by the center.

There is nothing magical about Tanzania. The same problems exist there that have led to departicipation elsewhere. To some extent Tanzania has followed the same path. The central government is more powerful than it was at independence. Opposition parties, weak though they were, found extralegal obstacles

129. These councils are different from existing workers' committees and are intended "to further industrial democracy in relation to the economic functions of the enterprise, and give the workers a greater and more direct responsibility in production." *Presidential Circular No. 1 of 1970,* 10 February 1970.

130. *Annual Reports of the Permanent Commission of Enquiry,* June 1966-June 1967 and July 1967-June 1968 (Dar es Salaam: Government Printer, 1968 and 1969). Kenya, by way of contrast, has restricted the possibility of challenge to administrative actions in court and "peremptorily dismissed" the proposal of an ombudsman. Ghai and McAuslan, *Public Law and Political Change in Kenya,* p. 515.

131. J. Nyerere, *Decentralisation* (Dar es Salaam: Government Printer, 1972).

placed in their way. Elections to the National Assembly were limited in scope and weight. Local government and voluntary associations lost their autonomy early, and it remains to be seen whether central administrators will respect local priorities in planning chosen by the new development councils.

The Tanzanian leadership decided to opt for a pattern of socialist construction in spite of the absence of popular consciousness of vested interests and privilege. This dilemma has meant that socialist measures have been introduced from the top with emphasis on political education. In theory Tanzanian socialism depends on mass involvement. The question is whether the current pattern of controlled participation will lead to that goal.

4. LIMITS OF DEPARTICIPATION

Though a symbolic commitment to participation encourages leaders to introduce newly designed channels for popular involvement from time to time, there is no longer much opportunity in Africa for most people to influence their governments. Given the continued existence of independent African polities, total departicipation, however, is impossible, since there cannot be a political system without involvement by someone at some level. The removal of participatory structures does not mean that those whom they previously serviced are totally or permanently outside politics.

Political struggle, in other words, continues in all African countries. To a small extent it remains public, often on an intermittent basis. The Ugandan constitutional debate of 1967, to a lesser extent the debate over socialism two years later, and the elections of UPC party officials in 1970 were sporadic spurts of participation. Vigorous debate in the Kenyan National Assembly compensated to a small degree for departicipation in other sectors. The Kenyan "primary" election of 1969 also permitted some political involvement. There were great efforts to secure symbolic participation in Ghana during the First Republic, though it remains unclear whether very many people were involved.

More striking, however, has been the reduction of politics to shadowy behind-the-scenes appeals on the basis of personal influence. Occasionally this sort of participation has erupted into violence – for example, the assassination attempts on Tom Mboya, Nkrumah, and Obote; the stoning of Kenyatta's car in Kisumu in October 1969 (in which incident at least ten people were killed and seventy wounded); and the defense of the Kabaka in May 1966.

Sufficient evidence also exists to show that many African military leaders permitted some participation and introduced new structures to channel it, though these often turned out to be heavily controlled. [132]   Since the institution of military rule in 1969, the Sudan has held three elections, two at the national level and one in the Southern Region, in addition to a presidential plebescite. Upper Volta held an election in 1971 that led to the appointment of a civilian prime minister. The Zairean leadership, like the Sudanese, invested heavily in building its new single party. The NLC in Ghana encouraged business and voluntary associations to articulate their grievances in the governmental decision-making process. The military has gone so far as to hand power back to civilians – though only temporarily in most cases. Civilian rule was restored through a carefully managed process in Ghana (1969) and more abruptly in Sierra Leone (1968) and the Sudan (1964).

The problem, then, is to identify the kinds of low-level involvement that take place after participatory structures established at the time of independence have been removed. The channels for participation created by the first military regime in Ghana and the forms of participation that have come to characterize military rule in Uganda suggest two different patterns – both becoming more frequent in Africa.

Shortly after it took power in Ghana, the NLC began to implement its promise to step down from office. [133]   The new political structures it introduced had the immediate effect of widening participation somewhat. A Political Committee was appointed in June 1966 (four months after the coup); and a

132. See Nelson Kasfir, "Bringing Back the Man on Foot: Civilian Participation in Military Regimes in Uganda and the Sudan," *Armed Forces and Society* 1, no. 3 (May 1975).

133. The argument is developed in Pinkney, *Ghana under Military Rule,* pp. 118-133, 136 (political schedule): 104-105 (decentralization); 18-36 (cases of popular involvement in decision making); and 158 (limitations on involvement).

Constitutional Committee that September. Members of a Constituent Assembly were elected in 1968, and national elections, which were held in September 1969, resulted in the hand-over of power to Busia, though the military held onto the presidency for a further period. The NLC even decentralized many administrative activities by delegating them to district authorities.

The NLC was also prepared to listen to the opinions of a variety of affected individuals and groups before making decisions. Chiefs, businessmen, farmers, gold miners, and local residents who stood to lose employment opportunities were able to persuade the government to meet some of their grievances and in some cases restore projects that had been cancelled. Since the military rulers did not have a rigid or even an explicit ideology, the scope of participation was surprisingly wide, though socialist alternatives that hinted of "Nkrumahism" were prohibited. On most occasions where involvement carried weight, the personae of participation were limited to the chiefs and the thirty to forty thousand who possessed secondary school education. Participation appeared to be controlled at far lower levels than in Tanzania, but it played a role in shaping governmental action and in achieving, temporarily, one of the NLC's goals – a civilian government.

The Ugandan situation differed from that of Ghana because there was virtually no effort made under Amin's regime to build and maintain structures through which participation could flow. At first Amin took a number of steps demanded by large and important segments of the population. He released some political detainees, allowed the Kabaka's body to be brought back for burial, banned miniskirts, and created two new districts. Later, in a move initially popular throughout the country, he expelled the Indians and Pakistanis.

However, the greatly enlarged political role of an army only intermittently under discipline suggests a different sort of limit on departicipation. Although Amin has removed or rendered meaningless most participatory structures in the country, it has become increasingly clear since the coup that soldiers are often laws unto themselves – uncontrolled in many of their actions by high officials, civilian or military. Thus, soldiers have increased their level of political participation in comparison with the level of the earlier Obote era, when they returned, albeit reluctantly, to their barracks after the 1964 mutiny, the 1966 attack on the Kabaka's palace, and the 1969 response to the attempted assassination of Obote.

After the first months of military rule, the weight of participation of the soldiers at individual and collective levels became far greater. Officers, some recently promoted from the ranks of NCOs, replaced most of the highly qualified ministers of Amin's first cabinet. Eight of the first ten provincial governors came from the armed forces (the other two were police and prisons officials), as did chairmen of many public bodies. A number of important and wide-ranging state decisions appear to have been made "with the advice" of the Defence Council, a military body. Soldiers supervised and often "won" the 1973 "elections" of Ugandan chiefs. But the appointment of soldiers to important positions did not mean that Amin took governmental structures very seriously. As in the case of the councils of elders discussed above, the personnel and responsibilities of these structures changed with such bewildering rapidity that it is hard to believe that they were capable of effectively formulating or implementing consistent public policies.[134]

In addition soldiers gained control of a large share of the national budget. [135] They acquired many of the businesses (not to mention the Mercedes Benzes) formerly belonging to expelled Indians and Pakistanis. They took the law into their own hands in countless personal situations — with the result that their opponents often "disappeared." In this fashion the personae of participation changed dramatically from the population in general and the educated (and predominantly Christian) elite in particular to the largely uneducated and Muslim soldiers. Much of the limited participation that did take place ceased to occur within existing structures. Instead, it amounted to unpre-

---

134. It seems clear that Amin's inability to gain a firm grip over the army was an important factor in his failure to stabilize the structures through which he could govern. The consequence of carrying out a coup with the support of a loosely organized faction within the army led to the widespread massacre of personally disloyal soldiers in his first year as president. The resulting distrust fed further turbulence.

135. Publicly announced spending on the security forces in 1971-1972 amounted to 25 percent of the recurrent budget and 35 percent of the development budget. The published estimates for the following year were lower. *Uganda Argus,* 21 June 1972, p. 1.

dictable personal action governed by no formal rules and only occasional penalties. Uganda has been characterized by a striking degree of political decay.

5. CONCLUSION

Strengthening central administration and dismantling participatory structures has greatly reduced the possibilities of popular involvement in most African countries. The removal of these structures does not necessarily mean the elimination of an individual's ability to participate. He might shift his activities to another means of participation. For example, the transfer of services from local to central government control might mean no more than transfer of the arena in which all who participated before continue to act. However, the center is farther away from most people and harder to influence.

Central governments have shown marked willingness to exercise significant control over those resources that might otherwise serve as bases of participation. They have greatly contracted the personae involved in politics as well as severely restricted the scope of the issues which can be openly considered. The wreckage of so many participatory structures – designed with little regard for the political conditions facing newly independent African nations – diminishes the weight of participation of all but those few with intimate access to high government officials. Individual calculations that a particular participatory act might meet with success occur far less frequently. Departicipation has become an established fact in country after country. Indeed, despite the careful political planning of the NLC, the history of the Second Republic of Ghana – and its culmination in another coup in February 1972 – suggests again how pervasive this pattern has been.

Still, it would be a mistake to assume that there are no limits to departicipation. Various structures have been recently introduced to elicit a low-level and easily managed volume of political involvement. The approaches of the NLC in Ghana and Amin in Uganda present contrasting variations on this pattern of shrunken volume. The first military regime in Ghana attempted to develop structures that could accommodate participation and in some cases give it significant weight. In Uganda, however, an important portion of what participation there was occurred outside any formal procedures established by the government.

Tanzania remains an important exception. There, too, many of the same participatory structures were removed. But these were replaced with imaginative new channels through which a controlled, but significant, volume of participation can be encouraged. Nevertheless, the leadership's careful management of public participation indicates that Tanzania faces the same pressures that have forced people out of politics elsewhere.

TEN

◇

ACHIEVING POLITICAL DEVELOPMENT: CAUSES AND DESIRABILITY OF DEPARTICIPATION

If political development means establishing a balance between participation and the political structures designed to accommodate it, then both sides of the equation must be investigated. The problem is broader than the question of how "to make power, to mobilize groups into politics and to organize their participation in politics."[1] Political development may be more likely if groups are demobilized and if leaders organize their departicipation from politics. Most African leaders, at any rate, have acted as if they were persuaded that this is so.

Since the achievement of departicipation has meant the elimination of most participatory structures, the central bureaucracy appears most likely to be the chief governing institution in the years to come — just as it was during the colonial period. It may turn out to be more capable of coping with low volumes of participation than the full panoply of imported participatory structures proved to be in the first years of independence. How long this simplified system of government will persist can at present be no more than a guess.

Let me hasten to add that the achievement of political development in this fashion may not be desirable. The consequence of getting people out of politics may entrench institutions so unresponsive to popular needs that existing government capabilities are poorly employed. The concern for stability can drive out all consideration of satisfaction of grievances or of economic improvement.

Furthermore, getting people out of politics is a risky venture

1. Samuel P. Huntington, *Political Order in Changing Societies* (New Haven: Yale University Press, 1968), pp. 144-145.

269

for rulers. It necessarily results in a significant reduction of the legitimacy of the surviving institutions. These can be weakened beyond the point of being able to cope with even radically lowered levels of participation. As the last years of Kwame Nkrumah's rule in Ghana — and perhaps those of Milton Obote's in Uganda — illustrate, departicipation can lead to political decay. To pursue this argument requires a look at the causes of departicipation that lie behind government policies to strengthen central administration and dismantle participatory structures and then at the grounds for judging whether departicipation is desirable.

1. CAUSES OF DEPARTICIPATION

If departicipation is as pervasive as I have argued above, the causes are likely to be equally widespread. It is not sufficient to observe that rulers have transformed their regimes without wondering why they do so. The explanation must take into account both the values that shape the operative norms of politicians at the top and the importance of poverty in the acceptance of departicipation by those at the bottom.

Certain general values held by members of the highest ranks of the political elite are discussed here because they seem directly relevant to a discussion of departicipation, though they are by no means comprehensive. They are general in the sense that they condition the specific attitudes of many African leaders toward policy choices. They include the desire to stay in power, habits derived from the colonial style of government, and the belief that economic development depends on central direction.[2]

The overriding desire to stay in power is the simplest and most obvious explanation of the trend toward departicipation. Uncertainty over the treatment one's successor is likely to mete

2. Focusing upon the social and economic interests that present-day political elites seek to protect provides an alternative explanation of departicipation. Many of these interests grow out of the stratified system of rewards originally introduced into colonial economies and presently nourished through links to European and North American countries. In addition, the dependency of African countries upon more industrialized states suggests that foreign firms or governments may play an active role in reducing the volume of participation in Africa. However, the steps in the argument supporting these assertions are far more difficult to substantiate than is the case for the explanations put forward here.

out cannot be absent from the minds of top political and military officials. Participation could mean opposition, which could develop into the loss of office and the high salaries that go with it. As a result, leaders develop vested interests that give them a closer identity with the colonial rulers they replaced than with the people they claim to be serving. "Populist behavior, in their reckoning, could hardly be permitted to threaten the transfer of this power."[3]

Chinua Achebe puts this extremely well in *A Man of the People:*

> A man who has just come in from the rain and dried his body and put on dry clothes is more reluctant to go out again than another who has been indoors all the time. The trouble with our new nation . . . was that none of us had been indoors long enough to be able to say "To hell with it." We had all been in the rain together until yesterday. Then a handful of us — the smart and the lucky and hardly ever the best — had scrambled for the one shelter our former rulers left, and had taken it over and barricaded themselves in. And from within they sought to persuade the rest through numerous loudspeakers, that the first phase of the struggle had been won and that the next phase — the extension of our house — was even more important and called for new and original tactics; it required that all argument should cease and the whole people speak with one voice and that any more dissent and argument outside the door of the shelter would subvert and bring down the whole house.[4]

A further consideration in the minds of rulers develops from the novelty of their position. Under the intense glare of publicity, leaders everywhere presumably fear failure. But when the nation is new, the desire to eradicate all potential threats is probably all the stronger: "An ever-increasing display of author-

3. Martin Kilson, *Political Change in a West African State: A Study of the Modernization Process in Sierra Leone* (Cambridge: Harvard University Press, 1966), p. 192.

4. (New York: John Day, 1966), p. 42.

ity is necessary to obtain minimal reassurance that things will not fall apart."[5]

The political struggle between local and central governments illustrates why national leaders use departicipation to stay in power. Departing colonial rulers wrongly assumed that the central government would allow local governments to learn from their own mistakes. National leaders, however, were concerned that these mistakes would cause a loss in their own popularity. Local councillors tried to focus their expenditures on popular social services and leave to the central government investments in long-range productive development measures which could not be easily converted into political capital. Furthermore, they attempted — for example in Uganda — to make the central government take public responsibility for cutting budgets. It is little wonder that national leaders moved quickly to dismantle the participatory aspects of local government.

A second important cause of departicipation in Africa is the heavy influence of the colonial legacy on the beliefs of political leaders. "Authoritarianism in the new African states . . . is — perhaps paradoxically — a feature of government in which there is a basic continuity across the great shift from colonial to African control."[6] Colonial administration followed military patterns of organization in both French and British territories. [7] The first and second generations of African officials grew up under this system. They were habituated to government justified by an Austinian "command" theory of law — that laws are obeyed only because adequate force backs them up. "Law was second only to weapons of war in the establishment of colonial rule, . . . both were useful implements to coerce the African." [8]

5. Aristide R. Zolberg, *Creating Political Order: The Party States of West Africa* (Chicago: Rand McNally, 1966), p. 66. The quotation ironically recalls Chinua Achebe's first novel, *Things Fall Apart* (London and Ibadan: Heinemann Educational Books, 1958).

6. Francis Sutton, "Authority and Authoritarianism in the New Africa," in *The Nigerian Political Scene,* ed. Robert O. Tilman and Taylor Cole (Durham, N.C.: Duke University Press, 1962), p. 277.

7. Ruth First, *The Barrel of a Gun: Political Power in Africa and the Coup d'État* (London: Allen Lane The Penguin Press, 1970), pp. 31-35.

8. Yash Ghai and J. P. W. B. McAuslan, *Public Law and Political Change in Kenya: A Study of the Legal Framework of Government from Colonial Times to the Present* (Nairobi: Oxford University Press, 1970), pp. 506-507. They brilliantly contrast the two opposing philosophies of law that distinguished settler from African

Another intellectual legacy that colonial administrators transmitted to the people they ruled was the overriding belief that government – in Africa, at least – stood above "politics." Their definition of politics was restricted to the struggle of special – and selfish – interests. This distinction served colonial administrators well because it insulated them from the people they ruled while they carried out activities that would be regarded as ''political" by almost any other definition.[9] The institutionalization of this belief worked against the political elite's acceptance of new participatory structures, other than those giving tactical advantage in the struggle for independence. Consequently, as African regimes emerge from their brief and unfamiliar interlude with participatory devices that now seem to be little more than an artifact of independence, they return to the instruments of rule used by the colonial governments from which they are descended.

The resemblance has its limits, however. African regimes cannot become colonial governments however much some of their leaders may desire the power and lack of accountability that characterized their predecessors. The fundamental reason is that the new leaders are indigenous and thus subject to the pressures of a society which they, unlike colonial officials, cannot legitimately leave. Second, whether or not these leaders were originally elected to office, all of them (with a few conspicuous exceptions) are committed to the mass franchise, at least in theory. This commitment requires them to modify the colonial legacy through at least some measure of symbolic participation. Third, African leaders by and large have insisted upon a more rapid rate of development than colonial administrators. One example of all three points is the rise in expenditures intended to improve the lives of a wide range of citizens in most African countries since independence.[10] Departicipation

administration in Kenya and bring out the consequences for constitutional development. Ibid., pp. 506-514.

9. See Nelson Kasfir, "Development Administration in Africa: The Balance between Politics and Administration," *Canadian Journal of African Studies* 3, no. 1 (Winter 1969): 97-98.

10. See Immanuel Wallerstein, "The Range of Choice: Constraints on the Policies of Governments of Contemporary African Independent States," in *The State of the Nations: Constraints on Development in Independent Africa,* ed. Michael F. Lofchie (Berkeley and Los Angeles: University of California Press, 1971), p. 23.

may be the product of the colonial legacy, but African leaders cannot reduce the volume of participation to quite the same point as their predecessors.

The belief that economic development and planning require centralized direction also seems to lead to departicipation. African leaders tend to regard questions of economic development in much the same way they view issues of national unity. In both cases they see the center as the vital actor holding the pieces together and local interests as irrational, selfish, and counterproductive. To permit local interests to be effectively involved in any aspect of planning or economic decision making would only add further difficulties."[11] Instead, planning (from a centrist perspective) means increased coordination and direction of peoples' social and economic activities because it is directed by a single authority.

The official response to the failure to meet planning targets is invariably greater centralization. Each East African five-year plan has been more ambitious than the one it replaced. "Having discovered that actual decisions diverge from planned forecasts, the East African governments have not reacted by abandoning their centrist premises, but rather have tried to tighten control over the economy from above."[12] Since this means that new projects will be carried out from the top downward, one unanticipated consequence is that the center is further strengthened vis-à-vis the outlying rural areas through the added financial and organizational input in the capital city. "With so much going on in Nairobi," Moris adds, "the high level officials can easily forget the periphery. . . ."[13] Given this perspective, de-

11. Uganda provides an interesting "exception that ended up proving the rule" – at least for central administrators. A new minister for planning and community development, Adoko Nekyon, decided in 1964 to encourage district councils to prepare three-year plans. What he received back were lengthy lists of projects extending social services and administrative infrastructure with no prospects of earning future revenue. In the case of one district, the "plan" had a total cost that amounted to over one and half times the district's total annual revenue without making any provision for consequential recurrent costs. Colin Leys, *Politicians and Policies: An Essay on Politics in Acholi, Uganda 1962-65* (Nairobi: East African Publishing House, 1967), p. 45.

12. Jon Moris, "Administrative Authority and the Pattern of Effective Agricultural Administration in East Africa," *The African Review* 2, no. 1 (June 1972): 118.

13. Ibid., p. 114.

participation is believed to be a sensible policy to adopt in order to clear the way for "rational planning."

Where the belief in rational planning is combined with a particular strategy for development, the probability of departicipation increases. Socialist reconstruction of the Tanzanian society and economy, for example, is necessarily a complex and long-term matter. But for the present it is far more the goal of leaders than of followers. "There have been stirrings certainly, but no dramatic push from below for socialism; there is a real sense in which the initiative has come from the top down." [14] Tanzanian leaders are not apt to permit participatory challenges that might interfere with such fundamental changes.

In general, then, there are diffuse beliefs based on the conditions of political combat prevailing in Africa today, on the pattern of government inherited from colonialism, and on the importance of keeping tight control on planning for development. These beliefs condition specific policy choices at every turn. Together they prompt political elites to reduce significantly the volume of participation.

However, without the acquiescence of those outside the small circle of high government officials, no departicipation policy could possibly succeed. Low levels of personal efficacy combined with ineffective political organizations also reduce the likelihood of participation. The poverty faced by all African countries is largely responsible for the significance of these additional causes of departicipation.

The widespread perception of a low level of personal efficacy in postindependence political life stems originally from the narrowly local world of the peasant. The absence of functional literacy among adults and their consequent inability to use tools of participation, such as newspapers — taken for granted in industrialized states — leave this situation little changed. When Western structures of participation were imported, not much allowance was made for these difficulties. Social and economic modernization and growing wealth are likely to reduce the significance of this cause in coming years and thus increase the

14. John S. Saul, "The Nature of Tanzania's Political System: Issues Raised by the 1965 and 1970 Elections," Part I, *Journal of Commonwealth Political Studies* 10, no. 2 (July 1972): 122.

volume of participation, though it is unlikely that increases from this change will be spread evenly throughout the population.

Of equal importance, habits of political participation in national and local organizations have not become deeply engrained. Although many subsaharan African parties can trace their ancestry through various predecessors to the early years of this century and in some cases back even further, none of them became effectively organized until well after World War II — that is, not until colonial governments, often in response to demands from local party leaders, introduced participatory structures. Because colonial rulers offered little resistance to independence movements, commitment to political participation probably has not penetrated deeply. African leaders "did not have to subvert a generalized public conscience into acquiescence: none had yet been brought into being." [15]

Seeming exceptions to this proposition, like the tax riots in Western Nigeria in 1968 and the peasant rebellions in Zaire in 1964, are important because they occurred outside participatory structures. They are further evidence of the shallow level of popular commitment to political institutions. In fact, where the polity decays to the point of breakdown, as it did in Zaire in 1960, participation is likely to rise somewhat.

In Guinea-Bissau and Mozambique, on the other hand, guerrilla leaders have been forced to build effective political organizations in order to gain popular support for their struggles against the Portuguese. [16] Postindependence parties based on these organizations are likely to sustain higher volumes of participation than elsewhere in black Africa. Not all liberation movements hold out this promise, however. Where conflicts within the movement lead to shallow alignments composed of competing factions, like those that bedeviled the Angolan, Rhodesian, and Southern Sudanese fighters, the chances for sustained participation at relatively high volumes later are less promising.

The third and most straightforward reason for individual

15. Zolberg, *Creating Political Order,* p. 90.
16. See Lars Rudebeck, "Political Mobilisation for Development in Guinea-Bissau," *The Journal of Modern African Studies* 10, no. 1 (May 1972).

withdrawal from material participation is that governments have made the costs far too high. Few of those enthusiastically involved a decade ago are likely to regard the rewards of political participation presently worth the risks they must run. The extensive control possessed by the state over economic rewards in the public and private sectors deters all but the most committed. In Kenya the government threatened civil servants, expatriate businessmen, and MPs who supported the Kenya People's Union or facilitated its campaigns.[17] Rural dwellers were warned that they could lose their plots in settlement schemes and that maize for famine relief might not be distributed in areas that failed to vote for KANU.

Ineffective political organizations compound the obstacles to participation posed by the widespread perception of a low level of personal efficacy. Participatory structures are weak partly because resources do not exist to make it possible for them to work. Available resources have been largely monopolized by the bureaucracies. In addition, departing colonial administrators gave scant consideration to the levels of "skilled political manpower" that would be required by the structures they introduced.

Thus, local councils failed because of irresponsible suggestions by new councillors, lack of adequate qualified employees, and lack of sufficient revenue. The same problem is at the heart of the poor performance of cooperatives in Africa. The result is disillusionment and voluntary departicipation by those who had previously been active. Poverty and departicipation have been closely related.[18]

The causal importance of poverty must not be overrated, however. The process of departicipation in relatively poor nations such as Uganda and Kenya has closely paralleled the process in Ghana, a wealthier country. Tanzania has a lower per

17. Susanne D. Mueller, "Statist Economies and the Elimination of the K.P.U.: A Critique of Political Party Analysis and the 'Center-Periphery' Argument" (paper delivered to the African Studies Association Conference, Philadelphia, November 1972) pp. 24-30.

18. As used here, *poverty* means low levels of wealth whether or not they are accompanied by high rates of economic growth. Participation often rises when rates of growth accelerate, though the continent-wide similarities in departicipation suggest that this proposition may have to be qualified. See Huntington's discussion in *Political Order*, pp. 39-56.

capita income than any of these three, but departication has made less impact there than elsewhere in Africa.

Poverty is more likely to be an important cause of departicipation where political involvement occurs within political structures. Poverty generally results in the absence of organizational resources, which in turn reduces the volume of continuing structured participation. If unstructured mass participation had been as high in black African countries as in other parts of the Third World, poverty might not have depressed the total volume of participation so much. There are occasional riots and rebellions, such as those in Nigeria and Zaire. The Biafran war led to mass involvement in certain types of participation. However, it is the unusual black African state that has masses who demonstrate other than on a signal from their leaders. Military intervention in the Malagasy Republic in 1972 and military withdrawal in the Sudan in 1964 were atypical because they were responses to unstructured participation by students and workers.[19] In the characteristic subsaharan African coup, the populace remains silent until the army is firmly in place.

In spite of these causes, there was nothing inevitable about departicipation in Africa. The response to the introduction of participatory structures toward the end of the colonial period showed that significant volumes of participation of varying weight, scope, and personae would appear where there was encouragement by officials and nationalist leaders. When the nationalist leaders took office, however, they discouraged participation which they could not control because of their general beliefs about how government should be conducted and how they might remain in office. Faced with governmental opposition, most Africans outside the political elite judged the costs of participation not to be worth the possible rewards, particularly where the political organizations on which they would have to depend turned out to be ineffectual.

2. IS DEPARTICIPATION DESIRABLE?

In the abstract few people would disagree with Niccolò Machiavelli's judgment that "every free state ought to afford

19. *Elite* unstructured participation occurs regularly in black Africa, as the plethora of military coups demonstrates.

the people the opportunity of giving vent, so to say, to their ambition; and above all those republics which on important occasions have to avail themselves of this very people." [20] The general commitment to participation has become so strongly entrenched in the Western liberal tradition that little attention has been devoted to the particular situations in which a contraction of the volume of participation might serve the public interest. However, when a specific decision has to be made, personal preferences for more or less participation turn out to vary considerably — especially in countries of the Third World. Considered solely as pure value choices, these preferences can neither be justified nor refuted by reasoned argument.

But the criteria on which the preference for departicipation may be judged are open to discussion. Even though partisans of democracy heavily stress participation in rhetoric that has been assimilated everywhere in Africa, additional increments of participation do not necessarily produce additional value. Like virtually every other good, participation is not desirable per se.

A large volume of material participation may help to clarify issues and build political community, or it may lead to paralysis of the government and possibly to civil war. The responsiveness of leaders to the wishes of citizens may or may not increase in proportion to the growth of political involvement. [21] Certain steps in policymaking require secrecy — for example, the process of negotiating treaties or complicated labor contracts. Implementation of laws requiring evenhanded application — such as the collection of taxes — would suffer if people were permitted to participate at that point. The adoption of complex legisla-

20. *Discourses on the First Ten Books of Titus Livius,* Book I, chap. 4, trans. Christian E. Detmold, ed. Max Lerner (New York: Random House, 1950), p. 120. Machiavelli's own position depends, of course, on how broadly he intended the category of "free states."

21. Much will depend on how threatening the leaders perceive new kinds of participation to be. Where threats are not a significant cost of participation and political institutions are secure, the sensitivity of leaders and participation of followers seem likely to reinforce each other. A study that compared the responsiveness of leaders in a large number of American communities exhibiting different volumes of participation found that responsiveness and volume of participation tended to vary directly, but with significant exceptions at lower volumes. Sidney Verba and Norman H. Nie, *Participation in America: Political Democracy and Social Equality* (New York: Harper & Row, 1972), pp. 316-318.

tion – particularly where it fundamentally alters social or economic relationships – cannot succeed if large volumes of participation are permitted at all stages. In some, though certainly not
all, cases, "the more persons involved in making a decision, the
more difficult it becomes to reach one." [22]

Thus, in certain circumstances participation, or at least a
portion of it, ought to be sacrificed in order to achieve other
goals. A complete discussion requires surveying all costs and
benefits of each component of participation, as well as ranking
their priority in relation to other goals in particular situations.
One of the first questions that would need to be asked is
"*Whose* participation is to be reduced?" Getting someone out
of politics is obviously a price that must be paid for a departicipation policy, and it may not be worth it. Once the issues have
been clarified however, it becomes easier to see the value
judgments that contributed to a specific decision. Controlling
participation in order to reduce the importance of ethnicity in
Uganda and to increase the importance of socialism in Tanzania
are two examples in which leaders translated their values into
policy.

From the range of possible issues that this question raises, I
want to focus here on two general considerations that affect
many specific policy decisions. The first concerns the relation
between departicipation and political modernization in black
Africa and suggests that a degree of departicipation is desirable
in certain situations. The second raises the problem of *overinstitutionalization* and indicates that departicipation is not desirable where it is carried beyond a certain point.

As modernization refers generally to control of problems, so
political modernization means the creation of procedures per-
mitting men to live peacefully together and to organize to solve
other problems. Thus, political modernization in the first instance is the establishment of effective authority. Only after
there is authority is it useful to discuss political modernization
as the rationalization of that authority, the differentiation of
structures and increased participation. [23] Where there is little

22. Daniel P. Moynihan, "The Relationship of Federal to Local Authorities," in
Annual Editions: Readings in American Government '72 (Guilford, Conn.: Dushkin
Publishing Group, 1972), p. 174.
23. Huntington suggests that political modernization "involves" the latter three
characteristics. *Political Order,* pp. 34-35 and 93.

political modernization, departicipation may make an important contribution — most dramatically where popular involvement is causing the disintegration of the state. The virtual destruction of political authority in Zaire between 1960 and the coup in 1965 appears to be such a case.

In strengthening central administration many African leaders are attempting to make more certain the exercise of state authority, though they often go to excessive lengths. Their actions suggest that "balanced political growth" — the simultaneous increase in constitutionalism and authority — may be impossible. By eliminating constitutional fetters, they open the possibility of extending political order throughout the nation. In this respect their behavior differs little from that of Louis XIV of France and the other great state-builders in seventeenth- and eighteenth-century Europe. "You must first enable the government to control the governed" the authors of the Federalist Papers remind us, "and in the next place oblige it to control itself."[24]

If political development is seen as a balance between participation and institutions, it may be enhanced in Africa by building central authority while contracting political involvement. There are many pitfalls in this process, and several African regimes have demonstrated the ease with which a government can slide into reliance on coercion alone, with a consequent decay in institutionalization. But what structural options are open to African leaders who take a long-range perspective of their responsibilities?

Faced with ineffectual governing parties (with the exception of TANU in Tanzania), leaders are making the bureaucracy, already institutionalized through fifty to one hundred years of colonial development, the vital core of their political systems. Students of Third World politics, who have seen one political structure after another fail, may miss this tendency in regime transformations. Huntington, for example, argues that antiparty strategies in modernizing countries increase the fragility of the state — that is, make governments more vulnerable to coups.[25]

24. Publius [Alexander Hamilton or James Madison], "The Federalist No. 51," in Alexander Hamilton, John Jay, and James Madison, *The Federalist: A Commentary on the Constitution of the United States* (New York: Random House, n.d.), p. 337.

25. *Political Order,* pp. 403-408.

But military rule is generally bureaucratic rule and often involves a significant civilian component — though regimes like Amin's in Uganda appear to be exceptions. In any event, where authority is fragile, reliance on the most viable institution they possess may give leaders the best chance to strengthen their polities.

Zolberg also overlooks the significance of the growth of authority in African bureaucracies when he stretches the discovery that African parties exist mainly on paper to cover all government structures; in effect he replaces the "no-party state" with the "no-state state."[26] The bureaucracy, however, despite its many deviations from anyone's ideal type, is becoming the repository for the authority of the regime. This does not mean that the authority of the state to penetrate the countryside and solve national problems is automatically increased. But the opportunity may be there.

Can the civil service undertake the functions normally carried out by a political party? Although they may be less effective in these respects than well-organized parties, bureaucracies can also generate change, absorb its impact, inspire loyalty that transcends parochial groupings, and even assimilate new groups.[27] It is all the more plausible that African bureaucracies might play this role since they have inherited significant political capabilities from their colonial predecessors and are further politicized by aspects of their social situation.[28]

In most African countries bureaucracies possess the best (and often the only) communications network. By supplying desired development projects and social services, bureaucrats may be able to assimilate people to national identity and at the same time generate modernizing changes in their lives. On the other hand, bureaucracies have less incentive than parties to mobilize people, and bureaucrats may fail to meet their political challenges for lack of effective administrative leadership or for other internal reasons. Also, bureaucracies lack an important political capability in that they are less suited structurally to solving the

26. "The Structure of Political Conflict in the New States of Tropical Africa," *The American Political Science Review* 62, no. 1 (March 1968): 71-72.

27. Huntington suggests that parties are particularly well suited to carry out these functions. *Political Order*, pp. 404-405.

28. This argument is developed in Kasfir, "Development Administration in Africa."

problem of leadership succession. But these are problems of degree, not of kind — and not problems at all by comparison with the present condition of most African parties.

African bureaucracies have the potential to accommodate low-level political participation. In the future, perhaps when economic and social modernization has progressed further, more effective structures may be necessary to cope with increased participation. In present circumstances, however, where much departication has occurred, the political capabilities of bureaucracies may be sufficient. In addition, given the poverty of African countries, the bureaucracy is the most reliable organizational instrument available for building the authority of the state. For these reasons a measure of departication resulting from the dismantling of political structures is a desirable goal to the extent that it frees bureaucrats to build authority.

Anxious over their personal security and tenure in office, strongly imbued with notions of their personal importance for achieving unity and development, and possessing little historical guidance from the short period of national independence, leaders in Africa often carry departication to the point of political decay. The dichotomy between "civic" and "praetorian" polities — that is, between states with high and low degrees of institutionalization — obscures this proposition by hiding cases of overinstitutionalization.

Civic polities, Huntington argues, exhibit development, and praetorian polities illustrate decay. [29] But civic polities include both those that strike a balance by having a volume of participation with which existing institutions can cope and those in which participation is suppressed to levels *below* the capacity of governing institutions. Polities in the latter category are overinstitutionalized. If the level of institutionalization that their governmental structures possess is relatively low, their volumes of participation are kept lower still. Some of these regimes may become more vulnerable to coups as a result of departication. Military intervention may lead to some experiments with controlled participation. But it is not likely to lead to much larger volumes of political involvement, particularly in Africa, since the populace appears to be prepared to acquiesce in most contractions of the political arena.

29. Huntington, *Political Order*, pp. 78 and 80.

Too much acquiescence, however, is not conducive to meeting important goals — including those that leaders set for themselves. An extremely low volume of participation means that leaders lose touch with ordinary citizens. Lack of communication often results in increasing reliance on an ideology or haphazard ad hoc proposals as the sole source of policy initiatives. The consequence is likely to be poorly designed policies and misallocation of resources. In addition, coercion becomes an ever more prominent feature of implementation in such regimes. Ghana and Uganda in the last years of rule by Nkrumah and Obote suffered from the consequences of over-institutionalization. In both cases their regimes became increasingly fragile, although Obote seemed to have plans to raise the volume of participation somewhat. Thus, departicipation can be carried to undesirable lengths.

A happy medium, then, of some departicipation but not too much would seem to be the most desirable goal for African leaders interested in political development. A pattern of a low volume of controlled participation may come relatively close to this norm. By this standard Tanzania has achieved so far a more effective measure of political development than any other African country.

Although parties seem to be the most plausible structures through which low-level participation can be organized there are few equal to the task. The burden might be successfully taken up by a bureaucracy — assuming its members are relatively responsive to national leaders. Whether a system of controlled participation under the aegis of either a party or a bureaucracy can remain stable for a long period of time remains an open question. The answer depends partly on the acquiescence in departicipation by those outside the tiny political elite, for they must accept their role as spectators who remain on the sidelines most of the time. It also depends on the willingness of leaders to encourage as much participation as the system can handle.

The broader possibilities suggested at the beginning of this chapter can now be sketched. By independence African states had added several new participatory structures to their bureaucracies. Over the previous half-century or more, these bureaucracies had achieved a significant level of institutionalization in spite of later nationalist opposition to their direct association with colonial rule. The new structures handled an appreciable volume of participation at the end of the dyarchy and during the first years of independence. [30] But they did not become deeply valued, and thus they were not institutionalized.

Most of these states rapidly reduced the volume of participation at the earliest opportunity by removing the new structures. The states suffered a small loss in institutional strength (and a much larger loss of legitimacy) but restored their bureaucracies to a position reminiscent of the colonial period. To some extent this regime transformation may have been necessary to establish more firmly the authority of an indigenous government. The new rulers certainly perceived this to have been so. But in many cases they removed all but the symbolic linkages between the people and their government: they lost contact while they maintained coercion. Other rulers not only removed these structures but also jeopardized the maintenance of continuous government authority.

However, Tanzania, the most conspicuous example of African states that have paid attention to the maintenance of participation, introduced a set of locally designed structures to replace those that had been dismantled. These structures have accommodated a volume of controlled participation of intermediate size and have begun to be institutionalized over the past ten years. In the process the involvement of citizens in political activities may have increased the legitimacy of the government far above that of its neighbors.

The question, then, is whether other rulers — perhaps no longer possessing the stimulus to build parties as effective as TANU — can bring participation and structures back into balance. In no case would their success be likely to bring volumes of participation as large as those expected on the eve of independence. Low-level controlled participation is the limit of realistic aspiration.

Nor would their strategies be similar — assuming they make

30. The volume of participation in industrialized states, though considerably higher than in Third World countries, should not be overestimated in drawing comparisons. The personae in American political participation, for example, never reaches more than a third of the available population for activities at any level of involvement carrying more weight than voting. Verba and Nie, *Participation in America,* p. 31.

the effort. For Kenyan or Ivory Coast leaders, the task would be to find ways to increase participation to the level of institutionalization already achieved by the bureaucracy. But for a ruler to guide Uganda to a balance between low-level participation and relatively institutionalized structures would require not only new participatory channels, but also more public confidence achieved by stabilizing government procedures and reducing the participation of soldiers. No head of state would be likely to introduce such changes unless they meant added support for his own security in office. Future participatory structures, therefore are likely to favor certain kinds of people and discriminate against others. And they are likely to be organized by bureaucrats.

Still, it remains possible that leaders could turn their policies on participation into tools of statecraft. They would need to give equal consideration both to the kinds of participation appropriate in different contexts and to the corresponding participatory structures. In other words, government strategies have to be concerned with the personae, scope, bases, weight, and individual propensities that together create the volume of participation in any specific situation. There is, of course, no guarantee that the most sensitive government can retain control over a volume of participation that it has evoked. To achieve political engineering of this complexity would require the most adroit statesmen that Africa can produce.

3. CONCLUSION

The relationships among political development, participation, and ethnicity have formed the basis of this book. My intention has been to demonstrate that participation is not an irreversible process and that departicipation on occasion enhances political development. It is sometimes difficult to know whether departicipation has occurred, since people may change their form of involvement in response to government (or other) pressures rather than either reduce it or leave the political arena entirely. To establish which is the case often requires an examination of the different components that constitute a given volume of participation.

The fact of departicipation is indisputable throughout black

Africa. The transfer of Western participatory structures on the eve of independence has been disrupted everywhere. Military and civilian rulers alike have given top priority to the task of building authority or sometimes just staying in power. In a few cases serious attention has also been given to building new and original participatory structures.

Of all the political forces with which African leaders have had to contend, ethnicity has been regarded as the most serious, the most unyielding, and the most uncontrollable. Ethnicity is thought to be the most prominent characteristic of the psychic identity of most Africans. And ethnic political involvement is assumed to rest upon primordial ties deeply laden with fundamental values. Although its existence is often deplored, ethnic political participation has usually been regarded as beyond political engineering — and thus the one social force beyond departicipation.

Anthropological evidence indicates that this view of ethnicity is seriously in error. Even in the precolonial period, ethnicity was a function of situations, a role sometimes assumed, sometimes ignored. Over the past century ethnicity has developed an ever more complex interrelationship with the uneven spread of both modernization and wealth. Because it is strongly affected by changes in situations, the force of ethnicity in politics can sometimes be altered by adroit political action. Leaders can reduce the scope of participation by making ethnicity illegitimate as a focus for public political assertion.

Uganda provides an important test for this argument. Forces of parochialism increased in strength even after independence. Mobilized as an ethnic group, the Baganda demonstrated the political advantages of ethnic definition. Others responded to this situation by organizing the political entry of new groups in local and national arenas on the same basis. Refusals by the central government to grant ethnic demands were met with threats of secession, which in one instance was carried out. Other groups were satisfied with establishing links with the government in the hopes of winning more limited rewards. Their linkages varied with their ability to present ethnic demands, the broker who forged the bond, and the attitude of the central government.

The Ugandan government tried to resist these demands in an

effort to strengthen its own authority. It succeeded in insulating entry into the civil service and the university student body — but not the cabinet — from ethnic demands, though the Baganda were generally perceived to have gained advantage from their head start in economic and social modernization.

Matters came to a head in the confrontation between the Baganda and the central government in 1966. Having first outmaneuvered his opponents in the cabinet, Obote used the momentum provided by the military defeat of the Baganda to mount an assault on ethnicity in Ugandan politics. The entrenched position of local government was eliminated, and the kingships were abolished. Finally, in the Acholi-Lango factory dispute, the government made it clear that public advocacy of ethnic considerations in any political appeal would result in rejection of the demand and dismissal from government service. The government's execution of this policy left something to be desired, however, and some ethnic maneuvering undoubtedly continued behind the scenes. But through its policy of ethnic departicipation, UPC leaders laid a foundation for reducing the importance of ethnicity in Ugandan political life. Following the military coup, Amin reinjected ethnicity into Ugandan politics without dropping all aspects of Obote's policy. Overall, Amin's approach appears to have helped to reify once again the perception of ethnicity by Ugandans.

A comparison of Amin's and Obote's policies toward ethnic participation demonstrates the important influence that a government has in restricting or expanding the different components of participation. For a variety of reasons involving many political problems in addition to ethnicity, Obote attempted to reduce the volume of participation to the point of overinstitutionalization. However, the elections that he was planning suggest that he may have wanted a high (though controlled) volume of participation. Amin's inability to control his soldiers, on the other hand, has resulted in much participation outside the structures of government. Heavy reliance on ideology, coercion, and terror have resulted in further political decay. Perhaps, the day will come when Uganda can renew itself.

A far more promising (and less extensive) use of departicipation has taken place in Tanzania, where controlled participation has led to a popular government and a relatively effective party.

By instilling value in participatory structures while strictly limit-ing the volume of participation, Tanzanian leaders appear to have achieved a viable balance and an impressive degree of political development. Other African countries have departici-pated to levels below that of Tanzania. Their chances of achiev-ing political development in the immediate future are slim.

Some military and civilian regimes have experimented with devices intended to permit a modest volume of participation. But if an attempt is to be made to institutionalize this level of participation, it cannot be left to political parties which exist in name only — if at all. The most viable institutions in African countries are the bureaucracies. The colonial legacy makes the supervision of low-level political involvement a possible role for civil services to undertake. If African leaders are to bring struc-tures and participation into balance, they appear to have little option but to learn how to use their bureaucracies as political instruments.

SELECTED BIBLIOGRAPHY

ONE: PARTICIPATION, DEPARTICIPATION, AND POLITICAL DEVELOPMENT

A. Books

Almond, Gabriel, and Powell, G. Bingham, Jr. *Comparative Politics: A Developmental Approach.* Boston: Little, Brown, 1966.

Almond, Gabriel, and Verba, Sidney. *The Civic Culture.* Boston: Little, Brown, 1965.

Anderson, Charles W.; van der Mehden, Fred; and Young, Crawford. *Issues of Political Development.* Englewood Cliffs, N.J.: Prentice-Hall, 1967.

Baran, Paul A. *The Political Economy of Growth.* New York: Monthly Review Press, 1957.

Bendix, Reinhard. *Nation-Building and Citizenship: Studies of Our Changing Social Order.* New York: John Wiley and Sons, 1964.

Binder, Leonard,; Coleman, James S.; LaPalombara, Joseph; Pye, Lucian W.; Weiner, Myron; and Verba, Sidney. *Crises and Sequences in Political Development.* Princeton: Princeton University Press, 1971.

Black, C. E. *The Dynamics of Modernization: A Study in Comparative History.* New York: Harper & Row, 1966.

Dahl, Robert A. *After the Revolution? Authority in a Good Society.* New Haven: Yale University Press, 1970.

————. *Modern Political Analysis,* 2d ed. Englewood Cliffs, N.J.: Prentice-Hall, 1970.

————. *Polyarchy: Participation and Opposition.* New Haven and London: Yale University Press, 1971.

Di Palma, Giuseppe. *Apathy and Participation: Mass Politics in Western Societies.* New York: The Free Press, 1970.

Halpern, Manfred. *The Politics of Social Change in the Middle East and North Africa.* Princeton:Princeton University Press, 1963.

Huntington, Samuel P. *Political Order in Changing Societies.* New Haven: Yale University Press, 1968.

Ilchman, Warren F., and Uphoff, Norman T. *The Political Economy of Change.* Berkeley and Los Angeles: University of California Press, 1969.

Jaguaribe, Helio. *Political Development: A General Theory and a Latin American Case Study.* New York: Harper & Row, 1973.

Lasswell, Harold D., and Kaplan, Abraham. *Power and Society: A Framework for Political Inquiry.* New Haven: Yale University Press, 1950.

Lerner, Daniel. *The Passing of Traditional Society.* New York: Free Press, 1964.

Lipset, Seymour Martin. *Political Man: The Social Bases of Politics.* Garden City, N.Y.: Doubleday, 1960.

Marshall, T. H. *Class, Citizenship, and Social Development.* Garden City, N.Y.: Doubleday, 1964.

Milbrath, Lester W. *Political Participation: How and Why Do People Get Involved in Politics?* Chicago: Rand McNally & Co., 1965.

Parry, Geraint, ed., *Participation in Politics.* Manchester: Manchester University Press, 1972.

Potholm, Christian P. *Four African Political Systems.* Englewood Cliffs, N.J.: Prentice-Hall, 1970.

Pye, Lucian W. *Aspects of Political Development.* Boston: Little, Brown, 1966.

Riggs, Fred. *Administration in Developing Countries.* Boston: Houghton Mifflin, 1964.

Rokkan, Stein; with Campbell, Angus; Torsvik, Per; and Valen, Henry. *Citizens, Elections, Parties: Approaches to the Comparative Study of the Processes of Development.* New York: D. McKay, 1970.

Rostow, W. W. *The Stages of Economic Growth: A Non-Communist Manifesto.* Cambridge: Cambridge University Press, 1960.

Rudolph, Lloyd I., and Rudolph, Susanne Hoeber. *The Modernity of Tradition: Political Development in India.* Chicago: University of Chicago Press, 1967.

Verba, Sidney, and Nie, Norman H. *Participation in America: Political Democracy and Social Equality.* New York: Harper & Row, 1972.

Whitaker, C. S., Jr. *The Politics of Tradition: Continuity and Change in Northern Nigeria, 1946-1966.* Princeton: Princeton University Press, 1970.

Zolberg, Aristide R. *Creating Political Order: The Party States of West Africa.* Chicago: Rand McNally & Co., 1966.

B. *Articles (in Books and Journals)*

Austin, Dennis, and Tordoff, William. "The Newly Independent States." In *Participation in Politics,* edited by Geraint Parry. Manchester: Manchester University Press, 1972.

Bendix, Reinhard, "Public Authority in a Developing Political Community: The Case of India." *Archives Européenes de Sociologie* 4, no. 1 (1963).

Braibanti, Ralph. "Administrative Modernization." In *Modernization: The Dynamics of Growth,* edited by Myron Weiner. New York: Basic Books, 1966.

Brass, Paul R. "Political Participation, Institutionalization and Stability in India." *Government and Opposition* 4, no. 1 (Winter 1969).

Cutright, Phillips. "National Political Development — Its Measurement and Social Correlates." In *Politics and Social Life: An Introduction to Political Behavior,* edited by Nelson W. Polsby, Robert A. Dentler, and Paul A. Smith. Boston: Houghton Mifflin, 1963.

Deutsch, Karl. "Social Mobilization and Political Development." *The American Political Science Review* 55, no. 3 (September 1961).

Deutsch, Karl W., and Dominguez, Jorge I. "Political Development toward National Self-Determination: Some Recent Concepts and Models." *Comparative Political Studies* 4, no. 4 (January 1972).

Doornbos, Martin. "Political Development: The Search for Criteria." *Development and Change* 1, no. 1 (1969).

Eisenstadt, S. N. "Bureaucracy and Political Development." In *Bureaucracy and Political Development,* edited by Joseph LaPalombara. Princeton: Princeton University Press, 1963.

Frey, Frederick W. "Political Development, Power, and Communications in Turkey." In *Communications and Political Development*, edited by Lucian W. Pye. Princeton: Princeton University Press, 1963.

Gibbons, David S. "The Spectator Political Culture: A Refinement of the Almond and Verba Model." *Journal of Commonwealth Political Studies* 9, no. 1 (March 1971).

Huntington, Samuel P. "The Change to Change: Modernization, Development, and Politics." *Comparative Politics* 3, no. 3 (April 1971).

————. "Political Development and Political Decay." *World Politics* 17, no. 3 (April 1965).

Inkeles, Alex. "Participant Citizenship in Six Developing Countries." *The American Political Science Review* 63, no. 4 (December 1969).

Kilson, Martin. 'African Political Change and the Modernisation Process." *The Journal of Modern African Studies* 1, no. 4 (1963).

Klinghoffer, Arthur Jay. "Modernisation and Political Development in Africa." *The Journal of Modern African Studies* 11, no. 1 (March 1973).

Mathiason, John R., and Powell, John D. "Participation and Efficacy: Aspects of Peasant Involvement in Political Mobilization." *Comparative Politics* 4, no. 3 (April 1972).

Morris-Jones, W. H. "Political Recruitment and Political Development." In *Politics and Change in Developing Countries: Studies in the Theory and Practice of Development*, edited by Colin Leys. Cambridge: Cambridge University Press, 1969.

Morrison, D. G., and Stevenson, H. M. "Cultural Pluralism, Modernization and Conflict: An Empirical Analysis of Sources of Political Instability in African Nations." *The Canadian Journal of Political Science* 5, no. 1 (March 1972).

Morrison, Donald G., and Stevenson, Hugh Michael. "Integration and Instability: Patterns of African Political Development." *The American Political Science Review* 66, no. 3 (September 1972).

Nie, Norman; Powell, G. Bingham, Jr.; and Prewitt, Kenneth. "Social Structure and Political Participation: Developmental Relationships." Part I. *The American Political Science Review* 63, no. 2 (June 1969).

Nordlinger, Eric A. "Political Development: Time Sequences and Rates of Change." *World Politics* 20, no. 3 (April 1968).

O'Barr, Jean F. "Studying Political Participation in Rural Africa." In *Survey Research in Africa: Its Applications and Limits*, edited by William M. O'Barr, David H. Spain, and Mark Tessler. Evanston, Ill.: Northwestern University Press, 1973.

Packenham, Robert A. "Approaches to the Study of Political Development." *World Politics* 17, no. 1 (October 1964).

Parry, Geraint. "The Idea of Political Participation." In *Participation in Politics*, edited by Geraint Parry. Manchester: Manchester University Press, 1972.

Parsons, Talcott. "Evolutionary Universals in Society." *American Sociological Review* 29 (June 1964).

Pitkin, Hanna F. "The Concept of Representation." In *Representation*, edited by Hanna F. Pitkin. New York: Atherton Press, 1969.

Riggs, Fred W. "Bureaucrats and Political Development: A Paradoxical View." In *Bureaucracy and Political Development*, edited by Joseph LaPalombara. Princeton: Princeton University Press, 1963.

Rokkan, Stein. "The Comparative Study of Political Participation: Notes toward a Perspective on Current Research." In *Essays on the Behavioral Study of Politics*, edited by Austin Ranney. Urbana: University of Illinois Press, 1962.

Rustow, Dankwart A. " 'The Organization Triumphs over Its Function': Huntington on Modernization." *Journal of International Affairs* 23, no. 1 (1969).

Seligman, Lester G. "Elite Recruitment and Political Development." In *Political Development and Social Change,* edited by Jason L. Finkle and Richard W. Gable. New York: John Wiley and Sons, 1966.

Selznick, Philip. "Coöptation: A Mechanism for Organization Stability." In *Reader in Bureaucracy,* edited by Robert K. Merton, Ailsa P. Gray, Barbara Hockey, and Hanan C. Selvin. Glencoe, Ill.: Free Press, 1952.

Uphoff, Norman T., and Ilchman, Warren F. "Development in the Perspective of Political Economy." In *The Political Economy of Development,* edited by Norman T. Uphoff and Warren F. Ilchman. Berkeley and Los Angeles: University of California Press, 1973.

Wallerstein, Immanuel. "The Decline of the Party in Single-Party African States." In *Political Parties and Political Development,* edited by Joseph LaPalombara and Myron Weiner. Princeton: Princeton University Press, 1966.

Weiner, Myron. "Participation and Political Development." In *Modernization: The Dynamics of Growth,* edited by Myron Weiner. New York: Basic Books, 1966.

————. "Political Integration and Political Development." *The Annals of the American Academy of Political and Social Science* 358 (March 1965).

Whitaker, C. S., Jr. "A Dysrhythmic Process of Political Change." *World Politics* 19, no. 2 (January 1967).

Willner, Ann Ruth. "The Underdeveloped Study of Political Development." *World Politics* 16, no. 3 (April 1964).

Zolberg, Aristide R. "The Structure of Political Conflict in the New States of Tropical Africa." *The American Political Science Review* 62, no. 1 (March 1968).

C. Government Publication

U.S., Commission on Civil Rights. *Political Participation: A Study of Participation by Negroes in the Electoral and Political Process in Southern States since the Passing of the Voting Rights Act of 1965: Report.* Washington, D.C.: U.S. Government Printing Office, 1968.

D. Unpublished Materials

May, Judith V. "Citizen Participation: A Review of the Literature." Stenciled. Davis: Institute of Governmental Affairs, University of California, 1971.

TWO: ETHNICITY

A. Books

Apter, David. *The Politics of Modernization.* Chicago: University of Chicago Press, 1965.

Bailey, F. G. *Stratagems and Spoils: A Social Anthropology of Politics.* Oxford: Blackwell, 1969.

Bell, Wendell, and Freeman, Walter E., eds. *Ethnicity and Nation-Building: Comparative, International, and Historical Perspectives.* Beverly Hills: Sage Publications, 1974.

Cohen, Abner. *Custom and Politics in Urban Africa: A Study of Hausa Migrants in Yoruba Towns.* London: Routledge & Kegan Paul, 1969.

Cohen, Abner, ed. *Urban Ethnicity.* A.S.A. Monographs no. 12. London: Tavistock Publications, 1974.

Enloe, Cynthia H. *Ethnic Conflict and Political Development.* Boston: Little, Brown and Company, 1973.

Epstein, A. L. *Politics in an Urban African Community.* Manchester: Manchester University Press, 1958.

Furnivall, J. S. *Colonial Policy and Practice: A Comparative Study of Burma and Netherlands India.* New York: New York University Press, 1956.

Klineberg, Otto, and Zavalloni, Marisa. *Nationalism and Tribalism among African Students: A Study of Social Identity.* Paris and The Hague: Mouton, 1969.

LeVine, Robert A. *Dreams and Deeds: Achievement Motivation in Nigeria.* Chicago: University of Chicago Press, 1966.

Little, Kenneth. *West African Urbanization: A Study of Voluntary Associations in Social Change.* Cambridge: Cambridge University Press, 1965.

McCulloch, Merran. *A Social Survey of the African Population of Livingstone.* The Rhodes-Livingstone Institute, Paper no. 26. Manchester: Manchester University Press, 1956.

Mitchell, J. C. *Tribalism and the Plural Society: An Inaugural Lecture.* London: Oxford University Press, 1960.

———. *The Kalela Dance.* The Rhodes-Livingstone Institute, Paper no. 27. Manchester: Manchester University Press, 1956.

Rudolph, Lloyd I., and Rudolph, Susanne Hoeber. *The Modernity Of Tradition: Political Development in India.* Chicago: University of Chicago Press, 1967.

Smock, David R., and Smock, Audrey C. *Cultural and Political Aspects of Rural Transformation: A Case Study of Eastern Nigeria.* New York: Praeger Publishers, 1972.

Southall, A. W. and Gutkind, P. C. W. *Townsmen in the Making: Kampala and Its Suburbs.* Kampala: East African Institute for Social Research, 1957.

Steward, Julian. *Theory of Culture Change: The Methodology of Multilinear Evolution.* Urbana: University of Illinois Press, 1955.

Vincent, Joan. *African Elite: The Big Men of a Small Town.* New York: Columbia University Press, 1971.

Young, Crawford. *Politics in the Congo: Decolonization and Independence.* Princeton: Princeton University Press, 1965.

B. Articles (in Books and Journals)

Anber, Paul. "Modernisation and Political Disintegration: Nigeria and the Ibos." *The Journal of Modern African Studies* 5, no. 2 (September 1967).

Apthorpe, Raymond. "Does Tribalism Really Matter?" *Transition* 7, no. 6 (October 1968).

———. "The Introduction of Bureaucracy into African Polities." In *Readings in Comparative Public Administration,* edited by Nimrod Raphaeli. Boston: Allyn and Bacon, 1967.

Arrighi, Giovanni, and Saul, John S. "Nationalism and Revolution in Sub-Saharan Africa." In *The Socialist Register 1969,* edited by Ralph Miliband and John Savile. London: The Merlin Press, 1969.

———. "Socialism and Economic Development in Tropical Africa." *The Journal of Modern African Studies* 6, no. 2 (August 1968).

Barth, Frederick. "Introduction." In *Ethnic Groups and Boundaries: The Social Organization of Culture Difference,* edited by Frederick Barth. London: George Allen & Unwin, 1969.

Chitepo, Herbert. "The Passing of Tribal Man: A Rhodesian View." *Journal of Asian and African Studies* 5, nos. 1–2 (January–April 1970).

Cohen, Ronald, and Middleton, John. "Introduction." In *From Tribe to Nation in Africa: Studies in Incorporation Processes,* edited by Ronald Cohen and John Middleton. Scranton Pa.: Chandler, 1970.

Colson, Elizabeth. "Contemporary Tribes and the Development of Nationalism." In *Essays on the Problem of Tribe,* edited by June Helm. Seattle: University of Washington Press, 1968.

Connor, Walker. "Self-Determination: The New Phase." *World Politics* 20, no. 1 (October 1967).

Cotran, Eugene. "Tribal Factors in the Establishment of the East African Legal Systems." In *Tradition and Transition in East Africa: Studies of the Tribal Element in the Modern Era,* edited by P. H. Gulliver. London: Routledge & Kegan Paul, 1969.

Diamond, Stanley. 'Reflections on the African Revolution: The Point of the Biafran Case." *Journal of Asian and African Studies* 5, nos. 1–2 (January–April 1970).

Dole, Gertrude E. "Tribe as the Autonomous Unit." In *Essays on the Problem of Tribe,* edited by June Helm. Seattle: University of Washington Press, 1968.

Edgerton, Robert B. " 'Cultural' vs. 'Ecological' Factors in the Expression of Values, Attitudes, and Personality Characteristics." *The American Anthropologist* 67, no. 2 (April 1965).

Evans-Pritchard, E. E. "The Nuer." In *African Political Systems,* edited by M. Fortes and E. E. Evans-Pritchard. London: Oxford University Press, 1950.

Fallers, Lloyd A. "Political Sociology and the Anthropological Study of African Polities." *Archives Européenes de Sociologie* 4, no. 2 (1963).

Fried, Morton H. "On the Concepts of 'Tribe' and 'Tribal Society.' " In *Essays on the Problem of Tribe,* edited by June Helm. Seattle: University of Washington Press, 1968.

Geertz, Clifford. "The Integrative Revolution: Primordial Sentiments and Civil Politics in the New States." In *Old Societies and New States: The Quest for Modernity in Asia and Africa,* edited by Clifford Geertz. New York: Free Press, 1963.

Gellner, Ernest. "Patterns of Rural Rebellion in Morocco: Tribes as Minorities." *Archives Européenes de Sociologie* 3, no. 2 (1962).

Greenberg, J. H. "Nilotic, 'Nilo-Hamitic', and Hamito–Semitic: A Reply." *Africa* 27, no. 4 (October 1957).

Grillo, R. D. "The Tribal Factor in a Trade Union." In *Tradition and Transition in East Africa: Studies of the Tribal Element in the Modern Era,* edited by P. H. Gulliver. Routledge & Kegan Paul, 1969.

Gulliver, P. H. "Introduction." In *Tradition and Transition in East Africa: Studies of the Tribal Element in the Modern Era,* edited by P. H. Gulliver. London: Routledge & Kegan Paul, 1969.

Gusfield, Joseph. "Tradition and Modernity: Misplaced Polarities in the Study of Social Change." In *Political Modernization: A Reader in Comparative Political Change,* edited by Claude E. Welch, Jr. Belmont, Ca.: Wadsworth, 1971.

Gutkind, Peter. "Preface: The Passing of Tribal Man in Africa." *The Journal of Asian and African Studies* 5, nos. 1–2 (January–April 1970).

Harlow, Vincent. "Tribalism in Africa." *Journal of African Administration* 7, no. 1 (January 1955).

Hlophe, Stephen. "The Significance of Barth and Geertz' Model of Ethnicity in the Analysis of Nationalism in Liberia." *Canadian Journal of African Studies* 7, no. 2 (1973).

Horowitz, Donald L. "Multiracial Politics in the New States: Toward a Theory of Conflict." In *Issues in Comparative Politics,* edited by Robert J. Jackson and

Michael B. Stein. New York: St Martin's Press, 1971.

————. "Three Dimensions of Ethnic Politics." *World Politics* 23, no. 2 (1971).

Janos, Andrew. "Ethnicity, Communism, and Political Change in Eastern Europe." *World Politics* 23, no. 3 (April 1971).

La Fontaine, J. S. "Tribalism among the Gisu: An Anthropological Approach." In *Tradition and Transition in East Africa: Studies of the Tribal Element in the Modern Era,* edited by P. H. Gulliver. London: Routledge & Kegan Paul, 1969.

Legum, Colin. "Tribal Survival in the Modern African Political System." *Journal of Asian and African Studies* 5, nos. 1–2 (January–April 1970).

Lemarchand, René. "Political Clientelism and Ethnicity in Tropical Africa: Competing Solidarities in Nation-Building." *The American Political Science Review* 66, no. 1 (March 1972).

Lewis, I. M. "Tribal Society." *International Encyclopedia of the Social Sciences.* Vol. 16. New York: Free Press, 1968.

Lloyd, P. C. "Introduction: The Study of the Elite." In *The New Elites of Tropical Africa,* edited by P. C. Lloyd. London: Oxford University Press, 1966.

————. "The Ethnic Background to the Nigerian Crisis." In *Nigerian Politics and Military Rule: Prelude to the Civil War,* edited by S. K. Panter-Brick. London: Athlone Press, 1970.

Lofchie, Michael F. "Political Theory and African Politics." *The Journal of Modern African Studies* 6, no. 1 (May 1968).

McCall, Daniel F. "Dynamics of Urbanization in Africa." *The Annals of the American Academy of Political and Social Science,* no. 298 (March 1955).

Mafeje, Archie. "The Ideology of 'Tribalism.'" *The Journal of Modern African Studies* 9, no. 2 (August 1971).

Mazrui, Ali A. "Violent Contiguity and the Politics of Retribalization in Africa." *Journal of International Affairs* 23, no. 1 (1969).

Melson, Robert, and Wolpe, Howard. "Modernization and the Politics of Communalism: A Theoretical Perspective." *The American Political Science Review* 64, no. 4 (December 1970).

Mercier, Paul. "On the Meaning of 'Tribalism' in Black Africa." In *Africa: Problems of Change and Conflict,* edited by Pierre van den Berghe. San Francisco: Chandler, 1965.

Mitchell, J. Clyde. "Some Aspects of Tribal Social Distance." In *The Multitribal Society,* edited by A. A. Dubb. Stenciled. Proceedings of the Sixteenth Conference of the Rhodes-Livingstone Institute: Lusaka (February 1962).

————. "Tribe and Social Change in South Central Africa: A Situational Approach." *Journal of Asian and African Studies* 5, nos. 1–2 (January–April 1970).

Moerman, Michael. "Being Lue: Uses and Abuses of Ethnic Identification." In *Essays on the Problem of Tribe,* edited by June Helm. Seattle: University of Washington Press, 1968.

Naroll, Raoul. "On Ethnic Unit Classification." *Current Anthropology* 5, no. 4 (October 1964).

————. "Who the Lue Are." In *Essays on the Problem of Tribe,* edited by June Helm. Seattle: University of Washington Press, 1968.

Parkin, David J. "Tribe as Fact and Fiction in an East African City." In *Tradition and Transition in East Africa: Studies of the Tribal Element in the Modern Era,* edited by P. H. Gulliver. London: Routledge & Kegan Paul, 1969.

Plotnicov, Leonard. "Rural-Urban Communications in Contemporary Nigeria: The Persistence of Traditional Social Institutions." *Journal of Asian and African Studies* 5, nos. 1–2 (January–April 1970).

Powell, John Duncan. "Peasant Society and Clientelist Politics." *The American Political Science Review* 64, no. 2 (June 1970).

Potekhin, I. "The Formation of Nations in Africa." In *Social Change: The Colonial*

Situation, edited by Immanuel Wallerstein. New York: John Wiley and Sons, 1966.

Rothchild, Donald. "Ethnicity and Conflict Resolution." *World Politics* 22, no. 4 (July 1970).

Sandbrook, Richard. "Patrons, Clients and Factions: New Dimensions of Conflict Analysis in Africa." *The Canadian Journal of Political Science* 5, no. 1 (March 1972).

Skinner, Elliott. "Group Dynamics in the Politics of Changing Societies: The Problem of 'Tribal' Politics in Africa." In *Essays on the Problem of Tribe,* edited by June Helm. Seattle: University of Washington Press, 1968.

Sklar, Richard L. "The Contribution of Tribalism to Nationalism in Western Nigeria." In *Social Change: The Colonial Situation,* edited by Immanuel Wallerstein. New York: John Wiley and Sons, 1966.

————. "Political Science and National Integration – A Radical Approach," *The Journal of Modern African Studies* 5, no. 1 (May 1967).

Smith, M. G. "Institutional and Political Conditions of Pluralism." In *Pluralism in Africa,* edited by Leo Kuper and M. G. Smith. Berkeley and Los Angeles: University of California Press, 1969.

Southall, Aidan. "Ethnic Incorporation among the Alur." In *From Tribe to Nation in Africa: Studies in Incorporation Processes,* edited by Ronald Cohen and John Middleton. Scranton, Pa.: Chandler, 1970.

————. "The Concept of Elites and Their Formation in Uganda." In *The New Elites of Tropical Africa,* edited by P. C. Lloyd. London: Oxford University Press, 1966.

————. "The Illusion of Tribe." *Journal of Asian and African Studies* 5, nos. 1–2 (January–April 1970).

Staniland, Martin. "The Rhetoric of Centre-Periphery Relations." *The Journal of Modern African Studies* 8, no. 4 (1970).

Swartz, Marc J. "The Middleman." In *Local-Level Politics: Social and Cultural Perspectives,* edited by Marc J. Swartz. Chicago: Aldine Press, 1968.

Tyler, J. W. "Education and National Identity." In *Tradition and Transition in East Africa: Studies of the Tribal Element in the Modern Era,* edited by P. H. Gulliver. London: Routledge & Kegan Paul, 1969.

Uchendu, Victor. "The Passing of Tribal Man: A West African Experience." *Journal of Asian and African Studies* 5, nos. 1–2 (January–April 1970).

Wallerstein, Immanuel. "Ethnicity and National Integration." In *Africa: Problems of Change and Conflict,* edited by Pierre van den Berghe. San Francisco: Chandler, 1965.

————. "Voluntary Associations." In *Political Parties and National Integration in Tropical Africa,* edited by James S. Coleman and Carl G. Rosberg, Jr. Berkeley and Los Angeles: University of California Press, 1964.

Winter, Edward. "The Aboriginal Political Structure of Bwamba." In *Tribes without Rulers: Studies in African Segmentary Systems,* edited by John Middleton and David Tait. London: Routledge & Kegan Paul, 1958.

Worsley, Peter. "Populism." Chapter 4 in *The Third World.* London: Weidenfeld & Nicolson, 1964.

Zolberg, Aristide R. "Patterns of National Integration." In *Governing in Black Africa: Perspectives on New States,* edited by Marion E. Doro and Newell M. Stultz. Englewood Cliffs, N.J.: Prentice–Hall, 1970.

————. "Tribalism through Corrective Lenses." *Foreign Affairs* 51, no. 4 (July 1973).

C. Unpublished Materials

Pain, D. R. "Ethnicity in a Small Town." Paper delivered to the East African Universities Social Science Council Conference, Nairobi, December 1972.

Weisner, Thomas S. "One Family, Two Households: A Rural-Urban Network Model of Urbanism." Paper delivered to the Universities Social Science Council Conference, Nairobi, December 1969.

THREE: UGANDA

A. Books

Apter, David. *The Political Kingdom in Uganda: A Study of Bureaucratic Nationalism.* Princeton: Princeton University Press, 1967.

Barber, James D. *Imperial Frontier: A Study of Relationships between the British and the Pastoral Tribes of North East Uganda.* Nairobi: East African Publishing House, 1968.

Beattie, John. *The Nyoro State.* London: Oxford University Press, 1971.

Burke, Fred. *Local Government and Politics in Uganda.* Syracuse: Syracuse University Press, 1964.

Elkan, Walter. *The Economic Development of Uganda.* London: Oxford University Press, 1961.

Gertzel, Cherry. *Party and Locality in Northern Uganda, 1945–1962.* London: Athlone Press, 1974.

Goldthorpe, J. E. *An African Elite: Makerere College Students 1922–1960.* London: Oxford University Press, 1965.

Gukiina, Peter M. *Uganda: A Case Study in African Political Development.* Notre Dame, Ind.: Notre Dame University Press, 1972.

Ibingira, G. S. K. *The Forging of an African Nation: The Political and Constitutional Evolution of Uganda from Colonial Rule to Independence, 1894–1962.* New York: The Viking Press, 1973.

Ingham, Kenneth. *The Making of Modern Uganda.* London: George Allen & Unwin, 1958.

Leys, Colin. *Politicians and Policies: An Essay on Politics in Acholi, Uganda, 1962–65.* Nairobi: East African Publishing House, 1967.

Low, D. A. *Political Parties in Uganda, 1949–1962.* London: Athlone Press, 1962.

Parkin, David. *Neighbours and Nationals in an African City Ward.* London: Routledge & Kegan Paul, 1969.

Richards, Audrey I. *The Multicultural States of East Africa.* Montreal: McGill-Queen's University Press, 1969.

Somerset, H. C. A. *Predicting Success in School Certificate: A Uganda Case Study.* Nairobi: East African Publishing House, 1968.

The Kabaka of Buganda [Edward Mutesa]. *Desecration of My Kingdom.* London: Constable, 1967.

Vincent, Joan. *African Elite: The Big Men of a Small Town.* New York: Columbia University Press, 1971.

Wamala, M. B. *Where Does Uganda's Wealth Come From? From the 1900 Agreement: Report 1904–1948.* Kampala: Uganda Growers Co-Operative Union, Ltd., n.d.

Welbourn, F. B. *Religion and Politics in Uganda: 1952–1962.* Nairobi: East African Publishing House, 1965.

B. Articles (in Books and Journals)

Alnaes, Kirsten. "Songs of the Rwenzururu Rebellion: The Konzo Revolt against the Toro in Western Uganda." In *Tradition and Transition in East Africa: Studies of the Tribal Element in the Modern Era,* edited by P. H. Gulliver. London: Routledge & Kegan Paul, 1969.

Bennett, George. "Tribalism in Politics." In *Tradition and Transition in East Africa: Studies of the Tribal Element in the Modern Era,* edited by P. H. Gulliver. London: Routledge & Kegan Paul, 1969.

Bundy, Emory. "Uganda's New Constitution." *East Africa Journal* 3, no. 4 (June 1966).

Byrd, Robert O. "A Portrait of Leadership in a New Nation: The Case of Uganda." *Queen's Quarterly* 69, no. 4 (1963).

Cohen, Dennis L. "Ryan on Obote." *Mawazo* (Kampala) 3, no. 2 (December 1971).

Cohen, Dennis L., and Parson, J. "The Uganda Peoples Congress Branch and Constituency Elections of 1970." *Journal of Commonwealth Political Studies* 11, no. 1 (March 1973).

Davey, K. J. "Local Bureaucrats and Politicians in East Africa." *Journal of Administration Overseas* 10, no. 4 (October 1971).

Doornbos, Martin R. "Kumanyana and Rwenzururu: Two Responses to Ethnic Inequality." In *Protest and Power in Black Africa,* edited by Robert I. Rotberg and Ali A. Mazrui. New York: Oxford University Press, 1970.

Edel, May. "African Tribalism: Some Reflections on Uganda." *Political Science Quarterly* 80, no. 3 (September 1965).

Engholm, G. F. "Buganda's Struggle for Power." *New Society* (2 June 1966).

Engholm, G.F., and Mazrui, Ali A. "Violent Constitutionalism in Uganda." *Government and Opposition* 2, no. 4 (July–October 1967).

Fallers, Lloyd A.; assisted by Elkan, S.; Kamoga, F. K.; and Musoke, S. B. K. "The Modernization of Social Stratification." In *The King's Men: Leadership and Status in Buganda on the Eve of Independence,* edited by Lloyd A. Fallers. London: Oxford University Press, 1964.

Gertzel, Cherry. "How Kabaka Yekka Came To Be." *Africa Report* 9, no. 9 (October 1964).

————. "Report From Kampala." *Africa Report* 9, no. 9 (October 1964).

Gingyera–Pinycwa, A. G. G. "A. M. Obote, the Baganda and the Uganda Army." *Mawazo* (Kampala) 3, no. 2 (December 1971).

Hancock, Ian [R.] "The Buganda Crisis of 1964." *African Affairs* 69, no. 275 (April 1970).

————. "Patriotism and Neo-Traditionalism in Buganda: The Kabaka Yekka ('The King Along') Movement, 1961–1962." *The Journal of African History* 11, no. 3 (1970).

Kakonge, John. "The Political Party, its Structure, Organisation, and its Members." In *Challenge of Independence,* no editor. Kampala: Milton Obote Foundation, 1966.

Kasfir, Nelson. "Bringing Back the Man on Foot: Civilian Participation under Military Rule in Uganda and Sudan." *Armed Forces and Society* 1, no. 3 (May 1975).

————. "Cultural Sub–Nationalism in Uganda." In *The Politics of Cultural Sub-Nationalism in Africa,* edited by Victor A. Olorunsola. Garden City, N.Y.: Doubleday, 1972.

————. "Organizational Analysis and Uganda Co-operative Unions." In *Co-operatives and Rural Development in East Africa,* edited by Carl Gösta Widstrand. New York: Africana Publishing Corporation, 1970.

————. "The 1967 Uganda Constituent Assembly Debate." *Transition* 7, no. 2 (October–November 1967).

————. "Toro Society and Politics." *Mawazo* (Kampala) 2, no. 3 (June 1970).

La Rue, Andre de [pseudonym]. "The Rise and Fall of Grace Ibingira." *The New African* 5, no. 10 (December 1966).

La Fontaine, J. S. "Tribalism among the Gisu: An Anthropological Approach." In *Tradition and Transition in East Africa: Studies of the Tribal Element in the Modern Era*, edited by P. H. Gulliver. London: Routledge & Kegan Paul, 1969.

Lofchie, Michael F. "The Uganda Coup – Class Action by the Military." *The Journal of Modern African Studies* 10, no. 1 (May 1972).

Mair, Lucy. "Local Government in Busoga." *Journal of Commonwealth Political Studies* 5, no. 2 (July 1967).

[Mazrui, Ali A.] "Mazrui on Amin and Obote." *East Africa Journal* 8, no. 6 (June 1971).

————. "Privilege and Protest as Integrative Factors: The Case of Buganda's Status in Uganda." In *Protest and Power in Black Africa*, edited by Robert I. Rotberg and Ali A. Mazrui. New York: Oxford University Press, 1970.

Middleton, John. "Political Incorporation among the Lugbara of Uganda." In *From Tribe to Nation in Africa*, edited by Ronald Cohen and John Middleton. Scranton, Pa.: Chandler, 1970.

Miller, Norman N. "Military Coup in Uganda: The Rise of the Second Republic." *American Universities Field Staff Reports*, East Africa Series, vol. 10, no. 3 (1971).

Nsibambi, Apolo. "Increased Government Control of Buganda's Financial Sinews since the Revolution of 1966." *Journal of Administration Overseas* 10, no. 2 (April 1971).

————. "Language Policy in Uganda: An Investigation into Costs and Politics." *African Affairs* 70, no. 278 (January 1971).

————. "The Rise and Fall of Federalism in Uganda." *East African Journal* 3, no. 9 (April, 1967).

Nye, Joseph S., Jr. "TANU and UPC: The Impact of Independence on Two African Nationalist Parties." In *Boston University Papers on Africa: Transition in African Politics*, edited by Jeffrey Butler and A. A. Castagno. New York: Frederick Praeger, 1967.

Obote, A. Milton. "Language and National Identification." *East Africa Journal* 4, no. 1 (April 1967).

————. "Myths and Realities." *The People* (Kampala), 29 August 1970.

————. "The Footsteps of Uganda's Revolution." *East Africa Journal* 5, no. 10 (October 1968).

Oryem, Otim. "The Role of a National Party Office in the Development of A National Party." In *Challenge of Independence*, no editor. Kampala: Milton Obote Foundation, 1966.

Parkin, David J. "Tribe as Fact and Fiction in an East African City." In *Tradition and Transition in East Africa: Studies of the Tribal Element in the Modern Era*, edited by P. H. Gulliver. London: Routledge & Kegan Paul, 1969.

Pratt, R. Cranford. "The Politics of Indirect Rule: Uganda, 1900–1955." In *Buganda and British Overrule, 1900–1955: Two Studies*, edited by D. Anthony Low and R. Cranford Pratt. Oxford: Oxford University Press, 1960.

Richards, Audrey I. "Traditional Values and Current Political Behaviour." In *The King's Men: Leadership and Status in Buganda on the Eve of Independence*, edited by Lloyd A. Fallers. London: Oxford University Press, 1964.

Rothchild, Donald, and Rogin, Michael. "Uganda." In *National Unity and Re-*

302BIBLIOGRAPHY

gionalism in Eight African States, edited by Gwendolen M. Carter. Ithaca, N.Y.: Cornell University Press, 1966.

Ryan, Selwyn. "Electoral Engineering in Uganda." *Mawazo* (Kampala) 2, no. 4 (December 1970).

Scott, Roger. "Trade Unions and Ethnicity in Uganda." *Mawazo* (Kampala) 1, no. 3 (June 1968).

Southall, Aidan. "The Concept of Elites and Their Formation in Uganda." In *The New Elites of Tropical Africa,* edited by P. C. Lloyd. London: Oxford University Press, 1966.

Twaddle, Michael. "The Amin Coup." *Journal of Commonwealth Political Studies* 10, no. 2 (July 1972).

————. " 'Tribalism' in Eastern Uganda." In *Tradition and Transition in East Africa: Studies of the Tribal Element in the Modern Era,* edited by P. H. Gulliver. London: Routledge & Kegan Paul, 1969.

Van Den Berghe, Pierre. "An African Elite Revisited." *Mawazo* (Kampala) 1, no. 4 (December 1968).

Whiteley, W. H. "Language Choice and Language Planning in East Africa." In *Tradition and Transition in East Africa: Studies of the Tribal Element in the Modern Era,* edited by P. H. Gulliver. London: Routledge & Kegan Paul, 1969.

Winter, Edward. "The Aboriginal Political Structure of Bwamba." In *Tribes Without Rulers: Studies in African Segmentary Systems,* edited by John Middleton and David Tait. London: Routledge & Kegan Paul, 1958.

Witthuhn, Burton O. "The Spatial Integration of Uganda as Shown by the Diffusion of Postal Agencies, 1900-1965." *The East Lakes Geographer* 4 (December 1968).

Young, Crawford. "Congo and Uganda: A Comparative Assessment." *Cahiers Economiques et Sociaux* (Kinshasa) 5, no. 3 (October 1967).

————. "The Obote Revolution." *Africa Report* 11, no. 6 (June 1966).

C. Government (and Party) Publications

bibliography

[Amin, Idi Dada]. "Speech to the Nation by His Excellency Major-General Idi Amin Dada." *The Uganda Gazette* 64, no. 8 (26 February 1971).

Annual Reports of the Education Department. Entebbe: Government Printer.

The Constitution of the Republic of Uganda. Entebbe: Government Printer, 1967.

Constitution of the Uganda People's Congress: Adopted by the Fourth National Delegates Conference 11th June 1968. Kampala: U.P.C. National Headquarters Secretariat, n.d.

"Declaration by the Officers and Men of the Uganda Army and Air Force Made to the Nation on the 20th February 1971." *The Uganda Gazette,* 64, no. 8 (26 February 1971).

"Education Statistics: 1967." Stenciled. Kampala: Ministry of Education 1967.

Evidence and Findings of the Commission of Enquiry into Allegations Made by the Late Daudi Ocheng on 4th February 1966. Kampala: Uganda Publishing House, 1972.

"Minutes." Stenciled. District Team Sebei, 10 May 1967.

"Minutes." Stenciled. Toro Rukurato and District Council, 1962–1969.

Obote, A. Milton. *The Common Man's Charter.* Kampala: Consolidated Printers, 1969.

————. *His Excellency the President's Communication from the Chair of the National Assembly on 11th February 1969.* Entebbe: Government Printer, 1969.

————. *Proposals for New Methods of Election of Representatives of the People to Parliament: Document No. 5 on the Move to the Left.* Kampala: Milton Obote Foundation, 1970.

Parliamentary Debates. Entebbe: Government Printer.

Peagram, R. C. *A Report on the General Elections to the Legislative Council Held in March, 1961. Entebbe: Government Printer, 1961.*

—————. *Report on the General Elections to the National Assembly of Uganda Held on the 25th April, 1962.* Entebbe: Government Printer, 1963.

Report of the Commission of Inquiry into the Recent Disturbances amongst the Baamba and Bakonjo People of Toro. Entebbe: Government Printer, 1962.

Statistical Abstract: 1968. Entebbe: Government Printer, 1969.

The Birth of the Second Republic of Uganda. Entebbe: Government Printer, 1971.

Uganda Census 1959: African Population. Entebbe: Statistics Branch, Ministry of Economic Affairs, 1961.

Uganda's Plan III: Third Five-Year Development Plan 1971/2–1975/6. Entebbe: Government Printer, 1972.

Uganda v. Commissioner of Prisons, *ex parte* Matovu. *Eastern Africa Law Reports.* 1966.

Work for Progress: Uganda's Second Five-Year Plan, 1966–1971. Entebbe: Government Printer, 1966.

D. Newspapers

The People (Kampala).

The Standard (Dar es Salaam). "Where Was Tribalism in Uganda?" 12 February 1971.

Uganda Argus, now *Voice of Uganda* (Kampala).

E. Unpublished Materials

Banyenzaki, Tarcise. "The Effects of the General and District Council Elections on Administrative Effectiveness in the Parishes of Katooma and Masheruka, Sheema County, Gombolola Kigarama, Ankole District." B.A. dissertation, Makerere University College, 1969.

Bowles, B. D. "Ethnicity and Integration: The Attitude of some Batoro, Banyoro, and Acholi to Uganda and its Unity 1955–62." Paper delivered to the Universities Social Sciences Council Conference, Kampala, December 1971. Stenciled.

Bundy, Emory. "Madi." Uganda District Handbook. Stenciled. Kampala: Institute of Public Administration, n.d.

Denoon, Donald. "The Perception of Ethnicity and Change." Paper delivered to the Universities Social Science Council Conference, Kampala, December 1971. Stenciled.

Griffith, Stephen. "Local Politicians and National Policies: The Secretaries-General of Uganda." B. Phil. dissertation, University of Oxford, 1969.

Gugin, David A. "Africanization of the Ugandan Public Service." Ph.D. dissertation, University of Wisconsin, 1967.

Hansen, Emanuel. "Busoga." Uganda District Handbook. Stenciled. Kampala: Institute of Public Administration, n.d.

Lee, Michael. "The Structure of Local Government." Paper delivered to the African Politics Seminar, Institute of Commonwealth Studies, University of London, November, 1973. Stenciled.

Low, D. A. "The Anatomy of Administrative Origins: Uganda 1890–1920." Paper delivered to the East African Institute of Social Research Conference, Kampala, January 1958.

Nsibambi, Apolo. "Some Aspects of Local Administration in Uganda Since the Revolution of 1966–68." n.d. Typescript.

————. "The Uganda Central Government's Attempt to Acquire Effective Control in Administering Education, 1962–70." Paper delivered to the Universities Social Science Council Conference, Kampala, December 1971. Stenciled.

Pain, D. R. "Ethnicity in a Small Town." Paper delivered to the East African Universities Social Science Council Conference, Nairobi, December 1972.

Segall, Marshall H.; Doornbos, Martin; and Davis, Clive. *Patterns of Self-Identifications among the Banyankole in Uganda.* Forthcoming.

Strate, Jeffrey T. "Post-Military Coup Strategy in Uganda: Amin's Early Attempts to Consolidate Political Support." Papers in International Studies, Africa Series no. 18. Athens: Ohio University Center for International Studies, 1973.

"The Background to the Events Leading to the 'Suspension' of the Uganda Constitution by Dr. A. Milton Obote, Prime Minister of Uganda in February, 1966." Mengo, 11 March 1966.

Young, M. Crawford. "Kingship in Buganda: Last Stand of the Monarchy." 1972. Typescript.

————. "Sebei." Uganda District Handbook. Stenciled. Kampala: Institute of Public Administration, n.d.

FOUR: AFRICA (OUTSIDE UGANDA)

A. Books

Achebe, Chinua. *A Man of the People.* New York: John Day, 1966.

Austin, Dennis. *Politics in Ghana, 1946–1960.* London: Oxford University Press, 1964.

Bienen, Henry. *Tanzania: Party Transformation and Economic Development.* Princeton: Princeton University Press, 1967.

Bretton, Henry L. *The Rise and Fall of Kwame Nkrumah: A Study of Personal Rule in Africa.* London: Pall Mall Press, 1966.

Coleman, James S. *Nigeria: Background to Nationalism.* Berkeley and Los Angeles: University of California Press, 1958.

de St. Jorre, John. *The Nigerian Civil War.* London: Hodder and Stoughton, 1972.

Dryden, Stanley. *Local Administation in Tanzania.* Nairobi: East African Publishing House, 1968.

Election Study Committee, ed. *Socialism and Participation: Tanzania's 1970 National Elections.* Dar es Salaam: Tanzania Publishing House, 1974.

Fallers, Lloyd A. *Bantu Bureaucracy: A Century of Political Evolution among the Basoga of Uganda.* Chicago: University of Chicago Press, 1965.

Fanon, Frantz. *The Wretched of the Earth.* Translated by Constance Farrington. New York: Grove Press, 1968.

First, Ruth. *The Barrel of a Gun: Political Power in Africa and the Coup d'État.* London: Allen Lane The Penguin Press, 1970.

Gerteiny, Alfred G. *Mauritania.* New York: Frederick Praeger, 1967.

Gertzel, Cherry. *The Politics of Independent Kenya, 1963–68.* Nairobi: East African Publishing House, 1970.

Ghai, Yash, and McAuslan, J. P. W. B. *Public Law and Political Change in Kenya: A Study of the Legal Framework of Government from Colonial Times to the Present.* Nairobi: Oxford University Press, 1970.

Green, Reginald H., and Seidman, Ann. *Unity or Poverty? The Economics of Pan-Africanism.* Harmondsworth: Penguin Books, 1968.

Grundy, Kenneth. *Conflicting Images of the Military in Africa.* Nairobi: East African Publishing House, 1968.

Hill, Polly. *The Migrant Cocoa-Farmers of Southern Ghana: A Study in Rural Capitalism.* Cambridge: Cambridge University Press, 1970.

Hopkins, Raymond. *Political Roles in a New State: Tanzania's First Decade.* New Haven: Yale University Press, 1971.

Hunter, Guy. *Modernizing Peasant Societies: A Comparative Study in Asia and Africa.* London: Oxford University Press, 1969.

Hydén, Göran. *TANU Yajenga Nchi: Political Development in Rural Tanzania.* Lund: Uniskol Bokförlaget Universitet och Skola, 1968.

Kamarck, Andrew M. *The Economics of African Development.* New York: Frederick Praeger, 1967.

Kilson, Martin. *Political Change in a West African State: A Study of the Modernization Process in Sierra Leone.* Cambridge: Harvard University Press, 1966.

Lewis, W. Arthur. *Politics in West Africa.* New York: Oxford University Press, 1965.

Listowel, Judith. *The Making of Tanganyika.* London: Chatto and Windus, 1965.

Lloyd, P. C. *Africa in Social Change: Changing Traditional Societies in the Modern World.* Harmondsworth: Penguin, 1967.

Luckham, Robin. *The Nigerian Military: A Sociological Analysis of Authority and Revolt 1960–67.* Cambridge: Cambridge University Press, 1971.

Maguire, G. Andrew. *Toward 'Uhuru' in Tanzania: The Politics of Participation.* Cambridge: Cambridge University Press, 1969.

Molnos, Angela. *Attitudes toward Family Planning in East Africa: An Investigation in Schools around Lake Victoria and in Nairobi.* Munich: Weltforum Verlag, 1968.

Pinkney, Robert. *Ghana under Military Rule 1966–1969.* London: Methuen & Co. Ltd, 1972.

Smock, David. *Conflict and Control in an African Trade Union.* Stanford: Hoover Institute Press, 1969.

Tordoff, William. *Government and Politics in Tanzania: A Collection of Essays.* Nairobi: East African Publishing House, 1967.

Wolf, Eric R. *Peasants.* Englewood Cliffs, N.J.: Prentice-Hall, 1966.

Young, Crawford. *Politics in the Congo: Decolonization and Independence.* Princeton: Princeton University Press, 1965.

Zolberg, Aristide R. *Creating Political Order: The Party-States of West Africa.* Chicago: Rand McNally & Co., 1966.

B. Articles (in Books, Journals, and Newspapers)

Alexandre, Pierre. "Social Pluralism in French African Colonies and in States Issuing Therefrom: An Impressionistic Approach." In *Pluralism in Africa,* edited by Leo Kuper and M. G. Smith. Berkeley and Los Angeles: University of California Press, 1969.

Allen, V. L. "The Meaning of the Working Class in Africa." *The Journal of Modern African Studies* 10, no. 2 (July 1972).

Apter, David. "Ghana." In *Political Parties and National Integration in Tropical Africa,* edited by James S. Coleman and Carl G. Rosberg, Jr. Berkeley and Los Angeles: University of California Press, 1964.

Berg, Elliot J., and Butler, Jeffrey. "Trade Unions." In *Political Parties and National Integration in Tropical Africa,* edited by James S. Coleman and Carl G. Rosberg, Jr. Berkeley and Los Angeles: University of California Press, 1964.

Bienen, Henry. "One-Party Systems in Africa." In *Authoritarian Politics in Modern Society,* edited by Samuel P. Huntington and Clement Moore. New York: Basic Books, 1970.

————. "The Ruling Party in the African One-Party State: Tanu in Tanzania." In

Governing in Black Africa: Perspectives on New States, edited by Marion E. Doro and Newell M. Stultz. Englewood Cliffs, N.J.: Prentice-Hall, 1970.

Busia, K. A. "Speech at the Inauguration of the Second Republic at Black Star Square, Accra." *Weekly News Bulletin.* Kampala: Ghana High Commission (15 November 1969).

Cohen, Dennis L. "The Convention People's Party of Ghana: Representational or Solidarity Party?" *Canadian Journal of African Studies* 4, no. 2 (Spring 1970).

Cohen, Robin. "Class in Africa: Analytical Problems and Perspectives." In *The Socialist Register 1972,* edited by Ralph Miliband and John Savile. London: The Merlin Press, 1972.

Coleman, James S. "The Political Systems of the Developing Areas." In *The Politics of the Developing Areas,* edited by Gabriel Almond and James S. Coleman. Princeton: Princeton University Press, 1960.

Davey, K. J. "Local Bureaucrats and Politicians in East Africa." *Journal of Administration Overseas* 10, no. 4 (October 1971).

Dowse, Robert E. "The Military and Political Development." In *Politics and Change in Developing Countries: Studies in the Theory and Practice of Development,* edited by Colin Leys. Cambridge: Cambridge University Press, 1969.

Emerson, Rupert. "Nation-Building in Africa." In *Nation-Building,* edited by Karl Deutsch and William Foltz. New York: Atherton Press, 1963.

————. "The Problem of Identity, Selfhood, and Image in the New Nations: The Situation in Africa." *Comparative Politics* 1, no. 1 (April 1969).

————. "The Prospects for Democracy in Africa." In *The State of the Nations: Constraints on Development in Independent Africa,* edited by Michael F. Lofchie. Berkeley and Los Angeles: University of California Press, 1971.

Fallers, Lloyd. A. "Africa: Scholarship and Policy." *World Politics* 9, no. 2 (January 1957).

————. "Are African Cultivators to be Called Peasants?" *Current Anthropology* 2, no. 2 (April 1961).

Feit, Edward. "Military Coups and Political Development: Some Lessons from Ghana and Nigeria." In *Governing in Black Africa: Perspectives on New States,* edited by Marion E. Doro and Newell M. Stultz. Englewood Cliffs, N.J.: Prentice-Hall, 1970.

Ferkiss, Victor C. "The Role of the Public Services in Nigeria and Ghana." In *Papers in Comparative Public Administration,* edited by Ferrel Heady and Sybil L. Stokes. Ann Arbor: Institute of Public Administration, University of Michigan, 1962.

Gluckman, Max. "Inter-hierarchical Roles: Professional and Party Ethics in the Tribal Areas of South and Central Africa." In *Local-Level Politics: Social and Cultural Perspectives,* edited by Marc J. Swartz. Chicago: Aldine Press, 1968.

Goldsworthy, David. "Ghana's Second Republic: A Post-Mortem." *African Affairs* 72, no. 286 (January 1973).

Grant, Stephen H. "Getting by with Nothing: Upper Volta." *Africa Report* 18, no. 3 (May-June 1973).

Hanna, William John. "Students." In *Political Parties and National Integration in Tropical Africa,* edited by James S. Coleman and Carl G. Rosberg, Jr. Berkeley and Los Angeles: University of California Press, 1964.

Hopkins, Raymond F. "Constituency Ties and Deviant Expectations among Tanzanian Legislators." *Comparative Political Studies* 4, no. 3 (October 1971).

Hydén, Göran. "Government and Co-operatives." In *Development Administration: The Kenyan Experience,* edited by Göran Hydén, Robert Jackson, and John Okumu. Nairobi: Oxford University Press, 1970.

_____, and Leys, Colin. "Elections and Politics in Single-Party Systems: the Case of Kenya and Tanzania." *British Journal of Political Science* 2, no. 4 (October 1972).

Kasfir, Nelson. "Bringing Back the Man on Foot: Civilian Participation under Military Rule in Uganda and Sudan." *Armed Forces and Society* 1, no. 3 (May 1975).

_____. "Development Administration in Africa: The Balance Between Politics and Administration." *Canadian Journal of African Studies* 3, no. 1 (Winter 1969).

Kawawa, Rashidi. "Foreword." In *One Party Democracy: The 1965 Tanzania General Elections,* edited by Lionel Cliffe. Nairobi: East African Publishing House, 1967.

Killick, Tony. "Cocoa." In *The Economy of Ghana.* Vol. 1 of *A Study of Contemporary Ghana,* directed and edited by Walter Birmingham, I. Neustadt, and E. N. Omaboe. London: George Allen & Unwin Ltd., 1966.

Kilson, Martin. "Authoritarian and Single-Party Tendencies in African Politics." *World Politics* 15, no. 2 (January 1963).

Kingsley, J. Donald. "Bureaucracy and Political Development, with Particular Reference to Nigeria." In *Bureaucracy and Political Development,* edited by Joseph LaPalombara. Princeton: Princeton University Press, 1963.

Kraus, Jon. "Arms and Politics in Ghana." In *Soldier and State in Africa: A Comparative Analysis of Military Intervention and Political Change,* edited by Claude E. Welch, Jr. Evanston, Ill.: Northwestern University Press, 1970.

_____. "On the Politics of Nationalism and Social Change in Ghana." *The Journal of Modern African Studies* 7, no. 1 (April 1969).

Lemarchand, René. "Social Change and Political Modernisation in Burundi." *The Journal of Modern African Studies* 4, no. 4 (December 1966).

Leys, Colin. "Politics in Kenya: The Development of Peasant Society." *British Journal of Political Science* 1, no. 3 (July 1971).

_____. "Tanganyika: The Realities of Independence." In *Socialism in Tanzania: An Interdisciplinary Reader.* Vol. 1 edited by Lionel Cliffe and John S. Saul. Nairobi: East African Publishing House, 1972.

Miller, Norman N. "The Rural African Party: Political Participation in Tanzania." *The American Political Science Review* 64, no. 2 (June 1970).

Moris, J. R. "Administrative Authority and the Problem of Effective Agricultural Administration in East Africa." *The African Review* 2, no. 1, (June 1972).

Mulusa, Thomas. "Central Government and Local Authorities." *Development Administration: The Kenyan Experience.* Edited by Göran Hydén, Robert Jackson, and John Okumu. Nairobi: Oxford University Press, 1970.

"News in Brief." *Africa Report* 3, no. 3 (March 1968).

Nye, Joseph S., Jr. "TANU and UPC: The Impact of Independence on Two African Nationalist Parties." In *Boston University Papers on Africa: Transition In African Politics,* edited by Jeffrey Butler and A. A. Castagno. New York: Frederick Praeger, 1967.

Nyerere, Julius K. "Democracy and the Party System." *Freedom and Unity.* London: Oxford University Press, 1967.

O'Connell, James. "The Inevitability of Instability." *The Journal of Modern African Studies* 5, no. 2 (1967).

"Out of Africa." *Africa Report* 16, no. 6 (June 1971).

Post, Ken. " 'Peasantization' and Rural Political Movements in Western Africa." *Archives Européenes de Sociologie* 13, no. 2 (1972).

Pratt, R. Cranford. "The Cabinet and Presidential Leadership in Tanzania: 1960–1966." In *The State of the Nations: Constraints on Development in*

Independent Africa, edited by Michael F. Lofchie. Berkeley and Los Angeles: University of California Press, 1971.

Rothchild, Donald. "Ethnic Inequalities in Kenya." *The Journal of Modern African Studies* 7, no. 4 (1969).

Rudebeck, Lars. "Political Mobilisation for Development in Guinea-Bissau." *The Journal of Modern African Studies* 10, no. 1 (May 1972).

Sandbrook, Richard. "The State and the Development of Trade Unionism." In *Development Administration: The Kenyan Experience,* edited by Göran Hydén, Robert Jackson, and John Okumu. Nairobi: Oxford University Press, 1970.

————. "The Working Class in the Future of the Third World." *World Politics* 25, no. 3 (April 1973).

Saul John S. "Marketing Co-operatives in a Developing Country: The Tanzanian Case." *Taamuli* (Dar es Salaam) 1, no. 2 (March 1971).

————. "The Nature of Tanzania's Political System: Issues Raised by the 1965 and 1970 Elections." Parts I and II. *Journal of Commonwealth Political Studies* 10, nos. 2 and 3 (July and November 1972).

Schiffer, Harriet B. "Local Administration and National Development: Fragmentation and Centralization in Ghana." *Canadian Journal of African Studies* 4, no. 1 (Winter 1970).

Skurnik, W. A. E. "The Military and Politics: Dahomey and Upper Volta." In *Soldier and State in Africa: A Comparative Analysis of Military Intervention and Political Change,* edited by Claude E. Welch, Jr. Evanston, Ill.: Northwestern University Press, 1970.

Standard (Dar es Salaam). "No Room for Racialism," 10 December 1968.

Staniland, Martin. "Single-Party Regimes and Political Change: The P.D.C.I. and Ivory Coast Politics." In *Politics and Change in Developing Countries: Studies in the Theory and Practice of Development,* edited by Colin Leys. Cambridge University Press, 1969.

Stryker, Richard E. "A Local Perspective on Developmental Strategy in the Ivory Coast." In *The State of the Nations: Constraints on Development in Independent Africa,* edited by Michael F. Lofchie. Berkeley and Los Angeles: University of California Press, 1971.

————. "Political and Administrative Linkage in the Ivory Coast." In *Ghana and the Ivory Coast: Perspectives on Modernization,* edited by Philip Foster and Aristide R Zolberg. Chicago: The University of Chicago Press, 1971.

Sutton, Francis. "Authority and Authoritarianism in the New Africa." In *The Nigerian Political Scene,* edited by Robert O. Tilman and Taylor Cole. Durham, N.C.: Duke University Press, 1962.

"T.A.N.U. Guidelines on Guarding, Consolidating, and Advancing the Revolution of Tanzania, and of Africa." *The African Review,* 1, no. 4 (April 1972).

Tiger, Lionel. "Bureaucracy and Charisma in Ghana." *Journal of Asian and African Studies* 1, no. 1 (January 1966).

Turner, Thomas. "Congo-Kinshasa." In *The Politics of Cultural Sub-Nationalism in Africa,* edited by Victor A. Olorunsola. Garden City, N.Y.: Doubleday, 1972.

Twumasi, Yaw. "Ghana's Draft Constitutional Proposals: An Aristotelian-Burkean Riposte to the Nkrumah Constitutionalists." *Transition* 7, no. 6 (October 1968).

Van Velzen, H. U. E. Thoden, and Sterkenburg, J. J. "Stirrings in the Tanzanian National Assembly." In *Socialism in Tanzania: An Interdisciplinary Reader.* Vol. 1. Edited by Lionel Cliffe and John S. Saul. Nairobi: East African Publishing House, 1972.

Wallerstein, Immanuel. "Elites in French-Speaking West Africa: The Social Basis of

Ideas." *The Journal of Modern African Studies* 3, no. 1 (1965).

————. "The Range of Choice: Constraints on the Policies of Governments of Contemporary African Independent States." In *The State of the Nations: Constraints on Development in Independent Africa*, edited by Michael F. Lofchie. Berkeley and Los Angeles: University of California Press, 1971.

Ward, W. E. F. "Tribalism in Ghana." *Venture* 18, no. 5 (June 1966).

Welch, Claude E., Jr. "The Roots and Implications of Military Intervention." In *Soldier and State in Africa: A Comparative Analysis of Military Intervention and Political Change*, edited by Claude E. Welch, Jr. Evanston, Ill.: Northwestern University Press, 1970.

Willame, Jean-Claude. "Congo-Kinshasa: General Mobutu and Two Political Generations." Translated by Claude E. Welch, Jr. In *Soldier and State in Africa: A Comparative Analysis of Military Intervention and Political Change*, edited by Claude E. Welch, Jr. Evanston, Ill.: Northwestern University Press, 1970.

Worsley, Peter. "Frantz Fanon and the Lumpenproletariat." In *The Socialist Register 1972*, edited by Ralph Miliband and John Savile. London: The Merlin Press, 1972.

Wrigley, C. C. "The Changing Economic Structure of Buganda." In *The King's Men: Leadership and Status in Buganda on the Eve of Independence*, edited by Lloyd A. Fallers. London: Oxford University Press, 1964.

Zolberg, Aristide R. "The Structure of Political Conflict in the New States of Tropical Africa." *The American Political Science Review* 62, no. 1 (March 1968).

C. Government Publications (Tanzania and Nigeria)

Annual Reports of the Permanent Commission of Enquiry, June 1966 — June 1967 and July 1967–June 1968. Dar es Salaam: Government Printer, 1968 and 1969.

Namata, J. A. *The Civil Service in Tanzania*. Dar es Salaam: Government Printer, 1967.

Nyerere, Julius K. *Decentralisation*. Dar es Salaam: Government Printer, 1972.

————. *Education for Self–Reliance*. Dar es Salaam: Government Printer, 1967.

"Presidential Circular no. 1 of 1970." Stenciled. Tanzania. 10 February 1970.

Report of the Presidential Commission on the Establishment of a Democratic One Party State. Dar es Salaam: Government Printer, 1965.

Statistical Abstract 1970. Dar es Salaam: Government Printer, 1972.

Unity in Diversity. Lagos: Federal Ministry of Information, Federal Military Government of Nigeria, 1967.

D. Unpublished Materials

Kjekshus, Helge. "Tanzania's General Elections, 1965 and 1970; Some Statistical and Cartographical Notes." Stenciled. Dar es Salaam: Bureau of Resource Assessment and Land Use Planning, University of Dar es Salaam, September 1972.

————. "The Elected Elite: A Social Profile of Candidates in the 1970 Parliamentary Election." Stenciled. University of Dar es Salaam, n.d.

Mueller, Susanne D. "Statist Economies and the Elimination of the K.P.U.: A Critique of Political Party Analysis and the 'Center–Periphery' Argument." Paper delivered to the African Studies Association Conference, Philadelphia, November 1972. Stenciled.

Skene, Danus. "The Peasant Factor in the Modern Politics of Eastern Africa." M.A. dissertation, Department of Political Science, University of Chicago, 1970.

INDEX

Abidjan, 157n
Achebe, Chinua, 271
Acholi, 96, 103, 105, 109, 112, 143, 154, 180, 181n, 183, 185, 189, 203-205, 215, 216, 217, 219
Acholi district, 37, 92, 117, 129, 154, 178, 179, 203-205
Acholi-Lango factory dispute, 154, 169-170, 203-205, 250
Action Group (AG), 66, 82
Administrative centralization: and growth in freedom of executive, 230; and constitutional changes, 230-232; increases powers of president, 232-234; and civil-military coalition, 234-235; and military regimes, 234-236; in Tanzania, 253; becomes chief instrument of government, 269
Africanization: of commerce, 184, 194; in Tanzanian industry, 254;
Allen, V. L., 66n, 70n
Almond, Gabriel 3, 23, 24n, 46n
Alur, 35, 62, 109, 142-143, 218, 219
Amin, Idi, 30, 49, 212n, 214-215, 217n, 218, 219, 220; and ethnic representation in cabinet, 180-181; Africanizes commerce, 194; contrasts with Obote's ethnic policies, 195, 196, 215-216; accused of smuggling gold, 198, 199; changes languages on radio, 210; enthusiasm of Baganda for coup, 212-213; introduces policy for economic development, 212n; releases accused assassin, 213; deals with problems created by coup, 215-216; deplores fighting in the army, 215n; makes ethnic references in government statements, 216, 219; consults with former kings and constituent heads,

217; introduces councils of elders, 218; discusses restoration· of Kabakaship, 219; strengthens central administration, 223; drafts ministers into army, 236; suspends district appointment committee, 251n; responds early to popular demands, 265; lacks authority in army, 266n
Anber, Paul, 56n, 63n
Anderson, Charles W., 36n, 63n
Angola, 276
Ankole, 65n, 67, 92, 94n, 98, 99, 102, 115, 117, 142, 161n, 222, 246
Alnaes, Kirsten, 130n
Anyoti, J., 180, 239
Apter, David, 49n, 102, 105, 114n, 121n, 122n, 179n, 228, 238n, 242n, 243n, 245n
Apthorpe, Raymond, 36, 160n
Area and regional commissioners (Tanzania), 169
Arrighi, Giovanni, 66n, 71
Arusha Declaration, 255, 261, 262
Ashanti, 49, 62, 66, 80
Asians, 147, 181n, 184, 220, 265, 266
Atura Ferry, 204
Austin, Dennis, 24n, 49n, 66n, 229n, 238n
Austinian "command" theory of law, 272
Azande, 35

Baamba, 34, 38, 78, 96, 98, 112-113, 115, 117, 130-134, 143, 144-145, 146, 148, 149, 154, 156, 159, 162, 163, 164, 169, 197, 217, 218
Baganda, 38, 43, 50, 64, 65, 78, 80, 98, 119, 123, 125, 136-139, 141, 144, 150, 174, 218; agents, 94, 98, 208; and

Tribalism. *See* Ethnicity
Tribal unions, 59, 61
Tshisekedi, Etienne, 236
Turner, Thomas, 236n
Twaddle, Michael, 94n, 112n, 139n
Twumasi, Yaw, 231n
Tyler, J. W., 100n

Uchendu, Victor, 34
Uganda: postindependence political
transformation in, xii-xiii; control of
·district councils in, 16-17, 209, 247;
outlaws ethnic parties, 49; state ownership of industry in, 69n; political parties in, 78, 113-116, 123, 176-177;
British officials in, 78, 94, 99-101,
103n, 109, 116, 120, 136-137, 143,
150, 220n; ethnic units in parallels
Indian castes, 91, 92-93; scope of
participation in, 93; precolonial contributions to ethnicity in, 95-96; widespread ethnic politics in, 95; and protectorate policy in Karamoja, 96; policy of indirect rule in, 96-99; in relation to Buganda, 101, 122; local government in, 101, 234, 249-251, 272;
federal status of, 102, 104, 123, 131,
197; constitutional heads in, 102-104,
126, 128, 146, 202, 217; missionaries
in, 105, 188; secondary schools in,
106, 112, 188; army in, 109, 214, 215,
234, 239n, 265-267; police in, 109,
112, 174n; Kenyans as police in, 109n;
district councils in, 114; Legislative
Council, 114, 115; 123 votes in national elections, 116, 229; widespread
demands in for separate districts, 117;
National Assembly, 124, 125, 138,
179, 180, 199-200, 228, 232; 242;
confrontation of May 1966 in, 126,
164, 195, 196, 200-201; alters local
boundaries, 128n; constitution of
1962, 141, 200; constitution of 1966,
200-201; constitution of 1967, 134,
141, 202-203, 222, 232; placed in
typology comparing states, 155, 156;
develops strategies to reduce ethnicity,
160-161, 163, 195-196; belief in ethnic
dominance in bureaucracy, 174; cabinet, 175, 198, 266; General Service
unit, 175, 185, 216; Africanization in,

182, 183, 248; distributes "expanding
pie," 193, 194, 211-212; confrontation
of February 1966 in, 195-198 passim;
presidency of, 200; High Court, 201;
exercises greater central control over
districts, 202, 228, 231, 248-251; develops economic policies, 203-204,
210-212; secretaries-general in, 205;
planned 1971 electoral system in,
206-208; lack of linguistic unity in,
209; policy toward languages used on
Radio Uganda, 210; 1971 coup in,
215-216; given "18 points" manifesto
for the coup, 215n, 216; massacres soldiers, 215n; provides symbolic rewards
to Baganda under Amin, 216; and role
of district commissioner, 218,
233-234; and role of councils of elders,
218-219; reorganizes administrative
districts, 217; and role of Nubians,
220; passes preventive detention act,
228; increases president's constitutional powers, 232; creates nationalization measures, 233; National Trading
Corporation, 233n; civil-military coalition in, 235; disappearance of parliamentary elections in, 239; elections of
UPC branch and constituency chairmen, 239-240; elections of chiefs, 239;
denies speaking permits to opposition
members, 241; increases government
control over trade unions, 243; increases government control over cooperatives, 244; local government contrasted with Tanzania, 253; parallels
Tanzania in fate of trade unions and
cooperatives, 254; 1967 constitutional
debate in, 263; low volume of participation under Amin, 265-267; fluidity
of government structures under Amin,
266; and military, 265-266; Defence
Council, 266; provincial governors,
266; districts fail to plan rationally,
274n; departicipation contrasted with
Tanzania, 280; military regime and reliance on bureaucracy, 282; devises
strategy for political development,
286; increases coercion under Obote,
284
Uganda Development Corporation
(UDC), 203

Bang

Aug
25 Aug 57